NAIL 67-68

By
Jerry Dwyer & Pat Sweeney
With
Ned Helm

PJSA, Inc.
Centerville, OH

Books are available at
http://www.lulu.com/

Published by
Patrick J. Sweeney and Associates, Inc.
958 Fawn Lea Trail
Centerville, OH 45459

Copyright © 1991
By
Jerry Dwyer and Pat Sweeney
Copyright © 2009
By
Pat Sweeney

All rights reserved. No part of this book may be reproduced
In any form or by any electronic or mechanical means
including information storage and retrieval systems without
the written permission of the publisher, noted above, except
by a reviewer,
who may quote brief passages in a review.
For further information contact the publisher.

ISBN: 978-0-578-01933-8

Printed in the United States of America
First Printing: April 2009

DEDICATION and INSPIRATION

This book is dedicated to Lieutenant Robert J. Dwyer, USN, an F/A-18 pilot. Bob took off on a combat mission from the USS Theodore Roosevelt in the Persian Gulf on February 5, 1991. He never returned from that Desert Storm mission. He was Jerry Dwyer's son. Jerry died of cancer four years later and we dedicate this to him also.

We also dedicate this effort to all Nails who have taken their "Final Flights"… "over the Trail" or with their boots off….

This book has been inspired by all of those whose creed is "To Fly, To Fight and To Win."

THE COVER

In early 1966 when the NKP FACs were working the Laotian area code named Cricket, Nail John Taylor contacted the Walt Disney people and asked them to design a unit patch with Jiminy Cricket. John described the mission to the illustrators in a letter. As a result of this contact Mr. Ward Kimball, one of Disney's famous "nine old men" did so and the "Nail" patch was born. Disney sold it to the unit for $1.00.

The original patch had a Blue background to represent the sky. As more and more Nails flew at night they wanted a "Night Patch" to go with their black flight suits. As a result the "Black" patch on the cover was born. At a later date it was decided that two patches was too confusing so the Nails voted and the "Black" patch became the "Squadron Patch".

Book cover design by Leslie Helm.

THE AUTHORS ... the Contributors ... and the Book

Jerry Dwyer (Nail Five Five) and Pat Sweeney (Nail Four Five) have been personal friends and professional associates since 1959, when they met at Vance Air Force Base in Enid, Oklahoma. Pat was completing Basic Pilot Training and would receive his silver Air Force wings within days of when Jerry, who was returning to Vance as an instructor pilot, decided to rent the same bungalow that Pat had lived in for 4 months.

Jerry Dwyer is a West Pointer with a MBA from Harvard Business School and is a graduate of the National War College. He served for twenty years in the USAF, rising to the rank of Lieutenant Colonel while serving in the USA and Europe. Since he retired from the USAF, he has worked in industry where he was an executive for a Fortune 500 company and president of several small manufacturing companies. He built a diamond factory in Dublin, Ireland for General Electric, built airport fire trucks on Long Island, NY, and manufactured rocket transporter "boxes" in the southern US.

Pat Sweeney graduated from Notre Dame with a BS in aeronautical engineering and later earned a MS in industrial engineering at the University of Missouri. He also served for twenty years in the USAF and retired as a Lieutenant Colonel. He earned a PhD in mechanical engineering from the University of Dayton, where he is now a tenured Professor and Director of the Engineering Management program.

They were both in the Vietnam conflict, serving as Forward Air Controllers in the 23rd Tactical Air Support Squadron at Nakhon Phanom Air Base in Thailand. Although they were at the same base in Pilot Training for a very short time, the assignment to the 23rd TASS in the Vietnam conflict was the only time they served together in the same unit.

Their combined experience and awards are extensive:
7,000 hours of total flying time.
1400 hours of combat flying time.
390 combat missions (97 in North Vietnam in propeller aircraft).
3 Silver Stars.
5 Distinguished Flying Crosses.
1 Bronze Star.
21 Air Medals.
1 Purple Heart.

Jerry was shot down twice. He escaped capture on his second shoot down by shooting several of his would be captors with his Combat Masterpiece .38 Special.

A special note of thanks goes to....Phil Maywald, Nail Four Eight, who was the On Scene Commander for Jerry's second SAR. Phil's heroic efforts resulted in Jerry's survival and thus the writing of this book. Phil was recommended for the Medal of Honor for that mission. It was "downgraded" to an Air Force Cross (this nation's second highest decoration of gallantry) because his O-2 was never hit by ground fire and because he was not wounded. He is a bona fide hero none the less....His comment after the mission was **"It was all in a day's work...for a NAIL FAC!"**

Jerry and Pat worked on this book for over twenty years. Shortly after they returned from Southeast Asia, they compiled the background data and attempted to write the story. Both were too involved in their Air Force duties and were at opposite sides of the world. Jerry was in Germany, Pat in Florida. In 1982 they tried a second time... still no luck. Finally, in 1991 and well after they retired from the Air Force they succeeded in finding the time to put the words to paper.

Originally three former NAILs who were all stationed at Wright-Patterson AFB, OH in the 1970s gathered to begin planning for a NAIL novel. Nothing happened.

Then in 1991 Jerry and Pat asked the other NAIL if he was still interested in participating in writing what is now the "NAIL 67 – 68" story. He was busy with other activities and opted out of this new book.

Probably the best part of getting this book started was the conversation heard at one of the very first meetings.

As the conversation was settling down and after about an hour the third NAIL says, *"I just finished writing about the history of Laos during the 60s as my thesis at the War College, so clearly I am the most qualified to write all this stuff."*

Jerry then chimed in, *"As I look around this group, I am clearly the best pilot so I will write all the flying stuff."*

Both then looked at Pat and Jerry said, *"What will you write?"*

Quickly Pat said, *"I will write the sex."* And with that the meeting was over for the day, but it was not over for Pat as he described the above scene to his wife.

Her reply is a classic. *"That will be a very short paragraph."*

This is the fourth rewrite and reflects inputs from their friends and reviewers of the previous versions.

Jerry Dwyer died in 1995 of cancer.

The book was put away and forgotten until someone on the Nail Net (an internet group where old warriors from the 23rd TASS chat and pass data to each other) mentioned that it existed. At that point Ned Helm, who is the unofficial Nail Historian started digging and found both Don Brown and Pat Sweeney (The actual pilots of the famous O-2 "Kudy Jay"). One thing led to another and the pile of papers was dusted off.

Files zapped across the internet...and the project was reborn....this history needed to be told.

Contributor and editor Ned "Crash" Helm (Nail 27) is also an ex USAF pilot with over 2500 hours of time in the KC-135 Tanker, the OV-10 Bronco (the O-2's successor) and the F-4 Phantom. He also served in the 23rd TASS at both NKP and Ubon where he flew as a Rustic FAC in Cambodia in 1973. His decorations include 2 DFCs and the requisite "I was there" ribbons... not to include the Purple Heart ....which... like many other FACs who sustained minor injuries...he turned down.

The Authors and Contributor make absolutely no apologies to anyone who is offended by this book. This is the way it was as we saw it. Thus that is the way it was written. The names were changed to protect both the guilty and the heroic. Some locations were messed with and the time line was ignored at times to make the story flow.

But...approximately 90% of the incidents in this book actually happened and are historically accurate...the rest could easily have happened...that's why it's called it a novel.

All the Nails ...from the First O-1's over the Trail in January 1966 through the OV-10's who saved the Marines during the Mayaguez affair over Koh Tang Island off the coast of Cambodia in 1975... lived this Novel.

All NAILs were Shit Hot! NAILs are Shit Hot!! NAILs will always be Shit Hot, even after more than 30 to 40 years.

The contributors include: Leslie Helm, Don Brown, Sam Weaver, John Doty, Ron Deep, Phil Maywald, Jerry Stephan, John Bollwerk, Al Matheson, George Bohlen ...and more than 75 readers who gave us ideas and encouragement.

PAT SWEENEY and JERRY DWYER, 1968

JERRY DWYER, 1967

NAIL 67 - 68

Prologue

In the summer of 1967, President Lyndon Johnson and Secretary of Defense Robert McNamara were assuring the American people that more troops, more planes and more resources of all types would bring victory in Vietnam. President Ho Chi Minh and General Giap were telling the North Vietnamese people the same. The North Vietnamese were depending upon their ability to successfully use a supply route in Laos between the Mekong River and the western Vietnamese border to deliver their resources to South Vietnam. This supply route was known as the Ho Chi Minh Trail, a network of dirt roads passing from North Vietnam through Laos into South Vietnam. Along these unpaved roads and trails the Viet Cong and the North Vietnamese army were well supplied for their war in South Vietnam.

The primary responsibility for the interdiction of these supplies fell upon the shoulders of United States Air Force air crews of the 23rd Tactical Air Support Squadron and the Air Commando units based at Nakhon Phanom Royal Thai Air Force Base, Thailand. The base was just eighty miles from the main sections of the Ho Chi Minh trail and only eight miles from the Laotian border.

The age of jets notwithstanding, propeller-driven relics of World War II, a single engine Douglas A-1 and a twin engine B-26, were the primary attack aircraft flown by the NKP warriors. These bombers were assisted by other relics such as the slow B-57 Canberra Bomber and the T-28, an attack version of the Navy and Air Force training planes.

During the daylight hours, the supply convoys of trucks would remain hidden in transfer parks under the triple-canopy jungle. In the daytime, the trucks did not move on the Trail as they were afraid of being spotted by the continuous aerial surveillance and subsequently attacked by the American jets.

At night, the trucks would slowly snake their way south with their lights dimmed, well protected by many strategically placed anti-aircraft guns. It was during the nights that the slow propeller-driven aircraft could attack the truck convoys with some assurance of survivability within the range of the many guns along the Trail. All the flyers believed that "If they can't see us, they can't hit us." Generally, this was true, but even a stopped watch is correct twice in 24 hours and some gunners were occasionally successful.

In late 1967, the O-2 was the aircraft of the forward airborne observers at NKP. It was twin engine pusher-puller Cessna 337 Skymaster, which flew five hour surveillance missions around the clock to locate moving convoys or even single vehicles. It was these courageous pilots who called for and directed the air strikes to stop the Viet Cong from being re-supplied. U.S. aviators damaged or destroyed approximately five percent of the vehicles seen on the Trail carrying their deadly cargoes south. However, after the early 1968 build up to support the enemy's Tet offensive, the damage to the enemy's supply line as measured by truck destructions nearly tripled.

President Johnson and Secretary McNamara never understood nor appreciated the significance of Laos and they left a legacy in America of defeatism and withdrawal. While our brave soldiers, sailors, aviators and marines won victory after victory, Washington and Saigon never understood. So our politicians and political generals literally "snatched defeat from the jaws of victory." In that chaotic and deadly arena, individuals could and did make a difference. Some fought, some didn't; some lied, some died and, sadly, some were left behind. It will be to the everlasting shame of those faithless politicians and political generals that when they decided to take the cowards route, they broke faith with their missing warriors and betrayed the survivors. In the spring of 1973, Lieutenant General Deane, Jr. USA, Acting Director of the defense Intelligence Agency, stated that "...At the present there are approximately 350 U.S. military and civilians listed as missing in action in Laos." None was ever accounted for by the Laotians or returned to the U.S. No one in Washington was ever called to account for the wasted and abandoned lives of their countrymen.

This is the story of some of those betrayed young men.

GLOSSARY OF TERMS

ADSID	Air Dropped Seismic Intrusion Detector
Air America	Private Airline in LAOS (CIA)
AK-47	Kalashnikov assault weapon
Alleycat	C-130 C&C Aircraft, Steel Tiger, Night Ops
Alpha	Interdiction Point in Barrel Roll
Arc Light	B-52 carpet area bomb drop
"A" FAC	Fighter qualified FAC
AUTOVON	Automatic Voice Network (DoD phone network)
"B" FAC	FAC with no fighter experience
Barrel Roll	North and Central Laos
Batcat	C-121 that passes sensor data to TFA
BDA	Bomb Damage Assessment
Bird	Any aircraft
Binh Thuy	Airfield in Mekong Delta
Birddog	Nickname for the O-1 spotter plane
Blind Bat	C-130 Flare ship – Ubon
Bomb Line	Free fire zone about 30 km from NKP east of the Mekong
BUDs	Friends, fellow warrior aviators
BUF	Big Ugly Fucker – B-52
Can Tho	Airfield in Mekong Delta
Candlestick NKP	C-123 Flare ship/FAC -

CBU	Cluster Bomb Unit
CIA	Central Intelligence Agency
C&C	Command & Control - Air and Ground
Chao Phraya Hotel	Bangkok hotel leased by the US Army
Church Key	Bottle opener
Covey	O-2A FAC – Danang, 20th TASS
Cricket	C-130 C&C – Steel Tiger, Day Ops
Cricket Club	23rd TASS club in town of NKP
Cricket West	Area of Laos adjacent to Mekong River
Crown	SAR Refueling Aircraft, HC-130P
Danang	Large US Air Base in South Vietnam
DASC	Direct Air Support Center
DASH-1	Aircraft operation manual
DEROS	Date of Estimated Return from Over Seas
DISUM	Daily Intelligence Summary
DMZ	Demilitarized Zone
Dullness	23rd TASS Ops call sign
FAC	Forward Air Controller
FACU	FAC school at Binh Thuy, SVN
FAN	Forward Air Navigator
Fence	Mekong River for NKP aircraft
Fire Can Radar	radar directed anti-aircraft guns

504th	Group HQ of 23rd TASS
FM	Frequency Modulated Radio
FNG	Fucking New Guy
Foxtrot	Interdiction Point in Steel Tiger
Funny Bomb	Air Opening Cluster Fire Bombs
GCI	Ground Control Intercept, radar
Golf	One of Many Interdiction Point in Steel Tiger
GREEN-EYE	starlight scope; light amplifying telescope, used to see at night
Gunfighter	Alert F-4 - Danang
Harley's Valley	Ban Karai Pass from N. Vietnam to Laos. Named for Harley who was shot down at that location
Hillsboro	C-130 C&C Aircraft, Barrel Roll, Day Ops
Hobo	A-1 - Day Attack - NKP
Hootch	house, living quarters or a native hut
Igloo White	Sensor derived intelligence program
Intrep	Intelligence Report
Invert	Radar site - NKP
Jinking	Continuously moving the aircraft nose randomly left and right of a general heading
Jolly Green	HH-3 or HH-53 Rescue Helicopter
Khe Sanh	Marine base in NW S.Vietnam

Klick, K	Short for kilometer (0.62 miles)
Lamplighter	C-130 Flare ship - UBON
LAPES	Low Altitude Parachute Extraction System
LZ	Landing Zone
M-16	US assault weapon
MACV	Military Assistance Command, Vietnam
Mike Mike	Millimeter, usually a measurement for guns
Misty	F-100 fast FAC
Moonbeam	C-130 C&C Aircraft, Barrel Roll, Night Ops
Mud River	Sensor program near DMZ a
Nail	O-2A FAC - NKP Call Sign
Nail 01	FAC Commander - 23rd TASS
Nail 02	FAC Operations Officer - 23rd TASS
Nail Common	FM frequency – 50.50
Nail Hole	Bar in front of one Nail hootch room
Nimrod	A-26 - Night Attack - NKP
NKP	Nakhon Phanom Royal Thai Air Base
NOSTAR	Flying at night without any outside lights
NUMBER ONE	good
NUMBER TEN	bad
NVA	North Vietnamese Army
O'Club	Officer's Mess/Club
Out Country	Any SEA country but SVN
Parrot	Slang for ID Friend or Foe

Parrot	Army aircraft (Mohawk) with SLAR
PCS	Permanent Change of Station
PDJ	Plain of Jars in northern Laos
PE	Physical Education (PT for some)
Porter	PC-12 Pilatus Porter aircraft
PJ	Para-rescue airman
Phan Rang	US Air Base in SVN
R & R	Rest-and-Recreation
Ranch Hand	C-123 Defoliation aircraft
Raven	O-1 FAC (CIA) - Laos
Redbird/Yellowbird	B-57 - Night Attack Jets from Phan Rang Air Base
Red Horse	AF civil engineering construction team
Route Pack	1 through 6, North Vietnam bombing areas
RTB	Return To Base from a mission
RVN	Republic of South Vietnam
SAC	Strategic Air Command
Sandy	A- Aircraft, Rescue Protection/Cover
SAR	Search and Rescue
SEA	South East Asia
7th Air Force	Senior Air Force unit in Vietnam (MACV)
781 Form	Aircraft maintenance record
Shack	Direct hit, usually with a bomb
Sheep Dip	Removing all indications of nationality
Skycrane	Army Helicopter – H-34

Skyspot	Radar controlled fighter bomb drop
SLAR	Side Looking Airborne Radar
Slick	Non-gunship helicopter
Smart Bombs	Guided bombs
SOF	Supervisor of Flying
Sortie	One aircraft making one takeoff and landing
Spectre	C-130 Gunship - Ubon
Spotlight	TFA report of sensor readings
Starlight Scope	Low light level scope, AN-PVS-2A
Steel Tiger	Laos - South of 18 deg 25 min North
TACC	Tactical Air Control Center - 7AF
Tan Son Nhut	Saigon Airfield
Tankers	KC-135, jet refueling aircraft
TASS	Tactical Air Support Squadron
Tchepone (many spellings)	"Village" in Steel Tiger on Route 9
TDY	Temporary Duty - away from unit/base
TFA	Task Force Alpha — Trail Sensors
TUOC	Tactical Unit Operations Center
23rd TASS	FAC Squadron based at NKP
Ubon	Large Air Base in Eastern Thailand
UHF	Ultra High Frequency Radio Band
VC, Cong	Vietcong

VHF	Very High Frequency Radio Band
WAF	Women in the Air Force
Willie Pete	White Phosphorous 2.75" marking rocket
Winchester	Out of ammunition
X-Band	Beacon device to enlarge Radar return blip
Zorro	T-28 - Night Attack Aircraft - NKP
ZPU	Raid fire anti-aircraft gun - NVA

AIRCRAFT

A-1 SKYRAIDER

B-25 MITCHELL

A-26 INVADER

B-52 STRATOFORTRESS

ANTONOV AN-2 COLT

B-57 CANBERRA

C-7 CARIBOU

C-123 PROVIDER

C-9 NIGHTINGALE

C-124 GLOBEMASTER

C-119 FLYING BOXCAR

C-130 HERCULES

C-141 STAR LIFTER

F-4 PHANTOM II

CH-54 SKYCRANE

F-86 SABRE

EC-121 BATCAT

F-86D SABRE

F-100 SUPER SABRE

H-34 CHOCKTAW

F-105 THUNDERCHIEF

HH-53 SUPER JOLLY GREEN

HH-3 JOLLY GREEN

KC-135 STRATOTANKER

O-1 BIRDOG

PC-12 PILATUS PORTER

O-2 SKYMASTER (DUCK)

T-28 NOMAD

OP-2E NEPTUNE

T-33 T-BIRD

T-34 MENTOR

T-39 SABER LINER

T-37 TWEET

U-10 COURIER

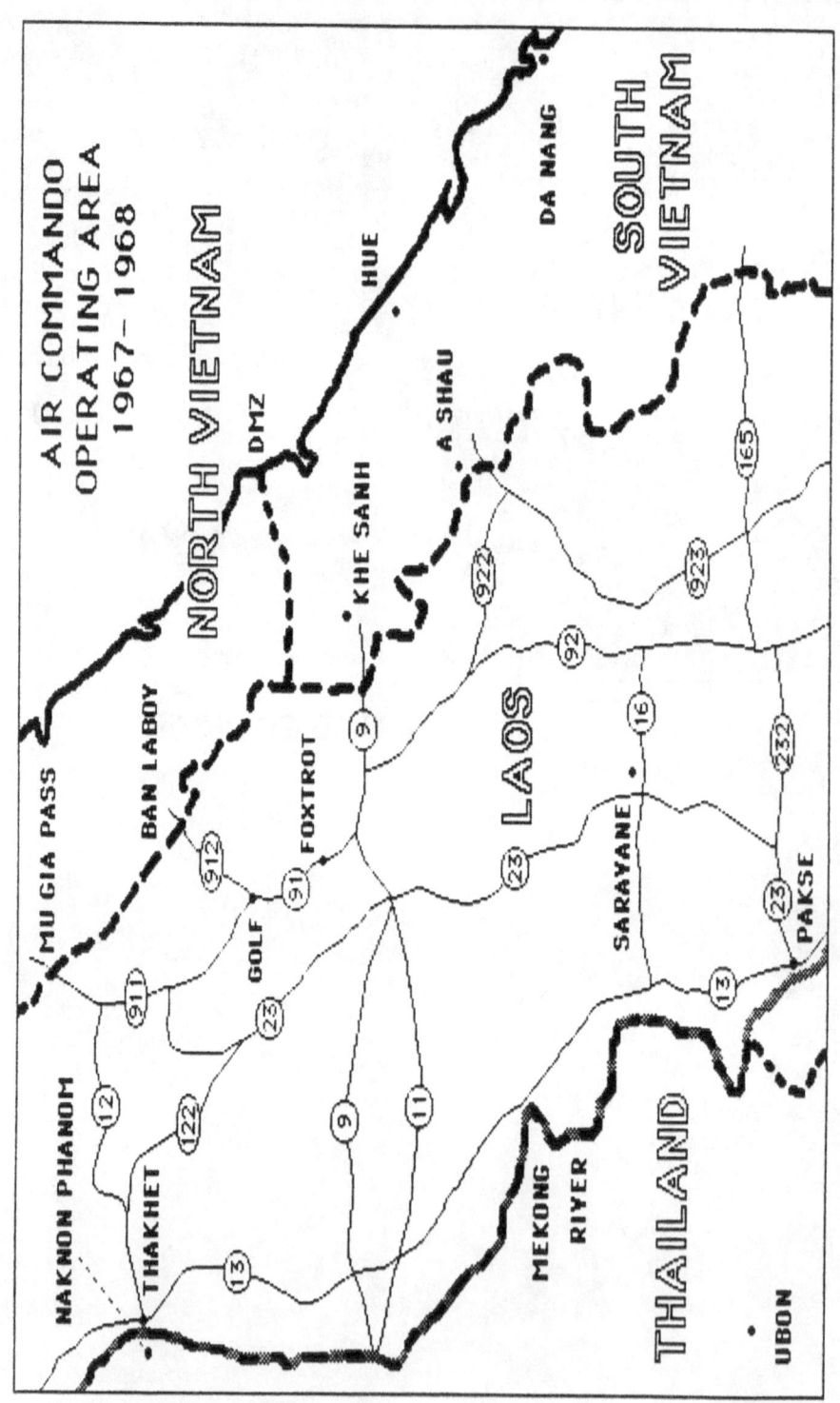

CHAPTER ONE
Binh Thuy Air Base
Mekong Delta, South Vietnam
12 October 1967, on the flight line

Captain William F. Thompson, USAF, stood in front of the small Cessna O-2A staring at the airplane. He was trying to decide if it was intentionally designed to be ugly or if it was an accident. Without the wings and front engine, it looked somewhat like the swamp buggy in Florida, although he'd seen some swamp buggies with better lines.

He was confused, disgusted, and upset. He thought *"Why am I, a great jet fighter pilot, stuck in this piece of shit in this asshole part of the world? I got more time in the men's room than I do in props? Why is Judy thinking about leaving me? She knew what she was doing when she married an Air Force pilot. She loved Europe. What did I do to deserve all this crap?"*

The twin engine propeller-driven airplane actually resembled a bathtub with wings. There was an engine at both ends of the tub; the front one pulled and the rear engine pushed. The twin booms extending back from the tub to the elevators and rudders looked like they belonged on an old airplane and the total effect was not graceful at all. The plane was squat and ugly. Kind of like an ugly duckling....which was appropriate... as the O-2's affectionate nickname was...."the Duck."

A cylindrical LAU/59 rocket pod with seven 2.75 inch folding-fin white phosphorous rockets was mounted under each wing. These could be fired one rocket at a time or salvoed one pod at a time. When the rockets exploded, they created a white cloud of phosphorous smoke easily seen by the fighters, and were used to mark targets for the Air Force attack planes.

Bill shook his head in dismay and walked to the cockpit door on the right of the aircraft. He put his parachute in the pilot's seat, the one on the left, and put his helmet and maps on the right seat, then walked around the plane and made the preflight inspection, taking special care to insure that the safety pins were installed in the rocket pods. These pins prevented accidental firing of the rockets or dropping of the pods and would not be removed until he reached the takeoff end of the runway.

With the walk-around inspection completed, he climbed into the cockpit and strapped himself into the seat. Today he was scheduled for a pattern ride to practice landings and he was headed for the US Army airfield at Can Tho, South Vietnam. Because he hadn't wanted to stay here at Binh Thuy and share the traffic pattern with four other O-2s, Bill had previously called Can Tho tower and they told him that they were not going to be busy for most of the afternoon.

Bill shook his head as if to clear the memories. Tinker toy or not, it could kill him. He had to fly and an airplane was no place for daydreaming. He reluctantly turned his attention to the Duck's checklist.

The O-2 was NOT an air-conditioned aircraft. Every flight started out as a steam bath. By the time he walked across the sun-baked tarmac from the parachute/weapon storage area to the plane, Bill's K2B flying suit (complete with all 11 zippered pockets!) was soaked in sweat. The worse part was getting into the plane after it had been sitting in the sun, baking. It was as hot and humid as an automobile got on a hot August day in Houston, but one couldn't just hop in and start moving. After you climbed into the O-2, you strapped into the parachute and tightened the seat belt and shoulder harness, and then you went through the seemingly endless checklist. After this Kabuki dance, if there were any dry parts left on his body, Bill had no idea where they might be. Fortunately, as soon as the front engine started, the vents provided a welcome but hot breeze. That was one advantage over a jet; it was like sitting behind a large fan.

He advanced the throttles and began taxiing, tapping the brakes to make sure they worked, and continued towards the end of the runway. In the arming area prior to takeoff, Bill placed his hands on the glare shield so the young armorer, an airman second class, could see that it was safe to pull the safety pins from his rocket pods. When the armorer was done pulling the pins, he held them up so Bill could count them.

He gave the airman thumbs up and taxied onto the runway. As he lined up with the runway centerline, he pushed the throttles forward full open to the stops and released the brakes. The O-2 quickly reached takeoff speed and Bill smoothly raised the nose. As soon as the plane left the ground, he checked his instruments and retracted the gear. He made an easy turn toward the southeast and Can Tho and climbed to 5,000 feet.

Can Tho and Binh Thuy were both located on the south bank of the Song Hau Giang River, as the southern extension of the Mekong was called in Vietnam. The mile-and-a half-wide river ran from northwest to southeast, from the Cambodian border to the South China Sea. The northern extension of the Mekong, the equally-wide Song Tieng Giang, ran roughly parallel until, at a point fifteen miles from Can Tho, it separated into two and then three outlets to the sea, forming the area known as the Mekong Delta. The land here was flat with rice paddies stretching as far as you could see in all directions.

For about an hour and a half he shot touch and go landings at Can Tho and began getting a feel for the Duck's handling characteristics in the traffic pattern. His first two flights in the aircraft had been at five thousand feet above the ground, turning, climbing and maneuvering the plane to get a feel for its flight characteristics. He had fired the rockets and dropped a flare, but this was the first time he was able to concentrate on takeoffs and landings. So far, his had been the only plane in the pattern, although he could see a large helicopter moving on the taxiway in front of the tower.

"Can Tho Tower, this is Bird Dog Three, on downwind for my final touch and go."

"Birddog Three, you're cleared for a touch and go landing on Runway 22." The tower operator replied.

In but a minute, *"Roger, Tower, Birddog Three is turning base. I'll be heading to Binh Thuy on the go,"* Bill called and lowered his gear for the landing. He made a wide descending turn to line up with the runway.

"Roger, Birddog. You're cleared for your touch and go, wind is from the west at six knots..., Army Heavy Four Six, hold short of the active runway."

At the tower's call, Bill glanced at the helicopter.

"Four six, holding."

The large ugly Skycrane CH-54 single-rotor helicopter moved up the taxiway and stopped near the takeoff/landing end of the runway.

As Bill flew down the final approach, he was aware of the large helicopter at the end of the taxiway but he wasn't concerned about it. That was the normal spot for aircraft to wait for takeoff clearance. When he reached the runway over run, he eased the throttles to idle, pulled gently back on the control wheel and prepared for touchdown. He was dumbfounded when the small aircraft suddenly rolled rapidly to the left. His right wing was up—way up—and the left nearly impacted the runway.

Bill's reaction was instantaneous. He quickly shoved the throttles to full power, pushed forward on the control wheel, and turned it all the way to the right. Fortunately, the little Cessna was light because it was low on fuel. It stayed airborne—barely—and he was able to regain control.

Bill was shaking, his heart was pounding wildly, and he realized that he was holding his breath. He was trying to hold the wheel gingerly, trying to determine what had gone wrong, and trying to get his composure back. The controls felt normal and none of the instruments were out of the green. He took a deep breath, let it out slowly and started to make a call, when he heard the tower's broadcast.

"Four Six, you did that on purpose."

"That's his problem," was the reply from the Army pilot. The voice was young—very young—and high pitched.

That was when Bill realized that the helicopter pilot had caused his wild gyrations by moving the giant Sikorsky's rotors to full pitch as his O-2 came in to land. The airflow from the large rotors blades created such severe turbulence for the small O-2 that it nearly flipped it on its back and splattered it onto the runway!

"The bastard almost killed me," he thought.

As Bill turned out of the traffic pattern, he reached up and armed the rockets in his starboard-side underwing pod which held seven 2.75-inch white-phosphorous marking rockets.

"Let's see if those Army sons-a-bitches like to play games by my rules," he muttered, his anger overriding any common sense.

By the time he turned back toward the runway, he could see the Skycrane flying north over the Mekong River. Bill lined up his sights on the departing helicopter, pulled the nose up...placed the pipper just over the Skycrane slightly to the right and hit the pickle button....*Whoosh!!* The 2.75 inch Willy Pete went over the helicopter. It impacted in the Mekong River, two hundred yards in front of the Skycrane.

"Birddog, that's one of ours!" screamed the tower operator.

In the right seat of the Skycrane, the young Army warrant officer was still giggling at his childish and dangerous prank when the 2.75-inch rocket blasted over his rotor and impacted the Mekong in a muddy, whitish blossom. His attention was gained! He swerved around the impact. He was VERY concerned... (Note: aviators are NEVER scared...just HIGHLY concerned!!)

"Hey, FAC...cease fire...cease fire.... you're gonna kill us all." His voice was now extremely highly pitched.

"Fuck you!" Bill shouted and fired another 2.75 rocket. This time he fired it down the left side of the Skycrane.

The supersonic whiplash crack of the 2.75 Willie Pete rocket passing the Sky Crane's open cockpit window and the bang of its impact in the muddy brown waters of the Mekong took all fight and fun from the Skycrane crew.

"FAC...FAC....cease fire.........please..."

The helicopter pilot's frantic, pleading radio calls were repeated over and over as Bill continued the chase. He didn't fire any more rockets, but the Army Chopper Jock really thought he would. When he was finished, he had fired only two of the Willy Petes from his starboard Lau-59. He had carefully placed them where they would not do any damage, but where they could be seen and heard by the Army crew.

As he continued the chase, he thought, *"Holy shit, what if I hit the bastards?"* He reached up and disarmed the starboard pod.

Bill had elected to disarm the pod, but keyed the VHF transmitter and said *"Skycrane, this is Bird Dog....have a nice day....Asshole!"*

Bill, soaked with sweat and still furiously angry, banked his Duck to the Northwest, toward Binh Thuy. Bill asked himself *"How in hell did I get here shooting at US Army helicopters?"*

Captain Thompson was thirty one years old and a career Air Force officer. He was five feet nine inches tall, weighed one hundred and seventy pounds and was well built, like a wrestler. He wore his sandy brown hair in a crew cut and had brown eyes and an ever- present grin. His expressions were rarely serious, although the smile or smirk often hid his real feelings.

After graduating from Ohio University, the Coshocton, Ohio, native went through Air Force Officer Indoctrination training at Lackland Air Force Base in Texas. He married his college sweetheart as soon as he finished the four-week training program and set off with a new wife and a Chevrolet convertible to attend flying school. When he arrived at Graham Air Base in Marianna, Florida, in the fall of 1957, he was one of hundreds of newly-married Second Lieutenants in the USAF Primary Pilot Training Program.

In six months he learned to fly a propeller-driven training aircraft; the T-34 and the T-28. Bill then went on to Basic Pilot Training and the faster T-33, a single-engine jet. There was no feeling quite like flying a speedy single engine jet, even the old T-33. (In 1958, the airlines still used propeller-driven airplanes). He flew well and progressed from the T-33 to a fighter, the F-86D Sabre Jet. The F-86F was the plane flown by USAF pilots in Korea and many of his instructors were veterans of the Korean Conflict. Bill was in awe of the men who flew these machines and decided that he wanted to be just like them.

When he arrived at Williams Air Force Base in Arizona for Advanced Training, he found that there were no two-seat versions of the F-86D. For the first time, Bill was uncertain about his flying abilities. The T-33 had two seats and an IP (Instructor Pilot) was in the plane while you learned to fly it. The F-86 had only ONE seat!!

He would never forget his first Sabre Jet flight. His Instructor stood on the wing and watched as Bill started the F-86. When he was ready to taxi, the IP shook his hand, wished him luck and jumped down. Bill was on his own and it was a glorious experience. The plane was a dream to fly and could even go supersonic, in a steep dive. When Bill returned to the pattern to make his landing, it was on the mark. His uncertainty was gone and he knew that he was going to be a fighter pilot.

He continued to fly fighters and upgraded to the F-100 Super Sabre (Hun) in the US and was transferred to Europe. In 1966 he volunteered to fly the Hun in Vietnam. Bill was assigned to the 352nd Tactical Fighter Squadron at Phan Rang Air Base, which was flying the F-100 Super Sabre, was and ordered to Vietnam with a ten-day stop in the Philippines for jungle survival training.

Two days before he was to leave the Philippines, his orders were changed and he was reassigned to the 23rd Tactical Air Support Squadron (TASS) at Nakhon Phanom (NKP) Air Base in Thailand as a Forward Air Controller (FAC). He was to check out in the new FAC aircraft, the O-2A, at a training base in the Mekong Delta, Binh Thuy.

When the Personnel Officer at Clark Air Base in the Philippines gave him his new orders, Bill was totally irate. He ranted and raved at the major to no avail….orders were orders. The Personnel major sat quietly and smiled at Bill until he had worked out his frustration. When Bill eventually calmed down, the major handed him back the orders and pointed at the door. He never said a word. Bill's supersonic days were over, at least for this war, as the O-2's top speed was less than 200 miles per hour.

Then Bill tried calling everyone he knew in Vietnam, attempting to get the orders changed again, with no success. So here he was in the hot, humid Mekong Delta flying this goddamned tinker toy. He couldn't believe that it was more important for him to fly this bathtub of a Cessna than a real fighter plane, doing what he was trained to do, dropping bombs and shooting guns.

He had left his very unhappy wife and two children three weeks ago and was wondering if had done the right thing by volunteering for combat duty in Vietnam. Nothing seemed to be going "as planned". Only five days earlier, he had been flown in a C-141 from the Philippines to Saigon and experienced for his first time its unbelievable heat, the humidity, and the putrid smells of Southeast Asia.

From Saigon, he was transported by bus to nearby Bien Hoa Air Base for processing into the 504th Tactical Air Support Group. All four of the FAC squadrons were part of the 504th, including the 23rd TASS in Thailand.

Before he went to NKP, he would have to go to Binh Thuy for check out and qualification in his new plane. He arrived at Binh Thuy on his second day in Vietnam. It continued to be very hot and sticky. (A pattern was forming here, he thought; it was always hot and sticky in Vietnam!)

Thirty-one-year-old Captain William F. Thompson nearly hadn't made it to thirty-two because of a stupid Army stunt. An experienced fighter pilot, he had flown over two thousand hours in aircraft capable of speeds of nearly one-thousand knots. To get killed in a one-hundred-knot Cessna Super Skymaster, in an avoidable accident, was incredible. He hadn't volunteered for Vietnam to die in a dumb accident, particularly one caused by his own side.

"Goddamned Army assholes," he muttered to himself. He sat slumped in his seat, slowly winding down both physically and mentally as he flew toward the Vietnamese air base at Binh Thuy. He reached up and removed his helmet. It was dripping wet and so was he. Using his handkerchief, he wiped his face and head and then the inside of his helmet. The close call had shaken him. He felt very tired…drained.

As the adrenalin dissipated, reason returned and he began to become concerned about the repercussions of his actions. If they threw him out of the school, he could end up as a staff flunky. Captains didn't have enough rank to get a responsible position at 7th Air Force Headquarters. He'd end up as someone's gofer. He was in for it now and there wasn't really any good excuse for firing rockets at a U.S. Army helicopter...at least he couldn't think of a good one. *"Hell,"* he thought, *"I could be court martialed and drummed out of the Air Force, maybe sent to Leavenworth."*

After he touched down and while taxiing to the de-arming area, he saw a jeep parked nearby. *"Oh, shit!"* The colonel was waiting for him with one of the senior maintenance sergeants.

As soon as Bill shut down the front engine, the sergeant walked to the starboard rocket pod, the one with the two empty tubes. He checked it carefully and then reached into his back pocket for something. Bill could not see what the sergeant was doing out there under his wing.

Lieutenant Colonel George T. Pirot, the tall, dapper, training school commander, was standing by the jeep. George always looked like he just stepped out of a recruiting poster. He was slim, blond and he kept himself in good physical condition by running every day. The colonel acknowledged Bill with a nod but did not approach the aircraft.

The sergeant finished with the rocket pod and stuck his head into the cockpit. *"Here's your problem, Captain. It was a loose connection in the firing circuit."* He was holding a small piece of wire. He winked at Bill and went back to the jeep. He and the colonel drove off.

Bill was still not sure what was going to happen...now or later. He received an "all clear" signal from the armorer and taxied toward the O-2 parking area. One of the instructor pilots running the checkout program, Major Fred Stebbins, was waiting for him. The major was a short, rugged-looking man who appeared to be about forty but was probably older. He had flown combat missions in Korea and even Colonel George listened to him when it came to aerial combat tactics.

"You really shot at him?" said the major, in disbelief.

Bill nodded. ***"Yes, Sir. The son-of-a-bitch nearly killed me!"***

"George and I were flying when Binh Thuy Tower called us about the incident. We came right back and he got on the phone with the local Army Commander. Can Tho Tower is claiming that it was an accident. Two rockets fired individually... some accident!"

Bill reddened. ***"I wasn't trying to hit him; just scare the shit out of him."***

"Come on, Captain. Let's see how George wants to handle this. He said he would meet us at the O' Club."

Historical Note: This all happened to Jerry Dwyer as he was checking out in the O-2 at Ben Hoa, but he did not fire any rockets at the US Army helicopter. Did chase him, but he did not fire.

CHAPTER TWO
Binh Thuy Air Base
Mekong Delta, South Vietnam
12 October 1967, later that afternoon at the "Officers' Club"

There were less than ten U.S. Air Force officers at Binh Thuy and they used a room off the mess hall as an Officer's Club. It contained a small bar, an old juke box, three four-place tables and half-a-dozen slot machines. It was air conditioned, as were most of the pilot's facilities in South Vietnam and Thailand. The mess hall building was an old wooden structure with a tin roof. During the monsoons, it was difficult to hear above the noise of the rain pelting the roof.

As they walked through the mess hall on the way to the club room, the few Air Force diners clapped and cheered.

"They don't seem to like the Army," Fred said, smiling at Bill, *"On the other hand, maybe they think that was normal fighter pilot shooting accuracy."*

Entering the club room, they met Captain Sean O'Malley. *"Nice going, Attila. Where did you think you were, on the gunnery range at Luke?"* Sean asked, grinning broadly.

"The son-of-a-bitch tried to kill me!" Bill said angrily and he sat down. Sean had never seen him quite so mad.

Sean and Bill had known each other since they were at Lackland for the four-week Officer Indoctrination Program in 1957. They were both single then and had enjoyed their liberty in San Antonio. Bill married after the program, but Sean remained a bachelor. Bill's career took him to fighters, and Sean's to the large refueling tankers.

Sean's flying career to date had been confined to one base in the Southwest U.S., where he flew KC-135 tankers in Strategic Air Command (SAC), followed by an eighteen-month assignment at the Air Force Institute of Technology where he earned a Master's Degree in Mechanical Engineering. A graduate of Purdue, he had applied for the Master's program to escape what was beginning to look like a one-airplane career. SAC was reluctant to lose good pilots and Sean was one of their best. He had been selected for Aircraft Commander and then Instructor Pilot several years earlier than his contemporaries. He was then selected for duty on the Wing Standardization and Evaluation team at Biggs Air Force Base, Texas. He had been facing a promising but virtually permanent and repetitive career, flying the same airplane from the same base doing the same thing every day for the rest of his career. He jumped at the chance to do something different and volunteered for the Graduate School program.

While in Grad School, the students were told that they were all going to Vietnam after graduation. Because of his multi-engine flying experience, Sean was programmed for the C-7 Caribou, a twin-engine, short-haul cargo plane. He was not at all pleased with the prospect of flying a small "trash hauler" and volunteered again, this time for the higher-priority and much more dangerous FAC program.

He was immediately accepted and received orders to report to Hurlburt Field upon graduation. He had kept in touch with Bill over the years and enjoyed it immensely when Bill would bring one of his fighters to Biggs on one of what seemed like many weekend training junkets.

Once Sean had been given a ride in the back seat of Bill's F-100, a common but unauthorized occurrence. Sean, in turn, had arranged for Bill to fly aboard the KC-135 and took him on an F-100 fighter refueling mission.

During the flight, Sean beat Bill out of dinner by betting that the KC-135 could out climb the F-100 as long as the fighter didn't engage its afterburner. Bill laughed and said **"No way!"**

When the refueling had been completed Sean called the Hun drivers and passed on the challenge. The F-100s had just finished refueling and were heavy with fuel and the KC-135 was at nearly minimum fuel. The big four-engine tanker easily out climbed the heavy fighters, much to Bill's chagrin. He hated to lose.

After nearly 10 years in "different Air Forces," Bill was surprised to find Sean in the same class at Jungle Survival School (known as "snake school") and even more surprised to find that they were both assigned to the same FAC squadron in Thailand.

Good friends, the two even looked somewhat alike; short brown hair, brown eyes, and stocky builds but, at five feet seven, Sean was a couple of inches shorter than Bill. They kept themselves in good physical condition, although their current appearance had more to do with the Jungle Survival Course, than with an exercise program. A couple of days in the jungle at the base of Mount Pinatubo tended to use up a lot of excess body weight.

Fred Stebbins came back from the bar carrying three beers. *"You don't understand, Captain,"* he said, handing out the cans.

"You just failed your first encounter with gross ignorance." Fred had an odd-looking smile on his face. He sat down and took a long drink.

"Gross ignorance?" asked Bill, curiously.

"Yeah, think about it. The average age of Army pilots over here is probably nineteen or twenty. The average age of an Air Force pilot is close to thirty. There is quite a difference in flying time, experience and maturity between the two groups. Most of the Army pilots are only high school graduates, while nearly all of our pilots have college degrees. That's why we wiser and more experienced heads consider "gross ignorance" to be.... one hundred and forty four Army helicopter pilots."

They all laughed. Major Stebbins was enjoying his moment but he was also teaching them an important and possibly life-saving lesson: don't depend on the young Army pilots to react or function the same way that Air Force pilots would.

Bill thought for a moment and said, *"You're telling us to stay away, far far away from the flying Army."*

"That's right, Captain. They're just kids and they'll pull kid's stunts. Know it and make allowances. You didn't have to stay in the pattern once you saw the helicopter. In reality, you created the opportunity for a disaster," Fred said and paused briefly.

"This is a war and there are very few rules in a war. In the future, don't allow any situation to develop which can lead to a problem you can't solve. You'll be surprised how easy it is to keep things like that from happening. Keep your head out of your ass; it may save your ass."

At that moment, George walked in and sat down. Bill said, *"I'm sorry, Colonel; I should've left the pattern when the helicopter showed up."*

George looked at Major Stebbins and smiled. *"I see you've explained the situation."* He turned to Bill. *"Sergeant Woodley has explained to the powers to be that it was a weapons malfunction, but I don't want any more dumb shit stunts. Bill, you owe the sergeant a bottle of bourbon… a bottle of Jack Daniels."*

Bill nodded, turning somewhat red.

There was no more said about the incident. George drank a beer with them and left to check on the next day's schedule.

CHAPTER THREE
Binh Thuy Air Base
Mekong Delta, South Vietnam
12 October 1967, dinner time in the "Officers' Club"

"Let's get something to eat. I want to talk to the two of you for a while," Fred said, suddenly quite serious. Bill and Sean were surprised, but said nothing.

They followed Fred into the dining area. All three picked up trays and walked through the serving line and selected their food. They took the trays to an empty table and went back for coffee.

"What's on your mind, Major?" Sean asked, after they had finished their meals and returned their trays to the pickup counter.

"This is mostly for Bill, but I suspect it also applies to you, O'Malley," Fred started.

"You both have short fuses, too short."

The two smiled. Fred was right. He looked at Bill. *"You flew the Sabre, didn't you?"*

"Yes, Sir, at Willy," Bill replied.

"So did I, in Korea. It's what I want to talk about. In 1951 I was a Second Lieutenant, just finishing my training in the F-86 and headed for Korea. I'd never been in combat but I was absolutely certain that I could handle the plane and the war," Fred continued his eyes unfocused and his voice softer than usual.

"In less than a week after my arrival, I was shot down by a MIG-15," he continued. Bill and Sean were listening intently. Fred had their attention now.

"Were you captured?" Bill asked.

"No. It was my good luck to be picked up by the Navy, but that isn't why I'm telling you this. I went back up the next day and, within another week, got my first MIG. I actually shot down three of them before my tour was over."

The two were impressed. Fred rarely spoke of his experiences. They waited while he sipped his coffee and lit another Marlboro. He looked at each of them in turn and continued, *"What I'm telling the two of you is that I was shot down because I didn't understand about combat and assumptions. I was too cocky and I lost a perfectly good airplane for a bad reason. It still bothers me, sixteen years later."*

"It's not wrong to be shot down, Major. It may be bad news, but it isn't wrong," Bill replied.

"What makes it wrong is what caused it. I've never told anyone this story, and I expect the two of you to keep it to yourselves. In the F-86, the gun-arming switch is on the left outboard panel, behind the throttle. It's guarded and you have to lift the guard, and then arm the guns by lifting the toggle switch. It isn't very difficult and the switch guard is the only one located there."

Bill nodded in agreement. He remembered the procedure and the switches.

"Some of the hot shots in my squadron did it another way. They pulled the gun-arming circuit breaker, which was located a couple of inches forward of the arming switch. With the circuit breaker pulled, you could leave the guns armed and when you wanted to shoot, just push in the breaker. The checklist warned against doing that, but the hot shots thought it was quicker and easier just to push in a circuit breaker. Well, I was a fighter pilot and I could do anything as well as anyone else so I pulled the circuit breaker. On my second combat mission, there were four of us on patrol and we were jumped by six MIGs. I was flying wing on my element leader and we turned into the MIGs. It was a real zoo. There were planes everywhere and I was having a hard time keeping my lead in sight."

Bill was nodding, remembering the F-86 and the air-to-air combat training.

"When we turned into the attack, I pushed in the circuit breaker and set the arming switch. It was a colossal error. The next thing I knew, we were mixing it up with two MIGs and Lead was yelling at me to get one off his tail. I slid over, lined up my guns and squeezed the trigger," Fred paused and looked at them. Both were engrossed in his story. ***"Nothing happened; not one goddamned thing. The guns didn't fire. I looked down and saw that the circuit breaker was in, and then I leaned over and looked at the arming switch. The goddamn thing was off! In my excitement, I turned it from 'ON' to 'OFF'. That didn't take very long, but when I looked up Lead was gone and so were the MIGs. I started to turn back when I was hit, the fire started and I ejected. End of story."***

Bill smiled. ***"I can see how that could happen."***

Fred got very serious and his eyes flashed angrily. ***"The reason I told you the story is not for you to sit there and agree with me, smart ass. I told it to you to illustrate how you can fuck up. Now, you did fuck up badly today and I am going to offer some advice only this once."***

Both Sean and Bill were taken aback by the force of Fred's words. They straightened in their chairs and waited for him to continue.

"Number one, I assumed that I was as smart as the other pilots in my squadron. I wasn't."

"Number two, I assumed that the people who wrote the checklist were assholes. They weren't. "

"Lastly, I assumed that the MIG pilots weren't very good. They were. My Lead didn't make it back."

Fred's words were being spit at them in short bursts. Both captains were turning red and they were squirming uncomfortably in their chairs.

"That's not all," he continued his short bursts, ***"You made some grossly stupid assumptions today, Captain.***

"First, you assumed that all of your rockets were good. How many times have you had one go

off on a tangent when a fin didn't open? You could have hit that helicopter."

"Second, you assumed that you and your O-2 were more important to this war than the Skycrane. You aren't!"

"If you asked 7th Air Force right now which they would rather have, a Skycrane or an O-2, the answer is obvious."

"Finally, you assumed that your opinions and feelings are important. They aren't! My words to the both of you might keep you alive. Grow up!"

"I am going to make a prediction. You, Captain Bill Thompson, are going to bust your ass somewhere in Laos because you think you have all the answers. Captain Sean O'Malley, you may make it, if you don't listen to him."

Fred was finished talking. He glared at them, then stood and walked into the club, leaving the two sitting stunned at the dinner table. After a moment, Sean said to Bill, *"You really screwed up this time. I don't understand. You screw up and I get a ration of shit."*

"Who knows? That's a side of our good major that I don't want to see again. I think he's angrier with himself than with us. Whew!" Bill replied.

"Do you think he's right? Are we doing things the wrong way?" Sean asked.

"I like Fred a lot," Bill replied. *"I think he's trying to help. He told us some things he hasn't told anyone else, and at least he did it in private. He's a friend, but he certainly succeeded in showing me what a dumbass I've been."*

Sean laughed at his friend's discomfort. *"I don't think he was concerned about your embarrassment. He was trying to get us to think about what we're* doing here. If you tried that rocket stunt in the states, you'd end up in Fort Leavenworth."

Bill nodded in agreement. "We definitely need to be very careful how we operate. Fred sure was right about the Army kids, but I don't know whether I share his views about combat."

"His views on combat? Jesus Christ, what kind of combat experience do you have? You shot at one fucking helicopter and it was on our side," Sean was as intense as Fred had been.

"We've been friends a long time, Bill. Fred's only known you for a week, yet he picked right up on your attitude. Shit, we've talked about your goddamned rotten attitude a lot in the past."

"What's wrong with my attitude?" Bill said, defensively.

"See what I mean? You can't handle criticism. I think what Fred was saying is that you better make big changes if you want to live through this war." Sean wasn't mincing his words.

"He said it to you, too," Bill argued.

"Not really. He only warned me about listening to you."

Bill scowled and sat quiet for a moment. Sean was looking at him intently, waiting for him to speak. "Damn! I guess you're right; no, I know you're right. I've got to give people more room and not be so critical or defensive. This is going to be a long war and some people are going to do dumb things. I better not be one of them."

Sean laughed at him. He really didn't think Bill would change, but Fred's talk had made him think about it. Sean would have to watch him carefully.

They sat for a while, talking about the war and combat in general. Of course, these were two topics that neither of them knew very much about. Fred's words bothered Bill far more than he was willing to admit and he promised himself to follow the advice and think before he reacted. When they returned to the bar, Fred was gone but Colonel Pirot and a couple of student FACs were sitting around a table. The colonel was explaining the "frag order" system when Sean and Bill pulled up chairs and joined them. He talked for another half hour about the war, particularly the importance of the FACs, and then rose and started to leave.

"Captain Thompson, how did you like the F-86 story... shoot down, three kills and the circuit breaker?" the colonel, asked, turning to look at Bill.

Bill sat with his mouth open, staring at Colonel Pirot. He couldn't speak.

Colonel Pirot smiled at him and then turned and left the room. Nothing more was ever said about his incident or about Fred's story.

CHAPTER FOUR
Binh Thuy Air Base
Mekong Delta, South Vietnam

16 October 1967, in the "Officers' Club" after dinner

For the next few days, the pilots avoided flying into Can Tho and remained near Binh Thuy. Sergeant Woodley's malfunction report seemed to satisfy the Army and there was no further action taken against Bill. He was still smarting from the lecture Fred had given him and was uncharacteristically quiet in the Officer's Club most of the time.

It was customary for the pilots to meet at the O'Club every evening after flying the daily schedule of training missions. They would sit around a table and talk about the flying or about the war. Generally one or two of the instructor pilots assigned to the school would be there. These bull sessions lasted a couple of hours and broke up when the bar closed, usually around 2200 hours.

Two days after the helicopter incident, they had been discussing their reasons for coming to Vietnam. The two majors in the class had not volunteered for duty in Vietnam. Bill, Sean and the other student, a lieutenant, had. The lieutenant was in SAC, like Sean, and volunteered to get away from the big bombers and tankers. Also, like Sean, he was single and did not care for the lifestyle at the SAC bomber bases, particularly sitting alert. He would be going to the 20th TASS at Danang and was looking forward to the challenge of flying the O-2 in support of ARVN ground troops.

Bill, on the other hand, had volunteered to fly fighters, not the O-2. It was expected that the men in the fighter squadrons would volunteer and he was no exception. His squadron was based in Germany and committed to NATO. It would not be rotating through Vietnam like many of the squadrons based in the U.S. When a call came in for qualified F-100 pilots, he had volunteered and was assigned to the F-l00 unit at Phan Rang, South Vietnam.

"Are you still sore about missing a chance to fly a fighter over here?" Sean asked.

"Damn right! As soon as I get to NKP, I'm going to see if there's something there that I can fly," Bill replied.

"Do you think they're running this war for your convenience?" Fred asked with a smile.

Bill looked at him and shrugged. *"No, but when I volunteered, we were promised fighter squadrons."*

"Things change, Captain," Major Willard replied.

"I could've stayed in Europe. I would have, if they'd told me I'd end up flying a bathtub," Bill said.

"What difference does it make?" Willard asked.

"I've been training for ten years to fly a fighter in combat. It's a waste for me to fly this Tinker Toy!" Bill was getting agitated.

"Someone thinks it's where you belong," Sean noted.

Bill gave him a disgusted look. *"I know. Some colonel in 7th Air Force that I never heard of, a goddamned SAC type marked my orders 'Priority' for NKP. That's all they would tell me. When I cleared in at the 504th they tried to get it changed to another FAC squadron. Even that wasn't allowed. No one tells me anything."*

Fred laughed. *"War isn't logical. The people who run it have their own priorities...and their own friends. Someone obviously wants you at NKP. Maybe you should be grateful. At least you won't have to worry about having the base overrun or being hit with mortars at night."*

Bill nodded in agreement. *"That's the one good thing about the assignment. Every time I look at those sandbagged revetments and bunkers, I think about the mortars."*

Fred was leaning back in his chair with an enigmatic smile. The others could tell he was remembering some event from Korea and waited for him to speak. He suddenly sat up and said, *"There's one other thing we all need to remember about combat."*

"What's that, Fred?" Major Willard asked. He had not been in Korea.

"The movies are wrong. John Wayne lied. War isn't fair, or logical, or fun...and the good guys don't always win."

"We surrender, Fred. Would you like another beer?" Sean asked, getting up from the table.

The conversation changed to orders for drinks and then switched back to flying. All the new FACs were now feeling comfortable with the O-2 except for Major Matthew R. Willard, who hadn't flown an operational aircraft in eight years.

Previously assigned to MAC Headquarters at Scott Air Force Base, the major's last operational flying was in the old, slow C-124 Globemaster, a giant plane used to carry men and equipment all over the world at very slow speeds. Major Willard was much more familiar with the sedentary life of a staff officer than the activities of a flying officer and even the survival school hadn't changed his chubby appearance. At five feet ten inches and one hundred and ninety pounds, with a cherubic face and sandy hair, he looked like a successful, well fed, small-town storekeeper. He was not a volunteer and once he was ordered to Vietnam he had worked diligently to secure what he believed to be a reasonably safe non-flying job. At thirty-nine, he knew his promotion to lieutenant colonel, if it ever came, would depend on his actions in Vietnam. He did not care much for the younger pilots and, unlike Fred, insisted that they maintain strict military courtesy. Major Stebbins was Fred. Major Willard was Major Willard.

Sean walked back to the table with the drinks just as they started to talk about night flying. He said, as he sat down, *"You know, Bill, I've never made a night landing."*

"Come off it, Sean. You must have two thousand hours in tankers," Bill stated, emphatically.

"In the big aircraft we didn't get many night landings, and my aircraft commander always took them for himself. You don't argue with Majors."

"I agree with that, but aren't night landings required?" asked Willard, pompously.

"Sure, Major. My flight records show plenty of night landings, but I never made one myself," Sean replied. *"Do you think it matters?"*

"It certainly does. You should've explained it to your aircraft commander," Willard answered, with a serious look.

Fred interrupted the exchange. *"Night landings aren't too difficult at seventy knots. The landing lights are good and the plane's easy to handle. You shouldn't have any problem if you managed day flying."* He was looking at Willard.

"I had some trouble with the O-2 at first," Willard agreed, nodding his head.

"We heard, Major," Bill said, laughing. *"Sergeant Woodley was afraid that they'd have to shoot you down on your first solo flight."*

"Don't be so sure of yourself, Captain. I have a lot more hours than any of you, except Fred," Willard snapped. He paused and then continued, looking at Fred. *"I don't know why it was such a problem. I never had any difficulty with landings before. I guess being out of a cockpit for eight years makes a difference."*

"Don't worry, Matt. They get easier with practice," Fred replied. *"Sean's the one with real problems."*

"How so, Major?" Sean asked, innocently.

"If you'll turn on the memory in your pea brain, you will recall that we flew together tonight and I made the only landing. I don't think you can make a night landing," he replied, sarcastically.

"Sure I can," Sean answered. *"They're just like day landings, aren't they?"* He looked inquisitively at Bill.

"It's obvious that my colleague requires my expert assistance and advice," Bill stated. He stood and took Sean by the arm.

The others watched as the two left the club. Bill had one arm around Sean's shoulder and was using his other hand to describe a night landing. Once outside the building, the two exploded with laughter.

"He believed every word," Bill exclaimed.

"Wait until tomorrow night. It gets worse!" Sean said.

CHAPTER FIVE
Binh Thuy Air Base
Mekong Delta, South Vietnam

17 October 1967, after dinner in the "Officers' Club"

The charade continued all the next day and that night they sat by themselves at a corner table. Sean became more forlorn looking and Bill kept up his constant instruction. The others could hear every word, but did not join in the conversation. Major Willard had made one night landing earlier that evening, after eight attempts. He kept sneaking worried glances at Sean and Bill.

Finally, Willard could stand it no longer. He looked at Sean and asked, ***"Who are you flying with tomorrow night?"***

Sean brightened, ***"Don't worry, Major. George is taking me up himself. They tell me you get to go with our most experienced old head, Major Stebbins."***

Willard looked extremely relieved. Fred Stebbins shook his head in disbelief and Bill gave Sean a puzzled look. **"How did Sean set up their final check flights?"** he wondered. Before he could say anything, Sean cut him off and the two left the club.

"How did you know about the schedule?" he asked Sean.

"I worked it out with George and Fred. They want Willard to request a transfer to a staff job.

They don't feel comfortable about him directing air strikes near our troops."

"I sure wouldn't want him anywhere near me. He isn't likely to be able to handle the plane and the strikes at the same time," Bill said.

The next afternoon, all of the pilots were in the training room being briefed on the operation of the Starlight scopes. The fat, cylindrical, telescope-like devices were light intensification aids and were used by the FACs at night to see targets on the ground. The group practiced in the semi-darkened room until they were familiar with the controls and operation of the scopes.

CHAPTER SIX
Binh Thuy Air Base
Mekong Delta, South Vietnam
18 October 1967, just before sunset at the "Officers' Club"

Prior to their final night flight, they went to the mess hall for supper. Sean was still at it.

"Major, you make sure the other major gets to practice his landings," Sean said. *"Don't hog all of the time."*

"No problem, Captain. I'm going to make sure he flies in the left seat. He can make them all," Fred said, smiling.

Willard was sweating noticeably. He was not having an easy time getting the O-2 on the ground during the day and his one night landing was more luck than skill. He was not looking forward to this last night flight.

"I'm going to let George make all of mine. No sense changing my perfect record," Sean stated, confidently.

"Would you guys please make an announcement when you get to the pattern?" Bill laughed. *"We want to watch a fiery crash."*

"Oh, Ye of little faith," Sean replied, grinning.

The pilots left the mess hall and walked to the flight line where they preflighted their aircraft. Fred Stebbins began the outside pre-flight. Willard climbed into the O-2 and was strapping himself in when Sergeant Woodley came up in the jeep. *"Major Stebbins, Colonel Pirot wants to see you right away."*

"I'll be right back, Matt," Fred said, and left in the jeep with Woodley.

Ten minutes passed. It was getting dark and Willard began to get worried. When he saw the jeep returning his spirits picked up, but when it stopped he realized that Fred was not in it. Sean was in the jeep with Sergeant Woodley. Willard watched with unbelieving eyes as Sean got out and walked to the aircraft.

"Hi, Major. Colonel Pirot can't make it. He sent me over to go with you. Fred isn't going to fly tonight."

Sean climbed into the right seat and strapped in. When he finished and was settled in his seat, holding the Starlight scope on his lap, he turned to the major. *"Let's go, Sir. I can really handle this Starlight scope."*

Sean busied himself with the checklist and did not look at the Major. That unfortunate soul was near panic. Willard started the aircraft and taxied to the end of the runway. When tower cleared him, he took off and they headed toward their assigned area, climbing to six thousand feet. The sun had set thirty minutes ago and it was now dark. Sean held the scope out the right window and spent the next half hour changing settings and looking for ground movement. When he finished, he handed the scope to the major.

"Your turn, Sir."

Sean took control of the aircraft and spent a half hour flying easy turns a mile above the ground while Willard experimented with the scope and wiped sweat from his face.

"Pretty neat, isn't it?" Sean said.

"Yeah," Willard replied, uncertainly.

"I think we should head back, Major," Sean said, reaching for the scope. Willard reluctantly handed the device to Sean.

Sean used the scope to look out the right side and ignored the major, who was now faced with getting the plane back on the ground. Willard was unsure of himself, but was not about to let a pilot who had never landed at night take control of the aircraft. On the other hand, he wasn't sure that he could make another safe night landing.

Willard turned toward the base and began a slow descent. As the plane started down, Sean looked at Willard with a funny expression, pushed his seat back and crossed his legs. Looking as nonchalant as possible, he turned to Willard and said, *"This is really great, Sir. You're flying so smoothly that I can't even hear the engines. It sure is peaceful up here."*

Willard smiled at him and then his eyes widened. There was no sound coming from the two engines. He looked at his instruments and they were in the black. They weren't in the green, or even the red; they were in the black! The engines were shut down, not running.

"They quit, they quit! The engines quit," he yelled at Sean.

"You don't have to shout, Major. I can hear you just fine," Sean replied. *"I kind of like it this way. What's next?"*

"What do you mean, what's next? Our engines have quit, Captain. Do something!"

"Was there something you wanted me to do?" Sean asked, still leaning back in his seat with his legs crossed.

"Why did they quit? What happened? What did you do?" Willard was getting very agitated.

Sean reached up and moved the two mixture-control levers from idle-cutoff, where Willard had placed them, to rich. The engines sputtered and caught, the instruments returned to the green and Willard sat transfixed.

"Sir, excuse me, Sir, there's something you need to know," Sean said, politely.

"What?" Willard croaked.

"Major, Sir, for a normal descent you retard the throttles, not the mixture-control levers."

Willard looked at Sean with a horrified expression. He suddenly knew what had happened. Instead of pulling back the throttles, he pulled the mixture levers to off. He had inadvertently shut down the engines. He didn't respond to Sean and continued with his descent toward Binh Thuy. Willard was sweating profusely and his arms ached from holding the wheel too tightly. He wanted to ask Sean to take the airplane, but did not want to embarrass himself by admitting that he was upset. Sean looked away.

When they switched to the tower frequency, they could hear two planes making touch-and-go landings. George must have changed his mind because they could hear both Bill and Fred talking to the tower.

They flew for about fifteen minutes and when the field was in sight, Willard called for landing clearance. *"Binh Thuy, this is Birddog Two. Request landing instructions."*

"Roger, Two. You're cleared to enter the pattern for Runway 23. Wind is from 240 degrees at five knots and the sky is clear. There are two other aircraft in the pattern," the tower replied.

"Roger, Tower. Birddog Two is entering downwind for Runway 23," Willard said, his voice shaking slightly.

"Tower, this is Birddog One. We're on final for a full-stop landing*.*" Fred's voice came over the radio.

"One, you're cleared to land. Two, extend your pattern*,"* the tower responded.

"One, Roger," Fred replied.

"Two, extending downwind," Willard said.

"Tower, Birddog Three is making a full stop behind One."

"Three, cleared to land. Two, make a right 360 on downwind."

"Three, Roger."

"Two, making a right 360," Willard responded.

Sean and Willard made an easy 360-degree right turn while the other two O-2s made their final landings. The Major was relieved. They would have the pattern to themselves.

"How do you feel, Sir?" Sean asked. ***"Are you nervous? You shouldn't be. I know you can do it."***

Sean's comments didn't help. Willard was still in a nervous sweating state. He was holding the wheel too tightly and his movements were erratic. Sean ignored it all.

By the time the aircraft turned onto final approach, they were much too high for a safe landing. Sean calmly asked, ***"This is going to be a full-stop landing, isn't it?"***

"Yes," Willard replied, his voice beginning to crack.

"Sir, don't you think we are a little too high and a little too fast for a landing?" Sean asked, innocently.

The Major was getting very agitated. He looked at his airspeed and it was twenty knots too fast. There was no way he could land now. **"I'll take it around."**

"I'll talk to the tower," Sean said, helpfully. ***"Tower, Birddog Two on the go for another pattern."***

"Two, you're cleared for another pattern. Will it be a touch and go or a full stop."

"A full stop, Tower," Sean replied.

"Roger, Two. You're cleared for a full stop."

This time Willard turned final too tight and they initiated their go around while rolling out on final approach. *"You're doing just fine. I always have the same problems,"* Sean said, nicely.

"Tower, Two on the go for another pattern," Sean radioed.

"Birddog Two, are you in trouble?" The tower sounded concerned.

"Negative, tower. We're just practicing approaches," Sean replied.

"You can do it, Major," Sean said, calmly.

Willard looked at Sean. He could not understand why the captain was so calm. Sean said he never landed at night and here they were, missing approach after approach. He tried to relax and told himself that it was easy. He could do it. The O-2 turned to downwind and settled at one hundred knots. Willard maintained the speed until turning onto base leg. He reduced power slightly and allowed the nose of the aircraft to drop. He kept his eyes on the runway.

"Aren't we a little fast?" Sean asked, maintaining his calm.

When the major looked at the airspeed indicator, it was showing one hundred and ten knots. He was much too fast and they had not turned onto final approach. He yanked back on the throttles.

"Ah, Major, Sir. It seems to me that we're not going to make the runway," Sean said, pointing to the airspeed. *"At least not at this speed."*

Willard was rapidly losing his concentration. He had reduced the throttles too much and when he rolled out on final, the O-2 slowed rapidly. They were at seventy knots and losing speed. He moved the throttles forward.

"Binh Thuy tower, Birddog Two on the go for another pattern," Sean reported.

"Roger, Two. You're cleared for another pattern. Should we alert one of the perimeter batteries? They'll be glad to shoot you down," the tower replied.

"Stand by, Tower," Sean said, laughing. He looked at the major. *"Let me try."* There was no reply.

"Major, Sir. We have a problem. You've missed three approaches and I've never landed at night," Sean continued. Willard was still unresponsive.

"We can climb to six thousand feet and bail out or I can try to land. What should we do, Sir?" Sean asked.

Willard was somewhere else.

"Sir, what should we do?"

"Birddog Two, are you in trouble?" The tower was now quite concerned.

"Uh, Tower. We are in the air," Willard came back from wherever he had been.

"Captain, give it a try. I could never bail out... You'd have to go first anyway. The door is on your side." He released the wheel and slumped back into his seat.

"It's finally my turn, by God! After ten years of this, I ought to be able to do it once, don't you think?" Sean asked, turning to look at the Major.

"I hope so," Willard replied, in a dejected voice.

Sean turned the aircraft smartly to downwind, leveled at one thousand feet above the ground and called the tower.

"Birddog Two on downwind for a full stop."

"You're cleared to land, Birddog Two. Do you want the fire trucks?" the tower was definitely worried.

"Negative on the assistance, Tower," Sean replied.

He turned the aircraft onto the base leg and lowered the gear. It was at that moment the major realized that he had forgotten the gear on his last two approaches. He sat quietly, staring wide eyed at the captain, prepared to take the aircraft if Sean couldn't land. He didn't know what he would do, but he wasn't going to let this dipshit captain kill him.

The O-2 came down final at eighty knots. The airspeed never wavered. When they crossed the overrun, Sean throttled back and gently eased the aircraft onto the runway. The tires bit smoothly and Sean let the aircraft roll. Approaching the end of the runway, he shut down the forward engine and slowly came to a stop in the de-arming area.

The major sat, staring straight ahead in his seat. He was grateful to be alive. Sean got out of the aircraft and walked over to a waiting jeep. He climbed in and the jeep drove off.

CHAPTER SEVEN
Binh Thuy Air Base
Mekong Delta, South Vietnam
18 October 1967, that night on the taxiway

It was several minutes before Willard realized that something was wrong. An airman was pounding on the window to his left.

"OK, Major. You are cleared to the parking area."

He looked around. Then he remembered that Sean left him without saying a word. He wasn't supposed to do that. The airman was grinning and so was the sergeant standing in front of the aircraft. Willard gave the signal to remove the wheel chocks and added power to start taxiing. On the way to the parking area, he realized that he'd been had.

Sean wasn't unqualified. The other pilots must have set him up! *'Those dirty little bastards,'* he thought, angrily.

When Willard stormed into the O'Club, George met him at the door and handed him a beer. **"Congratulations; you passed."**

All of the pilots were there, grinning, and Sean was in the middle. He was laughing. The major turned a deep shade of crimson and sat down. He felt like he was a hundred years old.

Major Stebbins leaned over and said, **"Don't feel bad, Matt. Captain O'Malley isn't normal."**

At that, the rest of the pilots nodded their agreement. They raised their glasses and toasted the completion of their training at 'FAC U'.

Major Matthew R. Willard resolved then and there to get himself in a staff job as soon as possible. There was no way he was going to fly in combat with these lunatics.

When George broke up the celebration, he shook hands all around, and wished them luck. He had another class arriving in two days. They were usually pretty much the same. Some old heads, some experienced, some scared and some too young to know better. This group was a little different. When he turned to leave, they all stood, raised their glasses, and sang the traditional Air Force Hymn.

"Him, Him, Fuck Him!"

Historical Note: The final night flight was flown as reported above by Pat Sweeney and the Major with the "silent engines." The Major did go directly to a staff job. That is the "unofficial" and traditional Air Force Hymn.

CHAPTER EIGHT
Nakhon Phanom Royal Thai Air Base (NKP)
20 October 1968, evening at Task Force Alpha Command Center

Brigadier General Ernest L. Holland, TFA (Task Force Alpha) Commander, scowled at the lieutenant colonel sitting across from him. His stomach started to burn again and he looked down to find the pack of antacids in his desk drawer. He took one and returned the package to the drawer.

"Well, Dave, I'm waiting for your answer," he growled.

Lt. Colonel David P. Benjamin (23rd TASS Commander) smiled and shook his head slowly from side to side. *"You can't send them back. This isn't like a department store or the BX, Ernie. They don't come with guarantees."*

Ernie let his irritation show and tried to intimidate the man in front of him. It wasn't working. *"We don't need uncontrollable fools flying our planes. One of them actually shot at an Army helicopter, one of our Army's helicopters!"* he continued, on the verge of shouting, *"They're both old enough to know better."*

"It's a war, no matter what anyone says, and I need warriors, not timid, well behaved pets." The colonel didn't raise his voice. After a short pause, he continued, *"You seem to have enough of those running around here already."*

"My people are skilled technicians, they look professional and they act professionally." Ernie was quick to defend his organization, TFA. It was formed to prove the Secretary of Defense's theory that an electronic wall could be emplaced across the Ho Chi Minh Trail to locate, track and stop the resupply convoys. Ernie Holland was justly proud of being selected as its commander. The stocky general was five feet eight inches tall and solidly built; his hair was cropped short, which slightly diminished the effect of the bald spot at the back of his head.

General Ernest L. Holland had been wearing a uniform for twenty-six years and had resigned himself to retiring as a colonel, when Task Force Alpha was formed by the Department of Defense. A non-rated officer, he joined the Army Signal Corps in WWII and was assigned to Army Air Corps aviation support. When the Air Force was formed in 1947, he transferred to the new service and spent his career in electronic communications and navigation systems. He was in charge of an electronic maintenance depot in Dayton, Ohio, when he was selected to oversee the implementation of the electronic wall and moved to the Air Force's Electronic Systems Division at Hanscom Field in Massachusetts. He also participated in the testing of this electronic wall that was conducted from a building built inside a hangar at Field 3 on Eglin AFB in northern Florida. Eglin, a 724-square-mile Air Force installation, was the ideal location to test secret Air Force concepts. In fact Jimmy Doolittle's B-25s did their aircraft carrier take offs and bombing training here before they left to bomb Japan. Gen. Holland knew the history and was pleased at being part of the new history.

With his selection came the single star of a brigadier general and the possibility of a second star ... if he was successful. Ernie thoroughly enjoyed the status and perks which came with his promotion to general. The one star made him the senior commander at NKP and he would make the most of it. These weekly meetings with the commanders and operations officers of the flying units were his way of showing everyone at NKP that he, Ernie Holland, was in charge and no one was to forget it even though he had little or no operational control over any of these units. He would let nothing spoil his importance or come between him and the next star.

"If they can't do the job then we can send them back, or put them in staff jobs," Dave Benjamin offered. *"Right now, we need pilots. The North Vietnamese supplies are still moving down the trail and we need to stop them."*

"Our wall will do that," Ernie stated, positively. *"With the ADSIDs (aerial delivered acoustic sensors) in place, we'll be able to pinpoint the trucks for the fighters to attack. Your FAC squadron won't even be needed. Colonel, these two new clowns of yours are not only big problems, they will soon not be needed...extra baggage."*

"Ernie, even if you can find the trucks, who will direct the strikes? At best, the wall will make the FAC's job easier. You can't replace someone flying low and slow over the roads. The jets move too fast to find a truck." Dave responded. He hoped he had succeeded in moving the subject away from the two incoming pilots.

"The Secretary and his experts don't believe that. They want the wall to operate without visual support and I'm here to see that it works. We'll replace all the FACs in Laos including your NAILs. We're the future. You guys are the past."

"It isn't that easy, Ernie. You don't understand how difficult it is to hit a target as small as a truck. The jets move pretty fast and the trucks are small. It's hard enough to hit a road that's twenty feet wide. How about an eight-foot-wide truck that may be moving?"

"Look, Dave. I know I've never driven a jet, but how hard can it be to hit a truck with today's weapons? The Secretary's people at the Pentagon don't think it's so hard and they have the figures to prove it. The problem here is that all of your equipment is outdated. The only reason this base is here is to provide a home for a bunch of old men flying outdated planes. You're an anachronism. You belong in the past... "

Dave flushed and started to respond to the taunt when they were interrupted by the telephone. Ernie picked up the phone, listened and then said, *"I'll be ready in five minutes,"* he looked at Dave who was getting up from his chair. *"I have a staff meeting in a few minutes. We'll make the final decision on these pilots when they arrive tonight. I want to see them as soon as they get on base. We don't want this project hurt because some stupid pilot fucks up!"*

"Yes, sir."

Dave nodded and left the office. He never felt comfortable in the Task Force Alpha compound in his rumpled fatigues. Everyone here was dressed in freshly starched uniforms and many wore the standard stateside tan short-sleeved cotton uniform. The young Ph.D.s and electronic whiz kids who walked these corridors with thick glasses and arms full of printouts were out of place on a combat base. He was relieved when he was back in his jeep and headed for his office at the 23rd TASS.

CHAPTER NINE
Nakhon Phanom Royal Thai Air Base (NKP)
20 October 1968, the same evening on the flight line

Lt. Sharon Stuart had driven the jeep from the TFA compound to in front of base operations on the NKP flight line as ordered by General Holland. She noted how dark this part of the flight line was at this time of night compared to the individual unit areas where the aircraft were parked. The latter were lit with many portable and a few permanent overhead lights.

She hoped that the C-130 would be on time and remembered that these flights that made the rounds of the Thai bases picking up or dropping off people and equipment ran either clockwise or counter-clockwise and that they were called the "Klong." This name was in honor of the Klong River, also known as the River Kwai, which flowed from Burma to the Gulf of Siam. Although she never had, many of her colleagues in TFA used the Klong to travel around Thailand.

It was about time for the Klong to arrive, but she could see nothing in the very dark sky and the noise on the flight line would make hearing the C-130 impossible. She was then startled when a plane's landing lights came on as the aircraft approached about 200 feet above the runway. The disembodied landing light flew down a short final approach until, at the last moment, she could see the dark outline of the C-130 transport. It was nearly on the ground and she smiled to herself, thinking, **"These pilots were not taking any chances with enemy fire, even though they were landing in Thailand. The shooting war was at least fifty miles east of NKP. Better safe than sorry."**

With a loud squeal, the main gear tires bit into the steel-planked runway. The four giant turboprops made a deep rumbling sound as they were reversed and the plane quickly slowed. The pilot turned off the runway at the center taxiway and headed toward Base Operations where parking spaces were set aside for visiting aircraft.

Lieutenant Sharon G. Stuart, Aide-de-Camp to Brigadier General Holland, was surprised to find herself in this role. When she went to the flight line, it was usually to pick up visiting dignitaries such as colonels, 7th AF staffers or congressmen, NOT captains. She'd been sitting in the back of the room at the TFA Commander's weekly status meeting when her boss interrupted the meeting and sent her out to pick up the two pilots. He wanted to see them as soon as they arrived. The TFA Commander's weekly meeting was held every Sunday evening at 1900 hours. The unit commanders met to review the coming week's schedules and support requirements with the TFA Commander and his staff. Usually, the meetings served to make sure everyone was aware of the comings and goings of senior military and government officials as well as any media representatives. They also reviewed changes in the operating units.

Tonight's discussion was running late because of the planned arrival of a new unit on the base and a discussion of where to put the aircraft, the crews, the maintenance personnel and their staff.

When General Holland interrupted the meeting and directed her to pick up the inbound new FACs, there were puzzled looks around the table. Only General Holland, TFA and the FAC squadron had received the uncomplimentary messages from 7th Air Force Headquarters in Saigon describing Bill and Sean's conduct at the FAC training base in South Vietnam.

The general didn't bother to explain and the others quickly returned to their discussion of the new unit.

Sharon didn't care too much for the cocky pilots she had met so far at the O'Club. They were much like those she remembered from Wright-Patterson Air Force Base, Ohio. Her father was a career civil servant in the Aeronautical Systems Division (ASD) located on that base and she had grown up around the people who lived and worked there. From her father, she had acquired a disdain for the rated officers who were in charge of many ASD projects. While they commanded the projects they generally lacked the technical knowledge to do any of the work.

When she finished high school, she enrolled at the University of Dayton where she studied Mechanical Engineering, one of the few girls in the Engineering School. There weren't many companies clamoring for female engineers so, when she graduated, Sharon reluctantly agreed to accept a commission in the Air Force.

The young lady who arrived at Lackland AFB, Texas, had no difficulty with the Officer Training program. Slim and athletic by nature, she handled the physical training with ease and breezed through the academic courses. The attractive five-foot-five-inch-tall officer candidate missed out on the special attention given to her heavier classmates and her engineering degree set her apart from most of her peers. She finished at the top of her class and found herself assigned to the research laboratories at Wright-Patterson AFB, a favor to her father from one of his former bosses.

The pretty, dark-haired, green-eyed young engineer had her own apartment in Dayton and her social life revolved around the university and the graduate school. However, working close to her father proved difficult. Her parents couldn't resist their matchmaking efforts and she was looking for job alternatives when she met Colonel Ernest Holland, commander of the electronic maintenance depot in Dayton. When he was promoted to general, he offered her the position as his aide-de-camp.

She spent the next year at Hanscom Field and loved the work. Most of the time she was taking care of visitors to the Hanscom facility, escorting personnel in for interviews with General Holland and the staff, and accompanying the general to status briefings at Andrews Air Force Base or the Pentagon. She was meeting a lot of people, many of whom could favorably affect her future promotions and assignments. Unfortunately, nearly all of the young men she encountered were pilots or they were married.

Lieutenant Stuart broke away from her reverie and watched as a ground crewman directed the plane to a parking spot with his illuminated yellow wands. She waited until all four engines were shut down and the props stopped turning, then drove the jeep around the plane to the rear loading ramp which was opening.

Inside the C-130, Captain Bill Thompson unfastened his seat belt, stood and waited as the ramp slowly lowered. As soon as it touched the ground, he walked down and stepped out onto the aircraft parking area. His buddy, Captain Sean O'Malley, followed him down the ramp.

"Jesus, Bill, we're in a time warp," Sean said, as he stepped out onto the ground, *"It's really 1943."*

"I know what you mean. All I can see are propellers. There isn't a jet anywhere in sight," Bill pointed at their feet. *"Not only that, look what, we're standing on. That's PSP, pierced steel planking, I think from World War II. I've seen it in the John Wayne movies."*

Bill and Sean stood transfixed on the ramp at Nakhon Phanom Royal Thai Air Force Base and stared at the entire fleet of propeller-driven aircraft. It was 2145, military time, 9:45 p.m., local time, and they were flabbergasted by the number of old aircraft on the busy flight line. They watched as an olive-drab pickup truck drove past them towing a string of four bomb carts, each holding a five-hundred-pound bomb. There was a rack in the bed of the pickup filled with rockets. The truck drove down the flight line and turned between rows of parked aircraft. There were Jeeps and pickups driving everywhere they looked. Portable lights illuminated individual aircraft and they could see ground crews working around the silhouetted aircraft.

As they watched, an unmarked, all-black, twin-engine plane took off. The deep roar of its reciprocating engines drowned out any attempt to talk. When the engine noise subsided Sean asked, *"What was that? "*

"I'm not sure," Bill replied, shaking his head. *"It looked like a B-25 or a B-26. I couldn't tell from here."*

"That was an A-26." a young female voice stated. They both jerked their heads in her direction. The transient

ramp lights were not bright but they clearly illuminated the speaker. She was getting out of a jeep parked behind them.

"I'm Lieutenant Stuart," she said, saluting them. *"If you are Captains Thompson and O'Malley, I'm to take you to meet the general."*

At that moment, another black plane started to take-off, its engine roaring. Bill turned away from the lieutenant and watched. *"There goes a T-28. I haven't seen one of those in ten years"* he said to no one in particular. *"What general?"* he continued sharply, looking back at the lieutenant.

"General Ernest L. Holland. He's the senior officer on this base. He runs TFA."

"What kind of planes are in a TFA?" Bill asked. *"What is a TFA,"* he added, sarcastically.

"TFA is Task Force Alpha, a ground operation. They don't have planes. It's a classified project, Captain." her reply was clipped and her voice sharp. She didn't care for the captain.

Bill made a disgusted snort, *"It figures."*

"What does the general want with us?" Sean asked, nicely, turning and moving to place himself between Bill and the lieutenant. He couldn't believe his eyes. Here he was, on the border between Thailand and Laos, hundreds of miles north of Bangkok, looking at a real live American female and a pretty one, at that. She looked about five-and-a-half-feet tall, slender and she was wearing an Air Force fatigue uniform that fit so well it had obviously been tailored for her. Sean liked the looks of this pert lieutenant. He wondered what the hell she was doing driving a jeep alone at night on a super-secret air base in Thailand.

"He didn't say. I do know that you two have been the subject of some messages back and forth with 7th Air Force and have caused some talk

around here. What kind of trouble did you get into at Binh Thuy?" she asked, frowning.

"Let's find the BOQ and get changed. There's no sense in meeting a general in these wrinkled flight suits," Bill interrupted, ignoring her question.

"The general said he wants to see you as soon as you arrive. He's still in a staff meeting at Headquarters." She was beginning to irritate Bill, but Sean hadn't quit staring.

"Come on, Bill, let's go see what he wants," Sean said, breaking away from his thoughts and climbing into the jeep.

"I'll bet it's over that Army helicopter thing," Bill replied. He threw his bag in the rear of the jeep and climbed in beside it. Sean was already sitting next to their driver.

"Let's go, Lieutenant." She started the jeep and drove down the flight line. *"Where are the guards?"* Sean asked, looking around.

"I don't see any but they must be here someplace. None of these people I can see are carrying weapons," Bill replied. *"This sure is different than Binh Thuy or Saigon. I don't see any sandbagged bunkers either."*

Sharon turned toward a road leading away from the flight line and said, *"There aren't any guards here, except at the gates. The war is in Vietnam and Laos. There isn't any shooting in Thailand. We don't need bunkers."*

Bill scowled again and sat back against the seat with his arms folded and said to himself *"What the hell are we doing at a base full of goddamned women? I came here to fight a war, not chase skirts."*

Sean sensed his mood and ignored him. He was trying to maintain a pleasant conversation with the attractive lieutenant. *"What're you doing over here, Sharon?"* he asked. *"We didn't believe there were any females assigned to the flying squadrons."*

"There aren't," she replied. *"I'm the General's aide."*

"Well, that's unusual, isn't it? Are you here for the duration or is this just a TDY location for you?" Sean continued. *"Is this the only base you stay at?"*

"Do all generals get female aides in wartime?" Bill interrupted, insultingly.

"I'm his aide, that's all!" she hissed. She definitely didn't care for that captain in the back. To Sean, she replied, *"We're here for the duration and this is our only location. It should be less than a year but we don't know. It depends upon the success of the project."*

"Don't pay any attention to my rude friend in the back seat," Sean said warmly. *"I'm just glad to see a girl from home."*

Sean got a smile from their driver. Bill didn't notice or didn't care. He was leaning back in his seat with his arms crossed, scowling as he viewed the buildings in the darkness.

CHAPTER TEN
Nakhon Phanom Royal Thai Air Base (NKP)
20 October 1968, later that evening at Task Force Alpha Command Center

"Here we are," Sharon said as she pulled the jeep into a reserved parking spot at a low, long building. *"Leave your bags; someone will take you to your squadron when you're finished."*

Sean and Bill followed the lieutenant into the building and past a sergeant seated behind a counter. He waved the lieutenant through without stopping them. Bill didn't think it was a good sign. **"It look's as though we were expected,"** he whispered to Sean, who nodded in agreement.

Sean's attention was still on the attractive lieutenant. He was not disappointed when he saw her inside the well-lit building. It confirmed his initial impressions...slender, walked with a confident air, brunette, he liked the swing of her hips and the slim legs. Walking behind her, he caught the faint trace of perfume. He was so engrossed in the pleasure of her nearness that he bumped into her when she stopped at a conference room with a "No Admittance" sign on the door.

Sharon smiled at Sean's clumsiness. She knew he was taken with her and she liked the feeling. He seemed like a friendly person but she wondered about the stories from Saigon. **"Maybe he wasn't really as wild as the stories she had heard."** She thought, but only momentarily.

She motioned for them to wait as she entered and closed the conference room door behind her. Within a minute, it banged open and a stocky, balding man with a cigar in his mouth came out. He was wearing a short-sleeved summer khaki uniform with one bright silver star on each collar. He frowned and looked at the two captains as if they had some incurable disease. **"Well, here are the two heroes of Binh Thuy. What a pleasure to meet you two assholes. What the fuck did you do?"** he barked as he passed them and continued into an office across the hall. It was marked, "TFA Commander."

They started to follow when the conference room door opened again and a lieutenant colonel emerged with Lieutenant Stuart. The colonel motioned for them to follow the general.

"I asked you a question," came from the general. He had entered a large office and turned to face them.

"We just completed FAC training at Binh Thuy, General," Bill answered. *"There wasn't any trouble."* He noticed that the general was not wearing pilot's wings, not even navigator's wings... *no wings*. He wasn't a flying officer.

"Which one of you tried to shoot down a U.S. Army helicopter," the General yelled, sticking his face next to Bill's.

"Neither one of us, Sir," Bill replied, loudly. It startled the general and brought a smile to the colonel's face. He was standing behind the general watching the exchange. Sharon looked confused. Even she had heard about that incident.

"What do you mean, Captain? Do we have the wrong pair of pilots? Aren't you Thompson and O'Malley? Are you trying to say that you didn't shoot at an Army helicopter?"

"I shot near an Army helicopter, but I did not shoot at an Army helicopter, Sir" Bill replied, slowly and distinctly. *"If I had shot at it, I would have hit it."*

"Well, I'm sorry, Captain. How did I ever doubt your skill with a rocket?" he paused, then put his face close to Bill's, *"What difference does it make?"* he hissed.

"I felt it necessary to teach a young Army pilot that he should use better judgment when he was operating his chopper on an airfield around small fixed-wing aircraft," Bill replied, crisply. *"I'm certain that he learned his lesson and it will most probably save a few aircraft from having unnecessary accidents in the future."* He didn't sound at all contrite.

"I don't really give a shit what you think, Captain. I don't want you on my base," the General replied *"or your friend, either. He doesn't seem to be able to get along with field-grade officers."* Sean started to interrupt, but thought better of it and closed his mouth without speaking. The general looked back and forth from one to the other several times.

Neither replied so finally when the general looked at the lieutenant colonel who said, *"I still need pilots, Ernie."*

"You're not going to need them for long," the general snapped back.

"Even if the sensors work, Ernie, you're going to need FACs to direct the strikes. If we don't get better with our marks, those Navy pilots aren't going to be able to drop the sensors in the right places," the lieutenant colonel continued.

"I've already told you that we won't need FACs after the sensors are in place. I don't see how these two will make a difference. They're nothing but troublemakers."

Colonel Benjamin paused and turned to look at the two captains. *"I doubt that I'll have much trouble with these two now that you have made your feelings known. Will I, Captains?"*

"No, Sir!" their replies were nearly in unison. Sharon was smiling with amusement. Benjamin maintained a neutral expression but Ernie Holland was red faced as he growled at them. *"Get out of here, you sorry sons of bitches. If either of you ever screws up, even once, even a little, I'll send the both of you to Greenland where you can freeze your asses off until you retire. Understand?"*

"Yes, Sir!" in unison again. They saluted and turned to leave.

"I'll see that they get settled, General." Sharon offered.

"Just drop them at TUOC and get back here," the general directed, *"They can get themselves checked in."*

"Dave, let's get back to our meeting."

The two captains watched as the general and the colonel walked back into the conference room. When the door closed, they both let out a sigh of relief. *"Whew! He looked like he meant it,"* Sean commented.

Bill nodded in agreement then turned to face Sharon. *"OK, Lieutenant Stuart, where to now?"* He bowed from the waist and motioned for her to lead the way.

Sean fell in beside her and let Bill follow along as they walked back out to the jeep. The two spoke quietly, excluding Bill from their conversation. He didn't seem to care.

CHAPTER ELEVEN
Nakhon Phanom Royal Thai Air Base
20 October 1968, departing TFA

Sharon drove back to the flight line and took them to another low dark brown wooden building. *"This is the base TUOC where the general said to leave you."*

Bill grabbed his bag and started for the door. Sean stood by the jeep for a moment. *"Where can I find you?"* he asked.

Sharon smiled. *"The general doesn't like us to mingle with the crews, but we sometimes go to the O'Club. It's the best place to eat on the base. When I do go there, it's only for dinner."* She started the jeep and waved as she drove off.

Sean picked up his bag and hurried to catch up with Bill. *"We were lucky that the son of a bitch didn't throw us off the base,"* he said as he reached his friend.

"The lieutenant colonel, spoke up for us. I doubt if the general could overrule him. That's our squadron commander, Colonel Benjamin," Bill replied, and then continued, *"He didn't seem nearly as upset as the fat little general, did he? I'll bet the little general doesn't really have much say about combat crews. He's not a pilot!"*

"He's no littler than you," Sean commented. He grinned and continued, *"a little fatter, a little balder and Hell, Bill, that's you in twenty years."* Bill ignored him.

They walked into TUOC and found themselves looking down a long hallway. Their entry triggered a buzzer and while they looked, a lieutenant came out of one of the rooms along the hall. He walked up to them.

"Are you new arrivals? I'm Lieutenant Zack North. I'm one of the Intelligence Officers assigned here to debrief you guys." He noticed the wings on their flight suits and assumed correctly that he was speaking to combat crews.

"Bill Thompson," Bill said and stuck out his hand Sean followed suit. *"We just arrived. What do we do now?"*

"The offices don't open until 0700. What unit are you assigned to?" Zack asked.

"We're FACs," Bill replied, *"assigned to the 23rd Tactical Air Support Squadron."*

"Who's assigned to the NAILs?" came from behind them.

They turned, *"What are the NAILs?"* Sean asked.

"You are, if you're FACs. That's their call sign," was the reply. A slender man in a black flying suit came

up to them and stuck out his hand. **"I'm Denny Cutter. I fly the Nimrods, the A-26s. Welcome to NKP and the NAILs."**

"Bill Thompson, Sir," was the reply. Bill caught the silver oak leaves on the tall man's shoulders. **"This is Sean O'Malley. We just arrived."**

"Any of their pilots due in soon?" Denny looked at Zack.

"No, Sir. Not for another couple of hours."

"Is there a VOQ?" Sean asked the Lieutenant.

"Of sorts, but they aren't open now either. Captain, you need to find a couple of empty beds in your squadron area for the night," Zack replied.

"I'll take them to the O'Club. We might find some FACs there," Denny said.

"Thanks, Colonel, We appreciate the help," Sean said.

"No problem. It's tough to find any of the base staff after duty hours. I don't think they know about the war," Denny replied.

"Isn't that a little odd?" Sean asked.

"Not here, not now, it isn't. Things were different when we had a flying senior commander. Now we have a nonrated staff-type general. There are over forty-five hundred support personnel at NKP to keep four hundred and fifty of us flying. The staff operates five days a week from seven to five, but all of the units fly around the clock, every day."

"It isn't that way in country," Bill said. **"At least we didn't come across any staff types."**

"It's peculiar to the out-country bases. You will find it true anywhere in Thailand where the senior commander doesn't fly combat missions," Denny said, with a disgusted expression.

CHAPTER TWELVE
Nakhon Phanom Royal Thai Air Base (NKP)
20 October 1968, evening at TUOC

They departed TUOC, climbed into Denny's jeep and drove from the flight line to the Officer's Club, a combination dining room and bar. On the way, they got a good look at Nakhon Phanom. It was built mostly between 1963 and 1965 by US Navy SEA-BEES and appeared more like the National Park Service camping grounds at Yellowstone than a forward combat base. There were tall pine trees everywhere and nearly all of the one-story buildings were constructed of redwood, or something that looked like redwood. The only thing missing was the distinctive Park Service wooden signs with yellow letters. The base was built on gently-rolling terrain. The runway and airfield were flat, but the remainder of the sprawling base was built on small hills. The two highest hills held the Officer's Club and a large radar station.

When they arrived at the club, they could see rows of portable trailers and "hootches" stretching for blocks from the club down the hill. The hootches were long one-story wooden structures with a porch along one side and a door every ten feet. They looked like rustic motels.

"Where are the forest rangers with the Boy Scout hats?" Bill laughed.

"It does look like a camp, doesn't it?" Denny agreed, smiling. *"Leave your gear in the jeep. Let's find out where you're going, before we move it."*

Entering the club, Denny led them to the bar where the flight crews, some in black flight suits and some in fatigues, were seated around several tables drinking and making considerable noise.

"You two are in luck, here are your NAILs," Denny walked up to one of the louder noisemakers.

"Joe, these two are new FACs. They came in on the Klong from Bangkok."

Joe stood and came over to them. *"Thanks, Colonel, I'm Joe Brown."* He extended his hand to them. Sean and Bill shook hands and introduced themselves, then met the other three FACs seated at the table.

"We need a place to sleep," Sean said.

"The room next to me is empty. You can use it," one of the NAILs said.

"Great. We'll take it for tonight. Let's get our stuff and put it in the hootch," Sean said.

Joe borrowed the keys from Denny and drove them to the hootch with the empty room. He waited while they stored their gear in the room and then drove them back to the club.

"Can you find your way back?"

"Yeah, it's not that far. What're you guys doing, drinking this late at night? It's nearly eleven. What happened to "12 hours between bottle and throttle?" Sean asked, looking at his wrist watch.

"We didn't get back from the trail until ten. The guys in the club already flew tonight. The staffies will bitch up a storm when they come in for breakfast and see the crews drinking and raising hell. The bar never closes and the seven-to-fivers think we sleep all day and drink all night. We don't want them to be disappointed, so we never say anything."

"You flew tonight?" Bill asked.

"Yeah. We destroyed two trucks. Denny was in one of the Nimrods that I was controlling," Joe said.

The three of them were looking for a table when they saw Denny Cutter in the dining room. He motioned for them to join him. *"Sit down a minute. I think I've heard stories about you two."*

"Not us, Sir," Sean replied, with a wide grin. *"It must have been two other pilots."*

"I'm sure it was," Denny answered. *"Why don't you tell me about them, as long as you're here?"*

"I haven't heard any stories," Joe interjected. He was looking at them with interest.

"These are recent, Joe. I doubt if they've traveled much. At least not yet." Denny looked amused.

"What did you do, Sean," Joe asked.

"I was night flying with one of the stateside staff types, you know the ones. They haven't flown in years and someone sent them over here to be a FAC. They're scared to death of making a mistake and not making it to twenty for their retirement. Or worse, they're afraid of getting killed."

"What's so bad about that? So am I," Denny interrupted.

"Me, too," Joe added.

"Their fear keeps them from doing their jobs, or so it appears. The one I was talking about was scared of night flying, although I must admit that I did give him a bad time. On our last night flight he got so nervous that he pulled back on the mixture controls instead of the throttles for a descent."

Denny interrupted again, *"That would shut off the engines!"*

"No shit, Colonel, It did just that. The dumb SOB didn't even realize what he had done for several minutes. Needless to say, by the time we got back on the ground he was a basket case," Sean added. *"They assigned him to the staff at the 504th."*

"Rumor says you are both troublemakers." said Denny.

Joe and Bill were laughing loudly, but Denny just shook his head.

"What did you do?" He asked Bill.

"I was shooting touch-and-go landings at the Army air field at Can Tho when some young helicopter jock tried to turn my plane upside down. He was waiting for me to land and as I flared, he put his rotors on full pitch. It almost flipped the O-2 over and I nearly bought it. Unfortunately for the Army pilot, I had two full pods of Willy Petes so while I chased him back toward Saigon, I shot two of the hummers at him, one at a time; one on the right side and one on the left. When I quit he was blubbering badly.

Colonel, I doubt if he'll try that again."

Denny Cutter's eyes were wide and he was shaking his head in disbelief. *"That's what the messages said. I just didn't believe it. What did our blustery TFA Commander have to say? He was fuming yesterday when the messages arrived from Binh Thuy."*

"He wanted to send us to Greenland. Fortunately, our squadron commander was there and he spoke up for us," Sean said.

"I like Dave Benjamin," Denny said. *"You two better not treat him like the people at Binh Thuy."*

"No, Sir," they answered in unison.

"Go listen to Joe and his friends. They can tell you how things work for the NAILs," Denny said. He paid for his meal and walked toward the front door. Bill and Sean followed Joe back into the bar. As soon as they entered the bar, they were hailed by two black-suited pilots. Joe made the introductions to the other NAIL FACs and they all sat down around the table.

Sean had been looking around the club since they returned from the hootches. He asked, **"How many American girls are here?"**

The reaction from the others was one of surprise. **"Two, I think,"** Joe answered after a long pause. **"We never see them. One is the TFA general's aide and the other is his secretary. At least, that's what I've heard. They live in trailers in the TFA compound."**

"Don't they come in here to eat?" Sean asked.

"Not very often. I haven't seen them more than once or twice a month," Joe answered. **"How come you two are interested? Most of the guys don't even know they are on the base."**

"Sharon picked us up when we arrived," Sean replied.

"Sharon!" Joe exclaimed. **"Who...or...what ... the Hell.... is Sharon?"**

"She's the aide," Sean answered, smiling. **"Lieutenant Sharon Stuart, with the green eyes."**

There were three pilots staring at Sean. **"You just got here and you were met by Sharon with the green eyes?"** The speaker shouted at Sean. **"What the fuck did we do wrong? I've been here three months and I've never seen one of those round-eyed honeys. He just gets off the plane and is met by a Sharon? Well, kiss my ass!"**

Joe was laughing at his friend's outburst. He turned to Sean, **"We've never been introduced to either of the girls or to the general for that matter. There are several thousand guys here who would probably kill for a chance to spend a night with a round-eye. What makes you two so special?"**

"Don't include me. She thinks I crawled out from under a rock," Bill said, holding up his hands in surrender.

"What did you do to rate such service?" They were all looking at a red faced Sean.

"I don't know. Anyway, it looks like it was an accident. I doubt if we'll be seeing her again from what you say," Sean sounded disappointed.

Historical Note: In 1967, NKP did look like an American National Park.

CHAPTER THIRTEEN
Nakhon Phanom Royal Thai Air Base (NKP)
21 October 1967, morning in the NAIL hootch area

Bill was the first to wake. He looked at his watch, which read 0755 and yelled across the room at Sean, ***"Get up, Deadhead. We need to get checked into the base. We don't want to be late for the war."***

Sean opened one of his eyes and then pulled his pillow over his head. Bill left for the communal showers at the center of the hootch. It took him a while to get used to the little Thai maids wandering in and out of the large "bathroom" and throughout the compound. There were Thais everywhere; sweeping, doing laundry, cleaning the toilets and showers, shining boots, cleaning individual rooms and cutting and raking the grass.

After they showered and shaved and put on fatigues, they left to find the 23rd TASS. When they reached the O'Club at the top of the hill, they could see part of the flight line, so after a quick coffee and a doughnut they headed in that direction.

Halfway there, they passed a building with a sign that read "Personnel In-Processing." Sean looked at Bill and shrugged. It looked just like a stateside personnel office. Obviously, spit and polish and assorted military customs would be in order in this office. They were not disappointed.

With processing completed on the main base, the two were directed to the 23rd TASS offices. They arrived there about 1030 and were met by a young airman.

"The commander is flying and he will want to meet you two sirs."

This young man was the apparent squadron clerk, a very courteous young three striper, an airman first class, who continued, *"I'm Eddie Jackson, the squadron clerk."*

"Glad to meet you, Eddie," Bill answered and shook hands. Sean followed suit.

Eddie then advised them that they were to go get physical examinations and come back after lunch.

They found the Flight Surgeon's office in a portable module adjacent to the main hospital. The entire hospital complex was assembled from air-transportable modular units much like those used for temporary classrooms or modular housing. The arrangement appeared unplanned, as if the units were assembled as received, rather than according to a preset plan. The modules were directly connected or within a few feet of one another. Raised wooden boardwalks connected the separated units to keep personnel up out of the mud and all of the modules were elevated about two feet on cinder blocks.

There were two large, prominently-displayed signs in the front of the hospital complex, a directory of the available clinics and medical offices and a list, by name and Identity Card number, of the local ladies who tested positive for a venereal disease.

Bill chuckled as they reached the signs, *"I don't remember John Wayne having this problem in any of his movies."*

"I'm sure he did. They just didn't show it on the screen," Sean offered, nodding his head.

"I don't see your friend's name on the list," Bill remarked with a grin, *"she must be OK..."*

Sean cuffed him in the back of the head. *"She isn't my friend,"* then almost to himself, *"but, I'm working on it."*

It took about an hour and a half to complete the brief physical examinations and meet with one of the doctors. With that completed, the two headed back toward the O'Club for lunch.

"Do you suppose the general actually takes his meals in the O'Club?" Sean asked.

"Nah, I'm sure he has his own dining area or maybe a special room in the back of the club," Bill answered. *"He might even have his meals done in his trailer. There are some big ones in the TFA compound. I thought we passed a couple of doubles last night."*

"I didn't see any," Sean challenged.

"You didn't see any because you couldn't take your eyes off the lieutenant," Bill grinned, then continued, *"Shit, Sean, she won't have any time for junior officers. I'll bet there's at least one colonel or lieutenant colonel servicing that honey, if the general isn't doing it himself. I wouldn't put it past them."*

"Knock it off! You don't know what you're talking about," Sean was disgusted. Bill was such a damn cynic when it came to females.

"Sorry," Bill held up his hands in surrender. *"We can ask at the O'Club."*

CHAPTER FOURTEEN
Nakhon Phanom Royal Thai Air Base (NKP)
21 October 1967, about lunch time at the "Officers' Club"

They entered the club and walked into the large dining room. It would easily seat two or three hundred people. Sean scanned the room but could find no sign of Sharon. He asked the Thai hostess and was told that they rarely ate at the club. They had their own mess in TFA and the General had a private room in the O'Club for his use.

The disappointment was still apparent on Sean's face when they were shown to the FAC table. Joe Brown was there with several other FAC pilots.

"What's the matter, Sean?" he asked.

"It's Sharon," Bill replied.

"Not again!" one of the other captains yelled. *"I heard more than I wanted to hear about her last night."*

"He can't find her," Bill continued.

"Aw, shucks. Here we thought Sean was different. We finally had a FAC assigned here who had a round-eyed girl friend," the loud Captain teased. *"He's just like us. He has horny dreams about girls from home. Only he thinks they are assigned here. Poor fellow."*

The group laughed while Sean turned a deep shade of red.

"I thought she was real," Bill said to the group.

Joe was shaking his head. *"No. This happens to some of the new guys. Every now and then they think they see a real American girl and everyone goes nuts. I'm sure it was just your imagination. Or, just maybe the TFA guys were playing a joke on you."*

"That's possible, I guess," Bill replied seriously.

"I'm sure that was it. Sorry, Sean. They aren't very considerate at TFA," Joe continued, smiling.

"You'll have to settle for these lovely Thai maidens, Sean," the other captain explained. *"Would you like me to introduce you to some of them?"*

"I think he can handle that himself," Bill interrupted.

"You sure?" Joe asked, looking at Bill.

"Pretty sure..., maybe," Bill replied, nodding solemnly.

CHAPTER FIFTEEN
Nakhon Phanom Royal Thai Air Base (NKP)
21 October 1967, Nail Ops Office

Lieutenant Colonel, David P. Benjamin, Commander of the 23rd TASS, walked into his office with his head down. He didn't speak to his clerk or to the lieutenant colonel; standing by the door and this was unusual for the colonel. He walked to his desk and sat down with a loud sigh. When he looked up, Ed Hardy was standing in his doorway with a puzzled look on his face.

"What's the matter, Boss?" Lieutenant Colonel Edward J. Hardy was concerned as Colonel Benjamin never ignored anyone. Ever.

"Close the door, Ed, and come in." Ed shut the office door and walked to the desk. Benjamin pointed to a chair.

"We aren't winning. We aren't even making a dent in the traffic on the trail. I just got back from the monthly intelligence summary and we aren't doing our jobs!" Benjamin replied, his voice rising as he

spoke and then as he obviously started thinking again his voice became very weak. He sat back and continued somberly, *"Maybe Ernie is right. Maybe we don't belong out there."*

"Damn, Boss. You just got here and we just got a new plane that will stay up longer than three hours. We've asked for some fighter qualified pilots to be assigned to the unit and we got our first one. We are ready to roll now?" Ed wasn't much calmer than his boss.

"Oh yeh, we're doing great. We get our first qualified fighter pilot and the dumb bastard shoots at one of our Army helicopters. It's just what we needed to make this perfect!" Benjamin shook his head slowly.

Lt. Colonel David P. Benjamin was an experienced and seasoned Air Force pilot. He had seen service in World War II and Korea and this was his third time in combat. An attorney at home in the state of Hawaii, he loved to fly and had joined the Reserves after being mustered out of the Army Air Corps at the end of World War II. He was recalled in 1950 and spent three years in the new Air Force, flying T-6 Mosquito spotter planes in Korea. The bald, deeply-tanned Colonel was five feet ten inches tall and fit. He exercised daily and looked ten years younger than his 54 years.

A recalled reservist, he had taken over command of the FAC squadron only five weeks ago and already he had lost one of the new planes and two of his young officers were dead, killed in action (KIA). He was not looking forward to the loss reports and the inevitable explanations. Even less, he did not relish the thought of being ineffective. They needed to find a better way to stop the North Vietnamese traffic on the Ho Chi Minh trail. He didn't think the answer was an expensive, sophisticated line of sensors but he was open minded. The only way to stop road traffic for certain was to put men on the ground across the road. Since the Geneva agreement prevented any non-Laotian personnel in Laos, this was not in the cards. As far as he knew, there were no other successful examples in history; clearly it could not be done by dropping bombs.

The Operations Officer, Lt. Colonel Ed Hardy, had first seen combat in Korea. A career officer and an experienced pilot, Ed had been flying the big Strategic Air Command B-52 bombers, BUFs (Big Ugly Fuckers) until he was assigned to the 23rd as Operations Officer. The tall, Louisiana native towered over his boss at six feet two inches. He was a lanky man in his early forties with curly salt-and-pepper hair and sharply defined features. He talked softly and usually slowly, with an unmistakable southern drawl. Ed had been in the 23rd for five months, overseeing the transition from the single engine O-1E Birddog to the twin engine O-2 Skymaster. He and Benjamin had become friends, which was more important to both of them than their differences in age or position.

"It isn't your fault, Boss," Ed continued. *"We have to do the best we can with what we have. We've got some decent planes, finally. Sooner or later someone has to send us more fighter qualified pilots. It'll happen; just wait and see."*

"We have a bunch of staff-type majors leading a squadron full of green lieutenants. If this new guy doesn't shape up in a hurry, we replace him. We need to get some experience in here with all of the new programs on the drawing board. According to the briefing this morning, we have less than a month until the Navy gets here to start laying the TFA ADSIDs. That will be a total mess if we can't direct them to the targets," Benjamin replied, intensely. He was leaning forward and hitting his fist on the desk.

"Where are our two notorious new guys anyway?"

"Well, Boss," Ed said looking at his watch, *"they should be back from lunch pretty quick. The hospital called in their reports about an hour ago and both are fit to fly. I expect the two to show up any minute. How do you want to handle them?"*

Historical Note: *This was the actual situation in Laos as the dry season of 67-68 was about to start. Only about 5 percent of the trucks spotted on the Trail were stopped and many, maybe most, were never seen.*

CHAPTER SIXTEEN
Nakhon Phanom Royal Thai Air Base (NKP)
21 October 1967, Nail Ops Office

"Colonel Benjamin is waiting to see you, Sirs," Eddie Jackson said, when they walked into the Orderly Room.

"Have you finished your physicals?" Eddie asked.

"We're all done. The only thing we don't have is our quarters," Sean answered. *"We're staying in an empty hootch in the squadron area. Captain Brown told us to use it last night but we need to get some permanent billets."*

"We do that here, Captain," Eddie replied. *"By the time you're finished with the colonel, I'll have your hootches for you. The Operations Officer makes those assignments."*

"Is he here?" Sean asked.

"Yes, Sir. He's with the commander now. You're to go in."

Bill knocked on the door to the commander's office.

"Come in," said a familiar voice.

Bill opened the door and saw two people in fatigues sitting in the office. The lieutenant colonel they had seen last night was seated behind a desk and another lieutenant colonel was in a chair in front of the desk. They stood when the captains entered. The colonel behind the desk was several inches shorter than the other colonel, but looked to be in better condition. Both appeared to be in their mid-forties.

"I'm Dave Benjamin; sorry we didn't get a chance to talk last night." The obvious commander stuck out his hand before either captain could salute.

They introduced themselves and were in turn introduced to the tall, lanky Operations Officer, Lieutenant Colonel Ed Hardy.

"Sit down," Colonel Benjamin said. *"Welcome to the 23rd TASS. Have you finished your in-processing and medical exams?"* He returned to his chair behind the large desk as they both nodded affirmatively.

"How was your training course at Binh Thuy?" Ed Hardy asked.

"Fine, Sir," Sean answered.

"The O-2 is a nice aircraft. It sure beats the hell out of the O-1 in performance," said Bill.

"It does that, but I still miss the old Birddog," Ed Hardy said, wistfully.

"Ed and I have been wondering about you two since we got the reports from the FAC School. They seem to think you two might be a bit hard to handle."

Bill and Sean exchanged surprised glances. *"Not at all, Colonel,"* Sean said seriously. *"We are ready to get into the action."*

"Bullshit!" Ed Hardy interrupted. *"Neither of you is old enough to know what action is."*

"Are you as good as you think you are, Captain?" Colonel Benjamin was looking directly at Bill.

Bill quickly tried to compose an answer that would satisfy the colonel, *"Yes Sir,"* he blurted.

"You'd better be," the colonel, suddenly lowered his voice and sat back. *"You damned well better be."*

Both captains were embarrassed. They had hoped that reports of their activities would not have preceded them but they were wrong. Now they had to defend and justify their actions at Binh Thuy.

"You're both getting a second chance and not because we need pilots. I can always get more of those," Colonel Benjamin paused and looked at each of the captains. *"Major Fred Stebbins thinks the two of you will be assets to our squadron, if you can be aimed in the right direction. Those are his words."*

"Is the major coming here?" Bill asked, quickly. He had visions of Ed Hardy and Fred Stebbins comparing notes:

"No, he called yesterday from Danang. He's assigned to the DASC there, but he'll be here for an orientation visit next month. He just happened to mention two unusual pilots he met at Binh Thuy," Colonel Benjamin continued, *"Well, will you two fit in here?"*

"Yes, Sir," they answered, quietly this time.

The Colonel looked at Ed Hardy and said, *"Let's assign them to Jerry Hersey's flight. He can get them checked out."*

Ed nodded at the colonel, *"Yes, Sir. I agree, he can keep them in line."*

The two captains stood and saluted the commander. He returned their salutes and reached for the paperwork on his desk. Lieutenant Colonel Hardy led them from the room.

CHAPTER SEVENTEEN
Nakhon Phanom Royal Thai Air Base (NKP)
21 October 1967, Nail Ops Room

"In here, you two. I'll turn you over to Jerry. When he's finished with you I want to hear more about your troubles at Binh Thuy."

They followed Ed Hardy into the operations room. A major was seated at a desk, talking on the telephone. He nodded to Ed and returned his attention to the telephone and the papers in front of him. Bill and Sean were introduced to two captains and a lieutenant. Both captains wore pilot's wings, but the lieutenant wore the wings of a navigator. Sean wondered why they had a navigator in the squadron. He couldn't imagine an O-2 needing one. It wasn't fast enough nor did he think it would go far enough to get lost.

"This is squadron Operations. We listen to TUOC reports on this UHF radio and follow the FACs with this one, the FM. Neither one will reach more than thirty miles due to the terrain. The FM radio is set to 50.50 which is "Nail Common", and the call sign here is "Dullness". Ed walked over to a large wall map, and began pointing.

"This map is our area of operations. We cover the area from Mu Gia Pass to just south of Route 9, from the Vietnamese borders to the Mekong River. The flight sectors are outlined in black. This is Steel Tiger. The area north of us is

called "Barrel Roll" and is usually controlled by both the Nails and the Raven's. You'll get the details at TUOC during your orientation briefings."

"I've heard about the Ravens. From what people say they are Wild Men...is that true?" Bill asked.

"They are volunteers taken from the best and most aggressive FACs who have completed around 6 months of their tour. They are experts and should be treated as such."

"How many sorties do you fly every day?" Sean asked.

"Thirty day missions and eight every night. Our job is to locate and destroy trucks carrying supplies south on the Ho Chi Minh Trail."

"How're you doing?" Bill asked.

"Lousy. If we get five percent of the trucks we see, we're doing well," Ed answered. "We don't see all of the trucks, either."

"That's not very good," Bill commented.

"Don't make snap judgments, Captain," Ed bristled. "You'll see for yourself soon enough just how hard it is to kill a truck."

He turned from the map, walked over to the major, who had finished with his phone call. "Jerry, these two are in your flight. Get them checked out on days, then bring them back for another meeting with Colonel Benjamin."

Major Jerry Hersey's eyebrows lifted. He wondered why they were to be brought back for a second meeting with the commander. That was very unusual. Jerry was a shorter version of Ed Hardy, just over five feet ten inches tall and one hundred and sixty pounds. He wore his sandy hair long enough to part, and unlike the others, his uniforms were starched and expertly creased. His home was Boston and his accent contrasted sharply with Ed's. He wore command pilot's wings, where Bill and Sean wore only senior pilot's wings. Ed and Jerry had similar backgrounds. Both were bomber pilots who had come to Southeast Asia from active SAC bomber units. Hersey was another BUF driver.

"*Sure. Ed, I'm finished with these reports. Why don't I take the captains now? We can get started this afternoon and I'll have them on their first orientation flights tomorrow. I have their hootch assignments,*" he replied.

"*Good,*" Ed Hardy said. "*I'll talk to you two later.*"

Jerry motioned for them to follow him. On his way out the door, he picked up two folders from the Operations Officer's desk and went to a cabinet where he retrieved two Cessna O-2 flight manuals.

"*They'll be in my two-ship at 0800,*" he said to the lieutenant, who was working on the daily flight schedule.

He handed each of them a flight manual and a folder. The two followed him to a jeep and the three climbed in. Jerry drove up the hill towards the club and then to the Nail hootches.

CHAPTER EIGHTEEN
Nakhon Phanom Royal Thai Air Base (NKP)
21 October 1967, driving to the NAIL hootches

"*What do the navigators do, Major?*" Sean asked.

"*They operate the Starlight scopes at night. We have seven of them. They're all young and inexperienced, but they're enthusiastic. You'll enjoy working with them; they're a big help at night.*"

As they reached the hootch area, Jerry said, *"You two have been split up. Bill, you're in this room with Captain Joe Brown. He's probably sleeping now, but when he wakes up you can move in."*

"How will I know when he's up?"

"He'll go to the club to eat."

"Sean, you'll be bunking with Lieutenant Ralph Langer. He's on days so you can move in now. Where did you leave your gear?"

They pointed to the room they slept in last night and walked in that direction. While Sean was retrieving his gear, Joe appeared. He was on his way to his room for some more sleep. He helped Bill with his gear and showed him the empty beds. Each ten foot by fifteen foot room had three beds; a single and a bunk bed. Only two officers were assigned to each room because the squadron was not at full strength.

Bill left as soon as he stowed his gear. Joe said he would meet them at the club around six. He had an eight o'clock takeoff scheduled for tonight.

Sean hung his uniforms in an empty locker and left a note on Ralph's locker, telling him that he had a new roommate and that he did appreciate the artistic touch of having the entire ceiling covered with more than 7 years of Playboy centerfolds.

Historical Note: In mid 1967 about 8 navigators (7 lieutenants and one major) were assigned to the 23rd TASS to assist in primarily the night fighting. They also served at Khe Sanh during the summer of 1967 in support of that mission with the Nails. Don Brown's wife, Judy, sent the Playboy centerfolds and Don covered the ceiling of his room with the pulchritude.

CHAPTER NINETEEN
Nakhon Phanom Royal Thai Air Base (NKP)

21 October 1967, "Officers' Club"

They returned to the club with Jerry, carrying their newly acquired flight manuals and folders. There, they entered the very large and nearly empty dining room. Jerry led them to a well-lit corner where they sat at a table without a tablecloth or silverware.

"There are always a few open tables in this corner. With people flying day and night and the maids working around the rooms all day, it's hard to get anything done in the hootches. Most of us use this area to work," Jerry said.

"Isn't there room at the squadron?" Bill asked.

"If you go there, Ed will find something else for you to do," Jerry said, smiling. *"You met him. You're all kids, to him. He doesn't think that you have important work to do unless he assigns it."*

"How about TUOC?" Sean asked.

"There are a few rooms there, but we use them exclusively for classified stuff. Mission briefings, debriefings, and special operations are in TUOC. This corner of the club is the most convenient place for everything else."

"Now, tell me about Binh Thuy. We heard some wild stories about you two," Jerry continued, after they were seated.

"They're all false major," Bill answered, quickly. *"What did you hear?"*

"The school report arrived yesterday morning. It said you accidentally fired a couple rockets at an Army helicopter and you," Jerry said, giving Sean a curious look, *"nearly had a major busted from the program. Don't you like majors?"*

"I told you that the stories were false," Bill replied, grinning. *"I had a Lau 59 pod malfunction*

and it sequentially fired two of the rockets before I could get it turned off. I was busy keeping it pointed at the river."

"I merely assisted an old desk jockey in mastering his fear of the dark, Sir," Sean replied, seriously.

"General Holland wanted to have you both sent to Bien Hoa, but Colonel Benjamin called a friend of his in Danang, who said that you were OK pilots? Crazy, but OK. If the major in Danang hadn't known you, you'd be living behind sandbags avoiding nightly mortar attacks somewhere in the mud in South Vietnam."

"Sir, is everything settled?" Bill was concerned.

"It will probably depend on the next few days. The commander wants to see you again after your day checkouts. He doesn't usually do that."

"I guess we better be on our best behavior."

"That's for damn sure. Now, am I personally going to have trouble with either of you crazies?" Jerry asked.

"No, Sir. Not me," Bill said, innocently.

"Nor I, Major," Sean replied.

"Bill, you can probably get away with some of these stunts. You're the first real fighter jock that we've had in the squadron and people expect fighter pilots to be a little crazy. I think the colonel believes you can help us with strike control. On the other hand, we have a lot of guys with four-engine time," Jerry said, looking at Sean.

Jerry turned to Bill. *"Fred Stebbins said that with all the fighter time you have, if you wanted to hit that helicopter, you would have."*

Bill nodded. *"It seems to me that an O-2 could hit a very slow moving helicopter, if the pilot was seriously trying to hit it."*

Jerry looked at the two. His first impression was a good one, but he didn't want to get crossways with Ed Hardy. Eyeing them sternly he said, *"The folders are our day operating procedures. Read them before morning and remember what you read. You've seen the flight manuals already. You're both scheduled to fly at 0800 hours. Be in TUOC at 0630. I'll leave the Club at 0625 hours in the jeep. If you want a ride, be there."*

"Anything more today?" Sean asked.

"No. Read those folders and be ready in the morning. Do you have survival vests?"

"No, Sir."

"Make it 0600. We'll get survival kits and 38s after the mission briefing."

"Thanks, Major," Sean said.

"No sweat, I'll see you later. I have a couple of things to do this afternoon."

"How do I get to TFA?" Sean asked.

"It's too far to walk. You'll need a jeep. When you get finished reading the procedures come down to the squadron. I'll lend you one of ours," Jerry Hersey replied... *"What do you need at TFA?"*

"I'm looking for a friend," Sean answered, trying to sound nonchalant.

"He looks like he needs a friend," Bill said to Jerry.

"They won't let you through the gate unless you have a pass," Jerry said. *"You better call first. If your friend is there, he'll have to escort you in."*

"I'm sure "he" will do that," Bill was grinning.

Jerry looked at each of the captains and decided that whatever they had going, he didn't understand and wasn't going to ask. He said,

"My offer is still good. If you need a jeep come down to the squadron when you're done studying these procedures."

CHAPTER TWENTY
Nakhon Phanom Royal Thai Air Base (NKP)
22 October 1967, morning, departing the O'Club

Sean wasn't in a talkative mood when they left the O'Club at 0600 the next morning. After he searched for Sharon at dinner to no avail, he borrowed Jerry Hersey's jeep and drove to TFA. When he arrived, he was stopped at the compound gate by an armed Thai guard as Jerry said he would be and was told that Lieutenant Stuart was not there. **'She gone!'** was all that he could get from the guard. He was in a funk when he returned to the O'Club and was still depressed at breakfast.

Ralph Langer was with them. He would be flying with Bill in the high position while Jerry Hersey and Sean were going together in the low or lead plane. This high/low was not normally the procedure for the NAIL combat missions, but for training new guys it seemed to work out quite well. Not only could the new guy practice but he was able to observe the other new guy and learn from that. Jerry drove the four of them to TUOC where they received their mission briefing and area maps.

From TUOC, it was a short walk to the personal equipment section where they drew their backpack parachutes, survival vests and weapons. They were each handed an M-16 rifle and a .38 caliber Smith and Wesson Combat Masterpiece revolver. Sean selected a holster that fit on his survival vest.

Bill looked through the available rigs and picked a web belt with bullet loops and a side holster. All four received two spare magazines for the M-16s. Sean's mood rapidly improved as they donned their flak vests and survival vests. This was real and they would soon be in the air on a combat mission. There was no time for personal problems. Sean didn't like the feel of the .38 on his chest so he discarded the vest holster and picked up a side holster. Now both of them looked like cowboys with their low slung gun belts.

Sean and Jerry headed in one direction on the flight line; Bill and Ralph in another.

At 0755 they pulled into the arming area to have the safety pins removed and at 0800 they took off. Sean was first, flying in the lead O-2 and Bill followed. He was climbing to the high position, a couple of thousand feet above and behind Sean.

For the next forty-five minutes they flew over what could only be called spectacular terrain. After crossing the wide brown Mekong River, they passed over lush green jungle dotted with small rocky outcrops. Halfway across Laos, the terrain became more rugged as the mountains or karst reached to nearly five thousand feet and was separated by wide green river valleys. Everything was beautiful, except the bombed out areas on and near the "roads." These areas looked more like moonscapes, brown dirt circular mounds filled with green water... and there seemed to be millions of them. Such beauty, such destruction and all in one place. This was Laos in 1967.

By 0845 hours they were approaching the Ho Chi Minh Trail, a primarily north-south complex network of dirt roads, trails, way stations and staging areas. Although the main roads were visible from the air, the side roads, trails and way stations were under the dense triple-canopied rain forest that covered most of central and southern Laos.

'So this is the Ho Chi Minh Trail,' thought Bill. **'It doesn't look like much. No asphalt, no concrete,**

no bridges. Nothing but dirt roads and this is the major supply line from North to South Vietnam.'

The day was clear and visibility was excellent. There was no activity on the main roads and the FACs had only one preplanned strike against a suspected truck park. When they received their fighter handoff from Cricket, the Airborne Command and Control Center (ABCCC), they were over the target area. Bill was at eight thousand feet, orbiting one mile to the east of the target. Sean flew at six thousand feet also to the east, but only a half mile out. There was a twenty-knot crosswind at their altitude and they were having some difficulty maintaining position near the target. When the two F-105s arrived, Sean rolled in to mark and fired a Willie Pete. It missed the target, the suspected truck park, by nearly a half mile.

It took Sean two more rockets before the fighter pilots understood where the target was located. Then they made three passes each, dropping their entire loads of seven-hundred and fifty-pound bombs into the jungle. There were bursts and multiple shock waves when the bombs detonated but no black smoke or large flashes from secondary explosions, which would have indicated trucks or fuel drums. The fighters considered their mission a bust and the FACs could not verify any damage. This was a dull and non-satisfying mission for everyone. The BDA or Bomb Damage Assessment was zippo…nada…nothing…zero.

Bill wondered, *"If that was a truck park, why didn't we see some secondaries?"*

At the end of their three hours on station over the trail looking for trucks, they were relieved by the next two FACs and headed back for NKP. Halfway home, Bill called Sean. *"Hey, Sean. Do you have any Willy Petes left?"*

"I still have eight," Sean replied.

"We have ten left. Let me show you something. See that karst outcropping to your

left?" Bill asked. The karst outcrops were common sights in the Steel Tiger area of operations. They jutted up from the jungle floor for hundreds of feet and were often completely covered with very green vegetation and trees. They reminded Bill of the mountains in southern Utah. Like the wind sculptured sandstone mountains in Utah, the karst were the remnants of limestone mountains in Laos. Over the centuries they had been eroding, more from the effects of water ... the monsoons ... than wind. They typically contained large caverns and caves which were often used by the North Vietnamese and Pathet Lao to store supplies.

"The big one standing by itself, about eleven o'clock?"

"That's the one. Let's see you hit it."

"What about it, Major?" Sean turned to look at Jerry.

"We have the fuel. A little practice would be good and this is a free-fire zone," Jerry nodded in agreement. Sean rolled in on the target and fired. His rocket went to the right and missed the karst by a quarter of a mile.

"My turn," Bill said. Ralph was puzzled when Bill made adjustments to the elevator and rudder trim settings. He flew to the left for a few moments and then rolled in on the target. When Bill fired, the rocket went straight for the karst. It impacted the karst about half way up and nearly in the center ... a bull's eye.

"I'm impressed," Ralph said. *"How did you do that?"*

"I'll show you, but wait a minute," Bill replied, then radioed, *"You try it, Jerry."*

Are you going to show us something new?" Jerry asked.

"I think so, but I want to see you shoot first."

"Hang on; I need to get in position." After a couple minutes, Jerry rolled in on the target. His rocket also went to the right side of the karst.

"OK. I do have something to show you. But first, Ralph gets a turn next."

"Ralph, are you ready?"

Ralph nodded.

"Ralph is going to fire one first. Then I'm going to have him fire a second rocket. Stand by."

Ralph also missed the karst. His rocket impacted at least a half mile to the same side of the target.

"Ralph, look at your smoke. Which way is the wind blowing?"

"Left to right."

"First, as a FAC, your position is variable. So pick a starting position that is directly into or away from the wind relative to the target. That way you eliminate fifty percent of the firing variables."

"You mean fly over there," Ralph said, pointing to a position that would place him with the wind directly on his tail, blowing in the direction of the karst target.

"Exactly."

Ralph flew the O-2 to the desired location, downwind from the karst outcropping.

"Now line up and aim half again as high as the karst is tall," Bill said.

"OK," Ralph replied.

"Hold it, hold it!" Bill motioned for Ralph to stop. ***"Turn around"***

Ralph reversed course and gave Bill a puzzled look.

"What speed are you going to fire the rockets at?"

"About a hundred and forty, I guess," Ralph replied.

"Add power and lower the nose. Pick up one forty," Bill said. As soon as Ralph did that, he continued, *"Now set the trim to hold you straight and level at that speed."*

Ralph added power and leveled off. *"It's set,"* He replied, as soon as he finished making the settings.

"Now let's go back and fire at the karst. Don't mess with the trim."

Ralph turned the aircraft and climbed to his original attitude. Positioning himself so that he was in line with the wind, he rolled in and pointed the plane at the base of the karst. He fired.

This time the smoke rocket hit the right edge of the karst, about one third of the way down. Ralph was jubilant. *"I want to do it again. I've never hit anything with these rockets before today."*

"Later," Bill replied, laughing. He switched to the radio. *"Come up on FM, I want to explain what we did."*

"We're on NAIL Common (50.50 FM), Bill," Jerry said as soon as he switched the radio frequency.

"OK. First, add power to hold one hundred and forty knots. That's the speed you want to be at when you fire a rocket. Then, trim the aircraft for straight and level flight. When you get the settings write them down. Remember, they're different for each airplane. The rudder trim is the most important."

"Why the rudder trim?" came back a voice from the other plane.

"If the ball isn't centered when you fire, the rocket will go to one side or the other of the target."

"We got it, Bill. What is next?" Sean asked.

"I'm going to pop a rocket in the general direction of the karst," Bill said, and fired. They watched it impact. *"Now, look at the smoke. When you get to the range ... I mean trail ... find some smoke or use your own. Remember the wind direction. Always fire directly into or away from the wind. It takes half the variables away from the shot."*

"OK. I'm going to try another shot." Jerry rolled in and fired. His rocket went over the top of the karst, but it was on line.

"One more thing. Add or subtract for the wind direction. Aim way high if your nose is into the wind or way low if it's on your tail," Bill said.

"How high?"

"Use half the height of the karst. Aim that much above it, if you're against the wind. Aim at the base, if the wind is with you."

Jerry's next rocket impacted the target.

"One last thing, Sir," Bill said.

"What's that?" Jerry asked.

There was a pause, and then Bill answered, *"Always pick great big targets."*

Historical Note: Jerry Dwyer, the fighter pilot, did show several NAILs how to shoot the Willie Petes.

CHAPTER TWENTY ONE
Nakhon Phanom Royal Thai Air Base (NKP)
25 October 1967, TUOC

For the next three days, Bill and Sean were scheduled to fly orientation flights each morning with experienced FACs. Their afternoons were for briefings at TUOC on combat air operations in the Steel Tiger area of Laos. Ed Hardy believed that the NAIL FACs overall effectiveness would be improved if they had some flying experience in the operating area while they were being briefed on the situation. That way they could relate what they were being told with what was actually happening in the area during their flights. Their orientation flights were always with experienced FACs and were never flown in high-threat areas.

"Do we need to take notes?" Bill asked when they were seated in the conference room with their coffee. Lieutenant Zack North was preparing to begin their briefings.

"No, Sir," Zack replied. *"I have handouts for you which cover all you need to know. While you're here, we'll prepare your personal area maps and set up your mission packets. You'll need them as soon as you finish your checkouts and are cleared to fly on your own."*

"We just listen?" Sean was curious.

"Listen and ask questions. This isn't a test. If you need to know something, you can come here anytime. It's our job to get you as prepared as we can in the time that we have available," Zack said. Then he grinned, *"Maybe it is a test. Only we don't give the exam: it's in Steel Tiger. If you pass, you live. If you flunk, you die."*

"What's the schedule?" Bill asked.

"I'll be handling the briefings for the first two days. On the third day, we use other experts from the base."

They both picked up on the "other experts" comment. Zack was letting them know that he considered himself a knowledgeable Intelligence Officer and they could learn from him. Bill glanced at Sean who nodded and smiled. Zack had promise.

"We're going to cover our combat area, Steel Tiger, and the Command and Control structure today. Tomorrow we'll review the assigned flying

units at NKP, including their normal ordnance loads and missions. We'll do the same for other bases and units that support the interdiction efforts. The last day we'll have presentations by Task Force Alpha (TFA), Invert radar, Search and Rescue, and the Base Commander," Zack continued.

"Why the Base Commander?" Sean asked.

"He requires it for all new crew members. He insists that one of the doctors warn you about VD and the local girls," Zack said, with a broad grin.

"You're kidding," Sean said.

"No, Sir. I'm not. The doctors don't usually come themselves. They generally send a corpsman."

"Let's talk about the Ho Chi Minh Trail, Zack," Bill interjected.

Zack went to the large map which covered an entire wall in the conference room. The two captains had been seated but rose and moved close to the map, where they could read the names of the features depicted there.

"I'm sure you know that Laos is divided into two main areas. Steel Tiger is the name used to identify operations in the Laotian panhandle, everything south of 18 degrees 25 minutes north. Barrel Roll is for all operations north of Steel Tiger. This northern area contains the PDJ (Plain of Jars). More on that later. On the map, our area of interest extends from Nape Pass at the north end, where Route 8 crosses into North Vietnam, to a little south of the A Shau Valley, where Route 923 enters South Vietnam, a distance of approximately one hundred and thirty nautical miles. The western boundary is the Mekong River, and to the east, the border with Vietnam. Operations across that border are controlled by the Tactical Air

Control Center (TACC) at 7th Air Force Headquarters in Saigon. To cross that border there, north of route 9, will take you into North Vietnam and you will need special permission from Cricket or Alleycat to go in there."

"Our primary operating area is much smaller," Zack continued, using a pointer to depict each location he was identifying. "We concentrate our efforts in what is known as the Muscle Shoals operating area. It covers the road network between Mu Gia Pass, Route 12, at the north end, to Route 9 in the south. Muscle Shoals covers the area east to Route 122. The only thing to the west of that is the river road, Route 13 that parallels the Mekong. That area is part of Cricket West. You will fly most of your missions in the Muscle Shoals area. Some NAILs work in Cricket west, but Colonel Hardy said you two won't."

"Do we have to know everything about these areas, and what's going on all of the time?" Sean asked.

"Not really. We handle most of it for you. The mission frags, your tasks, are sent to us every day by the TACC in Saigon. We convert the frags to aircraft sorties. When you come in here for your mission briefing, we'll have specific targets and route sectors for you to work," Zack said.

"Do you do that for all the units or just us?" Bill asked.

"We do it for all of the NAIL units. Rescue handles their own," Zack replied. "I handle the night NAILs and the Candlesticks, the C-123 FACs. The A-26 Nimrods and the T-28 Zorros are handled by another one of us. Day NAILs and Hobos, the A-1s, are taken care of by the third Intelligence Officer."

"Where is Cricket? We talked to them on our sortie today?" Sean asked.

"Cricket is the C-130 Airborne TUOC that controls the entire Steel Tiger area or all of Laos south of 18 degrees 25 minutes north during the days. Every time you fly, you report in and out of the area to Cricket. They're like an Air Traffic Control Center, controlling all aircraft movement in their area. They usually orbit south of us, over the Laotian panhandle. Alleycat is the same, but at night. Remember it is Cricket in the daytime and Alleycat at night."

"We have a lot to learn," Bill said. *"Where are the handouts and the maps?"*

They devoted the remainder of that day preparing their personal maps and organizing the data carried in their individual mission pouches. After they completed their maps, Zack brought in a survival vest. It was a mesh-and-nylon webbing which was worn over the standard armored vest and under their parachutes. He showed them the special containers on the survival vest.

There was a medical kit packaged in a tough plastic container and sealed with waterproof, tear-resistant tape. There were two small survival radios, a pen flare gun with ten small flares and another well-wrapped plastic container. One pocket held ammunition for their personal weapons. All of the NAILs carried Smith & Wesson .38 caliber, Combat Masterpiece handguns. They also would carry an M-16 rifle in the aircraft. When Sean asked about the kits, Zack showed them two sealed, glass-covered displays. One had all of the medical supplies displayed and identified while the other contained the specific items for their flying area. It had half-a-dozen gold coins and a blood chit promising a significant cash reward, in several languages common to the area, to anyone who returned a downed flyer to U.S. forces. The cost of these two kits was high and they were carefully controlled. Each crew member signed for the kits before every mission and turned them in, unopened, after the mission. They were kept in locked safes and inventoried daily. They were wrapped in the special tape to insure that individuals did not avail themselves of the gold coins or of the drugs contained in the medical kit.

They would also carry bright orange and white nylon panels and two smoke canisters to help rescue helicopters in locating them. When Zack had them get their pictures taken, they joked about police mug shots. Every crew member was required to have front and side-view Evade &Escape photos taken. These photographs were available to assist the rescue forces in identifying downed flyers. They were also used by intelligence analysts to identify crewmen who were captured and displayed to the public. In addition to this identifying info, each flyer was to provide a special number, saying or code that would identify each individual airman. In case of a helicopter rescue, this coding would be used by the rescuers to assure that they were picking up a specific American and not an enemy imposter. Zack was particularly serious when he explained that this code had to be secret, and under the most stressful conditions it must be remembered. He made sure that everyone he briefed selected numbers or codes they would never ever forget. By the time the first day's briefings were over, both Bill and Sean were convinced of the seriousness of the war and more than impressed with the expertise of the Lieutenant.

The next two afternoons were as Zack promised. By the end of the sessions, they were familiar with the scope of the interdiction effort and with the forces being used in their area. The NAIL FACs had a lot of support, but they were clearly on the hot spot. If Cricket was the Air Traffic Control Center, the FAC was the tower. NAILs were responsible for all aircraft activities in individual sectors. The FAC was clearly the HMFICC....Head Mother Fucker in Complete Charge.

It was obvious that air interdiction in Laos was taken seriously because it was dangerous. Even though they had flown in the Mekong Delta and on a couple of missions into Laos, they had not fully appreciated the personal risks, until Zack briefed them on the number of guns guarding the trail, gave them the survival kits and took their pictures. The picture taking got their attention as these would be used to identify them, if or when they were taken prisoner. When Captain Don Combs, a Sandy pilot, briefed them on search and rescue operations, they listened carefully to every word he said.

When a captain from TFA came to brief them, Sean was sure he would finally get some information on the missing lieutenant. He was mistaken. The captain doing their briefing rarely saw the general and had never seen the aide. He was no help at all. All they learned about TFA was that they used air-dropped acoustic sensors, ADSIDs, to listen for enemy movement along selected routes. These movement reports were passed to the TACC and the airborne TUOCs for use in targeting. The entire project was classified to protect the identity of the seismic sensors. The captain showed them two air-dropped sensors disguised as plants.

Bill started to laugh. ***"Are you telling me that those are supposed to look like real plants in the jungle?***

"Certainly," was the captain's indignant reply.

"Have you ever been in a jungle?" Sean asked.

"No. The people who made these are experts. They don't make mistakes," the TFA captain was irritated with the two pilots and the lieutenant, all whom were laughing at him or his sensor or both.

"It doesn't look like a plant. It doesn't even look like an artificial plant. It looks like something

disguised as an artificial plant, Captain. It sure doesn't look like anything I've seen in the jungle," Bill shook his head in wonder. *"For this they need a general?"* he continued, laughing.

The captain turned a deep shade of crimson, but maintained his haughty composure. He assured them that TFA would soon replace all of the FACs on the Trail because the sensors didn't lie. Their data would be accurate and exact. It was clear that he didn't think much of the FACs or of their sightings and or their impact on the war.

Before Bill or Sean could respond, Zack interrupted the briefing and thanked the captain for coming. He told Sean and Bill to take a break and get some coffee while he set up their final talk.

The last briefing on their schedule would be given by someone from the flight surgeon's office. A medical corpsman soon arrived at TUOC and Zack introduced him.

He walked to the podium, looked at the two new pilots and said, *"Flies breed disease. Keep yours zipped up."* Bill and Sean laughed, Zack smiled and the sergeant nodded, stepped down from the podium and left the room. That was the end of their VD briefing and their base orientation.

Historical Note: The medical briefing was exactly as described above.

CHAPTER TWENTY TWO
Nakhon Phanom Royal Thai Air Base (NKP)
30 October 1967, morning, over the Ho Chi Minh Trail

Bill and Sean's second meeting with the NAIL commander never materialized. They completed their day checkouts, were certified "combat ready" and Jerry added them to his daily schedule. They typically flew a four-and-a-half-hour mission, seven days a week, directing air strikes on the Ho Chi Minh Trail against trucks, guns and truck parks.

During their second week on the Trail, they ran into the "Field-Grade Bloc" as it was often referred to by the company-grade flying officers. Bill was marking a target for the strike aircraft, when Major Martin, one of the FAC Flight Commanders who was also flying at the time, called him on the FM radio.

"Five Five, you're flying too low."

"Say again," Bill replied, disbelief in his voice.

"NAIL Five Five, this is NAIL One Five. You're flying too low, Captain."

Bill was pulling up from his firing pass at forty two hundred feet. He was at least twenty five hundred feet above the road and nowhere near the tops of the hills. He decided to let it go until they were on the ground. *"Roger, One Five, I'm climbing back to six thousand feet."*

When they departed the Trail, Bill flew home at eight thousand feet and noticed that Major Martin was at least two thousand feet higher. He wondered about the radio call, but did not mention it again until they were walking to TUOC for their debriefing.

"Major, explain the altitude problem," Bill said.

"There's no need to go that low over the Trail," Martin said. *"You can mark just as well from eight thousand feet as you can from four thousand."*

"No, Sir. You can't," Bill replied. *"The winds are tough enough to figure out from four thousand. At eight thousand feet, it would be nearly impossible. There was no gunfire and we were trying to mark a possible truck park."*

"Captain, you only need to get a mark somewhere in the vicinity of the target. It isn't

necessary to hit it yourself. You're taking unnecessary risks. Anyone as good as you are supposed to be should be able to hit the target from eight thousand feet," Martin's smug response irritated Bill.

"What about the fighters? They need to know where to drop their bombs," Bill answered.

"If you can get a mark within a half mile, it's good enough," Martin said, matter of factly.

"Jesus, Sir. Who told you that?" Bill wanted to know.

"That's how we do it here. You better wise up. We have a lot more flying experience than you and we've been here a lot longer."

"How many bombs have you dropped, Major?" Bill asked.

"That isn't important, Captain. What is important is that you are to do as you are told. The decision isn't yours to make. I'll speak to Major Hersey about it," Martin turned and walked into the briefing room. Nothing more was said.

CHAPTER TWENTY THREE
Nakhon Phanom Royal Thai Air Base (NKP)
30 October 1967, evening, O'Club

That night, when they were having dinner, Jerry Hersey came to their table. Ralph Langer was sitting with Sean, Bill and Charlie Green, one of the Zorro pilots.

"I thought you were going to stay out of trouble," Jerry said, looking at Bill.

"What did I do, Sir? Did Major Martin talk to you?"

"*He did. You are reputed to have an attitude problem. What happened out there?*" Jerry asked as he pulled up a chair.

"*Nothing. I was marking a target for two F-4s and went to about forty two hundred feet on the pullout. It was a good mark.*"

"*Martin wants to make our altitudes higher. He thinks we should stay above eight thousand feet,*" Jerry replied, seriously.

"*If we stay at eight thousand feet, then we'll have at least a two-mile slant range for marks. It'll probably be closer to three miles for most of the FACs. You can't hit shit with a Willy Pete from three miles away,*" Bill replied.

"*A lot of FACs can't hit shit from one mile,*" Ralph said, "*Although I'm starting to get good with mine, since Bill showed me how to shoot them.*"

"*I brought up your comments at the last flight commanders meeting and they weren't interested,*" Jerry replied.

"*So what're you saying, Boss? Do we fly higher?*" Sean asked.

"*If necessary. Don't take dumb chances, but don't go any lower than necessary to hit what you're aiming at. I'll talk to Ed. Martin was filling his ear when I left. When you have one of the older heads out there watching you, stay a little higher than normal. A lot of them are nervous. They thought they were getting an easy and safe assignment when they came here. You should see their reaction when we schedule them to fly at night.*"

Jerry was shaking his head as he left the dining room.

"Charlie, you Zorros are out there at night. How do our old heads do when you work with them?" Bill asked.

"We don't. I've only worked with a FAC once. We usually work by ourselves along Routes 122 and 23. You guys stay out on Routes 91 and 911. From the debriefings, I would say that they must have pretty poor night vision. The young guys seem to have a lot more sightings," Charlie replied.

"They fly as high at night as they do in the daytime," Ralph said. *"Ask the navigators. They fly so high it's difficult to see the ground."*

"I don't see them very often," Sean said. *"Where do they spend their time?"*

"The flight commanders usually fly in the afternoon. They sleep late, do a little work in the squadron and fly in the afternoons. That way the war doesn't interfere with their cocktail hour," Ralph answered, smirking. *"Not many of them come here very often and several have tealocks in town."*

"Honeys?" Bill asked, quickly.

"Some of the older guys think they've died and gone to heaven. They've never met or seen anything like the girls over here. They do anything to please their men. I know three of the majors who actually live in town. They have rooms in the hootches and they keep flight suits there, but they really live in town," Ralph replied. *"Some sergeants are there too."*

Sean saw the look in Bill's eye and said, *"No trouble, OK. Don't cause problems,"* He was looking straight at Bill. *"We can do it right as long as we don't rub their noses in it. What they do is their own business."*

"I surrender," Bill said, holding up his hands. ***"I see nothing, I hear nothing and I say nothing."***

They went into the bar, where they joined other crew members. There was always an opportunity for informal bull sessions in the bar about flying and the war. As often as not, they would be joined by crew members from the night, flying Nimrods or Zorros. Bill and Sean had not flown at night nor experienced any gunfire so they listened intently as the night pilots related their war stories.

Jerry Hersey reported daily to Ed Hardy and the two of them talked to Dave Benjamin whenever Bill's methods and techniques needed to be implemented. They believed that the assignment of fighter-qualified personnel to the FAC program was definitely going to help their mission results on the trail. At least Captain Thompson was making a difference.

CHAPTER TWENTY FOUR
Nakhon Phanom Royal Thai Air Base (NKP)
8 November 1967, morning on the NKP runway

Sean lined up with the runway at NKP and slowly reduced the throttles for landing. He brought the O-2 down, touched firmly on the main gear and quickly lowered the nose wheel to the ground. He turned off at the end of the runway and pulled to a stop in the de-arming area.

Holding his hands up and in sight so the armorers could see that he wasn't about to fire a rocket, he waited for them to replace the safety pins on his ordnance. He'd only fired a couple of rockets so it took them a few minutes to safety the twelve he had brought back. When he received their thumbs up, he taxied toward the NAIL parking area.

Sean felt good. It was his thirteenth combat mission. He directed a strike which had successfully cratered the dirt road along the face of the cliff at Foxtrot, one of seven identified interdiction points in Steel Tiger.

Alpha to Golf identified the selected interdiction choke points because of the likelihood that a bomb crater in the road at these locations would stop the truck traffic. Most points were on the sides of steep hills so that going around a bomb crater would be impossible. Sean was pleased with the results as it would please the night flyers to have the trucks bottled up at Foxtrot. He made the strike at 1540 and the enemy wouldn't have time to repair the road before dark.

Covered with sweat, Sean climbed out of the plane and pulled his parachute from the seat. He threw the chute over his shoulder and checked his watch: 1700. He would have plenty of time to debrief and clean up before dinner. Picking up his helmet and maps, he turned away from the plane and bumped into something soft. He stepped back and looked close at the obstacle. He was only inches from a smiling Lieutenant Stuart. His face lit up and the grin spread from ear to ear. Sean dropped his equipment and picked the lieutenant up in a great hug. *"I thought something was wrong. Where have you been?"*

She kissed him lightly on the cheek, *"Ugh! Are all pilots this messy after a mission? No wonder there aren't any women assigned here. You smell awful."* She had both hands on his chest, pushing slightly.

"Well, you smell great," Sean replied, obviously enjoying her closeness. *"You look great, too. Where have you been?"* he asked again as he picked up his gear. He put it in the jeep and walked around to the passenger seat.

"We were at a conference and planning meetings in Hawaii. Our flight just got back to Danang this morning and we came over here in a T-39," she answered. *"I called the FAC squadron and they told me when you were due back. I thought you might like a ride."*

Sean noticed that the maintenance personnel had stopped work to stare at them. Not even their commander had a good-looking female meeting his airplane. He knew he was going to have a lot of explaining to do.

"I have to drop this equipment off and go to TUOC for debriefing. Can we meet for dinner?"

"Just us?"

"Yeah, just us," Sean replied, smiling.

"I'll drop you at PE. We can meet later at the O'Club."

"Great. It'll take me about an hour and a half. I'll see you at the Club at 1830."

CHAPTER TWENTY FIVE
Nakhon Phanom Royal Thai Air Base (NKP)
19 November 1967, in the O'Club

Bill walked into the O'Club and joined Sean, Ralph Langer and Joe Brown at a table in the dining room. *"Did you see the Navy bombers on the flight line?"* Bill asked. He had just returned from a day mission.

"Yeah. What're they doing here?" Ralph said. *"Some new project, I guess. There's at least one new one every week,"* Joe said, disgusted.

"Those aren't bombers, they're OP-2E Neptunes and they're designed for antisubmarine work. They use the old World War II Norden bombsights: have low light level TV, and a bunch of other electronic stuff. They couldn't be here looking for subs," Sean said, *"Could they?"*

"Before I got to NKP, I used to think that headquarters people knew what they were doing

but since I've been here, I really don't know," Bill replied.

"Have you met any of their pilots?" Ralph asked.

"No, not yet. We'll probably see them in the bar."

"We still don't have any jets. More old equipment," Bill lamented.

The four finished eating. Joe headed for the flight line and his night mission. The other three went to the bar, where they found a large group of Navy officers.

"Here, here!" Sean cried. *"Bartender, a drink for our Navy friends."*

When the round was served and introductions made all around, Sean stood on a chair. *"A toast, Gentlemen, a toast. Here's to the Navy. May they be congratulated for keeping us safe from submarine attacks in the Mekong River? Since their arrival, this base has not once been shelled from that hostile and dangerous body of water by any North Vietnamese submarines...none...a testament to their skill, cunning and bravery."*

Loud boos greeted his toast. It was the signal for good-natured barbs and jibes about the conduct of the war. Hearing the commotion, other crews wandered into the bar to see what was happening. There were Nimrods, Zorros and NAILs standing or sitting, watching the exchange between the Navy crews and the three FACs.

"What do you guys do?" Carl Mayes asked, after the exchange. He was one of the Navy pilots, a lieutenant.

"We're Forward Air Controllers or FACs. Usually we look for truck traffic on the trail and try to stop it."

"What's the symbol on your flight suits? A number with a spike through it?"

"That's our call sign," Sean said. *"See, mine is NAIL FOUR FIVE and Bill there is NAIL Five Five."*

"Who're the guys in the black suits?" Carl continued, motioning toward some of the crews at nearby tables.

"Night pilots. We have them as well," Ralph interjected.

"You guys fly those Cessnas at night?"

"Sure, that's when we get most of our truck kills."

"I'd like to go on a night flight," Carl said.

"You can't, at least not with us. At night there are two people aboard. One to fly and the other one to work the night scope," Ralph said. He turned toward some of the black-suited crewmen. *"Do the Zorros take up passengers? You guys have an empty seat at night?"*

"No fucking way! No way," Captain Martin Wesley Wilson yelled. Marty, one of the Zorro pilots, was a certified nut. The son of a Methodist preacher from Arkansas, he was spending his life demonstrating his manhood. Between his junior and senior years at high school, he hitchhiked to Venezuela following the west-coast highways. When he graduated from high school, he was actively skydiving and, as a final stunt before leaving for college, he jumped into a river from a two-hundred-foot-high bridge. While at college, cars and illegal back-alley drag racing were his hobbies. Marty joined the Air Force and learned to fly because he thought it would show everyone that the diminutive, five-foot-four-inch-tall preacher's son was a real man.

A tall Navy pilot made the mistake of chuckling at the size of the black-suited Zorro pilot. He stood and walked up to Marty and said, *"I'm sure we can manage to fly at night if you can, Shorty."*

The Navy crews laughed and-cheered, much to Marty's chagrin. He slammed his hand on the nearest table, **"OK, you bilge-drinking smart asses. Let's see if you can pass the night flyer's test."**

"Anything you can do, runt," the Navy pilot answered.

The Navy crews were cheering on their pilot, while the NKP crews who knew what was coming, laughed and prodded them on as Marty was about to pull one of his favorite tricks.

"Bring out the champagne," Marty yelled.

A bartender soon appeared carrying a tray with two champagne glasses and an unopened bottle of the bubbly. He obviously had seen Marty in action before. He set the tray down on the now-cleared table between the two seated pilots.

"Before you can fly at night, you must pass the grit test," Marty said. He had the Navy crowd's full attention. The noise subsided as they listened to him. **"This test is designed to verify your mettle and check your grit. Are you ready?"**

The Navy pilot, a full lieutenant, nodded and turned toward his crews. They cheered as if on cue. **"Anything the Air Force can do, we can do better—much better,"** he said to his screaming Navy audience.

Marty merely smiled. When the shouting died down, he took off his flight jacket and laid it on the table. **"What say we make this interesting? Let's bet our flight jackets on the test. If I can do it and you can't, then I get both jackets. If I fail and you do it, then they're yours. If it's a draw, we get our own back."**

The Navy jacket was immediately placed on top of the Air Force jacket. The bet was accepted.

Marty opened the champagne bottle and set it back between the two glasses. He picked up one of the glasses and handed the other to the Navy pilot. It was quiet now, quiet enough for everyone to hear the words. Marty was looking his challenger straight in the eyes.

The tall Navy pilot did not know what was about to occur. He held his glass out, expecting it to be filled with champagne, but Marty didn't touch the bottle.

"OK, you want me to be first," Marty said. **"That's fine."** He lifted the champagne glass and took a bite out of it. The Navy pilot and the Navy crews watched, stunned, as Marty slowly and carefully continued biting off more pieces and chewed the glass. When he finished chewing one bite, he swallowed and then took another bite. Two of the Navy crewmen who were watching closely threw up on the floor. Marty's challenger put his glass on the table and just sat there, mouth open, staring at the madman.

Finally, there was nothing remaining of the glass but the stem and base. Marty set it down on the table and took a large swallow of champagne from the open bottle. When he set it back on the table, there was a small trickle of blood running down the left side of his mouth. **"It's your turn, Navy,"** he said.

The Navy pilot tried to hold up his end. He gingerly picked up the glass and bit off a small piece. With increasingly wider eyes, he attempted to chew the glass. After three or four small bites, he quickly grabbed the champagne bottle, drank, and spit everything out on the floor. There was blood everywhere.

"I guess that settles it. The Navy is restricted to daylight hours," Bill announced as he picked up the two flight jackets and handed them to Marty. **"Nice job, Shorty."**

Marty bowed gracefully and sat down at a nearby table with Ralph, Bill and Sean. Ralph was shaking his head in wonder. **"No matter how many times I see you do that, I'm amazed that you don't die or something,"** Sean said.

"It pretty much goes right through you.... There's a risk, though," Marty answered.

"What's that?" Ralph wanted to know.

"You don't want to get constipated for the next couple of days!" was the reply. Bill and Sean roared with laughter. Ralph's expression was priceless.

Historical Note: Glass eating was done often by many different warriors and particularly well by Don Brown, who must have eaten at least 5 champagne glasses and 3 light bulbs in a six-month period.

CHAPTER TWENTY SIX
Nakhon Phanom Royal Thai Air Base (NKP)
19 November 1967, later in the O'Club

Marty got up and went over to the Navy crews. *"Welcome to NKP,"* he said, holding out his hand. *"I'm Martin Wesley Wilson."* Sean and Bill had followed him into the bar and introduced themselves to the Navy flyers.

The Navy crews acknowledged the Zorro and his two friends as they sat down with them. Soon these old heads were answering the many Navy questions about the war and night flying over Laos.

"When do you start flying?" Bill asked the Navy crews at the table next to theirs.

"We're supposed to get orientation flights with the FACs," Mike Kurten, another Navy lieutenant, said.

"We haven't heard about it. When is that supposed to happen?" Sean asked.

"Starts tomorrow, according to our commander," Mike answered.

"Maybe we'll see you then," Bill said. *"I've never heard of any FACs giving sight-seeing rides, though."*

"We're to be at TUOC in the morning for our briefings. I have a 0630 show time," Carl said.

"That's our briefing time. You might be with us, then," Sean remarked.

Walking back to their hootches Bill commented to Sean and Ralph. *"The Navy guys never told us what they were doing here."*

"I noticed," Ralph answered. *"The last group like that was here to put ADSIDs along the trail, using helicopters. The Army choppers did not have the range and never dropped a sensor."*

"Zack never mentioned the Army or acoustic sensors."

"Yeah, the Army choppers were to drop them for the TFA guys. They use them to listen for trucks. We heard that the sensors can even pick up voices."

"Big deal. You still have to locate them for the fighters. How are they going to run a strike from the TFA?" Bill asked. *"Most of that jungle looks like every other bit of jungle. I'll bet the fighters don't see twenty percent of the trucks unless they come down close to the ground. My guess is that they usually drop on the FAC's smoke."*

"Is it hard to see a road from a fighter?" Sean said.

"Not usually. But when you have all of the places looking like all of the other places, like out along the trail, it gets tough. A truck is a very small target when it's in and out of tree cover. I can't see the North Vietnamese driving large

convoys on open roads during the day. Could you?"

"Could you hit a truck with a bomb?" Ralph asked.

"One bomb? No way! I had a tough time getting a bomb to hit a two-hundred-foot-wide runway with an F-100. How big is a truck?" Bill said.

"Figure about eight feet by fifty feet and that would be a big one, an eighteen wheeler," Ralph said. "I never even got close to the roads with my Willy Petes until you showed me how."

"That's what I mean. Even if these TFA guys hear the trucks, someone has to set up the attack. If you want any success at all, you have to mark close enough to the target for the fighters to set up their bombing patterns. Half the value of the smoke is to let the fighters know the wind. It's tough enough on a stateside gunnery range with accurate weather data. Out here, trying to hit a single truck with a bomb is pretty much a waste of time and bombs, even with a good mark," Bill said.

"What the hell are we doing it for?" Ralph asked.

"We never use just one bomb. The fighters usually drop a string of bombs. Ideally, they drop about ten degrees off the road heading and the string crosses the road over the convoy. That should get a couple of trucks, even if the wind data is wrong."

"Are you telling me to run them in across the road, not along it?" Ralph wanted to know.

"Yep, every time. Give them run-in headings about ten degrees off the road direction. The smart ones are probably doing that already."

"You mean smart FACs?"

"No, the fighter pilots. They know how hard it is for you and they know that most FACs have never dropped a bomb or fired a gun."

"Should we ask them to use their guns?"

"Never! They have to come in too low. They're likely to run into antiaircraft guns along the trail and you could get them killed."

"We didn't get much of this in Florida," Ralph said.

"You didn't meet any fighter guys there, did you?" Bill said. *"You have to talk to someone who has done it for a while and also someone who will admit that the results aren't very good, even on a range."*

"Not very good?" Sean said, incredulously. *"You guys aren't very good? What about all you shit-hot fighter pilots strutting around like prima donnas? I was led to believe you could put a bomb in a barrel."*

"Not really. If we drop enough bombs, someone will hit the barrel but for pinpoint bombing, forget it. It's worse if we get only one or two passes."

Both Ralph and Sean were astounded. Here was the only squadron FAC with fighter experience and he was telling them that the strike pilots couldn't hit their targets. Hell, it sounded like they couldn't hit their own ass with both hands.

"We didn't usually drop real weapons on the range. We normally carried only four practice bombs for dive bombing and it usually took all four passes to get close to a target. And that's if we could drop them one at a time and correct our patterns each time. I don't ever remember getting shot at on the range, either."

"Don't you think someone should tell 7th Air Force?" Sean asked, seriously. *"Why do they send all those planes if they don't expect them to hit the targets?"*

"That, my friends, is why they drop in strings or use a bunch of bombs. One is bound to hit the target or at least be close enough to do some damage. It's like using a shotgun instead of a rifle. Fighter dive bombing in a war is strictly shotgun," Bill continued, smiling at them. *"Why do you think we're going to the smart bombs?"*

"Smart bombs? What the hell are smart bombs?"

"They are guided bombs. Guided by lasers or TV or something. I put in a couple on Mu Gia Pass a week ago. The fighter jock just said 'Watch this, FAC; we have a couple of the new guided bombs.' They hit dead center. Anyhow, right now we are doing the shotgun approach."

"That's why we have to give them good marks, to let them have more time to concentrate on the bombing run and a better chance to hit the target?" Ralph asked.

"Exactly. If you hurry the one or two passes that you're going to get, then they'll toss the bombs all over the countryside. It's even worse at night, when you can't see the plane drifting. At night there's no horizon, no up and no down. It's very, very difficult."

"Drifting?" Sean asked.

"Yeah. When you roll in, the plane is caught by the upper winds and you drift. The pilot has to allow for the drift in his drop pattern."

"I don't think I want to hear any more. My faith in fighter pilots has been shattered," Ralph said, shaking his head.

CHAPTER TWENTY SEVEN
Nakhon Phanom Royal Thai Air Base (NKP)
20 November 1967, early morning at TUOC

When Bill and Sean entered TUOC at 0630 hours the next morning, they found the Navy crews waiting. Ed Hardy was there with several of the FAC flight commanders.

"Everyone into the big briefing room," Ed said.

The room filled with NAILs, Hobos, Jolly Green crews and the Navy. As the room filled and the noise subsided, Zack North walked to the podium.

"Listen up! We have a short briefing for everyone," Ed Hardy said while standing before a front row seat, *"Beginning tomorrow, the Neptunes will be dropping ADSIDs on the trail. Pay attention."*

Lieutenant Zack North briefed them on the mission, using annotated maps and drawings of the sensors to be dropped. He identified the planned drop areas and passed out maps to each of the crews. Call signs were identified and the mission priorities explained. When he finished, Ed walked to the podium.

"Each of the NAIL sorties today will have a Navy crew member riding shotgun," he said. *"I want them taken to the planned drop areas and familiarized with the local landmarks. You'll be flying at typical FAC altitudes. Let them see what it looks like from there. You have the maps. Any questions?"*

"What about planned strikes in the area?" Bill asked.

"There won't be any during the drops," Ed answered.

"I didn't mean then, Colonel, What about today? Do we cancel all of the preplanned strikes or take these guys with us?"

"Take them with you. Any other questions?"

Bill found that he had Navy Lieutenant Carl Mayes with him. The FACs were going to be flying all over the place with twice as many FAC sorties as a typical day. The FACs would split the coverage of the trail and the airstrikes. Each would spend half the time orienting their passengers and half the time working their assigned areas.

Carl and Bill went to the personal equipment room to check out parachutes and pick up survival vests and weapons. They walked to their assigned O-2 and Carl followed him around as he pre-flighted the plane. Although Carl flew a multi-engine plane, it was nothing like the O-2. Bill answered his questions and showed him the emergency procedures in case they were forced to bailout. They took off and headed east toward the Trail.

They soon crossed the Mekong River and the Cricket west sector. Bill said. ***"Look down there."*** He banked the aircraft to the right and pointed at the ground on Carl's side of the plane.

"What am I looking for?" Carl asked.

"See those crops?"

"The rows? What kind are they?"

"I haven't got the foggiest. Just notice the rows. The Laotians don't plant row crops. They just scatter seeds all over in any which way. The rows tell you that someone from somewhere else planted these crops and from the size of the plants they have been around a while," Bill continued, rolling the aircraft back to straight and level. Carl noticed him making a mark on his map.

"So, who is it?" Carl asked.

"Probably North Vietnamese. Somewhere near those crops is an enemy camp or some sort of supply point," Bill said.

"Why don't you bomb it?"

"We may, but I'll pass it to Intelligence first. They can use it for a secondary target or send one of the other planes to check it out. It isn't close enough to the trail to be a major installation."

Carl looked pensive. He realized that there was much to learn from the pilots who flew here every day. He started to look for other signs on the ground.

"We're going to climb. I want you to see Mu Gia Pass but I don't want to get shot," Bill said.

He brought the aircraft up to ten thousand feet. *"Look up to the left. See those big cliffs? Now look between them. Can you make out the road?"*

"That's Mu Gia. No matter what anyone tells you, don't fly in there under ten thousand feet," he continued.

"What's there?"

"Lots of bad guys with a bunch of great big guns; 23, 37 and 57 millimeters and the big ones, 85s, have fire can radar."

"Any other bad spots?"

"One. Ban Laboy Ford, where Route 912 enters Route Pack One, but Mu Gia is the worst. Up north there are plenty of hot spots, but not down here. There are many heavily-guarded road sections in Route Pack One, but Mu Gia is the most dangerous place in our area. Up to the north is the Plain of Jars (PDJ). It actually has large stone jars all over the place. It also has an area where

the French burned a bunch of their trucks so the Vietnamese couldn't get them. You can see all of this stuff if you fly up there. We just don't have time today. That area is called Barrel Roll."

"Now, get out the maps that Zack gave you. We're at the north end of Muscle Shoals. All of your drops will be in this area. Here is where the interdiction program concentrated and where the gunners work overtime."

Bill spent the next forty minutes overflying the area and pointing out the major land features and road intersections. While he was near the trail, he continuously moved the nose of the plane randomly left and right of their general heading. This maneuver was called jinking and it made them a difficult target for the anti-aircraft gunners, because they did not hold a steady heading or constant altitude. They then descended to six thousand feet and went over the area a second time, excluding Mu Gia Pass. Carl now had a pretty good idea of the terrain and the major landmarks.

"NAIL Five Five, this is Dullness on Guard."

"Dullness, NAIL Five Five; go," Bill answered.

"Come up on FAC FM, Five Five."

"Five Five, Roger."

"NAIL Five Five on FM," Bill said, using the FM radio.

"This is NAIL Zero One; we have you in sight and will be at ten thousand feet. We are going to stay with you during your strike mission," came from Colonel Benjamin.

"Roger, Zero One. Who's with you?"

"I have Carl's boss with me."

"Roger, Zero One. I'm going to Cricket now for fighter info. If you need anything, I'll leave the FM on Nail Common."

"We just want to watch. Tell me where to orbit when you get the fighters."

"Roger, Zero One. I'm going to Cricket.

"Cricket, NAIL Five Five."

"Roger, Five Five. Are you ready to copy?"

"Five Five, ready."

"Bobbin flight of two Fox Four Echoes is inbound. Do you have the loads?"

Bill checked his notes from the morning briefing. He had Bobbin, two F-4Es with five hundred pound bomb loads. *"I have Bobbin. Are there any changes to the fragged ordnance?"*

"Negative, as fragged. What's your rendezvous point?"

"Have Invert give them a vector. I'll pick them up from there," Bill said. He would let radar get the fighters in position.

"Roger, Five Five. Passing Bobbin to Invert."

"Invert, NAIL Five Five, IDENT on." Bill hit the switch which caused his IFF beacon to double in intensity.

"Got you Five Five. Bobbin is with us now. Five minutes to rendezvous. They are on 257.3"

"Roger, Invert. Five Five going to 257.3. Pass the fighters to me at five miles."

"Roger, Five Five. Good hunting."

"Thanks," Bill changed to UHF 257.3.

"NAIL Five Five, this is Bobbin lead."

"Roger, Bobbin. I'm orbiting the target area. We have a truck park. I'm at six thousand feet orbiting to the east of the target. NAIL Zero One is also east at ten thousand. Do you have us?"

"Negative, NAIL. We're looking."

"Zero One, give them some smoke," Bill said on FM.

"Zero One, smoking," Colonel Benjamin replied as he activated his smoke selector. It fed a small stream of oil onto the hot exhaust manifold and a line of white smoke billowed out the rear.

"Bobbin, do you have the smoke?"

"Got it, NAIL. We're about two miles out and a few miles up."

"Set up an orbit. I'll mark with Willy Petes for the strike. Stand by for target data."

Bill gave the fighters the Intelligence estimate for the area. Target, terrain, winds and both known and suspected gun positions. On FM, he asked NAIL Zero One to watch for guns.

"Zero One, on the guns."

"Bobbin, any questions?"

"Negative NAIL. Restrictions?"

"Don't use east. The rest is up to you. Call in. I'm marking now." Bill pulled the nose up and then turned toward the area where the truck park was supposed to be located. He rolled out of his turn and fired a rocket. He then pulled up and stood the Duck on its wing as he watched for the Willey Pete to blossom in the green below.

"The mark is on target, Bobbin. String your bombs through the smoke. Mix up your inbounds if you can."

"Roger, NAIL. Two, use a ninety degree spread."

"Bobbin Two, Roger. I'll wait until yours hit."

"Lead's in."

"Do you see him?" Bill asked.

"Not yet. Which way is he corning in?" Carl wanted to know.

"I don't know. There he is!" Bill pointed and Carl saw the F-4E on its pullout. There were puffs of white behind the fighter.

"Bill, gunfire from the east! One or two guns. I've got them spotted," came over the FM radio.

"Thanks, Zero One, hold on," Bill replied, on FM.

"Bobbin Two, did you see the gunfire?" Bill quickly asked the fighters on UHF.

"I saw the fire, but not where it came from."

"Call in. Don't press your run. Lead, you were on the west edge of the target. Two, move to the east a bit."

"Roger, NAIL. Two's in." They didn't see Bobbin Two until they spotted the white puffs of anti-aircraft fire. The F-4 was above the flak. This time the bombs crossed through the target and there were many explosions as they hit.

"Bobbins, hold," Bill called, turning toward the smoke.

"Lead, holding."

"Two, holding."

"How much do you have left?" Bill wanted to know about their remaining bombs.

"Lead has six bombs..."

"Two dropped them all."

"You were right on, Two. We have some secondaries. I'll BDA in a moment. Bobbin Lead, how about a little surprise?"

"What do you have, NAIL?"

"We have the guns spotted. If the two of you will come in from the south, I'll mark the guns and Two can spray the guns with his 20 mike mike. Just spray 'em, Two. Hang high and kick the rudder.

"Lead, you drop on Two's bombs while Two keeps their heads down."

"You sure, NAIL?"

"Yeah. Two should lead by about five seconds. Pretend you are at Luke on the Tactical

Range and spray from altitude. We just want to keep their heads down."

"Done this yourself, have you, NAIL?"

"Yeah, Luke and Willy, F-86's and F-100s."

"Bill laughed, *"Ready?"*

"Bobbin is waiting for the mark."

"NAIL Zero One, mark the guns."

"Zero One, Roger," Colonel Benjamin sounded a little tense, since he worked mostly in Cricket West, where they rarely put in airstrikes.

"Bobbin Two, as soon as you see the mark, go!"

"Two, Roger."

Colonel Benjamin fired his rocket. On FM he said to Bill, *"I missed the target by a lot."*

"Don't sweat it, Zero One. They'll spray a big area, "Bill replied on FM.

"Bobbin Two, rolling in with guns."

There were small puffs and sparkles all over the karst where Two sprayed his 20 mike mike shells to the east.

"Lead is in."

In a few seconds Lead called, *"Off."*

"No gunfire, Lead. It worked, "Bill said.

"Nice work, NAIL. We'll orbit for a moment. Did we get anything?"

"Look at that!" yelled the Colonel, excitedly, on UHF for everyone to hear. A large black cloud was rising over the last string of bombs. Bobbin flight had hit a fuel storage area. The smoke continued to rise until it was over one thousand feet in the air and still rising ever more rapidly.

"Cricket, Cricket, Nail Five Five!!"

"NAIL Five Five, this is Cricket. What do you have?"

"Bobbin hit a fuel storage area of some sort. Can you see the smoke, Cricket?"

"They'll be able to see that from NKP. Standby, NAIL Five Five, we're sending you some more ordnance. How about gunfire?"

"I need some CBU. Can you get the Gunfighters?"

"We'll call them now. It'll take about twenty minutes to get them here from Danang."

"We better have them if you want more bombs on this target..."

"The Gunfighters will be rolling in one minute, Five Five. We'll have more bombs for you in about twelve minutes; there's a flight inbound from Korat"

"I'll be waiting," Bill answered.

Carl was staring open mouthed at Bill. This was his first combat mission and he was right in the middle of a fighter strike with anti-aircraft fire. He was watching it all from a front row seat. *"Are we in danger?"*

"Only if they start shooting at us. That's why I keep moving. I think it might be a good idea to climb a little."

"It's OK with me if you climb a lot," Carl replied.

"NAIL Zero One, can you wait?" Bill asked the colonel.

"Not really. Do you want another mark on the guns?"

"No, Zero One. I have the position. We can handle it by ourselves."

"NAIL Zero One departing. You don't need us in your way, Five Five. Good work."

"Thanks, Zero One," Bill said. He turned to O-2 toward the rising cloud of smoke, which now was over 3,000 feet and still rising.

"Invert, NAIL Five Five, IDENT," Bill said.

"Got you, Five Five."

"*Stand by for a permanent mark. We have a big one going.*"

"*We heard. Invert standing by.*" Bill flew directly over the billowing cloud of smoke.

"*Ready, mark! Beacon off. That's the center of the hit.*"

"*We have it, Five Five. We'll get a target number from Intel. Do you want the ordnance directed there?*"

"*Roger, Invert. Keep them at altitude. There are some real guns here.*"

"*Cricket, NAIL Five Five.*"

"*Five Five, this is Cricket.*"

"*Have the incoming passed to Invert for vectors and separation.*"

"*Roger, Five Five. We've got four flights inbound or committed to you.*"

"*Great. We can see if there's any more stuff here.*"

Bill remained in the area and climbed to eight thousand feet awaiting the arrival of the fighter aircraft. The first flight was a pair of F-105s carrying seven hundred and fifty pound bombs. They dropped high and scattered their ordnance over a wide area. There were more explosions and a second black cloud started to rise just north of the original smoke cloud.

The next flight was the Gunfighters, the alert F-4s from Danang, with anti-gun and anti-personnel ordnance. Bill held them to the east and cleared them for unrestricted runs east of the Trail. He moved west and kept the other flights with bombs orbiting to the west.

For the next half hour, he directed bombing runs from the west and let the Gunfighters attack the anti-aircraft guns at their own discretion. Two gun emplacements exploded and all gunfire eventually ceased. The two black clouds merged into one, which reached four thousand feet above the ground before starting to move away with the upper winds. There was little if any surface wind.

Bill was startled when he received a call on FM. *"NAIL Five Five, this is NAIL Six Eight. We're ten miles to the west."*

"Roger, Six Eight. Are you ready to take over?" He looked at his watch. He'd been directing strikes for over an hour and a half.

"We'll be there in a couple of minutes. What flights have you got?"

"None at the moment. There are a couple more inbound. Did Invert brief you on the situation?"

"We got it all. I have NAIL Zero One's marked-up maps."

"We've had only intermittent gunfire for the last twenty minutes and none in the last five. The Gunfighters worked over the eastern side and most of it stopped. Keep your eyes open, though. They could have more on the west."

"Thanks, Five Five. You guys did a hell of a job. We have you in sight. Crossing to the north."

"Tally Ho; we've got you, Five Five out. Cricket, NAIL Six Eight relieving Five Five."

"Roger on the change. Good work, Five Five. How did your passenger enjoy his first flight?"

Carl perked up and looked at Bill. Bill pointed to the radio.

"This is the NAIL passenger; do you have some of my friends with you?" Carl said, on the radio.

"Roger, Carl. There are a couple of us on Cricket."

"We'll see you guys later. NAIL out."

That evening, the NAILs and the Navy crews celebrated at the club. Carl was the envy of his Navy cohorts. None of them had seen or directed any flights since everything was diverted to Bill and dropped on the fuel storage area.

While they were celebrating, Ed Hardy entered the bar and walked directly up to Bill. *"The colonel wants to see you and Sean in his office at 0900 hours tomorrow. Be there!"*

Historical Note: The Nails did give many of the VO-67 crewmembers orientation flights over the Steel Tiger area prior to their initial ADSID drops.

CHAPTER TWENTY EIGHT
Nakhon Phanom Royal Thai Air Base (NKP)
21 November 1967, early morning in the NAIL Squadron Operations area

The two captains walked into the squadron at 0850 hours the next morning. Eddie Jackson was the only person in the administrative office.

"Where's the colonel, Eddie?" Sean asked.

"He said you two are to wait for him. He had to go to TFA for a meeting at 0800 and he should be back here about 0900 or maybe a little after."

"Thanks, Eddie. We'll be in Ops," Bill said, and walked into the Operations Center.

Jerry Hersey was there, monitoring the radio and working on the weekly flight schedule. *"You guys are screwing up a perfectly good schedule."*

"How's that, Sir?" Sean asked.

"Since you're now off days and on nights, I have to rework the whole damn thing."

"When did that happen, Major?" Bill asked.

"This morning," Jerry replied. *"Ed came in and said to take you off days and put you on nights."*

Bill looked at Sean and shrugged. *"Just like that?"*

"We usually wait for someone to get at least a couple of months experience before we put them on nights. Ed didn't explain. Of course, he never explains."

"It's the first we've heard of it," Sean said.

Jerry looked surprised. *"I thought you volunteered."*

"Nope. Ed told us to meet the colonel, here at 0900."

"They're both at a TFA meeting. The general is talking to them."

"What about?" Bill asked.

"I don't know," Jerry replied, with a shrug.

"How do you keep up with the big picture?" Sean asked.

"We don't. We just fly our fragged missions and try to stay out of trouble."

"So tell us about nights. What makes it so difficult?"

"First, you can't see shit. There aren't any highway lights or signs out there. Second, it takes two of you, a pilot to fly and a navigator to operate the night scope. Finally, it's dangerous. In addition to the mountains, there are a bunch of guys out there who try to shoot you down every chance they get and they shoot a lot." said Jerry, very slowly.

Bill laughed. *"You're scaring the shit out of me. Every night flight in a fighter is worse than that."*

"Did you ever try navigating with a Starlight scope being used by some one else and when some nasty bastard was shooting at you?" Jerry asked.

"No. Never, but we did use the scope in the delta, at Binh Thuy. It was easy."

"Great, just great! There aren't any navaids in Laos where we're flying. No one puts big beacons on the tops of those mountains out there and you don't have a big fucking river running through the middle of the area." Jerry continued the disgust showing in his voice.

"You just need to remember where they are," Bill said.

"It may be easy for you hot shots, but it's very difficult for us mere mortals."

"You should've flown a fighter. You get used to doing everything yourself. The trouble with you multi-engine guys is that there's always someone there to tell you what to do, where to go and get coffee and doughnuts," Bill said. *"I think nights will be simple. It's merely daylight flying without sunshine."*

"Simple, huh?" came from the door. Ed Hardy stood there, with Colonel Benjamin. *"In a week you'll be sorry your alligator mouth overloaded your hummingbird ass."*

"Yes, Sir," Bill said, grinning widely.

"I want to talk to the two of you," Colonel Benjamin said, turning and walking to his office. The captains followed.

"Sit down; I've got a project for you."

When they were seated, Colonel Benjamin behind his desk and the captains in chairs facing him, he began to speak.

"7th Air Force wants to do an interdiction capability and effectiveness test. They want to see how each of the night-flying units does when measured against each other and when using the TFA sensors. I've volunteered you two for the Task Force. You'll be our test FACs."

"We haven't worked with TFA or flown nights before," Bill said.

"Didn't I just hear you say it was simple?"

Bill reddened. *"It should be, Sir."*

"It will be, for two highly-trained and motivated pilots. Most of our FACs aren't fighter trained. They go out there and drop flares and fire rockets all over the country side. At best we're amateurs at night. We need to optimize what we do. You're the only fighter pilot in this squadron. So, use what you know and tell us how to improve our kills. The two of you are my choice. Ed agrees."

"Why me?" Sean asked.

"Two reasons. We need to know if we can use pilots without fighter experience at night. More important, you understand and get along with our resident smart ass."

"When does it start?" Sean asked, laughing.

"In two weeks. There'll be a plan published in about a week. We'll have another meeting then. So, go get checked out and get some feeling for night interdiction. See if you can come up with some pointers like you did on days."

"When do we get checked out?" Bill asked.

"Starting tonight. You two will be flying nights until further notice. Get some rest today. You'll be on the first night mission tonight."

"Thank you, Sir."

The two captains stood and saluted. Colonel Benjamin returned their salutes and shook his head. This would really be something to watch.

When they walked back into Operations, Jerry Hersey motioned them to his desk. *"You're scheduled for your briefings at 1630 at INTEL. Bill, you'll be with Milt*

Thomas and Sean, you're flying with Joe Brown. You'll both ride in the right seat for the first three nights so get familiarized with the Starlight scopes."

Bill and Sean left the squadron and returned to the hootches. They woke Joe and asked him to brief them on the night program.

"What do you mean, there aren't any procedures?" Sean asked. *"How do people know how to operate the scopes?"*

"Everything is taught by word of mouth. The navigators teach each other about the scopes and we run the strikes," Joe said.

Bill looked at Sean. *"Oh shit, how're we going to get this organized? The colonel wants it improved. How the hell do we improve something that doesn't exist?"*

"We'll write a manual. Beginning tomorrow, we'll spend an hour or so at INTEL after each mission. I'll lay out a format and we can fill in the blanks. I'll get one of the FANs (forward air navigators) to help," Sean said.

"A manual? Jesus, Sean, we don't need a fucking manual. A simple checklist should do," Bill was not happy.

"A checklist won't help until we get all we know down on paper. A manual is the only way," Sean continued.

"We don't want to start a paper empire. All we need is to get some standards set up," Bill said.

"I agree with Bill. We don't need a lot of written instructions. You can't read in the dark and at night we don't use lights because the gunners will shoot at you if they see you," Joe offered.

"Don't worry, I'll keep it simple. It isn't meant to be carried in the plane. You're supposed to study manuals before you fly. Preparing the manual will make us experts and we can write it so that people can understand it," Sean was so confident that Bill shrugged in agreement.

"I'll concentrate on marking and strike control. You get the damn procedures for flying and scope use. OK?" Bill asked.

"Consider it done. We've got a week to learn all we can about night operations and make some plans," Sean stated.

"A whole week? Sure, Captain Marvel. A week should be more than enough to memorize everything," Joe said, sarcastically. He looked at Sean, *"You're as bad as your friend, our resident fighter pilot idiot."*

"What about the flight commanders? I don't think they're going to like us preparing a manual on our own," Bill said, ignoring Joe's comments.

"Easy. We give them drafts to review after we are done writing it. If we ask them now, we'll get bogged down in politics," Sean answered with a grin.

"Isn't this going to cut into your love life?" Joe asked with a smirk.

"Don't I wish? I was supposed to meet her for dinner tonight. How long do you suppose this project will last?" Sean asked.

"At least a month. Probably longer if it's run by the staff types. They aren't likely to work much over the Christmas season," Bill replied.

"Are you two finished? Can I get some sleep? I suppose this means that I've got to fly with one of you paper shufflers tonight. I definitely need my rest if I'm going to be able to handle the strain." Joe

was pulling the covers over his head as he spoke. Bill and Sean left the hootch.

"I'll see you later. I need to make a call," Sean turned toward the O'Club and the telephones.

Historical Note: The Nails wrote several operational manuals during the 67-68 time frame. Jerry Dwyer, Jimmie Butler and Pat Sweeney wrote some of these.

```
                    DEPARTMENT OF THE AIR FORCE
                 23RD TACTICAL AIR SUPPORT SQUADRON (PACAF)
                       APO SAN FRANCISCO 96310
```

NAIL TACTICS

Night Tactics and Information for Crewmembers
of The 23RD TASS

Gerald T. Dwyer
GERALD T. DWYER, Major, USAF
Air Operations Officer

Patrick J. Sweeney
PATRICK SWEENEY, Captain, USAF
Stan/Eval Officer

CHAPTER TWENTY NINE

Steel Tiger, Eastern Central Laos
22 November 1967, that night over the Ho Chi Minh Trail

When the O-2s flew at night, there was a navigator or another pilot in the right seat with a night-vision scope. The right side window had been removed and in some aircraft a spoiler was riveted to the leading edge of the window frame to deflect airflow away from the right seater. The right seater hung his head and arms with the scope out of the window and was at the complete mercy of the pilot! He looked for signs of traffic on the trail and let the pilot know where they were and where the road was located. The pilot talked to the fighters, maneuvered the aircraft, dropped flares and fired the rockets. The right-seat guy generally didn't talk to the other aircraft.

Only two FAC aircraft flew at night at any given time. Sean flew in one of the planes with Joe Brown and Bill flew in the other with Lieutenant Milt Feldman, a recent Air Force Academy graduate. Milt had a couple of years of experience flying T-37s out of Bartow, Florida, as an instructor pilot in Air Training Command. He was short, aggressive and talented. Bill liked him.

"OK, Milt, I've got the road. I can see an intersection and a river paralleling to the east," Bill said, over the intercom. He was hanging out the right side of the aircraft looking through the scope. The night was clear with a quarter moon, perfect conditions for the Starlight scope. He continued to scan the road for several minutes.

"Not much action here. The road's clear, but I see some lights further north," Bill said. *"They don't look like trucks, more like a guy with a lantern or something for signaling. Hold it! Yeah, there's something going on up north."*

"Let's check it out," responded Milt.

"Stay out here to the west. I can see the road from here," Bill was getting excited.

"I have a truck! I have a truck!"

"Where, where? Give me a position!"

"Crossing the river just a little east of the road, about five miles out at two o'clock. I saw it when it turned the lights on for a second. They're out now, but it was crossing the river. Where's the map?" Bill was searching through his kit.

"Here, use mine; find Foxtrot. We should be close then look a little east. There are two bypass roads across the river here. It crosses twice. I think you saw the truck at the north ford. Which way was it headed?" Milt asked.

"South."

"Good. We leave the north bounders alone. They might be carrying prisoners."

Bill thought about that for a while. Prisoners. He decided that leaving the north bounders alone was a great idea. The thought of being a prisoner caused him to shudder involuntarily.

"Alleycat, this is NAIL Three Four. We've got movers," Milt said.

"Roger, NAIL. Nimrod Two One is inbound to your position. He'll contact you when he reaches Foxtrot. "Three Four's at six thousand feet."

"We'll pass six thousand to Nimrod Two One."

"Milt, I have two more trucks. They're crossing the ford to the north of Foxtrot, headed to the south."

"Keep watching. We've got a Nimrod on the way."

"NAIL Three Four, This is Nimrod Two One."

"This is Three Four."

"I'm at eight thousand over Foxtrot. What do you have?"

"We're turning our lights on, Nimrod. We're at six. Do you have us in sight?" The night O-2s were painted a dull black and had shielded navigation and anti-collision lights that could only be seen from above. Milt turned them on.

"Roger NAIL. You're right under me."

"We've got at least three movers southbound on the Foxtrot bypass. Are you familiar with it?"

"I know it."

"I'll flare and move east. You have it," Milt said.

"Hold it, Milt. Hold it," Bill said. *"Let me talk to him."* Milt nodded in agreement.

"Nimrod, this is the NAIL," Bill said.

"Go ahead, NAIL."

"How's your fuel?"

"I just got here; we've got a full load, NAIL." That meant about an hour and a half, Bill knew.

"OK. We recommend that you climb a little and throttle back. The trucks will be slowing soon to cross a river at a ford located about a mile south of our position. We'll time our flare to coincide with them bunching up at the river. They'll be to the north of the river, under our flare. We'll put the flare to the west of the crossing and it will drift east. You should have plenty of time to set up your run and acquire the trucks."

"That's great, NAIL, thanks. Keep your lights on and warn us when you release the flare," Two One radioed.

Milt was puzzled but did as Bill asked and in a few minutes they were in position to drop their flare and he called to the Nimrod. *"Flare away!"*

"Stay west, NAIL."

The flare gave off a few sparks when the parachute canister separated, then flickered twice and finally burst into life as a two-million-candlepower light bulb. Bill and Milt could see the ground and the trucks without the scope.

"We're west, Nimrod. Look at the east edge of the light. We can see three or four trucks getting ready to cross the river."

"I got them, NAIL. Watch this!"

"Gunfire from the east!" Milt's excited voice came over the radio. Bill got his first look at night tracers. The anti-aircraft rounds looked like big reddish-orange basketballs, slowly coming up from the ground. As they neared the O-2, they sped up and turned into streaks of light. The shells were not close, at least not close enough to be heard, but they were near enough to cause both pilots to flinch.

They never saw the black A-26. They were still looking for the black plane when the road suddenly erupted in multiple small explosions, and then larger ones, as two of the trucks exploded.

"You got two on the first pass, Nimrod," Milt radioed. *"They must've been carrying munitions. The other two should be damaged as well. Stay west, I'm going back in and will stay east."*

Bill and Milt watched the road. The flare had gone out but in the firelight they could see the two burning trucks clearly, as well as two stationary trucks sitting on the side of the road with their doors open. Those trucks weren't going anywhere until the drivers returned. *'Sitting ducks,'* Bill thought. The road suddenly erupted as the Nimrod made a gun pass. One of the remaining trucks exploded and the rear canvas covering of the other truck was shot off. Three guns fired tracer rounds at the Nimrod. Bill located one of the gun positions and Milt fired a Willy Pete rocket in its direction. The flash upon impact of the Willey Petes got Nimrod's attention!

"What was that, NAIL?"

"We fired a Willie Pete at one of the guns. There isn't enough light to see the smoke. The gun is less than one hundred meters from the two burning trucks and to the south, directly south. Aim a hundred meters directly south of the burners," Milt directed.

"Thanks. Any more movers?"

"We don't have any right now. I'll go back and see if we have some stopped at the north crossing. Do you have ordnance?" Milt asked.

"I have plenty," replied the Nimrod. He sounded happy.

Milt flew to the north crossing and Bill scanned the road for more movers. They saw nothing. *"OK, Nimrod, I'm dropping a flare. Let's see what's under it,"* Milt said, as he turned to the west. The flare ignited, hanging from the sixteen-foot-wide parachute. A cone of light spread out below the flare until it covered a circular area about a mile in diameter. From their altitude, they could see the road, the river and the ford. They didn't need the scope.

"We have the crossing, Two One. I've got one truck in the river and it looks like a couple others waiting to cross. We're at six thousand." Milt was excited.

"Stay west, NAIL. Two One is in."

The river crossing erupted in a string of small explosions as the Nimrod dropped his CBU. The truck in the river exploded, blocking the ford. Several guns were shooting and one stream of tracers came directly toward the FAC. They could tell that the tracers were aimed at them because of the trajectory of the shells. The orange balls looked as though they were going in front of the O-2, but as they rose they started to curve back toward the plane.

"Milt, they're shooting at us, move!"

Milt immediately turned the aircraft hard right. They could hear the shells passing the O-2 in the turn, the "pop, pop, pop" sound of popcorn on a stove.

Bill shuddered when he smelled the cordite and as Milt began climbing the O-2 to seven thousand feet.

"We moved up, Two One. We're at seven."

"Roger, NAIL. I'm RTB (returning to base). We've got an oil-pressure light. Is that you, Thompson?"

"Roger, Nimrod. Who's that?"

"I gave you a ride when you arrived."

"Yes, Sir, I remember. Good job tonight. Should we follow you home?" Bill asked.

"No. It's just a precaution. No need to worry. I like the way you set this up, NAIL. I'll see you at TUOC. Let's talk."

Milt looked at Bill. *"Who's that?"*

"It's Colonel Cutter. Sean and I met him when we arrived at NKP. He gave us a ride to the Club."

"He's one good pilot. What do you suppose he wants to talk about?"

"Maybe it's the way we're doing this night work."

"It sure was a good night. We accounted for four certains and two probables. That's excellent work. It may even be the best night any of the NAILs have ever had."

"Think we'll find any more?" Bill asked.

"Nope. They'll be off in the trees until things quiet down."

Milt was right. They looked for another half an hour, found nothing, and returned to NKP. When Bill and Milt arrived at TUOC, they were met by Denny Cutter. ***"Good work, Captain."***

"Thank you, Sir. You did quite a job on those trucks."

"The key was setting them up. You're the first FAC I've worked with who set it up like a fighter pilot."

"I have a lot of fighter time, Colonel. I just did what would've liked to have done for me."

"It shows, Captain, it shows. I'd like to see more of the NAILs work like that."

"We're working on a manual to standardize some of our procedures. It should be finished in a couple of weeks."

"Good. Let me know if we can help. I'd be glad to have some of our guys talk to your pilots."

"Thank you, Sir. We'll do it."

CHAPTER THIRTY
Nakhon Phanom Royal Thai Air Base (NKP)
30 November 1967, around the base

During that first week both Sean and Bill kept adding to their proposed night tactics manual. A rough draft was prepared and Bill gave copies to several of the more senior pilots and a couple of navigators in the squadron. He also gave copies to the Nimrods and Zorros.

Denny Cutter was surprised when Bill handed him a draft of the manual. *"You're the last person I would've expected to prepare a written manual."*

"Sir?" Bill said, puzzled.

"If you'd been in SAC, I'd have expected this. I didn't think fighter pilots ever even read manuals, let alone wrote them," Denny replied, grinning widely.

Bill reddened. *"It's Sean, Colonel. He wrote the basic manual. I only added comments."*

"That figures; I really didn't think you came up with this yourself."

"Sean spent a lot of time in SAC. He put the package together and I filled in the blanks," Bill admitted. *"He did a good job, didn't he?"*

"Yes, he did. Now can you make it work?"

"We can, Sir. If you and the others will help us."

"We will, Captain. We will."

By the time the 7th Air Force guidelines were established for the controlled test of night flying effectiveness, the FAC Night Flying Manual was drafted and out for review by the flying units. The comments from nearly everyone were positive and half of the copies were returned with good suggestions. The only source of negative comments came from the FACs. Several of the majors in the 23rd TASS said it was a waste of time and one of them, Major Tomasso, a FAC flight commander, came to Bill.

"You can't organize a war, Captain," said Major Tomasso.

"We aren't trying to. We just want to settle on some standard tactics that make our jobs easier and, at the same time, help us get more kills," Bill replied.

"It won't work," the major continued.

"Hell, Major, just try it..."

"I don't like it. It puts constraints on our flying."

"I understand, Sir. However, you don't have much choice. Colonel Hardy has approved them for the night FAC tactics and when you're a night FAC, you'll use them."

"Don't get out of line, Captain."

"I'm not. You'll follow the guidelines in that manual when you fly at night," Bill said, angrily. His eyes flashed and he was daring the major to object.

"We'll see, Captain, we'll see," Tomasso smiled, smugly.

"No, Sir. We won't see. The colonel told us to improve the kills and standardize the night tactics. We're doing that and everyone who flies at night will use them."

Major Tomasso reddened. He wasn't used to listening to captains. It didn't matter that the captain was better qualified; he was a major. He stomped out of Operations.

CHAPTER THIRTY ONE
Nakhon Phanom Royal Thai Air Base (NKP)
1 December 1967, morning in the NAIL Ops

"What'd you do to Major Tomasso?" Ed Hardy asked. *"He's in with the colonel; they're probably discussing your court martial."*

Bill shrugged. *"He's fighting every little thing. All I want to do is get the nights to be more standard and effective."*

"Don't sweat it. Cutter and Patterson have both talked to Benjamin. The Nimrods and Zorros both think you're doing a hell of a job out there. I doubt if our good colonel will pay any attention to an asshole like Tomasso."

"I sure hope not."

Eddie came into the Operations Office and said, *"Colonel Benjamin wants you two in his office, Sirs."* Bill looked at Ed Hardy and shrugged. He followed Ed into the colonel's office.

"What're you two up to?" David Benjamin asked.

"Nothing, Sir," Ed replied.

"Major Tomasso just left here. He wants to know why you don't have more majors working in operations."

"We don't have many good ones," Ed said.

Bill grinned. Benjamin looked at him and scowled. *"Knock it off, smart ass."*

"Most of the majors are coming here from some sort of desk in the states. Only a few of them have flown a real airplane in the past six years. In my opinion, they're not qualified to be Operations Officers."

"They don't like working for a captain," replied Benjamin.

"They aren't. Bill's only doing what we tell him to do. I've checked and approved everyone of his changes," Ed replied.

"Bullshit! He is scheduling the night flights and determining tactics!" David Benjamin replied. *"He even has Invert changing their procedures to*

accommodate his tactics. They were talking about Bill as if he were not present.

"We told him to fix the night program. How's he going to do that if he reports to a flight commander?"

"Who's his boss?" Benjamin asked.

"Officially it's Major Martin. But I've moved him to Operations." Ed said.

"What's his title?"

Bill watched the two as they argued. He interrupted when Ed paused and offered, *"Night Operations Officer, Sir."*

Dave and Ed both looked at him. *"We don't have a Night Operations Officer,"* Ed said.

"You do now. It's me. At least, that's the job I'm doing," Bill replied.

"How's the night interdiction test going?" Benjamin changed the subject.

"Good, Sir. We have a final briefing in three days. The formal test starts on Monday. I was planning to brief you on Sunday. Eddie has us on your calendar."

Colonel Benjamin turned to Sunday in his desk calendar. There was a two-hour block set aside for a TFA/Night Tactics briefing with Sean and Bill.

"Good. How's this manual thing coming?"

"The final draft is out for review. When I get it back, I'll bring it to you for approval," Bill said.

"Did you do it yourself?" Ed asked.

"No, Sir. Most of the work was done by Sean O'Malley. We had the Nimrods and the Zorros work on it as well as the guys in TUOC. I think it'll be pretty good. Next, we have to take it to the off-base squadrons."

"What squadrons?" Colonel Benjamin asked, frowning.

"All of the units that fly at night, including the Redbirds, Yellowbirds and Gunfighters. I sent a copy to a friend in the Yellowbirds and he promised to call me tomorrow with comments," Bill replied.

"What do you think that'll accomplish?" Ed asked.

"All I really want to do is get them to understand how the NAILs operate. If they know what to expect from our night descriptions, marks and flares, they'll do a much better job of hitting the trucks. I think we can save them fifteen or twenty seconds on a bomb run."

"Twenty more seconds to get lined up instead of trying to find the target?" Ed said.

"Yes, Sir," Bill replied, nodding. *"That's a lot of time for a fighter pilot."*

"OK, Captain. I'm anxious to see this tactics book. I'll see you at the briefing on Sunday."

Bill saluted and left the office. Ed remained with David Benjamin, who was now standing behind his desk.

"What do you think, Ed?"

"You know he's right, but he isn't cutting the old heads any slack. But, if he were more polite, they'd most likely ignore him. You gave him a tough job and he's doing it the only way he knows—flat out. Our truck kills have doubled in the past two weeks. Something is obviously working and working well. It can't all be luck."

"None of it's luck. I'm not sure about the Night Operations Officer thing? What do you really think?"

"I like it. I'll put Jerry in as Day Operations and Bill as Night. I still outrank all of the others," Ed replied.

"Make sure we cover him. Some of those majors have other friends."

"I will."

CHAPTER THIRTY TWO
Nakhon Phanom Royal Thai Air Base (NKP)
1 December 1967, late afternoon in the NAIL Hootches

Just as the little Thai maid finished her cleaning and left Sean's room, Bill entered saying, **"Sean, have you noticed that we now have more night missions than pilots?"**

"No."

"Well we do and as the "Night Chief," I think that is <u>my</u> problem and I will need to solve it if this night thing is going to work."

"Good luck, Chief. I need to get a shower as I have a dinner date with a round eye." Sean said as he reached for a towel and headed for the community shower.

"Hold on there; this is important."

"Important to whom?"

"Me and the war effort. Now, take a minute. How do we get more guys on nights?

"Hell, just order them out there. This is the Air Force, not a sewing circle. We can order people to do things. Have you heard of orders? Now I got to go."

"We don't want guys out there who are afraid or who don't want to be there. Shit, they

will cross the bomb line at 10,000 feet and never see anything or do anything. Man, we need volunteers. Guys who want to kill trucks. You don't see any trucks in the daytime, do you?

"*There ain't no day trucks so nobody sees any day trucks. Everybody knows that,*" said Sean, now getting quite exasperated with the "Chief."

"*We need night guys.*"

"*Bill, why would anyone want to go out there at night....it's dark, it's lonely and you eat breakfast at noon.*" Sean opened the door to leave, but was stopped by Bill's next comment.

"*You gotta help me,*" stated Bill in what seemed to be utter despair.

Sean shut the door and sat down on his bed across the room from Bill, "*Okay, I guess this is really important to you so let's see what we can figure out. If I'm late for dinner, I will unload an M-16 into your room.*"

"*Great! How can we get more night flyers?*"

After about 15 minutes of conversation that went absolutely nowhere, Sean exclaimed, "*I've got it! We make them want to fly nights by making it glory filled.*"

"*What??*"

"*Tom Sawyer did it with his whitewash. We do it with scores. It's coming to me now... let's have a hero's wall of fame. I got it now! We get a big sheet of poster board and cover it with white paper. We list all the pilots on the left side...about 2 dozen, right?*"

"*Something like that.*"

"*At the top we print in really big letters "KILLS." Under that, we put "TRUCKS" and then "GUNS." This will be the NAIL unofficial listing of* kills and by pilot. Next we hang it in NAIL Ops for everyone to see. What do you think?"

"I don't know; will it work?"

"Hell, I don't know either. Getting a major across the bomb line in the daytime below 10,000 feet takes a miracle. Getting one to volunteer at night...who knows?" Sean is beginning to think the idea is not so hot and it is showing.

"Shit, I don't need just the majors. I'll take anyone."

"Whatever."

"Don't give up. Let's try it. I will get Eddie to make up the "killer sign." Then I will hang it in Ops. Let's see if anyone takes it down." Bill was clearly excited; Sean could see the wheels in his head spin ever faster.

"Let see if anyone gets any trucks. Gonna look pretty silly with all those names and no kills." Sean was losing even more confidence in his idea.

"We'll get 'em, just watch, and we will kill a lot of trucks!"

As Sean picked up the towel for the third time and headed for the door, "I'm out of here and if she is gone before I get there, you are a dead piece of shit."

Historical Note: Don Brown and Pat Sweeney designed, produced and displayed the "killer board" exactly as depicted above. They never asked for nor ever received official permission to do this. It remained up for as long as they were NAILs and it was a very effective night-fighter motivator.

CHAPTER THIRTY THREE
Nakhon Phanom Royal Thai Air Base (NKP)
1 December 1967, early evening in the O'Club

While Bill and Sean were debating the Kill Board idea, Sharon stood on her bed, twisting and ducking to see how she looked in the small mirror over the dresser and wishing for the full-length mirror on the back of the closet door that she was used to having. She both wanted and didn't want to have dinner with Sean. She was attracted to him and wanted to get to know him better but she did not want this complication in her life. She'd been flattered and thrilled when the general had offered her the position as his aide. She expected to work long hours and to be totally focused on the demands of such an intense environment. But...after four months in-country, she was lonely. She missed her best friend, Caron; letters and phone calls could not make up for the distance between them. They had laughed about the similarity in their names and felt that they were truly sisters under the skin but, as their lives and interests diverged, the closeness they had once shared had begun to dissipate.

"**Well,**" she thought, "**I guess this is as good as it gets.**" She had debated about what to wear and for one moment had considered the sweater her mother had sent for her birthday. She wasn't sure her mother even understood where she was and could only stare in amazement when the sweater emerged from the box. Cashmere....well, cashmere is always good but when did her mother think she would ever wear it in Thailand's oppressive heat and humidity? And the color... shell pink was not a color she ever wore and not one she would choose for herself. Was her mother sending her a message? Her mother thought that she should look more feminine in order to attract a husband, to give her the grandchildren she so badly wanted. And, according to her mother, time was running out.

With her strong "Black Irish" coloring, Sharon tended toward very tailored, very understated clothing in solid colors. For this occasion, she had chosen simple, slim linen trousers in a pale pearl gray and a silk camisole in the exact same shade.

She threaded a plain Navy belt through her belt loops and pulled a Midnight Navy linen blazer off a hanger, knowing that she would welcome the comfort of long sleeves in the air-conditioned O' Club. She looked again in the mirror and laughed to herself; she wondered if she had subconsciously chosen what could almost pass for the civilian version of her daily uniform. Yeah, she probably had, not sure how much of a "date" this was and not planning to send mixed messages. She slung the strap of a small Navy Coach bag over her shoulder. She started toward the door, then turned back and opened the top dresser drawer. In flat leather box laid the few pieces of jewelry she had brought with her and she slid a wide silver bangle onto her right wrist. Her grandfather had thought it was never too early to learn to appreciate good jewelry and he had given her something on every Valentine's Day from the time she was thirteen until his death, two weeks after Valentine's Day, when she was nineteen. The silver bangle was his last gift. **"How perfect,"** she thought, **"I remember him with so much love when I wear these pieces."** Nestled in the hollow at the base of her throat was a fine silver chain with a large square sapphire, deep, deep blue, in a silver mount. That had taken her breath away the year she was seventeen. And then there was the silver and gold Rolex on her left wrist, a combination high school graduation present and congratulations-on-getting-accepted-into-the-Engineering-program present that same year. Glancing at the watch, she snatched up a bottle of Opium and gave a quick spritz down the front of her blouse, remembering Sean's comment that she "smelled good" the time she had picked him up on the flight line.

"OH. MY. GOD." blurted Sean, when he walked up to the front door of the O'Club and saw Sharon standing there, waiting for him. **"I've died and gone to Heaven! Wait until the guys see me walk into the dining room**

with a Goddess..., no, I mean an angel. You look GORGEOUS! And you smell WONDERFUL!"

Sharon laughed, *"Well, you're deprived and, therefore, easy to please!"*

As she turned and walked through the front door, Sean was transfixed by the flag of black hair that hung straight as a die halfway to her waist. He wondered how she hid it under that WAF hat she had to wear.

"I wish you'd get back to flying during the days." Sharon said to Sean later, rubbing her finger slowly up and down the stem of her wine glass. They sat back in their chairs, having finished dinner some time ago.

"I've only been at it for a couple of weeks. The test doesn't start until Monday and it's supposed to run for at least a month," Sean said, softly. He knew she was concerned.

"They told me that the only FAC losses have been at night. I'm worried about you."

"I'll be fine. We aren't taking any special risks. Bill has the whole thing worked out and we're really getting good at this night stuff. We will be sharing the night load as Bill and I have a scheme to get more night flyers so the few of us won't have to go out so often." Sean reached across the table and held her hand.

"That risk is what I'm worried about. I've seen the reports. There are more trucks being spotted and more guns shooting at you. You need to use the sensors and then we don't have to lose any people or planes," Sharon insisted.

"The fighter pilots can't hit what they can't see. We need to mark the trucks for them,' Sean explained.

"That's not true!" she raised her voice. *"The general said that the FACs were inflating their*

results to embarrass TFA. He knows that none of you want to be replaced by our computers and our sensors. That's why you have to get away from that program. He'll get even with the pilots who are trying to embarrass us. I've heard him at the staff meetings."

Sean laughed. *"What's he going to do? Send us to Vietnam? Don't worry, Sharon. The real decision will be made at 7th Air Force. They won't do anything that stupid."*

"It's not stupid! The sensors work. We don't need people getting killed trying to bomb trucks. We can do it by radar from here. No one needs to get hurt!"

Sean patted her hand. *"How're you going to bomb a truck from here? The pilots have a difficult time when they're right over the top of the trucks."*

"It's simple. We use the computers and the radars. The planes fly four or five miles above the ground and drop their bombs when the computer tells them to."

"How do you hit a target with radar that is eighty miles away using an airplane that is seven miles up that can't hit the targets when the pilots are looking at them?"

"There isn't any gunfire that high. The planes drop their bombs on the roads when we have trucks moving. It's not hard. We've been testing the procedures on the ranges at Eglin Air Force Base in Florida. SAC has been radar "bombing" American cities for decades using this technology and claiming they can hit a mailbox. They call this a Skyspot."

"Mailboxes don't move. Can you hit the moving trucks with a Skyspot?" Sean asked. *"How many bombs do you drop at a time?"*

"It takes a mix of bombs. They use five-hundred pounders to block the roads and CBU bomblets to get the trucks."

Sean looked incredulous. Sharon's eyes lit up as she explained the tests to Sean.

"What about the winds?" Sean asked. *"How will the computer determine the winds? We don't have any weather stations on the Trail."*

"I don't know how they do that. Maybe they get them from the fighters or from the control planes like Alleycat."

Sean sat back and smiled, *"Well, I hope you're right. I don't relish getting shot down unnecessarily. How soon will you begin using the Skyspots?"*

"Pretty soon. The sensors are working but we don't have them in enough places," she leaned forward and lowered her voice, *"Promise me you won't take crazy chances ...like your fighter-pilot friend."*

"I won't, I won't. I'd rather fly in the daytime anyway," Sean replied, taking her hand. He wished he were somewhere besides the O'Club dining room. There wasn't any privacy in the big open room.

When their Thai waitress finished clearing off the table, he asked, *"Would you like a drink?"*

"We can have one here. I don't want to go into the bar," Sharon answered, *"I don't care for the way they look at me."*

Sean chuckled, *"Do you blame them? Most of the people in that room haven't seen a round eye since they left the states. I'm considered the most fortunate pilot on this base. They all believe that we have a very close relationship."*

Sharon reddened. The attention embarrassed her and Sean's words made her feel warm. He hadn't pushed her too hard but she couldn't miss his desire for her. She wasn't about to go to bed with one of the pilots, even one she cared for. It wasn't time. She wasn't going to get involved with someone who could get killed tomorrow.

Sean watched her and smiled. He wanted to take her to bed in the worst way. So far, he'd managed a few kisses but she wouldn't go near the FAC hootches and she hadn't invited him into the TFA compound. He sighed and resigned himself to wait; it wasn't like he had any other choice.

CHAPTER THIRTY FOUR
Nakhon Phanom Royal Thai Air Base (NKP)
11 December 1967, afternoon in the O'Club

Bill and Sean were eating lunch in the O'club and noticed an unfamiliar face and some unfamiliar clothes on clearly a civilian sitting by himself eating a salad and drinking a Miller High Life from the bottle.

"This ought to be interesting. Look at that haircut." Said Bill as he pointed to the particularly long blond hair well over the guy's collar.

"Bill, he's a civilian, probably a contractor with the Red Horse guys. The few Air Force civil engineering guys surely can't manage all this

construction without some help. He's probably a construction manager, maybe a civil engineer. Why would he be interesting?"

"Hell, I don't know but I'm bored and maybe he would be." Bill got up and headed towards the new-found civilian. Walking up to him, he put out his right hand and said, *"Hi, I'm Bill Thompson; who are you?"*

The civilian had just put a forkful of salad into his mouth and could not immediately speak. Bill really enjoyed timing his *Howdy Dos* to the very moment that some one had a mouth full of food. Simultaneously dropping his fork and putting out his hand, he reddened when the fork fell to the floor. He swallowed and said, *"I'm Ed Garter from Westinghouse."*

"Our washing machine is fine, or is that GE?"

"No, I'm not in appliances."

"Well then, what are you selling?" asked Bill.

By this time Sean had joined them. Nudging Bill aside, Sean put out his hand and said, *"Hi, I'm Sean O'Malley. I'm his keeper; nice to meet you."*

"I'm Ed Garter and, like I was telling your friend ... it was Will, right?

"No, it's Bill, Bill Thompson."

"I am with Westinghouse, but not appliances."

Bill broke in, *"Okay, so what are you doing in this godforsaken place anyhow?"*

"I am trying to get my ... no, not mine ... the Westinghouse low-light-level TV into an airplane so we can see if it has any combat functionality."

"We got a lot of functionality around here. Didn't you see the waitresses?" said Bill.

Sean again jumped in. *"Ed, what is this low-light-level TV? Does low-light mean not very bright or does it mean limited light?"*

"Let me explain. We heard that since the Air Force and Navy do a lot of night flying and often are looking into areas of limited or no light, a device that would "help them see"... you know... "Lighten up the place" would be a great asset. Well good ol' Westinghouse engineers have designed and built a few of these things and I have one."

"You have one where?" demanded Bill.

"Right now it is at Base Ops where I left it when I got off the 130 from Bangkok."

"What are the dimensions and weight?" Sean asked. It was obvious that his engineer's mind was working in high gear. *"What electrical support does this thing need?"*

"Well it's about the size of the old bread box, you know 12 by 12 by 20. The 20 is the up/down dimension."

"Any other parts outside the bread box?" quizzed Sean.

"Not really, just the usual electrical cables. They designed it small and compact so it could fit into a fighter, I think. Actually I don't know a lot about this thing but if I could get someone to put it in a plane and fly some combat missions; I would be a big hero with Westinghouse."

"What about the power?" Sean asked.

"Just the regular 24 volt, the same as all USAF aircraft electrical systems."

"What was the weight?" Bill jumped in as he didn't want to be left out of this one.

"You got this thing at Base Ops?"

"Yep, in a box marked "Westinghouse tools." And it weighs about 30 pounds, Will."

"If you gave it to us to play around with, how long could we have it?" asked Sean.

"*Two weeks. A month. How much time would you want?*" replied Ed.

Sean looked at Bill and said, "*You know, Ol' Great Night Fighter, Ed here is going to make you a big-time hero with the USAF and with Westinghouse.*"

"*Yeh, I'll fly the box on my next mission and report that I could see to Detroit and Hanoi at the same time,*" snapped Bill sarcastically.

"*Ed, it is your lucky day! You are talking to the two most unappreciated but two most capable captains in the entire U.S. Air Force. We can make the impossible happen, and happen fast. We do it everyday. Sometimes two or three <u>times</u> a day.*"

"*B-Bill,*" Sean was nearly stuttering in his excitement,"*lets take Ed with us, steal a jeep, go to Ops, get the box and have Sgt. Ricardo put it in an O-2.*"

"*Are you nuts? Jesus Christ, we'll be hung out to dry after the court martial. I can just see them ripping the buttons off my blouse as the gates of Leavenworth open to invite us in.*"

"*Hey, hey, where are those fighter pilot balls?*"

CHAPTER THIRTY FIVE
Nakhon Phanom Royal Thai Air Base (NKP)
11 December 1967, about a half an hour later on the O-2 ramp

Sergeant Ricardo had his upper body well into the cockpit of an O-2 as he was trying to fix the left rudder pedal on the co-pilot's side of the aircraft. It was hot and humid and as Bill, Sean and Ed approached the scene they heard, *"God damn it; it was a snake."*

Sean peaked into the pilot's side window and said, *"What was a snake?"*

"Somehow a snake got up here and behind the rudder pedal and must have been squashed the first time the pedal was used. What a mess!" Sgt. Ricardo had pulled himself out by now and was wiping goop from his hands with a white towel that had been hanging out of his left rear pants pocket.

"Airman Hill, get over here and clean this mess up."

"What can I do for you sirs on this lovely day?" asked Ricardo to his new group of sightseers.

"Sergeant, this is Ed Garter of Westinghouse. Sergeant Ricardo." Both men nodded as shaking hands was not an option with the snake stuff and all.

"Nice to meet you, Sergeant."

"It's nice meeting you."

Bill jumped in, *"Sarg, my idiot friend and this Westinghouse guy want to put a TV in one of our O-2s. Ever hear anything so stupid?"*

"Now just a minute. We have the thing in the back of the jeep. It isn't too big or too heavy and it can use normal aircraft electrical lines. Why don't we just see if this is possible?" said Sean.

After retrieving the box from the jeep and uncrating the LL-TV it was obvious that it was smaller than the 12 X 12 X 20 that Ed had mentioned earlier. Actually the box it was packaged in was about that size; the individual parts were much smaller. The TV was a 12 incher and that means 12 inches diagonally. It was about 12 by 12 by 12. There was also a part that looked like a camera. It was small; about 6 inches cubed, but had an enormous lens that covered one entire side. The remainder was some wiring stuff and a twelve-page document comprising the installation and operation instructions.

"*We could put the TV on a small box and mount it under the yoke on the co-pilot side. Maybe we could set it up so it could be tilted and "aimed" at the pilot. This way the pilot could see the action,*" offered Sean.

"*That would work. Just push the seat all the way back and there's plenty of room. The scoper could ride in the back seat but how do we get the lens on the targets?*" Bill's enthusiastic input rather surprised everyone.

"*Hold on, everyone. Let's figure that out.*" said Sean.

Ed added, "*Cut a hole in the floor.*"

Bill was nearly screaming, "*Cut a hole in the floor?? Are you nuts?? Nobody cuts a hole in an Air Force airplane without the Chief of Staff's permission and his blessing.*"

"*Whoa, Bro! Let's settle down. As long as we don't mess with the structural integrity of the airframe, what's the difference?*" interjected Sean.

"*You gotta be shitting me! You, a captain, are going to grant permission to cut a big hole in a combat aircraft?*"

"*No, no. No permission needed. We just do it. What do you say, Sarg?*"

"*I don't know....why not? If they ain't happy with the hole, we'll fix it,*" replied Sergeant Ricardo.

Sean was now getting quite excited as he thought more and more about inserting this LL-TV into the O-2. "*Does that thing have its own gimbals?*" he asked Ed.

"*Yep, and it isn't too bulky either. Actually it's rather small and very light. Made out of titanium or something like that,*" said Ed.

"Now we've got the lens gimbaled but what do we control it with?" queried Sean.

They all started thinking about the control but this didn't last very long as Sergeant Ricardo said, *"Let's duct tape a sawed-off broom handle to it. That ought to work okay. What do you think, Captain?"* he asked, turning to Sean.

"Damn good idea. Let's try it. What the hell?" replied Sean. And so they found some duct tape and a broom, which they sawed off and attached to the lens mechanism.

"Captain O'Malley, I can take it from here. You don't need to be around here when I cut the hole in the bottom of this bird, tie this thing down and wire her up. I will leave a message for you at NAIL Ops when she's up and working fine. Just call Ops and ask if 418 is ready for a test flight."

The threesome returned to the flight line later that afternoon and checked out the Westinghouse LL-TV. On the ground it worked great, so Sean and Bill decided to check it out that evening. They flew it around in eastern Thailand near NKP for about an hour that evening, and again it worked quite well. The only limitation was that when the airplane was banked to circle a target, the bank was enough that the LL-TV lens could not remain on that target. This was a major problem, but the captains decided that it should be tested in combat and Bill, the great night fighter, volunteered to fly a few missions with this new "toy." Over the next few nights, Bill and a young lieutenant FAN, Olaf Svender, flew the LL-TV. They did see trucks and they did get enough ordnance to destroy two, but the banking limitations were enough of a problem to cancel any more flights with the LL-TV. With some better engineering and greater titling range, this LL-TV would be much better than the Starlight scope. The morning after the last test flight was completed, Sergeant Ricardo removed all the parts from the O-2, patched the hole in the bottom and Ed Garter departed with his box, heading for Bangkok.

Historical Note: LL-TV was used successfully in other aircraft during the Vietnam War. The story is true as reported above with the two pilots being Don Brown and Pat Sweeney. They never asked for permission, never were given any and no one ever said anything.

CHAPTER THIRTY SIX
Nakhon Phanom Royal Thai Air Base (NKP)
14 December 1967, the morning in Nail Ops

On the day the interdiction test was scheduled to begin, Colonel Benjamin received an unexpected visit from General Holland. The general arrived at NAIL Ops unannounced and alone at 0930.

"Good morning, General," Dave Benjamin said as he looked up to see who had walked into his office. He stood as he spoke.

"Good morning, Dave. I came down to see your operation before we get started on this test tonight."

"Come on in. I'll show you around. Do you want to see the planes?"

"Only the night ones, the black ones..."

The two left the squadron and climbed into the general's car. Dave gave directions to the driver who pulled onto the flight line and stopped in front of a black O-2. **"These are really little, Dave. I had no idea they were so small,"** Holland remarked.

"They certainly are. This is the military version of a four-passenger private aircraft, the Cessna 337 Skymaster. We usually have only two men aboard, but with the armament it is nearly overloaded," Benjamin answered.

"It's identical to the civilian version, except for a few alterations. It's painted all black with non-reflective paint. The cones on top are shields for the lights. They can only be seen from above and the fighters use them to rendezvous at night. Smoke isn't any good when you can't see it."

Dave continued, "The right side window is removed, permanently, and a wind deflector is installed to protect the scope operator. He sits in the right seat and looks out the window with a Starlight scope. Have you seen one of those?" Dave looked at the general.

"No. I haven't."

"We have a scope back in the squadron. I'll show it to you when we get back. For the O-2, the only other difference between it and the 337 is the armament. The big rack under the left wing is for flares. It holds six MK24 parachute flares. Under the right wing is the LAU 59 pod which holds seven marking rockets. Those are the 2.75 inch white phosphorous rockets that we use to mark the target."

Dave saw that the general was interested and he continued, "The inside pylons on both wings are used for additional flares. You can mount one on each pylon. That's about it for modifications that made the 337 a combat aircraft."

"I had no idea that the plane was so small or that it was so flimsy. It wouldn't stop a bullet, would it?"

"No way! The only armor in this plane is the one-inch ceramic seats. The crew sits on armor and they wear vests, but that's all. You pretty much hang it all out when you fly this thing in combat," Dave smiled as he watched the general.

"I had no idea it was so dangerous," Ernie Holland said. *"Do you fly at night yourself?"*

"Once in a while, just to remind me what they're going through," Dave answered. *"Maybe I should go out more often."*

"No, no! That's not what I meant. You shouldn't be flying at night. I was concerned about the people for our test."

Dave frowned and looked at the general. He wondered where Ernie was headed with the discussion. *"We have two lead pilots picked for the flights and two back-ups. Any of them can do the job."* Dave didn't want to remind Ernie of his discussion with Bill and Sean when they arrived.

"Let's go back to your office; we can talk there."

When they returned to the squadron, Dave got the Starlight scope and took it into his office for Ernie Holland to examine.

"I'm impressed, Dave. Your pilots have a hell of a lot of guts taking those planes out there at night. How're the two troublemakers doing?"

Dave Benjamin was surprised when Ernie brought up the two captains. *"Fine, Ernie. The fighter pilot is earning his pay. He's changed most of our tactics for the better. Our kills have doubled."*

"I've seen the reports... your unit has doubled its truck kills in the last month."

Dave nodded in agreement. He waited for Ernie to continue.

When Dave didn't speak, Ernie paused and then continued in a conspiratorial tone, *"I need a favor, Dave. It can't come out, but I need you to do something for me."*

"Sure, Ernie. What do you want?"

"Take Captain O'Malley off nights."

Dave Benjamin's mouth fell open before he could catch himself. He finally managed to say. *"Captain O'Malley?"*

"Captain O'Malley." Ernie replied, frowning. He hadn't expected this reaction.

"Do you mean no more flying or just no more nights?"

"Nights, just nights."

"Can I ask why?" Dave wanted to know.

"My aide can't function. She's so worried about that young man that she isn't doing her job. I don't want to let her go but she isn't going to concentrate on her work until she stops worrying about him."

Dave wanted to laugh but wisely decided that the general was serious. He said, *"No problem, General. We can move him to days. Ed Hardy and I've been trying to decide who should be in our new Stan Eval office. We'll put him there. He will never know she had him taken off nights."*

"Thanks, Dave. I'll see you at the next staff meeting," Ernie Holland said and walked from the office.

Dave Benjamin went into Operations and waved for Ed Hardy to come into his office. *"We have a minor problem, Ed. How close are you to getting the Stan/Eval Office set up?"*

"I'm ready to go. Major Mattaro will head it up and we need to put one pilot and one navigator in with him. Who did you have in mind?"

"Use Sean O'Malley, Ed," Dave said, and one more thing, *"get it set up today. I'd like to get it started as soon as possible."*

"Sean O'Malley? Are you serious? He's on the night test that's starting tonight," Ed looked at him curiously.

"Please, Ed, no questions. Just do it and do it now, as soon as possible. Take him off nights."

Ed Hardy broke into a wide grin. *"I'll be damned. He made you take the captain off nights?"*

"Ed, don't ask. I don't want to hear anything about this ...ever! Make the move this morning." Dave was as firm as Ed had ever seen him.

Sean O'Malley was appointed to the newly created Squadron Standardization & Evaluation Office. Ed Hardy told him it was because he'd been a Stan/Eval check pilot in SAC. Major Anthony R. Mattaro was made the Stan/Eval Chief and he reported directly to Ed Hardy. Like Sean, Tony and Ed were from SAC, so they were used to strict and demanding standards. Tony was tasked with getting a standardization program started in the 23rd TASS and it wouldn't take long for the rest of the pilots to learn that in SAC, you flunked your mother on a check flight if she didn't follow the rules.

Historical Note: The TFA Commander never ever interfered with internal 23rd TASS affairs.

CHAPTER THIRTY SEVEN
Nakhon Phanom Royal Thai Air Base (NKP)
15 December 1967

Bill recorded the first truck and the first two guns for the "Killer Board" as the tally board was soon to become known. Ben Miller then got three trucks and the kills mounted. It took but a few days of victories (kills) to excite all the pilots. Hell, no one (except a few majors) wanted to be on the board with no kills…that made you look like a wimp. In just under two weeks, the unit went from too few night pilots to way too many.

A few days later, navigator names and "kills" would also be added. This was suggested since the navs also flew the missions but also because fighter pilot's back seaters, their Weapons Systems Officers (WSO) or navigators, received "kill" credit when a U.S. fighter pilot with a WSO downed a MIG. That was clearly fair as the pilot didn't do it alone in either case.

Bill remained on night missions. He flew the right seat with every pilot, checking them out in the newly-approved NAIL night tactics and procedures and helping them standardize their control of air strikes. He flew the left seat with the navigators, observing their use of the scope and their ability to find targets. As with the pilots, he assisted them in getting the most out of every mission. By the time Bill had flown with each of the night crew members, he had established his credibility as a night FAC and as the Night Operations Officer. They found that when they followed his guidelines, they got more truck kills. They also received compliments from the strike aircraft.

Each night, the first two sorties were identified as control sorties for the TFA test. The planes would leave NKP at 1700 hours and arrive on station over the Ho Chi Minh Trail at 1800. They would remain in the area until 2100 and land at 2200. At Sean's suggestion, Joe Brown replaced him on the TFA control team for the test period, so Bill and Joe were always the pilots for these sorties. These early flights were the busiest and most active sorties. Truck traffic was the heaviest at dusk and most truck kills occurred during the first three hours of darkness. It appeared that the trucks were positioned to start moving at dusk and they only moved to the next truck park. Convoys were rarely seen after midnight.

The first two weeks of the interdiction test were to baseline the night units without the use of sensors. The second two weeks would introduce sensor data to see if it changed the effectiveness of the units. The results of the test were being tallied at TUOC using the reported BDA. So far the posted truck kills had the NAILs at the top of the FAC list. Although

Candlestick could light up an area for a long time with flares, without target marks the fighters were not as effective. The jet fighters often could not wait in the target area long enough to set up an effective strike. They typically had only ten minutes of fuel for an attack.

CHAPTER THIRTY EIGHT
Steel Tiger, Eastern Central Laos
22 December 1967, over the Ho Chi Minh Trail

On the eighth night of the interdiction test, Ralph Langer was with Bill, flying in the left seat. Bill was on the scope. They had a Nimrod A-26 following them on the Trail.

"Alleycat, this is NAIL Four Nine. We're at Foxtrot."

"Roger, Four Nine. We've got you on station at Foxtrot. We show you with Nimrod Three Two."

"We have Three Two, Alleycat." The Nimrod replied

"Good hunting, Four Nine. Alleycat, out."

"Let's go north to Golf," Bill said.

"Give me a heading," Ralph replied.

"Make it 355 degrees."

"Nimrod Three Two, we're headed north to Golf. Checking the Trail, maintaining six thousand," Ralph called over the radio.

"Three Two, Roger. I've got your lights, NAIL."

"NAIL Four Nine, this is Alleycat. We have a Yellowbird (B-57) inbound with funny bombs. Do you have any targets?"

"Negative, Alleycat. No sightings yet. Will let you know as soon as we get one."

As they approached Checkpoint Golf, Bill said, **"Ralph, give me an easy right turn. I see a light."**

Ralph turned the aircraft to the right. He looked out to his right side, but could not see anything. Bill was hanging out the window from the waist up. He motioned for more bank and leaned further out. Ralph increased the bank until he was at a forty-five degree angle. Bill pulled himself back into the plane and plopped into his seat. He had a big smile on his face.

"We have a convoy. They're passing under us. Stay in a right turn."

"Alleycat, we have movers! NAIL Four Nine with a large moving convoy," Ralph's excitement came across the radio.

"Roger, NAIL Four Nine. We're transferring Yellowbird One Three to your frequency."

"Thanks, Alley. Tell him to stay up for a little while. We want to set it up for good run. Tell him we've got a Nimrod for the guns."

"Roger, Four Nine. Will advise."

"Ralph, those trucks are moving through Golf without lights. I can see them in the scope. Get set to drop a flare; I'll tell you when. I'll work the radios until we're set up."

"Yellowbird One Three, are you up?" Bill called.

"I'm here, NAIL. What've you got?"

"Nimrod Three Two, you up?"

"I'm here; how do you want us to play?"

"We have a large southbound convoy at Checkpoint Golf. They're exposed and there's a bunch of trucks. Some look like fuel tankers. I'm going to pop a flare to the west. It will be opposite a small hill with a road along the base. A river also parallels the base of the hill; don't mistake the river for the road. Yellowbird, you're clear for a south to north run. Nimrod, you take the east and

watch for guns. We'll hold over the top of the hill to the west. OK?"

"Yellowbird, south to north."

"Nimrod has the guns to the east."

"I'll call flare release. Yellowbird, do you have my lights?"

"Got 'em, NAIL."

Ralph reached up and moved the station select switch to FIRE and then thumbed the pickle button on the yoke. The Duck gave a slight lurch as the flare fell away.

"Flare away. Five seconds to ignition. We're getting out of the way to the west."

"Move it, Ralph. Here comes the flare."

The flare lit its two-million-candlepower light and the road was exposed. On it was a convoy of twenty vehicles, moving south. Two of them were fuel trucks. Within two seconds of the flare igniting, it seemed like every gun in central Laos started shooting. It looked like Niagara Falls in reverse, tracers headed up in every direction. The gunners couldn't see above a flare, only below it. The flare was suspended under a sixteen-foot- wide parachute which blocked the light, hiding aircraft above the flare.

"Yellowbird One Three, in." The B-57 was on its bomb run.

"Nimrod's in on the guns."

The sky was filled with red-orange balloons, streaks and white explosions. The gunfire was a mixture of explosive and non-explosive shells. They were using 23mm as well as heavier 37mm and a few 57mm guns.

"Move it Ralph; break left. One of the guns is shooting at us; break left!!" Bill was hitting Ralph on the shoulder.

"I'm moving, I'm moving," Ralph said, through clenched teeth. The cockpit was illuminated by the tracers

whipping past. They heard the popcorn sound of passing shells. They smelled the cordite.

The B-57 dropped one of its large air-opening cluster fire bombs known to all as "The Funny Bomb." The clamshell split open at about fifteen hundred feet and a football-field-sized blanket of burning bomblets hit the ground. It covered the entire center section of the convoy and continued down the hill to the river.

"Nimrod, the fuel truck is getting away. Do you see it?" Bill called.

"I can't see anything, NAIL. I'm pulling off. Give me a second."

The A-26 was breaking away from its attack on the gun positions.

"I got it NAIL. I'll lay some CBU on it."

"Hold high, Yellowbird. Get set for another run on the southern edge of your last drop. We can clean up the tail end later."

"One Three, Roger."

Bill saw the cruciform shape of the black A-26 enter the dome of flare light, pass over the fleeing tanker truck and pull off to the east. The Nimrod's shadow was followed by a 100 foot wide swath of furious red and yellow explosions that swept over the tanker, which blossomed into a massive fireball that lit the valley and the surrounding karst!

"Nimrod off, to the east."

"Shit Hot!!! Look at that sucker burn" Ralph was almost wetting his flight suit with glee!! *"Shack, Nimrod, Shack!!!"*

"Yellowbird, you're clear for another run. NAIL is west.

"Nimrod is east..."

"One Three, Roger."

"One Three, off." The B-57 called as he dropped his second funny bomb. Short of the target a little flash and a puff

of smoke marked the opening of the clamshell dispenser and another blanket of burning phosphorous bomblets dropped on the road.

"Nimrod in on the guns."

A line of CBU bomblets started to explode along the east side of the road. The gunfire stopped.

"Everyone, get some altitude and hold. Let's see what we have." Bill called. *"Nimrod, eight or below. Yellowbird, above ten. We're at five."*

He turned to Ralph. *"Make an easy turn to the east. I want to get a good look at the road. Watch out for guns."*

Suddenly the safe enveloping darkness that hid the Duck was transformed into brilliant daylight!!

"Oh, shit! Where did they come from?" Bill yelled.

A string of six flares illuminated at about nine thousand feet directly above them. The NAIL and the Nimrod were clearly visible below the flares. The gunners now had targets that they could see and they took immediate advantage of their unexpected good fortune.

"Get us the hell out of here, Ralph! Climb, climb!"

Every gun in the valley deluged the Duck and the Nimrod with a huge volume of fire. Multi-colored streams of ZPU heavy machinegun fire and 23 MM cannon fire reached for them like undulating snakes of fire. Strings of yellow basket balls flew on all sides as clip after clip of 37mm shells sought them out. Not to be left out freight trains of bright red 57mm from the next valley blasted over their heads.

"Break right, break right! They have us zeroed in!" Bill yelled at Ralph.

"Break left, break left!"

There were shells exploding all around them and the little O-2 was being rocked by the air bursts and Ralph's jinking maneuvers. A round went off close to the right side of the O-2 and Bill felt something hit him in the head. He dropped the Starlight scope out the window and fell back into his seat. He couldn't hear anything but the wind and the O-2 engines straining.

As suddenly as it came the daylight vanished and was replaced by blessed darkness as the two Nails jinked out from under the western edge of the flare light.

Bill sat motionless for a few seconds, dazed, but feeling no pain. He reached up and felt his head. It was still attached, but it was wet, and he couldn't talk to Ralph. His helmet was gone and there was a banging noise coming from the bottom of the plane.

"Are you OK?" Ralph yelled loudly. *"Did you get hit?"*

Bill looked at Ralph. He shook his head no and motioned for Ralph to take off his helmet. Ralph handed it to Bill. He put Ralph's helmet on and reached for the radio leads. As soon as he connected the leads to his radio he could hear.

"NAIL, this is Nimrod Three Two. How badly are you hit? Come in NAIL."

"NAIL Four Nine is back on. We're climbing out. Stand by."

Bill heard a banging noise from the bottom of the aircraft and remembered the scope. He reached for the nylon line that secured it to his seat harness. As he pulled on the line, the banging noise stopped and the scope appeared at the window. Bill quickly retrieved it and wiped the sweat from his face with the sleeve of his flight suit. It was then that he knew he'd been hit. He could taste the metallic copper taste of HIS blood. It was running down his face. **"Must have taken some shrapnel in the head,"** he thought.

Bill sat back in the seat, shaken. He took off the helmet and felt his head again. He couldn't find where the blood was coming from. Putting on the helmet, he called Nimrod.

"Thanks, Three Two. Where did those flares come from?"

"I don't know. It must've been a flare ship."

"Alleycat, who else is in our area?" Bill called.

"Sorry, NAIL. Candle dropped a string of flares accidentally."

"Sorry isn't enough, Alleycat. What were they doing in our area without a call?"

"I can't answer that, NAIL. They told us they checked in with you."

"We'll settle it at NKP. Thanks Alleycat; NAIL out."

"Nimrod, are you OK? We saw you under the flares too."

"I'm a little faster than you, NAIL. I got to some of the guns before they could finish you off."

"Thanks. We better take it home. We may have some damage."

"I'll give you high cover on the way back. Did you finish the BDA?"

"Roger, Nimrod. I got it."

"NAIL, Nimrod One Three is recovering at NKP. See you there."

"Roger One Three, thanks."

"Alleycat NAIL Four Nine departing Golf for NKP. You might check for a recce bird. This strike should make for some good pictures."

"Roger, NAIL. Good work, we'll try to get you a few snapshots," Alleycat replied.

"Alleycat, this is Candle. We'll cover for the NAIL at Golf. We've got a camera aboard and will take any strike aircraft that you have available."

"Do you suppose they did it on purpose?" Ralph shouted. "They had to know we were down there."

"I don't know, Ralph. It sure doesn't make sense. They were in the wrong place, doing the wrong thing at the wrong time. That's too many coincidences," Bill yelled back.

"How are you? Some of those shells burst pretty close to us?"

"I'm fine," Bill answered. *"A little shook maybe, but fine. Do you want me to take it for a while?"*

"Yeah. I'm going to smoke a cigarette."

"NAIL aircraft headed for NKP, this is Zorro Two Six?"

"Roger, Two six. This is NAIL Four Nine. We're about sixty miles east of the river"

"Look to your right."

A T-28 was flying right next to them on the right side. It was totally blacked out. All that could be seen was the ghostly glow of the cockpit lights. Bill shook his head in amazement.

"I can just make you out. How did you find us?" he said.

"You have your rendezvous lights on."

"Thanks. We forgot to turn them off after the strike."

"No sweat. Alleycat asked me to shepherd you home."

"Thanks, Zorro. There's a Nimrod up there somewhere too."

Nimrod chimed in, *"I'm about five miles back and high."* "

Zorro, did you hear Nimrod Three Two?"

"I heard. Nimrod, Zorro Two six will fly the wing until we get to the pattern."

"I'll press on ahead when we get to the Mekong," the Nimrod replied.

"NAIL, this is Two Six. Were you hit? Alley thinks you might have damage."

"We got some and I'm bleeding. I can't tell where I got hit, but I can taste blood." Bill motioned to Ralph, who took control of the aircraft.

"Guys, we only have one helmet. I'm giving it back to Ralph," Bill said. He took the helmet off and wiped the inside with his handkerchief. Ralph put it on and hooked up his radio leads.

When Ralph took the helmet, Bill told him about the escort. He then reached down and adjusted his seat to the reclining position, leaned back, put his feet up on the instrument panel bar and closed his eyes. He was suddenly very tired and relieved to be finished with flying for the night.

Ralph watched as he leaned back and then panicked when Bill closed his eyes. *"I think he's passed out,"* he said over the radio.

"How bad is he hit?" asked the Nimrod?

"I don't know. The helmet's covered in blood."

"Get on the ground, Nail. Hurry up! Get the ambulance out. Is your plane OK?" the Zorro asked.

"I think so. Bill didn't think they hit anything serious. He didn't say anything about being hit, himself."

"NAIL, this is Three Two. I'm heading back now. I'll have the trucks and doctor waiting. Push it up."

"Roger, Nimrod. I've got it up as far as it goes. This thing doesn't go much faster."

"Zorro, you stay with them."

"Roger, Three Two. I'll be here. Nail, why don't you let the nose down slightly and pick up some speed?"

"What about ground fire?"

*"There isn't much around here. Just don't turn your lights on. Let the speed build up. You can go down to two thousand indicated in about

seven miles, without any risk." Ralph did as the Zorro suggested. He was thirty miles out when the squadron called.

"NAIL Four Nine, do you read Dullness?"

"I'm here," Ralph replied.

"How bad are you hit? Which one of you is hit?"

"It's Bill, he didn't say anything; just passed out on the way back."

"Can you tell where he's hit?"

"Negative. I can't see anything. The helmet was covered with blood though."

"Get back as fast as you can. The ambulance is headed for the runway. How far out are you?"

"I'm about twenty miles out, approaching the river now."

"We'll meet you on the runway."

"I'll clear the runway at midpoint. Have the trucks there."

"Roger, Ralph; hurry!"

The T-28 remained on the wing as Ralph called the tower and lined up on the runway. He made a straight-in approach and landing on Runway 33 and turned off toward the fire trucks and ambulance on the right side. When he touched down, he saw Bill moving out of the corner of his eye.

"Nice landing, Ralph, smooth," Bill yelled, and smiled at him.

When the bright emergency lights illuminated the cockpit, Ralph nearly threw up when he saw Bill was a bloody mess from his forehead to his waist. In the lights, the red blood was everywhere, making Bill look like a monster from some sort of horror movie.

As soon as Ralph turned off the runway, he shut down the front engine. When he came to a stop, men came running toward the plane from both sides. The door was yanked open and a medical orderly stuck his head in.

"How are you, Captain? We thought you might be dead."

"No such luck. What's all the fuss?" Bill asked. He unhooked his safety belt and started to get out when his legs failed him. He couldn't feel anything and would have fallen if the orderly hadn't grabbed him. Another man came up on his left and held him around the waist. The two assisted him toward the ambulance and into the back. The orderly helped him lie down and Bill saw Ed Hardy.

It was Ed who'd been holding him up. Bill laughed. *"Where did you get all the blood, Colonel?"*

Ed had blood on his arm, on his hand and on his side, where he'd held Bill. His expression was grave. *"Are you hurting?"*

"No, Sir. I can't feel a thing," Bill said, as the door closed and the ambulance sped off toward the hospital.

Ed went back to the plane and told Ralph to take it back to the parking area. He'd see him at the hospital.

When Ralph taxied into the parking area, the ground crew was looking and pointing at the right side of the aircraft. He parked and climbed out.

"What's wrong?" he asked the sergeant.

"Get a little flak, Lieutenant?" the sergeant said, pointing to the wing, boom and tail.

"Jesus! We had no idea. Some of those rounds came pretty close," Ralph replied.

There were holes in the starboard wing, the vertical stabilizer and in the horizontal stabilizer, as well as along the length of the starboard boom. Several anti-aircraft rounds must have detonated right beside the aircraft. There was blood on the door and on the right-side seat.

"Ralph, are you OK?" Sean asked, breathing hard. He had been in TUOC when the word came in about their hit. He had run to the parking area. His breath was coming in heaves.

"I'm fine. Bill got hit. He's at the hospital. He seems to be OK, but he bled a lot. Ed Hardy is with him."

Ralph stopped talking as another jeep came speeding onto the parking area. They both turned and looked at the rapidly approaching jeep. Its headlights were blinding them so they could not see who was driving until it screeched to a stop at the plane.

"Sean, Sean," a worried voice screamed and a slim figure threw herself at him, holding him so tight that he could barely breathe. *"They said a FAC had been killed."* Her voice was broken, tears running down her cheeks. *"I thought it was you. Our Operations said it was NAIL FOUR FIVE that was hit."* She couldn't stop sobbing.

Sean held her until she calmed. *"No, no, no, Ralph was flying. His call sign is NAIL 49, but Bill was the one who got hit. He's at the hospital. We're going up there now. Come on."*

Sharon slowly regained her control and reached out to hold Sean again. They stood for several minutes and then she said, *"I'll wait for you. Please come and see me after you get everything settled. You don't need me there."*

"Where will you be?" Sean asked.

"TFA; the guards will let you in," she replied. *"I'll leave a pass."*

CHAPTER THIRTY NINE
Nakhon Phanom Royal Thai Air Base (NKP)
22 December 1967, hospital emergency room

Ralph borrowed the maintenance jeep and he and Sean left for the hospital. They walked in to find a small group gathered in the emergency room. There was a trail of blood leading to a shower in the corner and the water running on the floor was pink. A wet flight suit, hanging on a hook, was being inspected by an orderly who was looking for holes. There were none. The flight surgeon, a nurse and Ed were watching as Bill showered. There wasn't a mark on him that anyone could see. He had his back to the group and was bemoaning the doctor's lack of hospitality and privacy.

"If you were a real doctor, you'd have a cold beer or some mission whiskey, or something," Bill said, loudly.

"If you were really a wounded hero, you'd have a hole in you, somewhere," the doctor replied. *"Cold beers are for the real wounded heroes."*

"Is it my fault you can't find the wound?" replied Bill, turning to face the group.

"Hold your arms out to your sides," the doctor said.

Bill did as he was told. There were now six people staring at him in the altogether, looking for a wound. *"Anyone see anything?"* the doctor asked.

"There isn't much to see, is there?" said Sean.

"Not that! We're looking for a wound. Something unnatural."

"Isn't that unnatural?" the nurse asked.

"No. It's a normal fighter pilot appendage," the doctor replied.

"Ugly and tiny, isn't it?" Sean offered.

"Do I get a beer, now?" Bill asked, lowering his arms and taking the towel offered by the nurse. He was beginning to turn a light shade of crimson.

"Where did the blood come from?"

"Ouch!" Bill yelled and looked at the towel. There was a bright red spot on it. There was also a trickle starting to flow from his right eyebrow.

"We found it!" the Doctor said, gleefully. *"Give the man a beer."*

"When do I get my Purple Heart?"

"You don't get one. Wounds have to be treated. Yours is doing just fine without our help. If you have a problem, take two aspirin and call me in the morning."

Sean O'Malley requisitioned some clean clothes from somewhere or some one and a pair of shower clogs from an orderly. While Bill was dressing, Ed Hardy and the doctor were talking.

"OK, Bill, the doc says you should get something to eat and then get some rest. We'll stand you down for a couple of days," Ed said, walking up to them. *"Sean, take Ralph to TUOC and debrief. I'll take Bill and meet you at the club."*

Ralph and Sean left in the maintenance jeep. Ed reached for Bill's arm, but he'd have none of it.

"I'm OK."

The two walked to Ed's jeep. When they climbed in, Bill noticed that Ed was having a difficult time keeping a straight face. *"I wish we had a photographer assigned to the hospital. Your pictures would be priceless."*

Bill was glad it was night. He was beet red.

CHAPTER FORTY
Nakhon Phanom Royal Thai Air Base (NKP)
22 December 1967, latter that night at the O'Club

Sean and Ralph stayed with Ed Hardy and Bill at the O'Club until Bill started to get drowsy. They'd been warned that this was likely to happen so Sean and Ralph took him back to his hootch. The doctor said that all Bill needed was rest. Ralph would check on him until Joe Brown got back from his mission.

It was after midnight when Sean left the hootch and drove to the TFA compound. He expected to find Sharon at her office and hoped that she had waited up. Instead, the guard gave him directions to Lieutenant Stuart's trailer.

Sean parked the jeep next to Sharon's. He climbed out and looked around. He was at the end of a U-shaped arrangement of trailers. The center was grass with several picnic tables scattered around a brick barbeque grill. It was a pleasant setting.

He checked his directions and noted that Sharon's trailer was the third one from the end on his left. He walked along a wooden boardwalk toward the trailer, being as quiet as possible. It was nearly midnight and there were lights in only two of the ten trailers surrounding the picnic, area, Sharon's and one other.

As he neared the entrance, the door opened and Sharon came out to greet him wearing a long robe over what looked like pajamas. *"Shhh,"* she whispered, holding a finger to her lips, ***"most of the people in the trailers are already in bed. I'm glad you came. I was so worried."***

He reached for her and pulled her close. They kissed and he could feel her under the robe. Sean was simultaneously aware of the feel and the smell of her, of touching and tasting. He realized that he wanted her more than he had ever wanted anyone. His body gave him away as he hardened and he turned slightly to keep her from feeling the pressure.

Sharon smiled at him and moved closer, intentionally pushing herself against him. She kissed him deeply and he could feel the heat rising.

He broke away, ***"I'm going to explode if you keep that up."***

Sharon took him by the hand and led him into the trailer and closed and then locked the door. Still holding his hand she led him into her bedroom and turned out the lights.

CHAPTER FORTY ONE
Nakhon Phanom Royal Thai Air Base (NKP)
22 December 1967, very late in the evening in the O'Club

The club was bulging, the liquor and beer flowing like Niagara, and the noise was unbelievable. It was amazing how this room with eight-foot wooden ceilings, wooden floors with no rugs and wood-paneled walls could make for a great drum effect. No noise ever dissipated. It just continued to bounce between walls, floor and ceiling.

It was in this environment that Ed Hardy began another of his "Bill Stories" and as usual he was surrounded by a cadre of younger NAILs. Ed was like a magnet when it came to operating at the O'Club. He had the stories, the personality, that southern accent and, since he was usually the ranking officer in the group, he bought much more than his fair share of the drinks.

Ed began his tale, ***"This one starts out as our hero, Mr. Fighter Pilot, turned low and slow FAC, is flying his O-2 to Saigon and he realizes that he will be about half an hour late for a meeting of*** senior tacticians at 7th Air Force HQ. He makes a call to Saigon approach control."

"Saigon Approach, this is NAIL Five Five, over."

"Roger NAIL. How can we help you?"

"Approach, I should be there in about forty-five minutes but I'm going to be late for a meeting with a two-star and some of his friends. Would you mind calling 7th and telling them that NAIL Five Five will be thirty minutes late for General Bohlen's staff meeting."

"Will give it a try, but you never know around here. Call us as you enter the pattern."

"Roger."

Ed continued, *"They did try but the general never got the message and began his meeting without his main attraction. It seems that our hero served under Bohlen when they were both in Europe someplace and this had a lot to do with why Bill was asked to brief the staff."*

"Was he late?" injected a new navigator. A very interested one at that.

"Of course he was late. Hell, he is probably better at estimating an ETA than you are. Only kidding."

Ed took a large swig of Bud, set the bottle down and continued. *"Our hero eventually gets to the meeting about thirty minutes late, just as he forecast. He knocks and is told to enter, which he does. Everybody with me so far?"*

Heads nodded but no one said a word.

"Now imagine this...We have a staff room. Think about the conference table in the West Wing of the White House. We have a two-star in the center, just like where President Johnson sits.

Around on all sides are other senior officers, three one-stars and maybe twelve colonels. Everyone is in 1505s. No blues and clearly no flight suits. Now you got that?"

More nodding.

"In walks our hero in a sweat-stained flight suit, jungle boots, no scarf, no patches on the flight suit, no folders. All he has is his normal shit-eating grin. He walks up to Bohlen, flips him a salute and then reaches out to shake hands. He got the salute returned. A handshake and—you may not believe this one—a hug. From a two-star. Is this guy a hero or what?"

"Bullshit, he ain't no hero. He just knows everybody in the goddamned Air Force," sang out someone from the far end of the table.

"Enough. Enough. Let me finish. Bill is asked to sit at the table and is directed to an open chair at the far end, off to the general's far left. The general then begins."

"We are specifically together today and at this time to find out what is going on out there in that out country war in Laos and especially the Ho Chi Minh Trail....."

He was interrupted by a colonel who thought he had finished. The colonel stated, *"The Trail is a network of unimproved roads that runs the length of Laos from the Plain of Jars to far into the south...."*

"One minute, Colonel. This is all very interesting, but when were you last on the Trail?"

"Ah, well...ah...er...ah, General, well, to tell the truth, Sir, I have never been on the Trail."

"Well then, Colonel, please shut the fuck up and sit down. Let us listen to the captain, who was there last night."

The stories about Bill never ended and they were repeated very often, especially when new guys joined the NAILs.

Historical Note: This is a true story and is nearly verbatim. The NAIL was Pat Sweeney.

CHAPTER FORTY TWO
Nakhon Phanom Royal Thai Air Base (NKP)
23 December 1967, morning in the NAIL hootch Area

Bill slept until noon and when he left his room he saw a big sign on the door. It read, "QUIET." Under the English, someone had written something in Thai. Bill couldn't read the words but it was definitely quiet in the hootch area. The maids and cleaning crew bowed politely, but did not speak. He thought it was some sort of Thai religious holiday.

When he walked into the squadron ops after he had eaten, it was nearly 1400 hours. Ed Hardy and Jerry Hersey were in Operations, working on the next week's flying schedule. Sean waved from his desk in the Stan Eval office.

"Good afternoon," Bill said, cheerfully.

"Hey there, Sleeping Beauty. How're you feeling today?" asked Jerry Hersey.

"Great, Jerry. The hootches were so quiet that I couldn't believe it. Is today something special?"

"Not really. The sign must have worked," Ed said, laughing.

"What sign?" Bill wanted to know.

"Colonel Benjamin had the base interpreter write a few Thai words telling the maids to be quiet. Jerry said that they probably threatened to cut off anyone's head if they woke you up."

"From the way they acted, it might be true. Jerry, how'd we do last night? How many trucks?"

"Counting your three, we got a total of twelve."

"What do you mean my three?"

"That's all that TUOC reported."

Ralph chimed in, *"But Candle couldn't find them."*

"Did Candle tell you why they flared us?"

"They said you requested the flares." Ed replied, *"Didn't you?"*

"Bullshit," Bill replied angrily. *"Those bastards flared us without warning."*

"Ralph said he thought Candle made an error, but that we should wait to talk to you."

"I'm going to TUOC to straighten this out," Bill said, as he bolted from the operations center. He was angry and visibly upset.

CHAPTER FORTY THREE
Nakhon Phanom Royal Thai Air Base (NKP)
23 December 1967, a few minutes later at TUOC

From Intel he learned that they received credit for only three trucks. Candle couldn't find any others that were damaged. The Candlestick crew reported that they put two more flights on the target to account for an additional seven kills. Bill was madder than hell. It appeared that the Candle flared them to drive them off and then took credit for their work. He could not believe it.

"Zack, are you sure about this?" he asked, frowning.

"We don't know. Mike said he got three trucks and two guns. The Yellowbird claimed seven trucks. Both of them reported that as your BDA," Lieutenant North said. "After they left here, we got the report from Alleycat. They want to talk to you."

"Who?"

"Alleycat. They want to talk to NAIL Four Nine."

"Do you have a radio?"

"We keep watch on Alleycat's frequency. You can call them here, but be sure they aren't busy."

"Thanks, Zack." Bill said and walked down the hall to the command center in TUOC. The NKP TUOC wasn't a large command complex like those in SAC or TAC; it was a one-story wooden building with a lot of rooms. There were official-looking signs outside each of the rooms, but inside they were much like the 23rd TASS Operations; a few desks, some telephones and occasionally a radio. Most of the offices were staffed by sergeants. The command center was in one of these rooms.

When Bill entered TUOC command center, the Duty NCO showed him the radio. Bill pulled up a chair, picked up the mike and called, *"Alleycat, this is NAIL Five Five."*

"Five Five, this is Alleycat."

"This is Five Five. I'm at the NKP TUOC. I was flying right seat with NAIL Four Nine last night. What do you have?"

"Candle said it took two more flights to get ten trucks."

"They're full of shit! I personally saw seven explode. There were three more on fire when we left. Did you get pictures?"

"Not for another forty-five minutes. By then Candle had put in two more flights. Do you guys have some sort of contest going?"

"No, Alleycat, we don't, but I feel like starting one. I'd like to file a formal complaint about their arrival in my area without notice. We got hit badly by the guns after they flared us."

"That's in our report. Are you OK? Our controller wants to know."

"Thanks, Alleycat. No sweat. I just got a small cut on my eyebrow, not even enough for a Purple Heart."

"Glad you're OK. You did a good job last night, NAIL. We don't see how the flaring could have happened."

Bill closed out with Alleycat, then went back to Zack's office and told him what happened. Zack North was surprised. **"Mike thought that it was strange that the Candle flared. He thought you were talking to them on another radio."**

"I better call the Candlestick people. Do you have their number?"

"Why don't you go see them? They're just a couple of buildings down the flight line, east of Base Operations."

"I better let Colonel Hardy or Colonel Benjamin handle that. Thanks for the help, Zack," Bill waved to the lieutenant as he left TUOC.

CHAPTER FORTY FOUR
Nakhon Phanom Royal Thai Air Base (NKP)
23 December 1967, minutes later in **NAIL Ops**

"Bill," a voice called out as he entered 23rd Ops. He looked up to see Ed Hardy waving him into his office. Jerry Hersey and Sean were sitting around Ed's desk when Bill walked in. He sat in an empty chair.

"Candle flared me and took credit for the trucks," he said. His voice was still angry.

"Hold it," Ed Hardy motioned for all of them to be quiet. *"Let's see if we can figure out what's happening."* He looked at Bill and added, *"TFA sent Candle to your area last night."*

"They have the authority to send anyone anywhere, regardless of who is working there at the time." Jerry Hersey added, *"New rules from 7th Air Force."*

"Now what?" Bill looked at Ed Hardy.

"So do we go back to days only?" Sean asked.

The others all answered at the same time, *"No!"*

"The area is big enough for all of us. We better get some sort of tactics panel going if we're going to keep from running into one another," Bill offered. He paused and added, *"It's like the range. If we don't coordinate our times on target, we'll start running into each other. We had to do that all of the time in fighters. It's easy."*

"TFA said they heard the sound of your attack but that there was a huge convoy moving right under where your plane was. You were after a small convoy and a big one was getting away so they asked Candle to go after it," Jerry Hersey sounded puzzled.

"Look, guys. There was no convoy under the plane. We checked the area first and the only thing moving was the one we were after. There were enough flares to see the roads without the scopes. The only convoy was the one we were after!" Bill replied, looking as puzzled at the rest.

"What did Candle say?" Sean asked. *"Did they find the second convoy?"*

"They reported that it merged with the first one," Jerry answered.

"OK, I've heard enough. We can't afford to get caught in a pissing contest with TFA. The Candles fly too high to do anything but light up Laos. They're dangerous because they're stupid. Like TFA they have to succeed, even if they can't do the job. So avoid them. I'll get a daily meeting set up with the Operations Officers to coordinate our flights. Even TFA will have to go along with that," Ed Hardy stood up and headed out of his office. The meeting was obviously over.

Bill and Sean headed for the coffee pot and then to Sean's desk.

"See you later?" Bill asked.

"Probably not tonight," Sean answered in a low voice.

Bill's eyebrows raised, *"Other plans?"* he inquired, grinning.

Sean turned bright red and Bill broke out in a loud laugh. The others in the Operations area turned to look. Sean's discomfort was obvious.

"Shit, shit, shit! I'll be damned. Well, little buddy, she sure is a looker. "

"Knock it off!" Sean snapped at him.

Before he could continue, Airman Jackson, the squadron clerk, came up and said, *"You have a visitor, Captain O'Malley. She's outside."*

"You stay here!" Sean hissed at Bill and then hurried out the door. Sharon was waiting beside her jeep.

"I have to go. We're leaving in a few minutes for Washington. Our schedule's been moved up from the first of the year. I won't be back until the first part of January," she said, quietly. *"I only have a minute."*

"Do you have to go?" Sean asked.

She nodded and reached for his hand. *"I have to go. Last night will have to do for a few weeks."*

Sean reddened. He was easily embarrassed and never quite sure how to act around Sharon. *"I'll still be here. I'm going to miss you,"* he said, *"a lot!"*

"Goodbye; you be careful," Sharon leaned forward and kissed him gently. Sean watched as she drove off and waved when she looked back.

He looked at the door to the squadron and decided that he didn't want to go back in there. Jamming his blue cap on his head, he turned toward the O'Club and started to walk up the hill.

CHAPTER FORTY FIVE
Nakhon Phanom Royal Thai Air Base (NKP)
25 December 1967, a couple nights later at the O'Club

The Thais celebrate Christmas so they made a valiant and successful attempt to make the Americans feel "at home" on this Christmas. The club was full of poinsettias, wreaths, candy canes, several well-decorated Christmas trees and strings of multi-colored lights.

"This is my last day off and all I want to do is get back out there," Bill said to Sean as the two of them were finishing dinner. Bill had slept most of Christmas Day but Sean had flown a check ride over the trail with a new NAIL. Both were still feeling the effects of the drinking the night before and were being reflective.

"Yeh, I would like to get out there at night myself," replied Sean. *"How many trucks do you have now?"*

"I think about 23, but maybe more like 22. Crazy, but I don't remember. You get away from NAIL Ops and the "killer board" and you forget. I always thought that I would get the most if I was lucky with the sorties but Karl has more than I do."

"Bill, that is only because he killed a thirteen-truck convoy. The Zorros and Nimrods still think you are the best NAIL. I don't, but they do."

They ordered a couple beers and were waiting for the delivery when Bill said, *"Let's paint our names with our kills on a black O-2."*

"What?"

"You know, just like WWII. All the pilots had their names on the planes. Hell, they even named them. Remember 'Enola Gay'?"

"You are the craziest son-of-a-bitch I ever met. They would hang us out to dry. We would pray for a court martial. That would be our best possible outcome. Hello, Leavenworth."

"Sean, think about it. We cut a hole in the bottom of an O-2, added a low-light-level TV, flew it for about a week and they never said anything— not a word. I know they knew what we were doing. Hell, they scheduled the flights."

"You're nuts."

"Are you in?

After a prolonged delay Sean said, *"Yep, now how do we do it."*

"We put our names on first. The number is already on the bird."

"The guys in WWII painted pictures on the noses. Remember the legs on some of them? We need a picture or symbol or something. How about a NAIL?"

"Hell, the NAIL on the flight suits looks pretty stupid. It would look worse on the plane and nobody would know what it was. Just like nobody knows what it is on the flight suits."

"All right, Mr. Brains, how about a cricket? Great symbolism. This used to be the Cricket squadron. Some of the guys like Colonel Benjamin fly in Cricket West. Disney's Jiminy Cricket is on our NAIL patch. Let's do a cricket."

"Done, Smart Ass. I do like that. We got names and the cricket symbol. What next?"

"We name it."

"Can we make something out of the letters WFT?"

"Yeh, Weally Fucked Tup. The Enola Gay was named after Paul Tibbets' mom. We could go that way."

Bill was clearly thinking about this and it took him a couple seconds to gather his thoughts and reply. *"I got it; we can use your mom because you ain't married and my wife. How about that?"*

"My mom's name was Kay and isn't your wife Judy?"

"You got it. Now we mash them together and get Kayjudy or Judykay. How is that?"

"Shitty."

"Alright, let me try again." Bill grimaces as he thinks deeply.

"Man, you are thinking too hard. How about Jaykudy?"

"Sounds like shit."

"How about Kudy Jay? Sounds like some kind of a bird and this is an airplane."

"I like that. Kudy Jay it is. Now we get someone to make stencils of a truck and one of a gun and we are off and running."

Bill again starts that deep thinking. *"We get Sergeant Ricardo again. We let him pick a black one. His guys can make the stencils. Hell, Man, we are in business."*

That night Sergeant Ricardo again selected 418, one of the black O-2s. He then painted in red on the left side of the plane, just aft of the cowling but in front of the wing: Bill Thompson, Sean O'Malley, KUDY JAY and a cricket. Aft of all this, in multiple rows, he painted small symbols representing trucks and guns. He stenciled in 26 trucks and 33 guns. Sergeant Ricardo would eventually add 42 more trucks and 27 more guns.

Historical Note: No one ever mentioned or questioned the fact that two captains and one sergeant had painted their names and their kills on a U.S. Air Force airplane, one that they named the Kudy Jay. No one else in the 23rd TASS ever did this.

The Kudy Jay, serial number 67-21418, was written off the Air Force rolls after a windstorm at Fort Bragg, North Carolina, flipped the aircraft over and on to its back on December 6, 1972 and it was declared too damaged to repair. The two NAIL pilots were Don Brown and Pat Sweeney

Captains Don Brown and Pat Sweeney with the Kudy Jay
 Note: Jerry Stephan (Nail 57) is refurbishing a Cessna 337 as the Kudy Jay (flat black paint, a red Cricket, the number 418, the names, Don Brown and Pat Sweeney, and, naturally, the truck and gun kills). This replica is on display at the Forward Air Controller Museum at Mecham Field in Fort Worth, Texas.

CHAPTER FORTY SIX
Steel Tiger, Eastern Central Laos
27 December 1967, early evening heading east at 6,000 feet

"Hello, hello, this is NAIL Five Five declaring that amateur hour is over," spoke Bill over UHF Guard channel.

"Tell the truck drivers and the gunners to look out because the old pro, NAIL Five Five, is on his way to the Trail to destroy trucks and kill guns. The first team is coming out. This is NAIL Five Five."

Bill had started doing this about a week previously and remained amazed that not one NAIL mentioned it to him...no one. Declaring amateur hour over was a clear slam at the FACs who were out over the Trail when he made the call. There were usually two FAC aircraft on the Trail at all times at night. He was puzzled by their lack of spunk. If that had been done to him, he would have been all over the SOB with the big mouth and bigger ego. But that is the way it was.

However, the amateur hour talk was only the beginning of his night time over the Trail charade; Bill explained this to the FAN, Lieutenant Benny Hallinan, a navigator flying the right seat and operating the Starlight scope. Ben was young but he was very experienced in night flying over the Trail. He had come to the 23rd TASS about six months ago and had transitioned from the back seat of the O-1 Birddog to the right seat of the O-2 Duck. He had amassed well over a hundred missions into Laos and most of these were at night where he became an expert on the operation of the night-vision scope.

"Here's the deal, Ben. I want the NVA or Cong or whoever is manning the guns to know that NAIL Five Five is in the sky. Since I now do this every time I come out here and they listen to all of

our communications, I believe they have gotten "know" me. That is they are or will begin to tie what I do to NAIL Five Five. So far you got it?"

"Shit, Bill, I don't have any idea what you are talking about or where this is going."

"I want these bastards to "know" NAIL Five Five. Maybe I mean FEAR NAIL Five Five. The next thing I do is load the air above me with Yellowbirds or Redbirds and then maybe a Nimrod or Zorro."

"Load the air above you? What the shit is that?

"I put phony airplanes up there. I know they're phony but the gooks don't. When they think I have three or four strike aircraft up here ready to kill them, they hold off on the anti-aircraft firing. Less ZPU, less 23 mm and less 37. It's great. Easy strikes when they don't shoot so much. And fewer losses on our side."

"Does it work? Do they fall for that shit?"

"Yep, every time. Now here is how we do it. I am NAIL Five Five and you are Yellow/Red/Nimrod/or Zorro. I will talk to you on the typical UHF frequency as if you are an attack plane. Then you answer as if you are. Any questions?"

"I guess not. It sounds simple.... Should I try to change my voice for different aircraft?"

"Why not? Why not lean right towards the open window as one and lean left towards me with the other one. The background wind noise will be different. Probably would even help to make it more realistic for our listeners."

A few minutes later and yet over twenty miles from the Trail, Bill begins the show. *"Redbird 44 are you on 247.8?"*

Ben replies, *"NAIL, this is Redbird 44. Read you loud and clear."*

"Redbird, give me an ETA to the fragged target area."

"Roger, NAIL. We are a flight of two. We will be there in about thirteen minutes at 21,000 feet. We have a full load as fragged and can stay in the area for about thirty minutes."

On intercom, *"Ben, that was great. Sure you haven't done this before?"* Ben shrugs his shoulders and smiles.

Bill continues, but now on UHF, *"Redbird, we will be on target in ten minutes and will be circling the target clockwise with our beacon light on. You should be able to see us in a few minutes. We will be at 7,000 feet."*

"Roger, NAIL."

Ben, with a "new" voice, chimes in, *"NAIL Five Five, this is Nimrod 32. I have been listening to your Redbird talk. I am behind you at 10,000 and have you in sight. As planned, I will concentrate on the guns. Let me know where you want me."*

"Roger, Nimrod 32. Stay to the east of the road at 10,000. You will be cleared in north to south or visa versa. Clear only to the east and stay below 20,000 and above 7,000."

"I got it, NAIL."

"Stay in position and as soon as one of those sons-a-bitches shoots, he's dead. I will clear you in immediately."

"NAIL Five Five, this is Redbird 44 and I have your beacon. We are at 20,000."

"Redbird, did you hear the instructions we gave the Nimrod?"

"Yes, should we also stay east?"

"Redbird, right on. Now don't come in on the guns until we clear you in. The Nimrod's bombs should make a good target area for you and the white phosphorous."

"NAIL, we are in orbit at 20."

"Okay, now what, Bill?" asked Ben on the intercom.

"Now we try to find some trucks. By the way...nice job on the UHF. Hell, even I believed that the Redbird and Nimrod are up there. You did this better than any other guy I have flown with. Let's get some trucks."

Bill began a slow right turn as they passed over the HCMT just north of Golf. Ben was on the scope and had the road, but no activity and no trucks. They continued in a southerly direction towards Foxtrot when they heard Alleycat, *"NAIL Five Five, we have a flight of three F-4s from Danang, Gunslinger 15. They will be on 247.8 and are inbound to your position at 25,000 feet. They are near bingo fuel so you will have to put them in fast."*

"Roger, Alleycat. Gunslinger 15, do you copy NAIL Five Five?"

"Roger, NAIL, we just heard all of that and we think we have your beacon. Please turn it off and on a couple times."

Bill reaches for the IFF Ident switch and moves it off to on to off to on...

"Gotcha, NAIL. Where do you want the bombs? We're in a hurry."

"Redbird and Nimrod hold your orbit positions and be ready to strike."

"Roger, NAIL," said Ben.

"Okay, NAIL," said Ben again, but with a deeper tone and leaning left.

"NAIL, how many planes do you have up here? This is Gunslinger."

"We got a lot but don't worry about it. I got them out of your way.

"Shit, shit, shit…shit …shit. We got trucks. We got trucks," screams Ben.

"Where?"

"They are almost to Foxtrot."

"Gunslinger, we have movers and they are approaching Foxtrot. I will flare from 7,000 feet and clear to the east. You will be cleared in about north to south and south to north. The flare will be west of the Trail and it will drift east over the road. You should be able to see the trucks as soon as the flare lights. Get ready."

"NAIL, we are ready."

"Ben, how is this position? We want to be a quarter of a mile to the west."

"Bill, this is perfect."

Bill reaches up and arms the station and pickles the flare, which drops away rapidly and ignites a two-million-candlepower flare below the large parachute. *"Flare away."*

"Tally Ho, NAIL. We got 'em. Gunslinger flight. Lock and load. Drop everything on one pass. One is in. FAC in sight."

"Bill, they haven't shot as us yet."

"They will. Wait until the bombs start going off."

"One is off." The first bunch of bombs was about fifty meters south and east of the trucks. However, one truck stopped and the driver got out and ran to the trees. Still no anti-aircraft fire!!!

"Two is in. FAC in sight."

"Two, move yours about 100 meters north on the road."

The 12 MK 82 500 pound bombs walked across the road, each one blasting a 20 foot crater and sending shrapnel and debris in all directions... levitating one truck which spun end over end into the jungle and causing two more to be blasted over on their sides.

"Two is off." One 37 mm fired one set of seven tracers but it was far from Bill and Ben and way behind the second Gunslinger.

"Two, you were a touch long. Three, put yours between the other two." Now another couple guns started, another 37mm and now a 23mm.

"Three is in with FAC in sight."

"Three is off." The gunfire was now concentrated in one area and it was still only three or four guns "firing at the moon" as they say when they have no visible targets. Three barely hit the ground with his bombs .... They were at least 500 meters west of the trail. He hadn't damaged any trucks but he <u>had</u> made lots of toothpicks!!

"Gunslingers go to 25,000 and join in a left turn. How did we do, FAC?"

"I got to give you credit. You all hit the ground. You guys got one burning and two others damaged. Appreciate your work. Fly safe; NAIL out."

"Redbird 44, are you still there?"

"Roger, NAIL. What do you want me to do?"

"Just hang in there. We are going after some more. Nimrod, you okay?"

"Roger, NAIL. Still have you in sight. Let's get some trucks," said Ben in that deep-toned voice.

Bill and Ben and the phantom flight of Redbirds and the Nimrod continued up and down the Trail for over an hour but saw no activity and, with fuel running low and time running out, began the trip back to NKP.

Historical Note: Pat Sweeney used this "phony aircraft" and "amateur hour" scenario very often soon after he realized that the keepers of the HCMT were listening to everything on the airwaves over Laos. It did seem to reduce the anti-aircraft fire.

CHAPTER FORTY SEVEN
Nakhon Phanom Royal Thai Air Base (NKP)
29 December 1967, mid morning in TUOC

The Navy Neptune crews were actively involved with the placement of sensors and had three of their dozen aircraft out of commission due to battle damage from antiaircraft fire in less than one month of combat. The competition among the Navy personnel was severe. One flight crew, eight men, had not been able to complete a successful drop and they were anxious to demonstrate that they weren't afraid to fly in such a hazardous area of combat. The hazing from the other Navy crews was becoming unbearable. Sean was scheduled to mark the drop for this crew on a particularly cloudy day.

The weather briefing at INTEL concentrated on the marginal weather forecast. **"The probability of a successful run is less than thirty percent, Commander,"** Zack North said, in answer to a question.

"Do we go?" Sean wanted to know. And then answered his own question, **"Why go? The weather stinks. We can do it tomorrow."**

"It's up to the Navy whether you go out to the drop area," Zack replied, looking at the aircraft commander.

"We go," Lieutenant Commander Hal Todd replied. His copilot, Lieutenant Mike Kurten, nodded in agreement.

"Come on, Commander. The flak-suppression planes can't fly under those clouds," Sean said, emphatically.

"We'll try, Captain. We'll go out there and see if we can make it."

"We can't get under a one-thousand-foot ceiling to give you any support," this from Dave Montgomery, the Hobo flight leader.

"We'll go in ourselves. They won't expect us in that weather," Hal replied.

"If you go in yourselves, there'll be no diversion and you'll be sitting ducks. Not only that, the mountains are sticking up into the clouds," Sean was getting disgusted. He knew this crew hadn't made a drop yet and they were being ribbed unmercifully by the other Navy crews. They had aborted three times and were totally embarrassed.

"If you're afraid, we'll go ourselves," Hal said, with too much sarcasm. He wasn't going to back down.

"No way. It's my call. The FAC's in charge of the drop," Sean replied, angrily.

"If you don't go, I'll call 7th Air Force and have you replaced," Hal was agitated and afraid of another abort.

"Talk some sense into him, Mike, he's your boss," Sean said looking at the copilot.

Mike shrugged and replied, *"Let's at least go out and take a look. Maybe it'll break up enough for us to make a run."*

"A look. I'll make the call when we get to the area. Do you agree, Commander?" Sean was looking at Hale

"I agree."

The crews left TUOC and headed for their aircraft. The rescue crews were alerted as was the normal routine and Cricket was notified that the mission was on a tentative go. They would fly to the area and check the weather first hand. Cricket alerted the fighters at Danang and Ubon to stand by for launch. Sean and Joe Brown took off first and headed for the target area. The OP-2E and the Hobos would take off thirty minutes after the FACs. All of the supporting aircraft were scheduled for launch to arrive at the target area at the same time. The total force consisted of two O-2s, two A-1s, the P-2 and four F-4s.

Sean arrived in the target area, flying above the clouds at seven thousand feet. *"Cricket, this is NAIL Four Five in the target area with Lindy 31 inbound."*

"Go ahead, Four Five."

"Roger, Cricket. Four Five is going down through a hole to check out the cloud cover. Keep the rest of the planes up here," Sean radioed.

"Roger, NAIL Four Five. The fighters are due in five minutes. We'll keep them at twenty thousand. The P-2 Lindy and its escorts are inbound at eight thousand. They estimate your position in seven minutes."

"Thanks, Cricket. I'm descending in an open area."

Sean kept the O-2 in the clear as he wound his way down around the clouds. He was concerned about the mountains and the height of the bottom of the clouds. They'd be very easy targets, if they were visible against the clouds and within range of the guns. Sean thought they were about five miles west of the Trail, but he wasn't certain.

"Invert, NAIL Four Five. I have my beacon on. Do you have a fix?"

"We have you NAIL. I show you a few miles west of the target," replied the radar controller.

Sean was suddenly below the clouds. The bottoms were at fifteen hundred feet. He got a quick look at the mountains to the north and then turned and climbed back up.

"This is NAIL Four Five. I bottomed out at fifteen hundred feet. The mountains are well above that height and the gunners will have a clear shot if you go down there," Sean radioed in the clear.

"This is Lindy 31. We can see the ground," Hal replied.

"The clouds cover about half the area. The openings are too small for the fighters and the Hobos," Sean replied. "

"We can see well enough for our run," Hal replied. *"If you can't mark the drop, we can find it ourselves."*

"You're nuts," came over the radio. It sounded like Dave Montgomery.

"NAIL Four Five, this is Cricket; will there be a drop? We've got 7th Air Force on the line."

"Negative, Cricket. NAIL Four Five is aborting due to weather," Sean answered.

"Negative, negative! This is Lindy 31, we are making our run," Hal replied in an excited voice.

"Break off! Break off!" Sean was shouting over the radio. He was looking at the OP-2E nosing down into the clouds. The two A-1s leveled off and remained above the cloud tops.

"Sean, we can't go down there," Dave said.

"Cricket, Lindy 31 is on its run, unescorted. You better put the rescue birds on strip alert. Hold the fighters at altitude."

"*Roger, NAIL. Didn't you abort?*"

"*We did, Cricket. The Navy decided to go in alone. We'll wait for them to come back up.*"

"*If they come up,*" it sounded like Dave again.

Sean flew wide orbits around the area at seven thousand feet and the Hobos circled above him, waiting for the P-2 to reappear.

"*Invert, do you have the Lindy?*" Sean called.

"*Negative, NAIL. We lost them when they went down for their drop. We have you and the Hobos, plus the F-4s.*"

"*Lindy 31, do you read NAIL Four Five?*" Sean called.

There was only silence. Ten minutes had passed since the OP-2E descended into a hole in the clouds. They should have called or reappeared. Another five minutes passed, and then Cricket called, "*NAIL Four Five. The F-4s have reached their minimum fuel. Do you want them to top off?*"

"*They can't get under the stuff anyway, Cricket. You might as well send them home,*" Sean's replied in a dejected voice.

"*Roger, NAIL. We're releasing the F-4s.*"

"*Dave, can you hang around?*" Sean asked the A-1 leader.

"*We've got plenty of fuel, Sean. We'll stay with you. What's next?*"

"*I'll go down and look for them,*" Sean replied.

The P-2 had been gone for twenty minutes and they had heard no calls. Sean was reluctant to descend if he had a damaged or lost P-2 wandering around in the clouds. He called Invert.

"*Invert, I'm going to descend to the west and then come back under the clouds. The Hobos will stay on top.*"

"Roger, NAIL Four Five. We still haven't picked up anything but you and the Hobos."

Sean descended in openings until he was again below the clouds. He turned to the east and carefully flew toward the Trail. He was looking for some sign of the P-2. When he reached the road, Sean pulled up into the clouds and reversed his course. He hadn't seen anything. He climbed above the clouds and returned to the area where the Hobos were orbiting.

"See anything, NAIL?" Dave radioed.

"Nothing, no sign of them. I didn't see any smoke either. I can't find the P-2. Cricket, have you heard anything?" Sean asked.

"Negative, NAIL. We haven't heard a thing. We'll keep a listening watch on this frequency."

"Roger, Cricket. We're returning to NKP. We better keep the rescue forces alerted. They could have been damaged and be limping home."

"Roger, NAIL. Cricket will advise rescue."

They flew back slowly looking for some sign of the big aircraft and its eight-man crew. When they landed at NKP, there was a large group waiting at TUOC. Colonel Benjamin and the Navy Commander were there as well as the TFA Commander, Brigadier General Holland. Sean and Dave Montgomery debriefed the mission and answered questions from all of the attendees. The P-2 was officially listed as missing. All crews headed for the Trail were to be briefed to look for signs of the aircraft and keep a listening watch on Guard Channel for any calls from downed crewmen.

The Neptune's wreckage was found two weeks later. It had hit the flat face of a high- rising karst near the top, and all the wreckage was at the bottom. No calls were ever received from any downed crew member nor were any recovered.

Historical Note: On 23 January 1968 (about two weeks after the actual crash) the OP-2E crash site was found. Two days later a NAIL FAC photographed the wreckage, which was identified as the VO-67 aircraft. The aircraft had hit a 4,583 foot karst about 150 feet from the top. No recovery team was inserted as this area was heavily occupied by the enemy, no emergency radio transmissions or beacons were ever heard, and the likelihood of there being any survivors was negligible.

CHAPTER FORTY EIGHT
Nakhon Phanom Royal Thai Air Base (NKP)
29 December 1967, dinner time at the O'Club

Sean and Bill were having dinner that night with Joe Brown and Jerry Hersey. Sean had just finished relating the events of the day.

Jerry shook his head in dismay. **"Ever since General Arnholt left, we haven't had a game plan,"** he said.

"What did you do before?" Bill wanted to know.

"Pretty much the same thing, but we didn't have the O-2s and the range for night missions. This sensor business is new, but Arnholt used to attend the briefings and make sure everyone had the same goals."

"Why doesn't Holland do that?" Sean asked.

"He's not really our boss. We answer to the 504th at Bien Hoa," Jerry replied. **"The Hobos answer to their unit at Pleiku. Rescue has their own chain of command. It leaves the Nimrods and Zorros in the 56th Air Commando Wing, with the Candlesticks operating as a special project. No one's really in charge."**

"What you're saying is that every one of the units up here is operating on their own. The

individual commanders decide what they will do?" Bill asked.

"That's pretty much the way it is," Jerry replied.

"Why don't we do something about it?" Sean asked.

"We don't have the authority," Jerry replied.

"We control the strikes," Joe piped in.

"Not really. We respond to a frag order from 7th Air Force. They typically issue orders for a certain number of sorties. It's up to the NKP TUOC to assign them to individual flights or squadrons. The TACC at 7th does issue targets to hit, like truck parks and storage areas, and they allocate a certain number of fighter strikes to our area but TUOC selects the way it's done. They do that in accordance with the unit's instructions. People like Candlestick are fragged for one or two sorties a night. They fly where they like, when they like," Jerry continued.

"I thought the TACC at 7th decided where to hit the convoys," Bill commented.

"No. It's up to our TUOC."

"Then, we're doing it very poorly," Bill said.

"Here comes the great words of wisdom from our resident genius," Sean said.

"It's an asshole stunt to attack the convoys in the same place every night," Bill snapped.

"Why? It's working, isn't it?" Jerry answered.

"It's lazy and it's dumb," Bill replied. *"I assumed that it fell into some overall design from the TACC. I didn't realize that we were doing it to ourselves. I was giving them credit for seeing the big picture."*

"Seems to me I heard someone warning you about your assumptions," Sean interjected. Bill reddened

a little. At that moment Ed Hardy and John Patterson appeared in the club. They joined the others.

"*What're you doing, picking on our resident fighter pilot? He looks a little flustered*," Ed said as he sat down.

Bill looked sharply at Sean and Jerry, and then he continued, "*We were talking about the attacks on the Trail. I think it's stupid, the way they're handled. Colonel, did you know that TUOC determines our attack strategy?*"

"*Strategy? Who the fuck uses strategy? We just go out every night and kill trucks. What fucking strategy?*" Ed was as incredulous as the rest.

John Patterson just shook his head back and forth. He didn't want to step in the middle of this one. Sean was laughing and Joe Brown looked confused. He was watching Bill with curiosity.

Bill looked up at the ceiling and said, "*I'm surrounded by them.*" He looked around the table. Everyone else was looking at him like he'd lost his mind.

He continued, "*OK. You win. We don't have a strategy. We should, but we don't. Are you interested in hearing one?*"

"*Don't you have enough to do with the night program? Do you want to run the entire war as well?*" Ed wasn't being receptive to Bill's latest contribution. In fact, he looked more than a little irritated.

Bill ignored the comments and began, "*As we all know, equipment and supplies are in short supply in North Vietnam. At least that's what we're told. It seems perfectly logical to me that we would want to limit the places that we attack so that they won't have a hard time getting the few guns that they do have set up at the right checkpoints. We probably should use just Foxtrot. That way it would be fair. They could put all of their guns there."*

Ed started to speak but changed his mind. John Patterson was nodding his head in agreement and from the looks on Jerry and Sean's faces, they realized that Bill was right. They were making it easy on the enemy by attacking the same places every night.

There was nothing said for a few moments. Bill was waiting for a reply. He looked around the table, but only Joe Brown and John Patterson were looking at him. Both grinned.

Ed Hardy finally spoke, *"Did you give your last commander this much trouble?"*

Bill only grinned at him.

"I think he's right. We're working the same spots every night to give better data to TFA. I agree with Bill. It probably isn't the smart thing to do," John said.

"Do you think he knows how hard it is to live with a smart ass that's smart?" Ed asked, looking at John.

"How'd you like to be his friend?" Sean asked.

John and Joe laughed. Sean was shaking his head. Bill had done it again. He managed to upset their view of the war and he was probably right.

"Why don't we fix it?" Bill asked the group.

"Don't tell me. If we make you general, you'll get it straightened out," Ed replied.

"That'd work, but I doubt that it's possible. Why don't we use the TFA Operations meeting as a tactics panel? It doesn't have to be formal. Get the squadron Operations Officers to meet after lunch every day and make a call on the location of the night's activities," Bill said. He was talking without a lot of preparation, but he didn't want to lose the idea.

"Why not do it at the night briefing?" Ed said. *"It would be easier to get them then. A lot of people sleep in the afternoons, particularly when they are flying at night."*

"The tactics need to be set up during the last daylight missions. If we're going to vary the attack locations, we need to get the roads blocked while it's still daylight."

"You're serious. You want to crater the roads at a different place every afternoon and set up the night attacks so that the guns have to be moved," Ed was interested.

"We have flare ships for the easily-identified places. A FAC will be most useful where there aren't a lot of identifiable terrain features. Let Candle light up Foxtrot. The fighter pilots all know it and can find the road. We could do more damage finding convoys on the alternate routes," Bill answered.

"Candle will get all the kills," Joe said.

"Only if we fail to get the routes blocked. Even then, if we're chasing them toward Candle, then we're going to destroy more trucks," Bill replied.

"I didn't think you cared for Candlesticks," John said.

"I don't. They'll do anything to look good. I don't really trust their BDA either but at Foxtrot they can't miss. Anyway, I'd like them to get shot at occasionally."

"I'll talk to the colonel. John, will you see if your commander is interested?" Ed asked.

"He will be. It'll get us some action away from the main trail. The Zorros aren't allowed out there anyway. We're too slow," John replied.

"If everyone buys it, we'll get something going tomorrow," Ed said.

"I'll give you recommendations when I see the results of each night's actions," Bill said.

"You stay away from the meetings. If they think you're involved, some of the people won't have anything to do with it. You aren't exactly their favorite person," Ed said.

"I can't act dumb. I don't know how," Bill replied.

"Just stay away. Don't tell anyone who thought this up. I can get everyone together tomorrow but they aren't going to like having some smartass captain calling the shots," Ed said. He paused, *"Even if he is, I don't like it either, come to think of it."*

The next morning, Ed Hardy was able to get the Operations Officers from the NKP squadrons together for a discussion. The idea of setting up one or two choke points for daily strikes was well received. The FACs would attempt to get the road cratered on the last sortie of the day and the night FACs would look for convoys delayed short of the craters. None of the units felt that their mission was being altered. They went after trucks wherever they could find them. If the NAILs could force the trucks to collect, then the strike planes would attack wherever the trucks were located. Candlestick was the only hesitant unit. They did not want to appear captive to the FAC actions. They agreed to assist, if they were in the area and available.

The first night was a success. The road was cratered to the north of Foxtrot and the strike aircraft were able to attack convoys with little threat from gunfire. Unfortunately, TFA did not agree with the new tactics. The night attacks were not in an area with sensors and the TFA could not calibrate and evaluate the data. General Holland was not pleased with the

FAC's attempt to alter his view of the war. The sensor program had priority.

Although TUOC was instructed to leave the nightly sorties scheduled for Golf and Foxtrot, the day FACs continued to crater the roads away from the primary choke points. They did this on their own and succeeded in forcing some of the guns to be relocated instead of concentrated at two or three major points along the trail. One of the disadvantages with this program was the increased threat to the Zorros. On the 28th of December, John Patterson was shot down over Route 23, in a location that had not previously been a threat. He was picked up uninjured the following morning.

The loss of the Zorro was attributed to movement of the guns away from the main trail. John didn't share TFA's view that it was the NAILs fault. He continued to support the unofficial road cratering program.

Colonel Benjamin defused the NAIL/TFA hostility by assigning Joe Brown as a FAC Liaison Officer with the TFA. Joe spent several hours each day at the TFA facility and assisted them in coordinating their drops and after-action reports with the day's flying activities. Golf and Foxtrot continued to be the main choke points, although at least a quarter of the night efforts continued to be conducted at other locations.

CHAPTER FORTY NINE
Nakhon Phanom Royal Thai Air Base (NKP)
30 December 1967, evening near base operations

Sean waited impatiently for the passengers to disembark from the T-39 Sabreliner. It was parked in front of Base Operations and General Holland's car was beside the plane.

The general and two lieutenant colonels got out of the small jet and climbed into the car. Lieutenant Stuart was the last one off the plane. She waved at the car as it departed and turned to pick up her bag.

Sean went to his jeep and drove out to meet her. She smiled and set her bag down as he stopped. They didn't speak until after they kissed. *"I really missed you and I'm so glad you're back early,"* he whispered.

"Me too," she replied, squeezing him tighter.

"I thought you might need a ride," Sean said, as he picked up her bag and put it in the back of the jeep.

"It depends on how many people are with us on these trips. If there's room for me, I go with the general. If not, I call TFA security to come pick me up or leave my jeep at Base Operations."

Sean drove to TFA and they were waved through the gate. It was 2012 hours and dark. He parked next to her jeep and reached for her bag. *"Have you had dinner?"* he asked.

"No. We ate lunch on the plane from Hawaii, but there wasn't time at Danang where we changed planes. Let's get something at the O'Club."

"Great. I'll drive," Sean said.

It was a few minutes before ten, 2151 hours, when they finished dinner. Sean listened while Sharon talked of her visit home for Christmas. He wanted to leave and take her back to her trailer, but she apparently wanted to talk.

"You had a bad time here over the holidays?" Sharon suddenly changed the subject. It caught Sean by surprise.

"Bill was hit, we lost a P-2 and John Patterson was shot down. It wasn't a really good holiday season. Actually, we didn't pay much attention to the season. It's been business as usual,

every day including Christmas, whenever that was."

"Didn't you care about the P-2?" she asked, her voice picking up a sharp edge.

Sean looked puzzled, *"Of course. They killed themselves. We couldn't do anything about it,"* he paused. When Sharon didn't respond, Sean continued, *"Didn't you read the report? "*

"We did. The reason for the loss was pilot error," Sharon answered quickly.

"That's right. The P-2 went in below the clouds when we told him to abort," Sean replied, sitting up straighter. He didn't know where this conversation was going and he didn't like it one bit.

"The pilot error was yours, Sean. You led the plane in when the weather was too low for the fighter aircraft to support it. It's all there in black and white," Sharon was angry and her voice was getting louder as she spoke.

"Who the hell told you that?" Sean's asked loudly.

"I read the Intelligence report. That's who told me about it!" she was snapping at him. *"Why are you so afraid to admit your mistake?"* She was angry and nearly shouting.

"Bullshit!" Sean found himself glaring at Sharon. Five minutes ago, he was hoping to be allowed in her bed. Now he was defending himself and his integrity against her attack.

"Am I interrupting?" came another voice. They both looked up to see Bill walking toward them from the bar; a beer can in his hand. He sat down at their table. *"Lieutenant,"* he said and nodded at her. *"Sean, can I get either of you a drink?"*

They were too surprised to do anything but shake their heads, no. *"Your conversation is depressing the fearless warriors gathered in the bar area to* honor their departed friends," Bill said, quietly, and then he turned to Sharon. **"Seriously, young lady, never confuse a real warrior with one of your pussy staff types. If you feel the need to call one of us a liar or coward, start with me. I'm so liberated that I'll knock out all of your teeth and not feel guilty,"** he paused, daring her to speak.

"Sean, you have a flight in the morning. Give me the keys. I'll see that the lieutenant gets back to her sanctuary," Bill held out his hand.

Sean realized that the two had been arguing much too loudly and that the crews in the bar had heard them. He turned bright red.

"Come on, Lieutenant," Bill said. **"Notice, Lieutenant, I gave you what might be construed as an order in many situations. The two bars up here,"** he pointed to his shoulder, **"mean that you had best pay attention."**

"Ralph, take a ride with us," he called into the lounge.

Sharon wisely kept her opinions to herself. She followed Bill from the club. Ralph hurried to catch up and continued out the door and climbed into the rear of the jeep.

Bill drove to TFA without speaking. When they reached the main gate, he swung the jeep around and said, **"This is as far as we go. Lieutenant, you'd better do your homework. It's hard enough here without a pussy staff type passing judgment on the real work. Check your facts and don't talk to me again unless it's to apologize. Now get out of our jeep."**

"You arrogant ass," Sharon started to say but he drove off before she could finish.

"Well, Captain Marvel, I think you've done it now," Ralph said, leaning forward. **"She's going to sic the general on you."**

"I don't really give a shit," Bill replied. *"The assholes in TFA must've written a report that blamed Sean for the P-2 crash. I think it's time to muddy the waters."*

"Sean looked like he'd just been hit in the gut with a bazooka round," Ralph commented.

"Shit, Ralph, he's in love. If he isn't careful, it'll get him killed. I just tried to get her aimed at me instead of him."

"I'd say that you succeeded," Ralph offered. *"Quite handily, I might add. Quite handily."*

They were still laughing when Bill parked the jeep at the O'Club and went to find Sean. He had left for his hootch. Ralph would go check on him.

CHAPTER FIFTY
Nakhon Phanom Royal Thai Air Base (NKP)
3 January 1968, late afternoon in TUOC

General Holland's return marked an increase in sensor reports along the trail and a shift in FAC effectiveness to Candlestick from the NAILs. The Candlestick kills were sharply increased during their nightly sortie over Foxtrot. NAIL results decreased slightly and then leveled off at an average about twice as high as their previous year. Overall truck kills in Laos rose sharply due to the success of the Candlestick/TFA partnership. The General was very pleased, to say the least.

Meanwhile, the informal Tactics Panel altered choke points every day on route segments without sensors. Except for Foxtrot, major anti-aircraft gun concentrations ceased to be a serious problem. The Nimrods, Zorros and NAILs enjoyed a break from the constant gunfire. It was still there, it just wasn't as ferocious as it had been. The Candlestick crews no longer shared night briefings with the other units. They worked exclusively with the TFA controllers.

Bill walked into the briefing room with his coffee, ready for the Intelligence Officer to update them on the day's status. The room was crowded with Zorros, Nimrods and NAILs. Since this was the routine nightly briefing, they joked with one another for a couple of minutes before the briefing began. Charlie Green was sitting next to Bill and leaned over.

"This is just like an old WWII movie."

"Do you think we're all playing roles?" Bill asked, grinning. *"Who am I? John Wayne?"*

"I was thinking more Mickey Rooney," Charlie said, laughing as Bill jabbed him in the ribs.

"It is similar. Or at least I thought so until I got to NKP. I thought they made all of it up!" Bill replied.

"Look around. I've seen this scene in a dozen old films," Charlie said.

"Hey, Joe, what movie does this remind you of?" Bill yelled across the room.

Joe Brown frowned and then broke into a wide grin. *"Command Decision. I'm Clark Gable,"* he replied, sticking his chest out.

"It can't be Command Decision," Mike said. *"Our general doesn't fly."* That brought loud cheers and laughter from everyone in the room.

"You're right. It must be "Flying Leathernecks," John Patterson said, very seriously. *"I remember it well...there we were, preparing to take on the yellow hordes."*

"You ought to remember it, you old fart. You were probably there," Charlie said.

"I'm not that old. I'm older!" John replied. *"It'd do you impudent young bastards well to heed the

advice and counsel of your wiser and more experienced colleagues."

"Hear, hear," they shouted in unison.

"Is that guy still shooting at you, John?" Bill asked, changing the subject.

"Every night. It's beginning to irritate me."

At that, the room broke into loud laughter again. John had been reporting the same thing every night for the past two weeks. Each night at dusk, about ten miles east of the Mekong River, a single round of anti-aircraft fire would be shot at him.

"Are you sure he's shooting at you, John. Maybe he's aiming at one of our satellites," Joe asked.

John gave the captain a disgusted look.

"Tomorrow, John. I'm going to be up at dusk and I will wait for you to come by. What altitude will you be at?" Bill asked.

"I'm usually at forty-five hundred feet by then."

"Give me a call after takeoff, John; I'll be waiting around Thakhet."

"It's a deal, little buddy. Now don't let me down."

"I'll be there."

After the briefing, they picked up their mission kits and left for their aircraft. Charlie and Bill walked out together. *"I don't feel right,"* Charlie said, almost to himself.

"What's the matter?" Bill asked.

"I don't know. It just doesn't feel right... "

"What doesn't feel right?"

"I don't know," Charlie repeated.

"Stand down. It isn't worth it for one mission," Bill replied.

"It's not that, I just feel strange. I'm usually up for these flights, but today things don't feel right."...

"Look, stand down. Get someone else or just abort."

"I can't do that. Some one else would have to fly it." Charlie said.

"Charlie, don't take any chances. If you don't feel right, then something's wrong. Look, if you have to fly, stay to the west. Go after the single movers. John will cover us if we need him."

"I don't know."

"Charlie, we're never far apart. What FM frequency do you use?"

"93.7"

"I'll give you a call in about forty-five minutes. Let's see how things are going. OK?"

"Thanks, Bill. I'll be all right, but give me a call anyway."

"Forty-five minutes."

Bill continued to his aircraft. Tonight he was flying with Ed Hardy. Ed was waiting for him at the aircraft. *"All set, Sir?"* Bill asked.

"Ready to go. What's with Charlie Green? I saw you two in deep conversation."

"Aw, nothing. He has the jitters tonight," Bill replied.

"I have the jitters every night, particularly when I'm flying with you," Ed said, seriously.

Bill looked at him. *"I make you nervous?"*

"No. It's just that whenever we fly together we always find a lot of trucks and more guns. Those guns make me nervous."

"Sir, did you ever think that we find a lot of trucks, because we work well together?"

"That never occurred to me. I just figured it was plain bad luck." Ed replied.

"Well, Colonel Hardy, Sir. When I fly with less capable pilots, I spend more of my time watching them and less time looking for movers. You have a good feel for location, so I don't waste any time finding the Trail. I've spent a lot of nights just trying to find where some damn fool got us to."

"OK, Captain. Your super pilot is ready to transport you to the wars," Ed chuckled. He liked Bill and was impressed with the way he worked the strikes. The captain was living up to his billing and the 23rd truck kills had doubled since Bill had been put in charge of the night program. Colonel Benjamin asked Ed to fly with Bill tonight to see how the captain was holding up. Sean had suggested to Benjamin that Bill might be taking too many risks. So far it didn't seem like much was bothering the captain. Ed would see about the risks during the mission.

Ed climbed into the O-2 first and settled himself in the pilot's seat. Bill followed and quickly strapped into the right seat. They started the engines and taxied to the arming area where the armorer pulled the safety pins from their rockets and flares. Ed called the tower for clearance and took off.

As they passed Thakhet, Bill called Charlie on the radio. *"Zorro Two Eight, NAIL Zero Two."*

"Hi, Bill."

"Where are you?"

"I'm past Thakhet and heading for Route 23."

"Stay loose. Let me know if you need any help."

"Roger, Bill. Be careful."

"Where's John tonight?"

"I'm on; listening to you two young squirts mess up radio discipline. I thought I taught you better."

"Check your mike, John. Your false teeth may be getting caught," Bill ribbed him.

"It's not his false teeth; it's his long gray beard. It keeps shorting out the mike," Charlie answered.

"Did your buddy shoot at you, John?"

"I told you he would and he did. Didn't you guys see it?"

Bill shook his head negative. "We didn't, John. Tomorrow for sure, same time, same place. I'll get here early and hold high."

"I didn't see anything either," Charlie said.

"Where're you headed, John?"

"I'm going to cover Route 12."

"We're off to Golf. Keep in touch. Two Eight, give me a call when you get to the intersection of 23 and 122. I'll fill you in on anything we see coming off 911."

"Thanks Zero Two. Call you later."

"Be careful, little buddy. It's dangerous out here now that they've brought in the big guns," John radioed.

"Take care, John. See you later."

"You three go back a few years, don't you?" Ed said, on the intercom.

"Charlie and I were in the same basic class. John was our military check pilot. When the civilian instructors figured we could fly, John gave us our check rides. That was almost ten years ago," Bill replied.

"Why do you know so many people?"

"It isn't that big an Air Force. I spent a couple of years as a general's aide. It got me around quite a bit since I was also his pilot."

"No wonder," mused Ed.

"It isn't just that. Can you name everyone in your pilot training class?" asked Bill.

"God, no!"

"I can. I have a funny memory. It won't let go of some things. It doesn't work all of the time, but it's good at names and maps."

"Maps?"

"Yeah, I get a good look at a map and I can recall it almost exactly."

"That explains why you have an easier time at night," Ed said, shaking his head.

"Probably. I can remember where the high spots are."

"More than a few people spend all of their time out here watching for mountains. They never bother looking for trucks," Ed nodded in agreement.

"I'm not surprised. How're the navigators doing?"

"You better start giving them some check rides."

"Are you trying to tell me something, Colonel?"

"See for yourself. Fly with Lieutenant Comers if you want a real experience, enough. Let's see what we've got tonight."

"Can you make out the road?" Bill asked.

"It's still light enough. I can make it out, but I can't see any detail," Ed answered.

"OK. Start an easy right turn. Keep the road to our right. I'll see what we have."

"Break right! Break right!" Bill yelled into the mike. Ed banked the aircraft hard right and pulled back on the stick. A stream of tracers raced by on the left.

"Where did <u>they</u> come from?"

"I don't know. What the hell are they shooting at us for? We don't have any bombs or guns on this plane."

"Alleycat, NAIL Zero Two," Ed called.

"Roger, Zero Two. What's all the action?"

"The action is us giving them some target practice. We haven't even got a mover. Something must be up. Where's our Nimrod?"

"Coming up fast. He has a visual on the gunfire. They weren't just shooting ZPUs. Those rounds exploded above you." Alleycat answered

"No shit! It seems to have stopped, now. I saw two separate streams," Ed said, over the radio.

"Nimrod told us he saw over a dozen bursts, NAIL. That's two clips worth. Did you do something to make them angry?"

"I don't think so. That's the first time I've been the target right at dusk. It's tough seeing those tracers in this light. We better be careful in the future and stay higher until it gets dark. I suspect that they could see us against the residual light in the west..."

"Makes sense, NAIL. We'll put it in the report."

"NAIL Zero Two, Nimrod Two Five."

"Hi! Mike. Did you see the guns?" Bill answered.

"I saw the bursts. I didn't see where they came from."

"Stay east. I'll keep looking to see if we can find what they don't want us to see."

"NAIL, we have a Redbird inbound, standard load."

"Thanks, Alley."

"Joe, are you up on FM?"

Bill didn't get an answer.

"Alleycat, NAIL Zero Two. Are you in contact with NAIL Three Seven?"

"Roger."

"Ask him to come up on FM 93.7, please."

"Roger, NAIL, 93.7."

"Zero Two, this is Two Four on FM."

"Joe, where're you?"

"Route 9."

"Did you sight anything unusual?"

"No. We don't have a thing."

"Well, we got two clips of 37mm or 57mm fired at us as soon as we got here. Something is up, be careful. Stay on this FM. The Zorros are on as well."

"Roger, Bill. Don't push it."

"Colonel, do some ziggies over the road. Don't make normal turns. I'll check it as we cross."

For fifteen minutes they flew back and forth across that section of the road. They found nothing. Suddenly, about ten miles to the west, the sky lit up as a string of flares illuminated. Immediately after the flares showed, the sky filled with red-orange balls and multiple small white explosions all going up and fast.

Ed Hardy looked at Bill, *"I wonder what they're shooting at? Do you suppose someone's under those flares?"*

"Yes, Sir. Someone's definitely under those flares and visible to the gunners. I can't tell how far away they are, but I'll bet it's Candle up there, those assholes!" Bill shook his head in dismay.

"Alleycat, this is NAIL Zero Two," Bill radioed.

"Roger, Zero Two. Alleycat here."

"Please ask Candle to hold up on the flares. They must've someone trapped under...."

Then on Guard they heard the screaming transmission....

"Bill, I'm hit! I'm hit!"

Bill immediately flipped the UHF to Guard (*All military planes have a receiver permanently set to receive transmissions on the UHF Guard channel, 243.0. In order to transmit on Guard, the radio had to be reset to 243.0.*)

"Charlie, I hear you. Are you OK? Is that you under those flares?" He turned to Ed.

"Head for that flak, Sir."

As soon as the call was received, Ed had banked and headed the O-2 to the west.

"Nimrod, we're moving west. Please cover us."

"I have your lights. I'll be here."

"Joe, pick up point Golf. We're heading for Charlie," Bill said on Guard.

"Roger, I'll advise Alleycat," came over their FM radio.

"Charlie, can you read me?"

The voice on the radio was strained. ***"I'm hit, Bill. The plane's on fire. Can you see it?"***

"Not yet, we're on the way. Turn west. What's your heading?"

"I'm turning west. The planes on fire," Charlie's voice was high and strained.

"Charlie, turn on your beacon. Invert, Nail Zero Two, get a mark on that beacon," Bill was barking out instructions on Guard Channel.

"Candle! No more flares! Do you hear? No more flares, you dumb shit!"

Candle didn't respond.

"Bill, I got to get out of here? The plane's burning."

"Hang on, Charlie. Are you OK? Were you hit?"

"I'm OK, but the engine's on fire. It's starting to come in the cockpit..."

"Invert, do you have a plot?"

"Invert paints the beacon at 075 degrees and sixty-seven miles."

"Give me winds, quick, Invert," Bill continued.

Bill turned on his flashlight and pulled his survival map from his left leg pocket. It had the radio aids and radials marked. Quickly, he found the position given by Invert and the nearest landmark. He tossed the survival map on the floor and opened his mission map. Charlie was right over a suspected enemy encampment.

"Charlie, turn to 260 degrees, repeat 260; acknowledge."

"Turning to 260, Bill. The flames are coming into the cockpit. When can I go?"

"Not yet. I'm going to put you on a hill. We'll get you in the morning. Can you hold out for a few more minutes?"

"The flames are in the cockpit!!!!" Charlie screamed.

"Get out on the wing, Charlie. Fly from there. Climb out and be sure the radio stays plugged in. Be careful!"

Charlie trimmed his burning T-28 for level flight.... unstrapped from the seat and then climbed out onto the bird's right wing ...the flames were rapidly encroaching the cockpit...he was being battered by the slip stream..... holding his position with his right hand and feet he could just reach the tip of the stick with his left hand.

He and his T-28 flew on...a literal ball of fire.

"Invert, give me target position."

"We have the beacon and skin paint, NAIL. He's heading 256 degrees at fifty-eight miles. Reported winds are from the east at twelve knots. Surface wind is estimated light and variable. Copy?"

"Copy, Invert. Charlie, are you still there?"

They could barely make out the words with the slipstream howling in Charlie's mike...

"I'm on the wing. I can hold it for a little longer. The flames are in the cockpit. Hurry, please hurry."

"Soon, Charlie, soon. Invert, position?"

"He's at fifty-five miles, NAIL."

Bill looked at the map and yelled, *"Jump, Charlie, jump!"*

Charlie released his hold on the canopy rail and the stick and let the slipstream tear him from his engulfed T-28. The roaring stopped...he was falling silently into the night above the Ho Chi Minh Trail....

Bill slumped back in his seat soaked with sweat. His mouth was dry and he couldn't move. He'd put his friend out over Laos in the middle of enemy-held terrain. If he was wrong, Charlie wouldn't have a snowball's chance in Hell.

"NAIL, Nimrod Two Five."

"Roger, Two Five," Ed replied.

"I hope you know what you're doing."

"Me, too," Ed said softly, to himself. He couldn't see a thing on the ground. He looked at Bill slumped in the right seat and shook his head in wonder. Bill had handled the bailout as if he'd practiced it every day. Ed didn't think he'd have had the courage to tell someone to jump on a radar plot, particularly a jump that was adjusted by figuring wind drift in his head.

"NAIL, Nimrod Two Five is going back to Golf. If you need anything, call."

"Roger, Nimrod. We can't do much here until morning. I'm going to wait," Ed answered and flew toward the place where Charlie had been told to jump. He was monitoring both FM and Guard.

"Bill, this is John on FM."

"Did you hear?" Bill answered, his voice cracking slightly.

"I heard. Has he called yet?"

"Not yet. Where are you?" Bill asked. *"We're at six thousand feet ..."*

"Coming down from the north at five thousand. I saw the plane hit and explode."

There were now two planes in the area listening for Charlie.

Charlie's chute had opened violently....he quickly checked the canopy....then as he started to look to see where he was.....he crashed through the tops of the jungle and came to a sudden stop suspended in the trees on the side of a small karst.

"Well, shit!!!!"

It was only a few minutes but it seemed like an eternity before the NAILs above heard his voice.

"NAIL Zero Two, this is Zorro Two Eight on Guard, do you read?"

The transmission back was weak, but it was Charlie!

"We got him! We got him!" Bill yelled over Guard channel.

"Charlie. Are you OK?"

"I'm fine, Bill. I'm in the trees on the side of a karst. I can hear movement and yelling down the hill."

"OK. Hide. Turn off the radio and don't turn it on again until first light. I'll be up here with the Marines at 0600."

"Roger."

"If you need something or get in trouble come up on the hour. Someone'll be listening. Hide and be quiet. Were you hurt?"

"I'm not hurt.

"Five Five, it was Candle. They lit me up. I never got a call or anything. They just lit me up and left me to die!!!!"

"I hear you, Charlie. We'll settle with them when we get you out. See you tomorrow."

"Is John up there?"

"I'm here."

"You were right, John. See you guys in the morning. Two Eight out."

"Alleycat, NAIL Zero Two," Ed called.

"Roger Zero Two, Alleycat is here. Very good work, NAIL."

"Thanks, Alleycat. Have you advised Rescue?"

"They've been alerted. Briefing for Sandys and Jollys is scheduled for 0430 hours at NKP. You are coordinating."

"Thanks, Alleycat. Will you maintain a listening watch for two eight? We're going back and get some rest."

"We can't pick up his radio; it hasn't got enough range. But we'll keep planes clear of the area and have someone in range every hour. "

"Thanks, Alleycat. Some night," Ed replied.

After thinking for a moment Ed added," You better get Candle on a leash. This is the second time Candlestick has flared the night fighters. Please, keep them in their own area."

"They reported that they were under the control of TFA."

"That's not likely. Are you going to do anything about this flare dropping?" Ed asked.

"Negative Zero Two, you can solve your problems at NKP," Alleycat replied.

Ed didn't reply. He shook his head in disbelief as he flew the plane. Bill was exhausted and said nothing all of the way back to NKP.

After landing Ed said**, "We better both go to TUOC now but then you get some rest. I'll stay at TUOC tonight to work with the rescue planners. You go out in the morning."**

"Yes, Sir thanks. Will you take care of the Candle thing?" Bill asked.

"I'll talk to their commander," Ed replied. He wondered why Bill seemed so calm about the flaring. It wasn't like him to ignore the Candle error that had resulted in his friend getting shot down. He shrugged off his thoughts. There wasn't any time for worrying.

There was a lot of activity at TUOC where preparations had already begun for the morning rescue attempt. It was 2008 hours when Charlie bailed out and 2130 by the time Bill left TUOC for his hootch. He stopped by the NAIL Hole, one of the rooms in the NAIL hootch area where two guys lived in the back half and the front half was a bar. He grabbed a beer, tried to relax and found Ralph there relating the story to half a dozen FACs.

"Hey, Bill. Colonel Hardy said you found the only safe place within thirty miles for Charlie to jump."

"We won't know until morning if I was right..."

"Did Candle really flare him on purpose?"

"They were only following their orders from TFA. It wasn't their fault," Bill answered, *"It was just one of those things."*

The group thought it was unusual for Bill to give TFA or Candle any credit, but no one wanted to chance his anger, so they let it pass.

"*Bill,*" Ralph asked, changing the subject, "*how did you know to have him stand on the wing?*"

"*One of my instructors in primary told me about doing that to shake up his students.*"

"*You gotta be shitting me.*"

"*No, it's true. It just came to me when he said the flames were in the cockpit.*"

"*Captain, I hope you're up there if I get in trouble,*" said one of the young lieutenants.

Historical Note: Jerry Dwyer related during one of the many evenings in the Nail Hole that he had seen a civilian instructor in primary pilot training actually get out on the wing of a T-34.

CHAPTER FIFTY ONE
Nakhon Phanom Royal Thai Air Base (NKP)
4 January 1968, early the next morning

At 0400 hours, the alarm shattered his deep sleep. He swung his feet off of the metal bunk bed....located his flip flops ....and padded down the deck along the front of the hooch to the bathroom. Afterwards he dressed in his flight suit, jungle boots and NAIL Go-to hell-hat and walked to TUOC, stopping briefly at the club for a quick cup of coffee. Breakfast could wait.

He'd slept for just less than four hours and felt on the edge of adrenalin high. The night was clear and cool and as he walked towards NAIL Ops he thought about Charlie. He'd had to spend eight hours in the jungle at night. Bill shuddered and increased his pace.

"Any word?" Bill asked, as he entered the briefing room.

"Charlie talked to Zorro Three Five once, at midnight and to NAIL Seven Three at 0300. The slopes are looking for him but he's OK," Zack replied.

"How far's the crash site from his position?"

"At least ten miles. Most of their search is probably concentrated nearer the wreckage," Zack said, confidently.

"Who's Nail Zero Two?" A big blond, chunky captain asked, walking into the room.

"It's Five Five and I'm Bill Thompson."

"I'm the rescue commander, Don Combs," he said, sticking out his hand.

"How do we do this?" Bill asked, shaking hands.

"You go out and find him. When you positively identify him, we come in and get him out…. a piece of cake."

"OK. Where do you want me?"

"As soon as you locate him, get out of the area. We've got our patterns with the Jollys and you'll be in the way. Go up to eight thousand feet if you want to watch."

"Great. I know where I tried to put him and we should find him in good shape. He'll be on the top or on the side of a small karst."

"How do you know that? It was a night bailout…"

"I told him where to jump," Bill said.

Don Combs looked at Bill skeptically. Zack North called for everyone's attention and introduced Bob Friend, a young second lieutenant from Invert, the radar site at NKP.

"We plotted his hit here and then tracked him to this position where Captain Thompson told him to jump. The plane impacted approximately here,

or at least that's when the beacon stopped, and we estimate from the winds that he's here." Lieutenant Friend was pointing to the east side of a karst, two thirds of the way up.

"How'd you find that at night?" Don asked.

Everyone was looking at Bill.

"I had him turn on the beacon and called Invert. They gave me a plot of his position. We turned him toward that hill and told him to jump when he was approaching it. The radar guys did all the work."

The Invert lieutenant was beaming. It was the first time he had participated in a rescue and he was pleased to be getting some credit.

"We do a lot of work with the controllers at Invert. They have a lot of practice picking up beacons and marking targets. Right, Lieutenant?" Bill asked.

"Yes, Sir. We mark some beacons every day. Our equipment is accurately calibrated and I'm certain of this plot."

"Captain Combs, it's your turn," Zack said.

Don stood, proceeded to the podium and went through the standard rescue briefing. Call signs were assigned and responsibilities reviewed. It was thorough and very professional. Bill was quite impressed with the rescue team. When he got to his aircraft, he found Sean waiting for him. *"I figured you could use some help. The bird's pre-flighted. I thought I'd fly and you can look. I had them pull out the right window,"* Sean said.

"Great. Let's go."

It was 0530 when they crossed the Mekong. Sean took the O-2 up to eight thousand feet as they flew east toward the karst. When Bill pointed out the area, Sean turned the aircraft to the south of the hill to mislead anyone on the ground watching them. They continued to fly straight and level about three miles south of the bailout area.

At 0550, their radio came to life. *"NAIL, this is Zorro Two Eight."*

"Charlie, it's us," Bill took a deep breath and sighed.

"Hi! Bill. Glad to see you. What happens now?"

"Are you in any difficulty?" He asked Charlie, while motioning for Sean to turn to the north.

"No. I'm at the edge of a clearing and looking at you to the south, headed east. Now you're turning north."

"Anyone around?"

"I heard people last night but there hasn't been any noise for at least an hour. They never got close to where you put me."

"Do you have a panel?"

"Roger, orange and white."

"Two or one?"

"An orange one and a white one."

"Stand on the orange one. Don't wave it around."

"I got him," Sean said, almost immediately. *"See..., by the large tree at the right edge of the clearing about two thirds of the way up the east side!"*

"Tally Ho, Zorro Two Eight. Stand by." Bill switched to the rescue frequency. *"Sandy Lead, this is NAIL Five Five."*

"Sandy Lead."

"We've got him identified and located. He's OK. There are no known hostiles in the immediate vicinity. We'll remain at eight thousand and direct you to him."

"Sandy Lead, I've got you in sight, NAIL. Describe his location," Don sounded calm and businesslike.

"Look at the clearing on the east side of the hill. Find an orange panel at the north edge of the clearing. He's standing on the panel."

"Roger, NAIL. I've got the clearing. I'm going in for a closer look." There was a pause, and they watched as the A-1 flew over the clearing.

"I've got the orange panel and I see the survivor... break... break...Jolly One Four, start your run."

Bill watched the A-1s as they circled the clearing. There was no apparent ground activity. The two Jolly Green HH-3 helicopters approached from the south. One turned to the west and the other came toward the clearing, dropping rapidly down to a hundred feet above the trees.

"Sandy Lead's going to layout some CBU. Keep your eyes open. Sandy Two, cover me."

Don flew along the base the hill dropping CBU. As he finished, Two yelled, ***"Ground fire! I've got it. It's coming from the base of the hill."***

While the two Sandys made repeated 20mm strafing runs and dropped a pair of white phosphorous bombs to screen the Jolly Green, the big Jolly Green helicopter hovered over Charlie. A jungle penetrator was lowered and the PJ in the Jolly saw Charlie fold down the seat, clip his snap link on his harness to the penetrator and give him a thumbs up.

"Survivor is on the penetrator.....survivor is in the door....let's get the fuck out of here"

Bill and Sean were both holding their breath waiting for the helicopter to move off to safety. They watched as Charlie was winched aboard. Immediately after he was in the helicopter, it rapidly moved away.

"This is Jolly One Four. The pilot is aboard and OK. We didn't get any ground fire."

"Roger, Jolly. We got a bunch from the base of the hill," said Sandy Lead.

"Excuse, me, Sandy Lead. Would you be so kind as to put a Willy Pete on that gun position that's been bothering you. We've got a little surprise for them," Sean said, over the radio.

"Roger, NAIL. Sandy Lead marking."

They watched as a 2.75 inch Willy Pete rocket hit the trees at the base of the hill. *"Thank you, Sandy Lead. All rescue aircraft clear the area. NAIL Four Five is going to put a strike on the hill."*

"Alleycat, NAIL Four Five," Sean radioed.

"Roger, NAIL. We have your aircraft. It's a flight of four 105s with full loads of 750s. Call sign is Thunder. They're waiting for you on 296.4."

"Roger, Alleycat. 296.4"

"Thunder, NAIL Four Five," Sean called, as soon as he set the frequency.

"Hey, Sean. We've got your mark. Where do you want 'em? We're on top of you at fifteen thousand."

"Thanks, John. Each of you take a side of the hill. String them out along the base. NAIL is clearing the area to the south. We're going to six thousand feet. Winds are from the east at ten knots."

"We have you in sight, NAIL. Thunder flight, Lead'll take the east side; Two has north, Three west, and Four south. Two passes each. Lead's in to the north."

Sean watched as the lead Thunderchief passed his altitude and then pickled off a pair of 750-pound bombs. The 105 then was enveloped in white mist as the G forces of its rolling pullout ripped the humid air. Sean turned his attention to the two bombs as they continued their fall to the base of the hill.

"Lead's off."

The two bombs impacted the base of the hill. The explosions erupted in the green jungle in dark orange and black and the visible shock waves blasted through the trees.

Thunder, you are cleared random runs and breaks. Call in and off.

The smoke was heavy as the four 105s worked over the area. When they finished dropping their bomb loads, Thunder Lead called…

"Thunder, rejoin at fifteen thousand, left turn. Sean, did we get them?"

"I'm sure you did.

Holy shit!!! Thunder…Look at that!!!! Did you see it?"

Below NAIL Five Five's twisting O-2 the entire west side of the karst exploded like a volcanic eruption.

"Take a look. The side of the hill just blew up."

"I'll be damned. It must've had tunnels or caves. It looks like they had some ammo stored there."

"Thanks, Thunder. See you next time we're in Bangkok."

"Glad to help. Pass the BDA to Alleycat."

"Who was that?" Bill asked.

"John Gross. He was my roommate in Primary Pilot Training. Right now he's at Korat. I called him last night and we arranged to get some bombs down here."

"Small world."

"Ain't it, though?"

"Let's go see Charlie."

A small aerial armada followed the helicopters as they returned to NKP. The F-105s made a high-speed pass across the field and turned southwest toward Korat. The two Jolly Green helicopters were next, gliding in over the runway and then turning to the center taxiway and stopping in front of the waiting vehicles. The two Sandys also made a low pass over the field, pulling up to downwind as each plane passed the parked helicopters.

Sean turned onto initial approach and made a normal pattern. He was followed by Colonel Benjamin. The O-2s returned to their parking area and the pilots headed for the hospital to see Charlie.

When they arrived, they were told that Charlie was with the flight surgeon and would be remaining in the hospital for several hours. The corpsman thought he'd be released that afternoon. Bill left word for Charlie that they'd meet him at the club that night. Bill and Sean then went back to the club for their missed breakfasts and then went to the NAIL hootches and crashed onto their bunks…with smiles on their faces.

CHAPTER FIFTY TWO
Nakhon Phanom Royal Thai Air Base (NKP)
5 January 1968, mid afternoon in TUOC

At 1500 hours, Bill walked into INTEL.

"You ready to fly, Lieutenant?" He asked Zack North.

"Yes, Sir. We have your mission on the board as an orientation," Zack was still excited and a little concerned.

"Do you have area maps?"

Zack held up his case. It was large enough to carry maps of the entire world. Bill smiled. **"Come on, we don't have any specific mission and I want to be ready when John takes off."**

"Do you think someone's really shooting at him?"

"I haven't got the foggiest notion. But just in case, I've requested some assistance."

Bill led Zack North to the O-2 and explained things to him as he preflighted the aircraft. They were using a normal O-2, rather than one of the black, night aircraft. He showed Zack the door-jettison procedures and explained how to jump out if it should be necessary. They strapped in; Bill started the engines and taxied to the end of the runway. They took off and turned towards the Mekong River and Laos.

It was 1600 hours. John was scheduled to cross the river at 1800. He had two hours to show the area to Zack and be in position to watch for John's shooter.

They flew at ten thousand feet, well above the level for ground fire. Zack had taken out his maps and was following their progress over the ground. When they got to Mu Gia, his eyes were as big as saucers.

"Is it dangerous?"

"Not really. There isn't anything going on at the moment and they aren't likely to shoot just for the fun of it. Look over there." As he pointed to east of the pass. **"That is North Vietnam. Now look straight ahead of us."**

"What am I looking for?" Zack wanted to know.

"See the peak in front of us to the east of the pass?"

Zack nodded. **"I see it..."**

"Ok. Now look out your side and watch the way we're moving over the ground," Bill continued.

"We aren't flying straight," Zack said. *"The plane's pointing at the mountain, but we're moving to the left of it..."*

"Right. If some gunner aims ahead of us, he'll shoot off to our right. This doesn't fool a radar-controlled gun but there are only a few of those around here," Bill said. He banked away and headed to the south. *"I want to show you Golf and Foxtrot before we head back."*

Zack got a good look at both interdiction points and at the cliff face at Foxtrot. They both looked like lunar landscapes, barren of any vegetation and ringed with hundreds of round bomb craters.

"Seen enough?"

"Thanks, Captain. I've been briefing you people for over six months about these places and this's the first time that I've seen them."

"Think it'll help?" Bill asked.

"Yes, Sir. It sure will. Particularly when we try to pinpoint the locations and the BDA."

"It's time to get ourselves set up for John's shooter."

Bill turned the O-2 to the west and they flew toward NKP at eight thousand feet.

"Alleycat, NAIL Five Five."

"This is Alleycat. We have a flight for you, Five Five."

"Roger, NAIL Five Five is ready to copy."

"Hobo One Five will meet you at six thousand feet over the west end of the rooster tail, on 302.8. Their ETA is 1750."

"Thanks, Alleycat. Hobo One Five at 1750 on 302.8."

"Good hunting, NAIL."

Bill continued toward the shooter's position descending until he reached sixty five hundred feet. When he was over the ridge line known as the rooster tail, he called on the UHF radio, *"Hobo One Five, this is NAIL Five Five."*

"Hi, Bill. We're waiting for you. Look out to your right."

"Thanks, Dave. Who's with you?"

Two A-1s were flying about a half mile away and a little below him. *"Another one of John's old students. Call sign One Seven. How do we do this?"*

"I want to stay to the south. You two get on my left side and stay south of me. We don't want to scare off the shooter. I'll pick up John when he takes off and keep him in sight. If anyone fires at him, I'll mark and clear to the east. You come in south to north and clear straight ahead or a little west. Recover to five thousand. I'll go to four thousand."

"Roger, Bill. What about lights?"

"No lights."

"Invert, NAIL Five Five."

"NAIL Five Five, this is Invert... "

"We're set up on 302.8. I have two Hobos, One Five and One Seven. Please advise when Zorro Two six is airborne."

"Roger, NAIL Five Five. Will advise."

Bill turned to Zack. *"Now, we wait for John to take off. Get your map out and be ready to mark the gun location."*

It was less than five minutes when Invert called. *"Zorro Two Six is airborne. He'll be at the river in one minute."*

"Thanks, Invert. Have him come up on 302.8. Tell him about the Hobos," Bill radioed.

"Roger, NAIL."

A moment later they heard, ***"Bill, this is John."***

"We're waiting for you. What's your position?"

"I'm at three thousand starting across the river."

"I have him," Hobo 15 called, ***"He's over the river climbing.***

"John, what altitude are you climbing to?"

"I'm going to five thousand. Who's with you?"

"We've got a couple of Hobos. Dave's in the lead."

"Buenos noches, compadre," came over the radio.

"Bien, bien. Como esta. Quien es?"

"Theese ees Jose. Ees somebody peeking on poor Juan?" came over the radio.

"Is that really you, Jose?" John's voice.

"None other. Dave and I wouldn't miss this. We've got you covered."

"You're a long way from Pleiku," John replied.

"OK, you guys, enough of that crap. We can bullshit later. Dave, do you have him?" Bill interrupted.

"We have the Zorro."

"John, is it usually in the same place?" Bill asked.

"Every night."

"Give us a call a few seconds ahead."

The three aircraft paralleled John's course as he climbed. Bill was a mile south of John and the Hobos were south of Bill. Bill set his trim for rocket firing and waited.

"Anytime now, Bill," John radioed.

It was dark as Bill looked at the ground beneath John's aircraft attempting to spot the telltale muzzle flash from a weapon.

Several things happened at once.

Bill saw a flash and turned immediately to the north. He kept his eyes on the ground spot. Zack yelled, **"Look Out!"**

Bill saw the flash from the airburst out of the corner of his eye, but he didn't turn the aircraft away. He kept the ground mark in sight as he reached up and armed his rockets.

"Did you see it? Did you see it?" John was shouting over the radio.

"We saw it, John. Climb to five thousand and stay east. Hobo, are you ready?" Bill's voice was terse.

"We saw the flak but not where it came from," Dave's voice came over the radio.

"I will mark and pull off to the east at four thousand. John, stay above me. Hobo…. lay in CBU on a north/south line. I am marking now!"

Bill rolled in and fired the Willy Pete rocket. As It blasted from the pod, Bill quickly shut his eyes to avoid the flaring motor's intense light….as he rolled and pulled off to the left, he watched it impact short of the target, but on line.

"Dave, it's a good mark. The target's on a north/south line through the smoke. Start at the smoke and lay the CBU north."

"Hobos are in."

Bill pulled up sharply and rolled to the east. He leveled his wings, cleared and rolled hard left. As soon as he was pointed toward the north, he rolled out. The sun had set but the afterglow was enough for Bill to continue to watch the billowing cloud of white smoke from his Willy Pete and look for the Hobos.

Neither he nor Zack were able to spot the A-1s but suddenly there were two streams of CBU bomblets exploding from the smoke north for several hundred yards. A larger explosion erupted out of the middle of the eastern stream of CBU.

"You got him, Dave. Something went up on the east side."

"That was Jose. We dropped together. Want us to come around?"

"Roger. Lay east/west through the hit. John, go ahead on your mission. We'll clean it up and I'll have a night NAIL check it out later. We don't have a scope."

"Thanks, little buddy. Adios, David, Jose."

"Anytime, John. See you later. Jose's recovering at NKP for the night," Dave radioed.

"Any ordnance remaining, Hobo?"

"Only guns. We used all our CBU."

"Thanks, Hobo. See you at TUOC. We're RTB."

"See anything else, Zack?"

"The only thing I saw was the CBUs and the explosion. What'd we hit?"

"It was a pretty small explosion but it was right where the shot came from. Did you see the size of the airburst?"

"It was close!" Zack replied. He hadn't expected to be shot at.

"Not really," Bill smiled. *"It's getting dark and everything looks closer at night. It didn't look like an anti-aircraft shell. I can't imagine them shooting only one shell in any case. It was more like a signal."*

"A signal?" Zack was curious

*"Yeah. It could've been a mortar shell with a cut fuse, timed to go off at altitude as a signal to someone. I doubt if they were trying to hit John. More than likely, they signaled every night when they saw the first of the fighters take off. John always flies the first sortie and he gets here

before the NAILs. The Nimrods don't take off for another thirty minutes."

"That makes sense. I wonder why we didn't consider it before. John's been reporting these things for weeks."

"Wait until we get back and talk to the others. In any case, we probably destroyed the shooter's ammunition."

"Are you going to wait for another NAIL?"

"No. I'm not sure we could find the spot now. It's too late and there isn't much sense wandering around in the dark. I don't want to turn the lights on since they're not shielded and we'll stand out like a Christmas tree. Let's go home."

They returned to NKP, entered the pattern, landed and taxied past the NAIL aircraft parking area to a spot near TUOC where Bill stopped the aircraft. Zack unbuckled his harness and began picking up all his maps and equipment. With this accomplished, he opened the right-side door and stepped out.

Zack leaned back into the Duck and to Bill said **"Thanks for the ride, Sir."**

"You're most welcome, Zack."

CHAPTER FIFTY THREE
Nakhon Phanom Royal Thai Air Base (NKP)
5 January 1968, minutes later in the Nail aircraft parking area

Bill had dropped the lieutenant off near TUOC and then taxied to the NAIL parking area. Instead of removing his equipment, he waited while the ground crew installed large flare racks on the outboard pylons and two rockets on each of the inboard pylons. As soon as the ground crew was finished and the plane refueled, he started up and taxied back to the runway.

As soon as the arming crews pulled the safety pins from the flares and rockets, he checked to see that the active runway was clear and nothing was approaching to land. It was clear so he taxied onto the runway and took off without any lights and without any clearance from the tower. In the dark, no one noticed that it wasn't a regular night aircraft. Most likely, no one even noticed that an O-2 had taken off.

Bill set out for Foxtrot, climbing the little plane to ten thousand feet. He didn't report to Alleycat or to anyone else. When he was about twenty miles from the Trail, he began to climb again. At twelve thousand feet, he eased the throttles back and leveled off. He armed the flare racks and set up an orbit to the west of Foxtrot.

As soon as he was set up, he made one call on the NAIL Squadron FM. *"Frequency,"* was all he said.

"Three Zero One Four," was the reply.

Bill switched to UHF and set in 301.4, the Candlestick frequency for that night. Then he listened. After a few minutes he heard what he was waiting for. *"Candle, this is Alleycat. I've got a flight of two F-4s inbound for you."*

"Thank you, Alleycat. We have a convoy for them."

"I'll pass them to you on 301.4 when they're five miles south of Foxtrot," came over the radio.

Bill looked down intently, trying to see the large C-123 aircraft but he couldn't pick it out in the darkness. He knew the wind was from the southwest and he positioned himself a couple miles west for the best flaring position. He started to make tight turns to stay as close to that position as he could.

Bill heard the fighters check in, *"Candle, this is Canasta flight with two."*

The Candle reply followed immediately, *"Roger, Canasta. Candle has a convoy at point Foxtrot. There are a reported twenty vehicles on the road under us. We'll be dropping a string of six flares in two minutes. They'll be at eighty five hundred feet moving west to east. The road is underneath and runs generally in a north/south direction..."*

Bill triggered his flares one at time on a northerly heading. By the time the first one started to flicker, he had dropped all four and was circling to the west, watching.

"Who's that? Stop! Stop! We're underneath, stop!" the Candle pilot screamed—literally screamed—over the radio. Even at their altitude, which was half again as high as the night NAILs flew, they were in range of the antiaircraft guns.

The skies over Foxtrot were again lit by the red-orange balls, streaks of red and many, many smaller white explosions. As Bill watched, the big airplane headed in a southwesterly direction, the closest escape from the light. The fighters saw the flak and wisely remained at altitude. They decided to wait and see what was happening.

It looked as though Candle would make it without damage when one of the gunners got lucky, found the range and hit them. Two airbursts peppered the right wing and one shredded the top of the vertical stabilizer. Bill did not see the explosions or the small pieces of the plane falling off.

"We're hit! We're hit**!" the pilot screamed. He didn't sound very composed. ***"Alleycat, we're hit!"

"Say again, Candle. Are you still flying? What happened?"

"Candlestick, this is Canasta. You could always sue them, couldn't you?" The fighter pilots were amused by Candlestick's reaction to the gunfire.

"Alleycat, this is NAIL Four Nine. We'll pick up the Foxtrot convoy and Canasta flight. "

"Roger Four Nine. Contact Canasta and go to 297.4. Canasta, did you read?"

"Canasta going to 297.4."

"NAIL Four Nine to 297.4 and covering Foxtrot."

Bill turned his plane toward NKP and lowered the nose. He let the speed build up and stopped just short of redlining the engine. He wanted to be back on the ground before Candle reached the base.

He continued to listen as the Candle crew talked to Alleycat.

Candle had headed southwest for several miles while they made sure they had control of the big C-123. When they were sure they had no major damage, they slowly turned west toward NKP. They had taken shrapnel hits from the airbursts in the port wing and high on the tail but apparently did not have any serious damage. They were taking it slow to be sure, because they couldn't really see very much of the damage in the dark.

Bill continued to fly without any exterior lights and since it was night, no one saw the O-2 enter the traffic pattern and land. Bill landed and turned off the runway into the de-arming area. As soon as he pulled to a stop, a pickup screeched to a stop and two sergeants jumped out and removed both flare racks from the plane. The racks were thrown in the back of the pickup and it sped off.

Bill taxied in without comment or lights just as he had taxied out a few hours before. While he was parking the O-2, he saw fire trucks hurry to the runway and watched as the C-123 made its landing. The plane came to a stop on the runway and the crew exited it running.

Bill left the plane and the flight line. He walked to the O'Club allowing himself time to cool down. It'd been quite a night.

CHAPTER FIFTY FOUR
Nakhon Phanom Royal Thai Air Base (NKP)
6 January 1968, morning in the Nail Ops office

Colonel Benjamin and Ed Hardy walked into Operations in the middle of a conversation. They were still talking when they walked up to Jerry Hersey's desk.

"Good morning," Jerry said, standing up, which is the military custom when joined by a senior officer.

"The general doesn't like our after-action reports. He thinks the FACs are making up incidents to protect their jobs," Dave Benjamin said, shaking his head.

"What do you expect from a, a ... what's he call them?

Yeah, a Staff Woosie," Ed Hardy added.

"So, what's the problem?" Jerry asked. *"The real decisions are made at 7th Air Force, not here."*

"The problem is that the non-flying general and his team of Whiz Kids believe they can find trucks and destroy them without FACs. They're sending reports directly to the Pentagon without going through Saigon. I see the potential for a real disaster," Benjamin said.

"What do you want to do? What does the general want us to do?" Jerry looked puzzled.

"We don't really know. He flew off the handle this morning, when he read the Intelligence report about the gun that Bill blew up yesterday. He thinks we fabricated the entire signal business to thwart TFA.... his words," Ed Hardy reported.

"The incident with Candlestick didn't help his attitude either. Someone flared Candle and they were nearly shot down. It's a good thing Bill was on an orientation flight when it happened. There's no way an O-2 could get up to twelve or thirteen thousand feet with LAU/59 pods on it. We can't carry a lot of flares either," Ed commented.

"What kind of orientation flight?" Dave Benjamin asked, frowning at Ed.

"I don't know. Something to do with taking an Intel officer for a ride.

CHAPTER FIFTY FIVE
Nakhon Phanom Royal Thai Air Base (NKP)
6 January 1968, later that afternoon in the Nail Ops

"General Holland doesn't care much for the way we handle his Spotlight reports. Our pilots think a lot of them are phony. They call and tell us they have trucks. We look and the road's empty. He thinks we're calling it empty to frustrate TFA. Candle never contradicts the TFA reports. Well, no matter. He doesn't care for us and I'm afraid he doesn't care much for our resident fighter pilot. His aide doesn't help much either. She goes ballistic whenever she hears his name," Benjamin

commented. He shook his head, *"Whatever he did to the young lady, she really didn't like it."*

"The way I hear it, Bill invited her to keep her woosie ass out of the O'Club. He asked her if she knew the difference between one and two— one being the number of bars on her shoulder and two being the number of bars on his shoulder," Jerry replied, laughing.

"Well, he isn't helping the cause. Ed, will you ask him to stay away from the TFA people for a while and to avoid the general and his aide for the next century?" Benjamin was smiling.

"We'd better brief Sean. I think those two are getting pretty serious," Jerry remarked. Benjamin looked at Ed and he nodded in agreement. *"Since they got here, the very first day,"* Jerry continued. *"She and Sean hit it off when she took them to meet the general. He borrowed my jeep the next day to go looking for her."*

"Jerry, you talk to Sean. I don't want to get involved with that side of things," Benjamin directed. *"Let's make sure she isn't carrying tales back to TFA or the general."*

"I'll talk to him right now," Jerry said. He turned and walked toward the Stan Eval office.

CHAPTER FIFTY SIX
Nakhon Phanom Royal Thai Air Base (NKP)
6 January 1968, late afternoon in the NAIL aircraft parking area

Sharon was waiting for Sean in the NAIL aircraft parking area when he returned from his afternoon check-out flight for a new lieutenant. He debriefed the maintenance crew chief and turned toward the jeep. He put his gear in the back seat before getting in next to her.

"I'm done. This was an easy check ride and he passed so I told him to go to TUOC and do the out brief by himself. Can we stop by PE while I drop my gear off?"

"Sure. After that you can change in my trailer. I've got something special planned for tonight. I've prepared dinner myself," she was smiling.

Sean said, *"Great. I'm hungry. I'm always hungry after a flight."*

"I know," she nodded, *"I'm finished for the day, so we can be by ourselves for the rest of the night."*

"Where's your boss?"

"He had to go to a briefing in Saigon. There wasn't room on the plane for me and all of his staff, so I stayed home."

"Outstanding," Sean leered at her and she blushed.

"There's plenty of time for that," she chided him.

When they arrived at her trailer, Sean waited for her to close the door then reached for her. She pushed him away, wrinkling her nose. *"You smell just as bad as always; go take a shower while I fix us something to eat."*

"Ok, Ok. I'll clean up first," he said and walked to the bathroom. He was in the shower when he saw the door opening. He moved back as she stepped in with him.

"I need one, too," she said and reached for him.

"This is definitely the way to shower," he answered softly, holding her close.

They didn't finish dinner until much later that evening. Sean didn't even remember what Sharon fed them…he was so completely taken by the lovely lieutenant.

243

At 0600 the next morning, he was getting ready to return to the FAC area. Sitting with coffee, watching Sharon dress, he smiled and said, *"I have a great idea. Will you marry me?"*

She turned in surprise, *"Why? I don't want to be a widow."*

Sean was surprised by her reply. *"I'm not planning on dying,"* he protested.

"Seriously, Sean. I don't want to be married to a pilot. I'm not the pilot's wife sort of person. All of you expect your wives to be old fashioned stay-at-homes. You live in the past, when women only wanted to get married, have children, and stay at home. Can't we just enjoy ourselves? Have fun and leave it at that?"

Sean was completely taken back by her response. He felt like he had been punched in the stomach hard and it hurt. He'd been confident that Sharon would marry him and had been trying to find the right time to ask her for the past month. He suddenly felt deserted.

Sharon saw the expression on his face and tried to soften the effect. *"This isn't the time, Sean. We're in the middle of a war and you are flying out there every day. You don't need to be worried about a wife."*

Sean couldn't think of a response. He smiled weakly and drank his coffee. So much for that good idea.

CHAPTER FIFTY SEVEN
Nakhon Phanom Royal Thai Air Base (NKP)
8 January 1968, early afternoon in the Nail Ops Office

Colonel Benjamin left word for Sean to meet him after the colonel returned from his usual morning flight in Cricket West. The colonel flew in the mornings with one of the Laotian observers. They made a circuit of the western part of Laos, Cricket West, while the observer talked to the friendly forces on the ground. His reports went to Vientiane, for General Vang Pao and the Laotian Government and for the U.S. Ambassador, William H. Sullivan. These few daily sorties were all that the ambassador could depend upon being fragged by 7th Air Force. He had constantly requested the authority to order a constant and specific number of sorties to targets he selected in Laos. He believed that if he controlled his own air force that he could allocate these resources more efficiently in his area of responsibility. General Momeyer was fighting three wars (South Vietnam, North Vietnam and Laos) and was not about to lose control of any of his air assets. These few sorties every day into Cricket West were not related to the interdiction campaign on the Trail. Rather, Cricket West was just another one of the many special missions assigned to the NAILs.

Walking into Operations after lunch, Sean met Ed Hardy. *"Hi, Colonel. Is Colonel B in?"*

"He's waiting for you. There's an Army major with him."

Sean knocked on the colonel's door and entered. A heavy set Army major in a neatly- pressed summer uniform was sitting in a chair in front of Benjamin's desk.

"Sean, I want you to meet Major Walters. He's from MACV and they have a test they'd like to run."

Sean and the major shook hands although the Army officer did not get up out of his chair. Sean then sat in the vacant chair also in front of the colonel's desk.

MACV was the acronym for Military Assistance Command, Vietnam, and the senior U.S. military organization in Vietnam. Although each service had its own chain of command for the units involved in the conflict, they were all technically subordinate to MACV. Unfortunately, MACV was nothing but a bunch of various staffs. It had no real combat units and its staff officers often had no combat experience. Sean immediately anticipated a problem...probably a big problem...and a field grade problem.

"Captain, I've been sent by MACV to oversee a special, highly-classified test mission assigned to your squadron. Colonel Benjamin tells me that he's giving you the responsibility for flying the mission."

Sean glanced at the colonel, who was leaning back in his chair, watching the exchange. His face was expressionless. *"Go ahead, Sir. We're always glad to help the U.S. Army,"* Sean replied in his friendliest manner.

"That's a good attitude, Captain. I know you'll be proud to participate in this top secret mission," the major said, pompously, not realizing that everything that the 23rd TASS did was top secret. Hell, the war in Laos was top secret...the secret war.

Sean instantly disliked the major, maybe it was his *"I am wonderful and a major so listen up, kid"* attitude. The man wasn't an Army pilot and wore no combat decorations or qualifications on his very neatly-pressed uniform. His lapels carried the insignia of the Ordnance Corps, the "titless WACS" as they were called in the Army. Sean and the colonel were wearing fatigues.

"What kind of mission, Major?"

"We want you to test a "People Sniffer." It'll be mounted in one of your aircraft and tested over Laos."

"A People Sniffer?" Sean asked his expression and his voice both displaying incredulity.

"It's not funny, Captain! It's vital to our war efforts in country," the major replied, huffily.

"What in God's name do you want with a People Sniffer?"

"We intend to use it to locate Vietcong and North Vietnamese troops hiding in the jungles."

"Why not test it with your Army helicopters?" Sean asked.

"We have. We can't tell the difference between friendly and enemy troops. We need to calibrate the device where there aren't any friendlies."

Sean was becoming more and more skeptical. "Why here, major? We don't have any VC and damn few NVA."

"The test is designed to be flown in Mu Gia Pass, because we know it is full of North Vietnamese regulars," the major replied, reaching into his briefcase and retrieving a classified document folder.

"What can you smell from a mile above ground, Major?"

"We plan to use it much lower than that in our helicopters."

"Why test it here? We rarely get below five thousand feet, except in western Laos. We avoid Mu Gia Pass, Major. It's dangerous as hell below ten thousand feet."

"This mission profile calls for you to fly through Mu Gia Pass one hundred feet above the trees."

"Did you bring some Kryptonite from Saigon? We'll probably need it," Sean said, laughing, "and the red cape, too."

"It's not funny, Captain. This is a required mission. We've determined that the input from this test is vital to the war effort."

"What else does this mission require, other than Mu Gia?" Sean wanted to know.

"We have a team here to install the device in an O-2. They'll finish today. As soon as they complete the installation, we'll fly the plane locally to calibrate the sensors. Then we'll fly into Laos. We expect you to complete all sorties before the end of the week."

Sean looked at Colonel Benjamin. He hadn't offered any comments and his expression hadn't changed. Benjamin was an unusual commander. He'd flown in WWII and Korea and had seen it all. He watched the exchange between Sean and Walters but didn't indicate approval or disapproval. Sean turned back to Walters.

"Major, get your equipment installed. Let's see what we can do short of committing suicide. Colonel, I'll take the major with me to the flight line."

"It's your project, Sean. Do what's needed," Benjamin said.

"Yes, sir. Major, let's go."

Sean led the major from the room. When he glanced at Colonel Benjamin, the colonel was rolling his eyes.

The two walked to the O-2 ramp and overweight Major Walters was soaked with sweat by the time they arrived. He wasn't used to the temperature and the humidity and missed his air-conditioned office in Saigon.

"Has the aircraft been checked for gross weight limits?"

"The weight limitations have been waived for this test, Captain," Walters said.

"Who did that?" Sean asked.

"General Westmoreland's staff."

"No sweat, I'll check it out with 7th Air Force," Sean replied. *"They keep pretty close tabs on the things we put on these planes."*

"It's a classified project, Captain. You're not authorized to talk to anyone about it, except me and your commander."

Sean smiled at the major. He was thinking, *'Is this guy real? How can they come up here and send someone on a completely useless suicide mission, without getting 7th Air Force approval?'* He'd make some calls, regardless of the major's instructions.

"Captain O'Malley, how're you today?" Major Ari Comers, the Maintenance Squadron Commander, called out, as they walked into the O-2 hangar.

"Fine, Ari. This is Major Walters from MACV."

"We've met," Ari said and looked at Walters, *"Your engineers and my maintenance guys are about done. The plane is nearly one thousand pounds over gross weight limits."*

"The gross weight has been waived," Walters replied.

Ari looked at Sean, who shrugged. *"Why don't we pull everything we can, Ari? Drop the pods, the spare radios—everything possible."*

"We already have, Sean. It's still a thousand pounds overweight."

"Think it will fly?"

"Yeah, but don't jerk it around."

"When you get the equipment loaded, I'll take it for a spin around the local area. Let's see how it handles."

"That's better, Captain. A real professional attitude," Walter's demeanor and pompous attitude were almost more than Sean could tolerate. He felt sorry for the ground troops who were at the receiving end of this officer's staff work.

Later that day, they were ready. Sean took the plane up and flew several patterns, checking its handling characteristics.

The plane needed an additional ten knots on takeoff and landing but it didn't feel awkward. However, it climbed only three hundred feet per minute, a third of its usual performance. Sean landed and taxied to the hangar where the two majors were waiting.

"OK, Major Walters. We're ready to test the equipment. Who goes with us?"

"We'll show you how to do it. There'll be two of you required for the sampling missions," Walters stated.

"Two of us? None of you?" Sean asked, puzzled.

"That's right," Major Walters replied.

"I should've guessed," Sean commented, sarcastically. He told himself that he had better shape up. He was beginning to sound a lot like Bill.

CHAPTER FIFTY EIGHT
Nakhon Phanom Royal Thai Air Base (NKP)
9 January 1968, the NAIL flight line

The next day, Sean got one of the young navigators (he had selected the lightest one in the squadron) to fly the right seat. The right forward seat was removed for the test device and one of the rear seats removed to reduce weight. They took off and headed for the Mekong River with an A-1 Hobo flying top cover in case of ground fire. The lieutenant calibrated the device according to his instructions and they recorded grid coordinates with each reading.

Sean flew an east and west course between Thahket and an intersection on Route 12, thirty miles east of Thahket. He started at three thousand feet above the ground and lowered his altitude five hundred feet for each leg. When they were at one thousand feet, they started to get occasional readings. Sean then dropped to five hundred feet indicated, which was two hundred feet above the ground and they were getting a strong signal response.

Luckily they encountered no ground fire...and the Hobo... had been bored to tears.

They returned to base and proceeded to TUOC to brief the MACV major, who had found the fully air-conditioned TUOC building much more to his liking than the steamy flight line. After some time, Major Walters pronounced that he was pleased with the results. Sean and the navigator were then allowed into the secure room at TUOC where an Army lieutenant and a civilian tech rep were decoding the readings.

"What do they show? One reading was right over a small group of farmers along the road. They were probably waiting for their transportation," Sean said.

"That has to be one of these two, Captain. What kind of area were you over on the second one?"

Sean looked at the navigator, who answered, *"That was over a field. There was nothing in it but a large compost pit or something like that."*

"It figures. It's the same problem we had in the south. The machine can't tell the difference between people and dung," replied the tech rep, sarcastically.

"What do you mean? What're you testing for?" Sean asked.

"That's classified," Major Walters said.

"Methane," answered the Tech Rep.

"If I understand correctly, you're trying to find hidden Viet Cong and NVA troops by sampling the air for methane. The only problem is that you

can't tell the difference between live troops and piles of elephant shit? Do I have it right, Major?" Sean asked, very loudly.

The tech rep laughed aloud and the Army lieutenant reddened. Major Walters blustered, *"It isn't your decision to make, Captain. Your job is to fly the missions. We make the decisions on what is and what isn't important..."*

Sean didn't answer. He turned to the navigator and said, *"You're all done. I'll handle it from here."*

"You need someone to operate the equipment, Captain." Walters said, angrily.

"You have three that I can see, Major. One of you can run the equipment. I'll fly the plane."

"Looks like you've run into someone who isn't impressed with your title, Major," said the tech rep, smiling broadly. *"You may get some combat experience yet."*

"I'll see you thrown out of the service, Captain," Major Walters threatened. He ignored the civilian tech rep.

"What're they going to do, Major, send me to Vietnam?"

Walters stomped from the room. The lieutenant looked at Sean. *"I can't go with you, Captain. I'm scared."*

"Don't sweat it, Lieutenant. I'm sure the major is on his way to see Colonel Benjamin. This may turn out to be a wild day for everyone. Now, does this really work?"

"It does. We just can't tell whether we've picked up VC, NVA, piles of elephant shit...as you put it...or our own troops," answered the tech rep.

"If you have to send in someone to verify every sighting, then you might as well not have it.

That's why we wanted to see if it gave different readings for NVA alone," said the Army lieutenant.

"Why don't you use prisoners? Or send it to Hanoi with some of our good friends?"

The tech rep laughed, but the lieutenant remained serious. *"They determined that Mu Gia Pass was the best place to check a large sample,"* he said.

"Not likely," Sean replied. *"Not on my watch. Close up for now. We'll see what they want to do tomorrow. I'll let the crew chief know."*

Sean walked to the flight line and told the sergeant to wrap it for the day but to be ready in the morning for another flight. He returned to the 23rd TASS offices.

Walking in, he was met by Ed Hardy, who grabbed him by the arm and led him from the building. *"Come on. Let's go have a beer."*

"Is Colonel Benjamin with the major?" Sean asked.

"He is. They're talking to some general at MACV. You're the subject of their conversation."

"What a mess. A stupid scheme, managed by an inept and uncaring SOB," Sean said. *"That major doesn't give a shit about anything but his test."*

"Welcome to the real war. The major's just doing his job as he sees it. He isn't supposed to be concerned about you and your problems."

"Why did you and the colonel decide to do this thing?"

"We didn't. We left it up to you. Benjamin didn't figure you'd let them make you do anything stupid. This way we can pretend that you did it on your own and we can get the generals at 7th Air Force involved. If we turned it down right off, they would've come down on us...hard. Now you've

rejected it as unnecessarily dangerous. We can handle that...

Sean grinned. *"Politics! Always politics."*

"Part of life, Sonny, part of life."

CHAPTER FIFTY NINE
Nakhon Phanom Royal Thai Air Base (NKP)
9 January 1968, later that night at the O'Club

That night Sean was at the club with some of the Nimrod and Zorro pilots when Bill walked in. *"What're you doing back so early?"* Sean asked. It was only 2130 hours.

"I was a bad boy, so they sent me home early," Bill said, sitting down. *"I require a large drink of spirits. What're you doing here?"*

Sean reddened slightly. *"She's busy tonight. They have some sort of meeting going on."*

"Didn't you have a TFA special bomb drop tonight?" Mike Miller asked. *"How was our great aluminum overcasts?"*

"The B-52s missed Golf by over a mile. When I told Alleycat that they missed, I was sent home. They brought in Candle for the BDA. The great FAC in the sky put them right on target. I tried to get a photo run but Alley said they were all committed."

"I didn't think those guys ever missed. I think it's against SAC policy," Charlie Green piped in.

"They missed tonight. I don't know whether they goofed or if TFA gave them the wrong coordinates. I went out to check the target before the drop," Bill continued. *"The coordinates were one mile north and one mile west of the roads. I'm sure someone goofed when they gave them the drop point. I never checked it in TUOC. They said Golf,*

and I wrote down the map coordinates but I didn't check them against the map until I got out there; then I found that they were wrong."

"Someone moved Golf, did they?" Sean asked.

"Nah. It's right where we left it. The Arc Light bomb drop was supposed to be on Golf. As soon as I saw the error, I tried to get someone to listen. TFA, Alleycat, the bombers... anyone."

"You called the bombers?" Mike asked, surprised.

"On Guard. I gave them the change but all of the bombs fell out in the jungle, a mile off target. When I gave Alleycat a miss, they told me to take off. On the way back, I heard them vectoring Candlestick in. They hit the assigned coordinates all right but the coordinates weren't the target. What a mess."

"Did they hit anything?" Charlie asked. *"Sometimes we get a storage area that way."*

"I checked. All they did was set some trees on fire and make tons of toothpicks. A few trees were burning but there wasn't a road anywhere in sight. I used two of my flares checking it out."

"They won't like that," Sean said. *"No one in SAC dares make a mistake."*

"It probably wasn't theirs," Bill said, *"More than likely your buddies in TFA gave them the wrong data."*

"They're not my buddies."

"You could always fly your Sniffer over there and see if anyone is around," Mike added, looking at Sean.

"How's that going?" Bill asked.

"They want to calibrate it over Mu Gia," Sean replied.

"*Lovely,*" Mike replied. "*How're they going to get it out there?*"

"*They want me to fly through Mu Gia in the day time at two hundred feet and calibrate the damn thing,*" Sean said, with a disgusted tone.

"*You've got to be shitting me,*" Mike said. "*What kind of a fool would fly through Mu Gia at two hundred feet in the day time?*"

"*The Army major assured me that it was possible.*"

"*What Army major?*"

"*I think it's probably the one coming this way, right now. Look!*" Charlie said, pointing to the door.

"*Captain O'Malley, you're scheduled for the test at 0800 hours tomorrow,*" Major Walters said. "*The run will be as we briefed and General Teddler will be here for the briefing.*"

"*Yes, Sir. Be sure to tell General Teddler to bring his flight suit,*" Sean replied.

"*Who's General Teddler?*" Mike asked.

Walters frowned at Captain Miller. At that moment another voice chimed in. "*Yeah, Major, who's General Teddler?*" It was Ed Hardy, who walked up and pulled a chair to the table. He was with Major John Patterson. They both sat.

"*General Teddler is my boss. He's on his way here, right now. You'll fly the mission as briefed.*"

"*That's up to the captain. How are you going to handle it, Sean?*" Ed asked.

"*I don't think it's safe but I'll fly it if the general goes along.*"

"*Seems fair to me,*" Ed replied. "*What were your guys doing to the plane this afternoon, Major?*"

"*We installed two transmitters.*"

"You're nuts, Major," Mike said, shaking his head.

"I wouldn't fly through Mu Gia at two hundred feet even at night," Charlie added.

"You have your orders, Captain. I'll see you at 0800 hours," Major Walters said and strutted from the lounge.

"What're you going to do, Sean?" Bill asked.

"If the major or the general won't fly with me, I plan on taking it up myself and going somewhere else. If they do agree to fly, I don't know what I'll do."

"We need to be sure you get a full briefing at TUOC," Ed said.

"I'll take care of that," John replied. *"We're flying top cover for Sean."*

"Thanks, John." Sean said.

"Colonel, what did you hear about the TFA Arc Light?" Bill asked.

"The official report is a hit. TFA's estimating ten trucks destroyed and the road cratered in three places."

"I wonder what world they're living in. That sure wasn't the same place I looked."

"Denny Cutter flew over after you left. He agrees. They missed completely," Ed said. *"Leave it alone. The decision's been made and no one's going to change it. The words don't count anyway. What we need is results. We're already killing more trucks than they have. At least it seems that way from the reports."*

"What's going on, Colonel? We go out there every night, and we're lucky to find three or four trucks to hit. Candle sights large convoys every night and they're flying twice as high as we are.

The B-52's get credit for ten trucks that aren't even there. Does anyone care?" Mike asked.

"The key, my young friends, is to recognize that this is a war. Everyone over here believes that they're doing their jobs," Ed answered.

"Some people over here are acting just like it's another stateside assignment. That's the root problem. This is my second shooting war and Colonel Benjamin's third."

"You're saying that it doesn't matter?" Charlie said.

"Almost, but not quite. Of course, it matters to you and me and to the poor SOBs in the trenches. Real targets are important to the guys in this war that are fighting it. You, all of you, are forgetting that ninety percent of the people over here aren't fighting it. They're supporting it. Their views aren't our views and they've got their own perspectives and agendas."

"That's not a very good call to arms, Colonel," Sean said.

"There's one more very important aspect of the ninety percent that you haven't considered," Ed continued, *"Most of the officers in that support role outrank you."*

The group was quiet for a moment. Then, Mike spoke up. *"Colonel Cutter was in Korea as well. Does he agree?"*

"Agree with what?" Denny Cutter said as he walked in. *"Bill, I checked out your BDA; the B-52 Arc Light missed by miles."*

"Thanks, Sir. Colonel Hardy told us."

"What else did Ed tell you?"

Mike answered. *"He said that everyone in the war has their own agendas and that most of the people in the staffs have a different view than us. Not only that, but they outrank us."*

"I must agree with my colleague," Denny replied.

"Is that why you two are here, in the field?" Bill asked.

"We're here by choice. We prefer to deal in realities; right, Ed?" Denny asked.

"You better believe it," Ed replied, grinning.

"So, the whole point of this is that I should fly through Mu Gia and that Bill should drop the BDA thing?" Sean asked, frowning.

"Definitely, drop the BDA thing. A lot of very senior people, including Ambassador Sullivan and General Holland, had to approve the B-52 drop in Laos. I can't see any of the generals admitting that they didn't assign the correct coordinates or that they didn't check them," Ed said.

"What about Mu Gia?" Bill asked.

"No way!"

"You have to find a way for them to save face, though," Denny replied.

"What about right and wrong?" Sean was getting angry.

"Did I use the words right and wrong anywhere in my explanation? They don't apply in a war. Legal and illegal apply but right and wrong are not considerations. They're matters of individual and cultural perspective," Ed said.

"It's not wrong to fly through Mu Gia at two hundred feet?"

"It's stupid, but not wrong," Denny answered for Ed.

"I should go get killed, because some asshole major tells me it isn't dangerous?" Sean was red faced and his eyes flashed angrily.

"Colonel Cutter, do you detect a most improper attitude on the part of a young Captain?" Ed said, looking at Denny.

"I most certainly do, Colonel Hardy. It's apparent that these young warriors haven't learned that anyone with more rank than they have is smarter than them," Denny replied in a serious tone.

"Bullshit, Colonel, Sir," Bill said.

"They aren't very respectful either," Ed said to Denny.

"Would you care to join me for dinner, Colonel?"

"I would, Colonel."

Ed and Denny left the young pilots and went to the dining room. John Patterson went with them. *"Shit!"* Mike Miller said.

"Now what?" Sean asked.

"That's not like them. They must want us to figure this out and come to a decision on our own," Bill replied.

"What's this "our" shit? You got a mouse in your pocket?" Charlie said, to Bill.

"Yeah. What're you going to do about Walters and his mechanical nose?" Mike added.

"I don't know."

"I plan to be at the briefing in the morning. I don't want to miss this!" Charlie said. "

"Did you have some trouble with Candle tonight, Mike?" Sean asked.

*"Not really. I hit a four-truck convoy and got two of them. On my way back, Candle reported

twenty to thirty movers south of my hit. I was there and the roads were clear all the way to Tchepone, yet TFA was arranging a Skyspot drop. I'll bet they report another big success."

"The trucks could've come out after you passed."

"Yeah, sure. I can't figure why Candle always has such large sightings and yet there are rarely any burned out trucks visible in the mornings. They can't seem to get photos either."

"I think you answered your own question, Mike," Bill said.

"One of us is sure screwed up," Mike replied.

"So, Bill, you forget your BDA and Sean, you fly through Mu Gia," Charlie prompted.

"Ed made it quite clear that the BDA's a dead issue. He talked around the Mu Gia thing, though," Bill said, *"Have you thought about having the plane break down? I can get Ari to fix it."*

"That's a good option. We better have it as backup. The real problem will be if I lose my cool," Sean said.

"I'll handle that. I'm going to be there. I will speak up. All they can do is replace me on the sortie," Charlie said.

"Thanks, Charlie. I'm going to get some sleep; see you guys at 0800," Sean said and left the room.

CHAPTER SIXTY
Nakhon Phanom Royal Thai Air Base (NKP)
10 January 1968, TUOC briefing room

There was standing room only for the 0800 briefing. Sean sat with Ed Hardy and listened as the Intelligence Officer presented data on the target area. Charlie was the assigned Zorro escort and Major David Montgomery was leading a flight of two Hobos for additional support. Major Walters and General Teddler were sitting in the front row.

When Lieutenant North covered the known threats, everyone chuckled aloud. General Teddler looked around the room, frowning.

"What're the odds, Zack, of getting hostile gunfire in Mu Gia?" Charlie asked. He was going to be difficult, as promised.

"One hundred percent, Captain."

"Do you have a survival probability for our flights through there?" Charlie wanted to know.

"Zero percent for the NAIL, twenty percent for the Zorro and forty percent for the Hobos," Zack replied.

At that, the room quieted. The people in the briefing were waiting for Sean or the Army officers to speak. General Teddler stood.

"Are you finished, Lieutenant?" He asked Zack North.

"I am, Sir. Are you going?"

"Everyone not on the mission is to clear the room," the General said.

No one left.

"Do you want to risk losing four aircraft, General?" Zack asked.

"Our intelligence differs from yours, Lieutenant," responded Teddler, icily.

"This's our area, General. Our information is as current as last night," Zack North responded.

"Captain O'Malley, are you ready?" Major Walters asked.

"I am, Sir, as soon as you deliver your observer."

"What observer?"

"Excuse me, Major. I'm prepared to ignore our intelligence in the face of your superior data, but I have doubts on the credibility of the information you presented. I'll fly the mission as briefed, to the letter, if you or the general will accompany me," Sean said.

"If we don't?" Walters asked.

"I have a call into the TACC at Saigon. General Momyer is currently being apprised of this mission and its risks. If you choose not to fly, then my launch must be approved by the TACC."

General Teddler looked at Major Walters, who was ashen. He turned to Captain O'Malley. *"Who authorized you to disclose the nature of this mission?"*

"No one, Sir... I didn't."

"Why did you contact the TACC?"

"We have standing orders denying us authority to fly within five nautical miles of Mu Gia Pass. I merely requested waiver of those orders," Sean said.

"What did the TACC say?"

"The prohibited area stands unless we receive 7th AF Orders to the contrary."

"Are you going?"

"I can't, Sir. I was willing to try, if you'd accompany me, but it seems like we'll have to wait for 7th Air Force approval."

"Colonel Hardy, order the captain to fly," General Teddler said to Ed.

"No can do, General. Since he contacted 7thAir Force, it's out of our hands," Ed replied.

"How long has this prohibition been in effect?"

"Since 0600 hours this morning," Zack North replied, smirking.

General Teddler was furious. He turned bright red and began to berate Major Walters. The rest of the pilots left the room. Ed Hardy walked with Sean. When they were clear of TUOC, he asked, *"How'd you get that done?"*

"Bill arranged it last night. He called one of his fighter buddies and found that they had a limit on Mu Gia for the F-4s. They just got the TACC to issue one to all of the units."

"What makes me want to believe that some lowly captain on night duty did this all by himself?" Ed asked.

"It's certainly possible, Colonel. And, it's legal."

"So it is, Captain. So it is," Ed said, grinning broadly. *"Colonel Benjamin'll be pleased. He was prepared to cancel your flight if you couldn't find a way out of it. This way, the Army isn't going to be mad at us, only you."*

"Gee, thanks, Colonel. If you ever need a friend, don't ask."

Ed laughed and said, *"Take the rest of the day off. I don't want anyone to find you. OK?"*

"I'm outta here," Sean said and started walking away towards the hootches. Then he remembered that the Invert guys had invited him to visit the radar site for the cook's tour. He then thought that he might stay there until Sharon finished work. He continued towards Invert.

After they left TUOC, Dave Montgomery saw the general speaking with Major Walters and walked up to him and said, *"Sir, have you ever seen our area?"*

"Not recently, Major. Why?"

"I'd like to take you for a ride. My A-1 has an extra seat and I've got a two-hour sortie scheduled. May I take you for a look at the area?"

"That's a good idea. I really would like to do that."

"General, Dave can show you where Charlie was shot down last week," John Patterson said.

"Was it near Mu Gia?"

"No Sir, it was about halfway across. Forty miles from Mu Gia. We can take a look at the area from way up. That way you can see what it's like," commented John.

"Sounds good to me," said the general with some excitement in his voice.

"Let's go. Do you have a flight suit?"

"I'm about the same size as you, Sir," John Patterson chimed in again. *"Use one of mine. Come on. I'll get you the suit and a parachute and help get you settled in the plane."*

To everyone's surprise, General Teddler and Major Patterson walked up to Dave's A-1. Dave was preflighting and the ground crew watched as John assisted the general strapping into the right seat. When Dave climbed into the cockpit, John patted him on the shoulder. *"Stay above five thousand."*

Dave nodded and hooked up his intercom.

"Ready, Sir?"

"I'm ready, Major."

For the next two hours, Dave took the general on a tour of Central Laos. They viewed Mu Gia Pass from ten thousand feet and five miles distance. It was a formidable location with high cliffs on both sides of the road and little cover. When they started to return to NKP, they were called by Alleycat.

"Hobo One Five, we have a strike scheduled for Golf in five minutes. NAIL Six Seven said you could watch."

"Thanks, Alleycat. We'll go to NAIL FM." In only a few minutes and several miles south Dave and the general watched as NAIL 67 directed a flight of two F-4s against interdiction point Golf. They could see the planes diving and the explosive puffs from antiaircraft shells. The bombs hit the road and caused one large secondary explosion. Something must have been parked or stored just off the road.

On the way back General Teddler was quiet. Dave started to talk about the area but soon stopped as he got no response from the general. He did point out where Charlie spent the night in the trees.

After they landed, they went to TUOC for debriefing. General Teddler listened but didn't offer any comments. When they finished, he shook hands with Dave, thanked him and then went to find Major Walters. He departed the base soon afterward.

CHAPTER SIXTY ONE
Nakhon Phanom Royal Thai Air Base (NKP)
10 January 1968, that evening at the O'Club

At dinner, Ed Hardy walked up to Sean and Sharon at their table. *"They're taking the test equipment out of* the plane. Walters and his people will be gone in the morning."

"That's good news, Sir. Did they decide it wasn't worth it?"

"The general got back from the flight with Dave and told Walters to take the equipment and go back to Saigon."

When Ed left their table, Sharon said, *"I'm glad you didn't have to fly that machine again."*

"It was a real mess. There isn't any way we could've flown it through Mu Gia Pass. Someone would've been killed, most likely someone named O'Malley,"* Sean said with a shrug.

"Are you still leading the P-2 drops?"

"I'm still at it even though your boss thinks we don't do it right. Does he really believe that the FACs are unnecessary?"

"He's adamant about it. The sensors work and our computers can pinpoint locations to within a few yards anywhere in Laos,"* Sharon responded confidently.

"You're just repeating the bullshit that your boss dreams up,"* Sean said with a twinkle.

"I am not!"* Sharon was quick to get defensive.

"If you can tell where things are in Laos to within yards, why does the general still need us to mark the drop zones for the Neptunes? It'd be a lot safer for the Navy if we didn't fly around with a big damn armada every time you schedule a drop."

Sharon quieted noticeably. She didn't want to get in another argument, particularly in the Club. Sean's friends didn't show her the deference she was used to in TFA.

Relations between the two were awkward at times. Sean couldn't accommodate her reluctance to make a marriage commitment and Sharon wasn't able to overcome her general dislike of pilots. The chemistry was there, both knew that, and they took great pleasure in each other's physical attractiveness. Their sex was both satisfying and enjoyable.

Sean was staring at her with obvious desire and Sharon blushed. She leaned forward and whispered, **"Let's go. I'm ready for some privacy."**

Sean took her hand as they walked out of the O'Club.

Historical Note: This sniffer was flown in Laos, but never over Mu Gia Pass. As in the story above, the device could not tell the difference between the enemy and animal shit!

CHAPTER SIXTY TWO
Nakhon Phanom Royal Thai Air Base (NKP)
10 January 1968, a few hours later in the O'Club

The noise was building in the bar as it was nearly 3am and the night fighters were mostly in and drinking too much. But this was not the problem as a very loud noise was emanating from the "non-flyers" area as they began pounding their empty beer bottles on the tables and all in unison. **"What the hell are they doing?"** said Ross Parker, a new NAIL FAC, to the group of guys sitting along the bar.

"It is just two old colonels trying to see who is the toughest. That son-of-a-bitch from the Air Commando group is doing it again." Said Bill as he downed his fifth Budweiser and flipped the bottle in the trash behind the bar.

"What do you mean again?"

"Every time we get a new Colonel, in here, like this new Personnel weenie, the big commando has to show he is tougher than they are. Watch this; it'll be fun."

The festivities began immediately as the big commando yelled, **"Grease pencil, grease pencil."** He raised his right hand knowing full well that some one would stick a grease pencil in it as they always did. And they did it again.

With grease pencil in hand, the big commando walked…if you could say that is how a drunken 56 year old would walk…to the wall at the end of the bar room and, with the pencil, drew an "X" about 12 inches square. He then turned to the crowd, stretched out his right hand with the grease pencil clutched in his fist, bowed to a lieutenant sitting near the wall and said **"Lieutenant, I commission you the keeper of the grease pencil. You will guard this with your life and give it only to me. Should you fail, you will be shot….tomorrow morning. Any questions?"**

"No, Sir," replied the lieutenant very loudly.

The old commando relinquished the pencil, stepped up to the wall, took a deep breath, and then plunged his head through the ¼ inch plywood wall. As he extracted his head from the wall, some of the splintered wood caught his left ear and caused some bleeding, but that did not stop this guy. He returned to the lieutenant and said, **"Lieutenant, the pencil, please."**

The Lieutenant gave the pencil up and the old commando walked back to the wall and drew a similar "X" about six feet to the right of the hole in the wall. He then threw the pencil off into the crowd of onlookers and returned to the table where the other colonel was still sitting. Not surprisingly, the new colonel's eyes were big as saucers…blood shot and big.

"Colonel, I have marked your target and assume that you will want to show us all how tough you are."

"You bet your sweet ass, Colonel. Don't bother getting up; just order me another Jack on

the rocks." He then got up and proceeded to the wall, not walking any better than the first wall banger.

He got within arms length of the wall, stopped, took a deep breath (because the other guy had done that), and crashed his head against the wall....and bounced off. He shook it off, then reset himself, took a deep breath and crashed his head into the wall again. Same result. Now it was clear that he was really concerned, and really hurting. He had split the skin on his bald head, but nothing was going to stop him and he hit the wall again, harder this time. He fell unconscious to the floor in a heap.

Several onlookers immediately jumped to assist the fallen colonel. Some one threw a pitcher of beer in his face, apparently to wake him up. And it did. He was very groggy, wobbly and weak as he was helped up by the lieutenant and a captain and mostly carried back to the original table.

"I guess I am the toughest old bastard in the bar," screamed the old commando as everyone began cheering. The noise was unbearable as it seemed like every beer bottle in Thailand was being slammed on the tables. It was one of the few times that the non-flyers really seemed to enjoy the bar scene here at NKP.

Back at the bar with the NAIL contingent Ross said, *"He almost killed himself."*

"Yeh, you can do that when you try to butt your head through a stud."

Historical Note: *This head butting occurred nearly every time a new colonel arrived at NKP. The instigator was Air Commando One, Colonel Henie Aderholt. Many at NKP during these times have attested to these incidents, but as best we know Col. A. has never admitted that he participated.*

CHAPTER SIXTY THREE
Steel Tiger, Eastern Central Laos

10 January 1968, nearing midnight at 7,000 feet over Route 91 near Foxtrot

Bill and Sean were together as a night team for the first time in weeks. Sean needed to log a night mission every three weeks or so in order to keep current on the latest night tactics and procedures. These occasional night flights were critical to his Stan Eval work and the new update of the night tactics manual.

Tonight Bill was on the Starlight scope and Sean was in the left seat. They had been airborne now for about three hours and had put in one flight of F-4s that cut the road near Foxtrot, but they hadn't even seen a truck. Since Bill was on board, they used the "amateur hour is over" ploy and stacked a flight of two phony Yellowbirds overhead. Subsequently, there was little gunfire as the F-4s dropped. The up side is that they did not get shot at, but, the down side of this was that there are few enemy guns to shoot at. All in all though, no gun fire is a good deal for the FACs.

"NAIL FOUR FIVE, this is Alleycat. Do you read?"

"Alley this is 45, what's up?"

"NAIL we have a friendly camp in western Laos about 20 klicks south east of NKP being attacked and they have requested some air. This is a serious emergency. Can you assist?"

"Roger, Alleycat. NAIL FOUR FIVE is turning west now. Do you have any assets we can use?"

"Roger, NAIL. We have a Candlestick and he is moving towards the camp. We also have a Nimrod. We will be trying to get some fast movers soon. What is your ETA?"

Sean looks at Bill, who smiles and announces over UHF, *"Alleycat, NAIL FOUR FIVE will be at the* camp in 17 minutes. Will they be able to hold on that long?"

"NAIL, we have no idea as communications to these sites is minimal. The controller is surprised we were notified of the difficulty."

"Candlestick, if you are on this frequency acknowledge and go to 248.6, this is NAIL FOUR FIVE."

"NAIL, Candle going to 248.6."

"Candlestick on 248.6, do you read, NAIL FOUR FIVE?"

"Candle you are loud and clear. Do you know what is going on?"

"No, just that a friendly camp is being attacked and it is about 20 klicks out of NKP."

"That is all we know, so…"

"NAIL, this is a friend; we are on 248.6. The camp is at 22 klicks on 100 degree radial from Channel 89, the NKP TACAN."

"Roger, friend. Where are you and what is your altitude?"

"We are at 3,000 feet directly over the camp. We are moving to the south and will hold here about a mile south at 3,000 feet. We will stay out of your way, but hurry. The gooks may make a final try here soon. We can see what is going on with our scope but can't do anything about it. That's why we called Alleycat."

"What frequency will the camp be using?"

"Unless you can speak Lao don't bother. They will be listening but they won't talk unless you speak Lao."

"Do you have a Laotian with you?"

"Yep, we always do."

"Friend, have the Lao talk with the camp on something other than 248.6 so they don't overcrowd us with their talk. Have him ask them what they want us to do and then pass that to us."

"That ought to work."

"Candle, this is NAIL FOUR FIVE. When you get to the camp, set up an orbit at 10,000 feet about a quarter of a mile west of the camp. You have a Starlight scope, right?"

"NAIL, yes we have a scope."

"Candle, we now have the camp in sight. When can you flare?"

"We are ready now, FAC; what is your altitude?"

"We are at 5,000, but don't worry. They don't have any big guns here. They will be able to see us under the flare but not able to hit us. Not to worry. Flare away. Let's try to keep the place constantly lit up."

"NAIL, this is friend. Do you have any ordnance? The camp wants a drop on the north side. That is where they think the most of the NVA are coming from."

"Friend, not yet."

Sean asks, *"Who the fuck is this friend?"*

"It is probably an Air America Porter, but who knows."

"NAIL FOUR FIVE, this is Nimrod 22 and I have the flare in sight and I am about three klicks out from the camp. Help me out with a Willy Pete. I want to make sure where this stuff goes."

"Nimrod, I want you to come in east to west. We have the Candle at 10,000 and he will stay off to the west. We have an unknown to the south

about a klick at 3,000. We will also stay south, so an east/west or west/east run will be okay."

"NAIL, I would prefer to go north/south."

"Negative, Nimrod. That is too chancy. You might hit the friendlys with a long or short drop. Let's go east to west."

"Roger, NAIL, makes sense. I am ready and in position east at 7,000. Where are you? Oh, I see you now. Is that light shielded?"

"Not to worry, Nimrod. No big guns here. I am rolling in now with the mark."

Sean fired the Willy Pete. It impacted just off of the north edge of the Lao base. *"The mark is right on. You are cleared in hot. Clear north and call off."*

"FAC in sight; Nimrod in."

The Nimrod was carrying a load of 250-pounders and he dropped about half on the first run, or at least that is what it looked like. His bombs were within 100 meters of the edge of the camp.

"Nimrod is off; no gun fire noted."

"Roger, Nimrod; now set up and do another one. This time move out from the camp about 50 meters further north."

The Nimrod dropped his other half load and called bingo fuel as he departed for NKP. About that time, Sean noted their fuel situation and decided they were also bingo. He called NAIL Ops on NAIL Common 50.50, *"Dullness, this is NAIL FOUR FIVE, do you read?"*

"Roger 45, how can we help?"

"We are bingo fuel and must leave the war out here. Have Ari get another O-2 ready for us. We are heading back but will need to get back here fast. Taxi the replacement O-2 in front of Base Ops. Load a full load of Willy Petes, both pods. Pull all the pins. When we approach Base Ops,

have them start the rear engine. We'll jump out of this one and get into the replacement and we'll have maps and guns. Any questions?"

"45, we got it. Good luck."

As soon as Sean and Bill had landed, they swapped aircraft, took off and were approaching the camp again, which Candle still had lit up. *"Nice job, Candle. This is 45. We're back with a full load of gas and rockets. Friend, what's new?"*

"NAIL, we need to put more ordnance on the north side of the camp, and up close."

"NAIL FOUR FIVE, this is Zorro 61; can I help? I have a full load."

"Roger, Zorro, where are you?"

"I'm over Candlestick at 11,000. I see the camp and copied the strange airplane's request. Is that what you want?"

"Roger, Zorro. I want you to drop as close to the camp as you can. Use an east/west run. There are only small arms here, no 37s or 23s. I suggest that you come in as low and slow as you can to get the best drop we can. The elevation here is 1200 feet. Let me know when you're ready and have me in sight."

"NAIL, I'm ready and I have you in sight."

"Zorro, you are cleared in east to west. Call off and clear north."

"Zorro 61 is in hot with FAC in sight."

This was the perfect drop, within 50 meters of the camp fence. Several NVA could be seen running north after this drop. *"Zorro off"*

"Zorro, great drop; right on target. I actually saw some of them running. You're cleared in again. Same east/west. Move these about 100 meters north. You're cleared in hot."

"This is Zorro 61, FAC in sight, and in hot."

Another perfect drop. *"NAIL, Zorro is off, Winchester, and heading for home. Hope this helped our guys on the ground."*

"Great drop, perfect. See ya' back at NKP."

"NAIL, this is your friend. The camp commander says that the NVA are now running off. I guess they're heading back north to tell Uncle Ho not to mess with the NAILs. It's all over, NAIL. The commander says thanks. Nice job."

"Thanks, friend. If we can be of assistance in the future, you know the call sign. Since this is now over, we're heading for NKP. Candlestick, nice job. See ya' at the club."

"Well, Sean, I guess we got 'em. Let's go home."

And then out of the dark night and on UHF guard channel, they heard in what seemed to be the voice of an Asian, somewhat experienced in the French language, **"Vive L' Aviateur. Vive L' Aviateur."**

Historical Note: Don Brown and Pat Sweeney actually participated in a similar mission with the two O-2 aircraft, the unknown and unseen friend, and Candlestick. As they departed the camp, they did hear on Guard "Vive L' Aviateur. Vive L' Aviateur."

CHAPTER SIXTY FOUR
Steel Tiger, Eastern Central Laos
15 January 1968, late morning flying at 6,000 feet

Sean and Ralph Langer were the assigned FACs on a scheduled Navy sensor drop. Sean was flying the low position and Ralph backed him up in the high position. They were leading a P-2 and two A-1s and had a flight of two F-4s on call for gun suppression.

"Ralph, do you read me on common?" Sean called.

"I'm here," Ralph answered.

"I can see the drop area. Stay out of the way to the west and watch for guns. Keep the Hobos with you. I'm going to get set up for my run," Sean said.

"NAIL Four Five, this is Alleycat," came over the radio.

"Roger, Alleycat. Four Five's marking the drop. Lindy Two One is descending to drop altitude," Sean responded.

Sean checked his position. Route 912 stretched away to the North towards Ban Karai Pass.

Sean rolled in and fired a Willy Pete rocket. It impacted about thirty yards from the road, near an intersection which marked the beginning of the sensor drop run. *"Do you have my smoke?"*

"We have the smoke and the drop point, NAIL. We're beginning our run," came from the Navy plane.

The big Navy patrol bomber descended to one thousand feet above the ground, lined up for its run, and then dropped to five hundred feet. Sean was to the east at four thousand feet watching the Navy plane make its approach. He saw the gunfire as soon as it started.

Sean watched as 37mm golf-ball-sized tracers streaked past the Neptune on both sides. The P-2 could not take evasive action in order to insure the sensors were properly dropped. It was no contest.

A 37mm round entered the radar compartment and exploded.

"We've been hit!" came screaming over the radio.

"Get away from the road," Sean called. ***"Turn left away from the road! Head toward the west."***

They watched as the P-2 started to climb and turn away toward the west. Suddenly smoke billowed from the fuselage. They were on fire.

Sean started to make a call when he saw the parachutes. The crew was bailing out.

"Ralph, get a mark on the chutes. Give me a count as soon as you can," Sean called.

Navy crew members were bailing out and chutes were blossoming all over Laos. The plane continued to burn as it lost altitude very gently. Then the Neptune lost flying speed and slowly rolled off on its port wing and crashed into a hill beside the road, just short of the ford at Ban Laboy.

"Cricket, Lindy Two One has been hit and the crew has bailed out. I've counted six,... make that seven...parachutes. We have seven chutes. The plane impacted the side of a hill. Repeat, Lindy Two One has crashed. There are seven 'chutes. Get the rescue people here as soon as possible."

"Rescue's been alerted, NAIL. Do you require additional gun suppression," came from Cricket.

"Negative, Cricket. The guns are too close to the 'chutes. We'll wait for the Sandys," Sean answered.

On FM he spoke to Ralph, ***"Do you have all of the positions marked?"***

"I've got them. You can see all seven of the chutes. I didn't see anyone else get out. Didn't they have nine aboard today, eight crew members and an observer?" Ralph replied.

"Yeah. Ralph, you head back to NKP as fast as possible. Get your map to TUOC so they can pass it to the rescue guys. I'll wait here and watch for trouble," Sean said. ***"If this takes a while, have another FAC lined up."***

"I'm on the way. Be careful, Sean. You better ask Alley to refuel the fighters," Ralph said as he headed back toward NKP.

"This is Cricket, NAIL Four Five. We have a tanker enroute for the fighters and Crown is airborne for the helicopters. We'll keep a flight of F-4s available at all times. Crown's ETA is one hour and forty minutes."

"Roger, Cricket. One plus forty for Crown. Where're the Jollys?" Sean asked.

"We have two inbound from NKP, ETA twenty minutes. The Danang and Udorn Jollys are about twenty minutes behind NKP," Cricket responded. *"Sandys are with the Udorn Jollys."*

"Thanks, Cricket. We'll get started with the NKP birds. Please advise when the Sandys are a couple of minutes out. Give the incoming rescue aircraft our UHF frequency. We'll stay on it... "

"Roger, NAIL."

Sean then called his A-1 escort... *"Hobo Four Two, do you have me in sight?"*

"Roger, NAIL Four Five. We've got you and some of the chutes. What's the plan?"

"We'll wait for the Jollys. When they get here, we'll begin by picking up the two crewmen at the south end of the drop. They're across the road from the other chutes. If we start with them, it may mislead the ground troops into thinking that they're all on that side of the road."

Sean switched his radio to Guard Channel, *"Attention, all P-2 crew. We have your 'chutes in sight. Stay off the radios and stay near your chutes. The Jolly Green helicopters will be here in twenty minutes. Stay quiet and wait. We'll pick up everyone as fast* as we can. This is NAIL Four Five. I'll be overhead where you can see me."

After about 15 minutes, *"Jolly One Zero; do you read, NAIL Four Five?"*

"We read, NAIL. We have you in sight. One One is about a mile back. Are those the Sandys?"

"Negative, One Zero and One One. We have two Hobos from NKP. There are two crewmen down to the southeast of my position. They're the only ones on the east side of the road. I'll have the Hobos make a low pass and you be ready to go after those two crewmen," Sean said.

"Where are the Sandys?"

"They're due in about fifteen minutes, Jolly. Will you try for the two crewmen?"

"We aren't supposed to go until the Sandys release us."

"Hobo Four Two, make a pass and check out the area," Sean radioed. There wasn't time to wait.

"Hobos are in," came the reply. The two A-1s made a pass over the parachutes on the east side of the road.

"No ground fire, NAIL. Both the crewmen are visible and appear to be OK," Hobo 42 called.

"Jolly One Zero, you're cleared for pick up of the two crewmen to the east," Sean said, hoping they wouldn't delay.

"Jolly One Zero's in to the east. Cover us."

"Hobo Four Two, set up above and west of the Jolly. If you see gunfire, make your runs to the east and drop ordnance east of the road only," Sean radioed.

"Roger, NAIL. We're covering the Jolly."

The two A-1s entered a circling orbit above the descending helicopter. Sean watched as the helicopter hovered and lowered its jungle penetrator. The metal device was suspended from a two-hundred-and fifty-foot-long steel cable. It seemed to take forever for the Jolly crew to lower the penetrator to the jungle. He saw the penetrator start back up with a crewman on the seat.

"Jolly One Zero has one coming up. As soon as he's aboard, we'll go to the second parachute."

"Roger, Jolly. Good work. Hobo Four Two, keep your eyes open," Sean replied.

"We have the Jolly covered, NAIL. So far, no ground fire," Hobo Four Two answered.

The big helicopter winched the downed crewman aboard and immediately moved to the second parachute. *"We have the second crewman in sight, NAIL. Initiating recovery."*

"Roger, Jolly. Pull off to the east when you get him aboard. Hobo, make sure that the Jolly doesn't cross the road below five thousand," Sean called. He watched the big helicopter hover and begin lowering the jungle penetrator.

"We got it, NAIL. We'll stay with Jolly One Oh and keep to the east," the Hobo answered.

"Jolly One Zero is over the second crewman, NAIL. Where are the Sandys?"

"We'll check, Jolly. Keep to the east."

"Cricket, this is NAIL Four Five. Do you have the Sandys?"

"Roger, NAIL Four Five. Sandy Lead's coming up on your position now. The Sandy will take over control of the recovery."

"Roger, Cricket," Sean breathed a sigh of relief. The experts were here. His relief was short lived. Almost immediately Guard Channel blared, *"This is Sandy Lead... all aircraft stand off until we check over the area. Advise that you are clearing."*

Sean couldn't believe what he was hearing. Sandy was jeopardizing the rescues in progress. He quickly switched his radio to Guard Channel, *"This is NAIL Four Five. Disregard the last transmission. Remain on 278.4. Sandy lead, come up 278.4."*

"This is Sandy Lead on Guard Channel. All aircraft come up on Guard," came over the radio.

"Remain on 278.4," Sean said. He was more than a little irritated at the Sandy pilot. They were in the middle of a rescue with six different types of aircraft and the Sandy blundered into the action without getting a briefing. Sean wasn't going to allow the A-1 pilot to foul up a smooth rescue.

"Cricket, this is NAIL Four Five. Advise the Sandy to pull back and wait for me to transfer control. I'm not relinquishing control of my area." Sean's voice was shaking with anger.

"Roger, NAIL. We will advise the Sandys. There are four helicopters inbound. What channel do you want them on?"

"Send the Jollys to me on 278.4," Sean replied. *"Does the Sandy have FM?"*

"We'll check, NAIL."

"Four Five, the Sandy has FM. We sent him to you on NAIL common," Cricket replied.

"Hobo Four Two, where's your Jolly?" Sean asked.

"We've got him at five thousand, NAIL. Where do you want us?"

"Cross to the west but stay back. The Jollys from Danang are coming in. You stay west and high. Cover the Jollys that are holding and watch for the Crown C-130."

"Roger, NAIL. We'll guard the corral."

"Thanks, Hobo."

"Sandy Lead, this is NAIL Four Five on FM," Sean called.

"Get out of the way NAIL; we're in charge here," came back.

"Very briefly, Sandy, what's the situation?" Sean asked.

"The situation is that I'm the mission commander. You're in the way," Sandy Lead replied.

Sean didn't respond. He switched his radio back to the UHF frequency and called Cricket. *"Please get another Sandy team here as soon as possible, Cricket. I'm not releasing control to the one we have. He isn't qualified to handle this rescue effort..."*

"It's unusual, NAIL, but you have operational control of the sector. We'll advise Crown," Cricket replied.

"Hobo Four Two, please make a pass over the west side of the road. We have the Danang and Udorn Jollys inbound. I want to get the other four crewmen as soon as possible. Sandy Lead isn't cooperating."

"Roger, NAIL; we heard. We're making a run now." The two A-1s flew a low pass over the west side.

"No fire, NAIL, but that's probably because they're waiting for the Jollys," Hobo 42 called, as they pulled up.

"Lay some CBU along the east side of the road. Maybe it'll confuse them. I'll get the Jollys in as soon as you're done. Pull up and hold to the east. Watch the hills for guns," Sean replied.

"NAIL, this is Jolly Three One. Where are the Sandys?"

*"Roger, Three One. Do you have us in sight? There are two A-1s working over the east side of

the trail," Sean responded. He wasn't going to get into an argument about the Sandys.

"*We have you, NAIL and we have the A-1s. Where are the Sandys?*"

"*The Sandys are not in on this one. They can't handle the number of chutes. We've got five more down on the west side of the trail. Two have been recovered so far and are aboard Jolly One Zero. Two crewmen are unaccounted for but we have the other four chutes. You'll see them easily as you approach from the south. If you come in to the north, one of you can pick up the two closest to the road. The other Jolly can go for the ones higher up the hill. As soon as Jolly One Zero refuels, we'll bring them back in. How's your fuel?*"

"*We've got about seventy-five minutes, NAIL. We need the refill from Crown but we've got time for a pickup.*"

"*Jolly Three One, you're cleared in from the south. The Hobos are covering you from the east. One One, follow them in.*"

"*Three One and Three Two are in, NAIL. We've got the parachutes.*"

"*One One is right behind them.*"

The three big helicopters descended and approached the visible parachutes.

"*Gunfire, gunfire!*" yelled Hobo 42. "*Stay back, Jolly. We're rolling in on the guns.*" The helicopters turned back, but remained at the lower altitude.

Sean watched as the two Hobos flew over the jungle streaming CBU bomblets behind their aircraft. They were flying almost on top of the road, several hundred yards from any of the downed crewmen.

The A-1s broke to the east, wrapped in vapor as they pulled hard to confuse the gunners.

"Hobos are off and turning east."

"Better keep holding, Jollys. Let's see if there's any more gunfire," Sean called.

"Jolly Three One holding to the south."

"Make another pass, Hobo Four Two. See if they're still shooting," Sean said.

"Four Two's in. We'll make an east/west pass and come back around to the south if they start shooting."

"Roger, Hobo. You're cleared for your pass. Get a look at the chutes on your way by. Watch out for the Jollys."

Then on Sean's FM, the banished Sandy Lead said, *"NAIL, this is Sandy Lead. We can help with the guns."*

"Get set, Sandy. Pass will be south to north along the road. The nearest crewmen are two hundred yards to the west. Don't drop over fifty yards west of the road. Hobo, what do you see?"

"Four Two's receiving some scattered fire. We're on the way around and will come down the road from the north."

"Roger, Four Two. You're cleared. Turn to the east as soon as you release your ordnance."

"Roger, NAIL. Four Two's rolling in. Will exit to the east... "

"Sandy Lead and Two, you're cleared south to north as soon as the Hobo breaks off."

Sean was the ringmaster, totally in his element. He was flying by rote, directing two sets of A-1's, talking to Cricket, controlling three sets of Jollies…and evolving his plan as it developed. He was God on a Thunder Throne: when he pointed, it died!!!

"Sandy Lead, roger."

"Make your break to the west, Sandy. Let me know if you can see any of the downed crewmen."

"Hobo Four Two's off to the east."

"Sandy Lead's in."

Sean watched the Hobo sharply roll off towards the east side of the road, he then rolled left and picked up the Sandy "coming down the chute" underneath him...

"Sandy, you are cleared hot!"

"Any ground fire, Four Two?"

"None on that pass, NAIL. What's next?"

"Sandy's off to the west. No ground fire. I picked up the chutes, but no joy on the people."

"Sandy, stay west. Cover the Jollies. Hobos, you stay east. Watch along the road. If there's ground fire, the Hobos are cleared to run north and south to the east of the road. Sandy, you stay west and make your runs west of the chutes."

"Hobo Four Two, Roger. We have the east."

"Sandy has the west."

"Jolly Three One, are you ready for a run?"

"Three One's ready."

"This is Three Two. We're ready, too."

"One will take the closest chute."

"Jollys come in from the south. Everyone alert. Call ground fire. Now move!"

Sean was busy. He could see the helicopters coming in to hover over the downed crewmen. There were three helicopters hovering, lowering the penetrators, when someone yelled,

"Ground fire!"

"Jollies, hold your position. Who has the ground fire?" Sean called out. There was no answer. *"Stay alert, stay alert. Jolly Three One, are you OK?"*

"Three One's OK. We're winching one man aboard now."

"Jolly Three Two. How're you doing?"

"Three Two made the call. We thought we were getting fire but it was a false alarm. Our man's almost aboard."

"Four One is winching up. No fire. We got ours."

"Three One is heading for number four. How many more?"

"We've got all of them accounted for. There are four aboard the Jollies and two on the penetrators. We're still missing one."

"Did anyone see the parachutes?"

"Negative. We only counted six chutes and we've got all six accounted for. NKP and Danang Jollys, RTB at NKP. Sandy, cover the Jollies. Udorn, do you read NAIL Four Five?"

"We read you, NAIL. This is Two Five and Two Six. We've topped off with Crown and are holding to the south."

"Roger, Two Five. We'd like you to wait and let us look around for a while. The Hobos will stay and we have some F-4s up high."

"Jolly Two Five can give you another hour and a half, NAIL."

"Roger. Sandy Lead, what's your position?"

"Sandys are with the Jollies. We're heading for NKP. All of us are heading to the west."

"Roger, Sandy. Thanks for your help."

"We'll discuss that when you get back."

"Tsk, tsk. It doesn't sound like he's too pleased, Four Five. What do you want us to do?" came from the Hobos.

"How's your ordnance?"

"We have enough to keep their heads down. I think the F-4s are getting anxious though. They haven't been able to help."

"Ground fire, ground fire!"

"Who was that?" called Sean.

"Hobo Four Three," came the sheepish voice. *"It startled me, sorry. Just as we crossed that ridge back there, I caught some fire from my right. Should we go back and check it out?*

"Go ahead," Sean replied. *"Cricket, how are our fighters?"*

"They just topped off. You've got a fully loaded and anxious pair of Gunfighters up here."

"Send them to me, please."

"Roger, NAIL. The Gunfighters are coming up on 278.4."

"Ground fire, ground fire! I'm getting it again," the excited voice of Hobo Four Three came over the radio.

"Hey, NAIL. This is Gunfighter lead. Do you have some work for us?"

"I got a chute! I got a chute!"

"Who has a chute?" Sean called out.

"Four Three. That's what they didn't want us to see. There's a chute just below the crest of the ridge. I can't see anyone but I've got a chute and they're shooting at me."

"Move out of the way, Four Three. I'm coming through below you. Where's the chute from your position?" came from Hobo 42.

"Look to the east. About fifty yards down from the top. There he is! There he is! He's in some rocks and they're climbing toward him." 43's voice was shrill with excitement.

"I have the chute. Where's the crewman?"

"Up the hill, fifty or sixty yards up from the chute."

"Tally Ho, NAIL; I have him."

"Gunfighters, get down here. Set up an orbit about ten thousand feet. The mountains here reach up to about forty five hundred feet."

"Gunfighters going to ten thousand. Guns are hot. We have you in sight, NAIL."

"Thanks, guys. Be careful. There are two Jollies and two Hobos down here."

"Roger, NAIL. Tell them to stay below eight thousand. We'll stay above."

"Hobo Four Two and Four Three, Roger we'll stay below eight."

"Jollys are at six."

Sean flipped his UHF to GUARD Channel and yelled….

"Beeper….Beeper…come up voice….," the SEA standard call for the survivor to come up on Guard Channel.

There was no response.

"Can you reach the downed crewman on Guard?"…. Hobo asked

"Negative," Sean replied. *"I've been trying."*

"Let's go get him. He's got his hands full," Hobo 42 replied.

"Hobos, hold back. Gunfighters, can you see what we're doing?"

"Negative, NAIL. Give us a mark somewhere near the ridge you're looking at."

"Roger. I'm marking at the base of the ridge. There's a friendly at the top." As soon as the rocket hit the radio came to life.

"We have your mark. NAIL. I have the chute. Two, do you have the Chute?"

"I got it, Lead."

"OK, NAIL. Where're the bad guys?"

"Below the chute. The crewman is fifty or sixty yards up the hill from the chute. The bad guys are at the chute and below it. You're cleared in."

"CBU, Two. Lay it along the hill. Watch drift."

"Two, Roger."

"Jolly Two Five, are you ready?"

"Jolly Two Five's ready. Am I cleared in?"

"You're cleared as soon as the F-4s make their pass."

"Gunfighter Lead's in."

Sean watched as Danang Phantoms screamed by the base of the hill with CBU bomblets streaming behind them. The waterfall of grenade-sized bomblets blasted along the side of the hill parallel to the crest and about one hundred yards down the hill.

"Gunfighters are off. That's all of our CBU, NAIL. We have twenty mike mike remaining."

"Roger, Gunfighters. Hold at ten thousand and be ready to come in if we get in trouble."

"Jolly Two Five, are you ready?"

"Roger, NAIL, Two Five's in."

"Thanks, Jolly. Hobos, you have the cover."

"Four Three, stay off to the west. Keep the CBU hot. There aren't any more friendlies around so lay it anywhere you see gunfire. Wait until the man's in the lift... "

"Four Three, Roger."

"Jolly Two Five is picking up light fire, small arms probably. It seems to be coming from down the hill. Can you get them off our back?"

"Four Two's in. Four Three heads up."

Sean watched as the Hobo made a pass along the side of the hill, CBU streaming from under his wings.

"Four Three is checking the other side of the hill. The Jolly will be exposed during hover."

"Roger Four Three. Be careful," Sean replied.

The HH-3 Jolly Green raced towards the hill. At the last instant it rotated, nose up, as it shuddered to a halt directly over the survivor.

"Jolly Two Five hovering. We have the downed crewman in sight. Keep those guys busy. We're still picking up some sporadic gunfire."

"Four Two and Four Three keep making passes. The Jolly's still under fire," Sean called.

"Four Two's in. This is the last of my CBU."

"Four Three's in."

Almost immediately, *"Four Three's hit! I got hit!"*

"I see you, Four Three. How bad is it?" came the calm voice of Hobo Four Two.

"I'm bleeding. There's some sort of automatic weapon on the back slope. Tell the Jolly to be careful. They stitched my cockpit and I took a couple of rounds."

"Can you keep flying, Four Three?" Sean asked.

"I don't know," Four Three replied, *"I can get out of the area, though. I'm heading west."*

"We have Four Three in sight, NAIL. This is Jolly Two Six. We'll stay with him."

"Cricket, we need some more help," Sean called, anxiously.

"It's coming, NAIL. Two more fully-loaded Hobos are one minute out. Hobo One Five and One Seven are on the way and are on your frequency when you need them. We have two more Gunfighters scrambled and due here in three minutes."

"Thanks, Crick. You're one up as usual."

"We've been monitoring, NAIL. Trying to help."

"Gunfighter Lead, NAIL."

"Ready, NAIL. We can give you gun support and we have the target."

"Hobo Four TWO, clear off to the west and stay with Four Three. Be careful."

"Four Two, Roger. See you back at the ranch, Four Five"

"NAIL, this is Cricket."

"Go, Cricket."

"The first Jolly reports that the P-2 aircraft commander was still flying the AC. He didn't have a chance. Only seven got out."

"Thanks, Cricket. We're after the seventh man now"

"Gunfighters, you're cleared in. Jolly Two Five, watch for the fighters. They'll keep you cleared."

"Roger, NAIL. The crewman is injured. We had to send down pararescue. Keep us clear."

"Hobo One Five, did you read?" Sean wanted to know. He needed some help and he needed it now!

"Gotcha, Four Five. We're thirty seconds out on a run down both sides of the hill. We'll be on target as the Gunfighters clear. We're looking for those guns."

The Phantoms, gun smoke streaming from the 20mm gun pods under their centerlines, strafed both sides of the hill.....sparkling trails of explosions racing ahead of them....then both pulled hard right as they blasted past the hill.

"Gunfighters off. That's our load, NAIL. Sorry we have to leave."

"Good work, Gunfighters. We've got a couple more of your guys due in any minute. How about filling them in."

"Will do, Four Five. Cricket, give us the Gunfighter frequency."

"Hobo One Five's in. I have the guns."

"Jolly Two Five, we've got the crewman in the seat with the pararescue. Winching them in now. Crewman is hurt but alive. Tell the Hobos thanks. They just blew something up on the side of the hill."

"Did you get that, Hobo? You must have hit some ammunition."

"Roger, NAIL. Let's get out of here before we get a nasty surprise,"

"Jolly Two Five, we've got them aboard and are egressing to the West ..."

"Hobos, cover the Jolly. Four Two, do you read?"

"Yeah, Four Five. We're on the way home with Jolly Two six. Four Three looks like he can make it."

"Don't take any chances. If he's losing blood he could pass out. You have a good Jolly with you and there aren't many bad guys to the west."

"This is Four Three. I'm OK. It hurts but I don't think it's serious."

"Thanks, Four Three. You did great. One Five, stay with the Jolly and take him back to NKP."

"Hobo One Five and One Seven are riding herd on Jolly Two Five. See you back at NKP, NAIL."

"Gunfighters, this is NAIL Four Five. Do you read?"

"We read loud and clear, NAIL. Have you got something for us?"

"Roger, Gunfighters. I would like one pass, all ordnance on the top of a hill where they picked up the last crewman. It's covered with bad guys."

"Mark the hill, NAIL, and consider it done."

Sean put a Willy Pete near the top of the hill and pulled off to the west, starting his climb to a safe altitude. He watched as the two F-4s cover the hill with hundreds of CBU bomblets.

"Gunfighter is off Winchester CBU....we have pistol left"

"On target, Gunfighters. Thanks a lot. Take the guns home. NAIL is headed back to NKP."

"Did we hit anything, NAIL?"

"You put it on top of the target. It will take a ground team to come up with the BDA. That ought to teach 'em to be more polite when we're running a rescue."

"Roger, NAIL. Gunfighters going back to Danang. Gunfighters button four go"

"Two!" the Gunfighter wingman replied

"NAIL Four Five, this is Crown on Guard. Please come up 269.5."

Sean changed frequencies. "Crown, this is NAIL Four Five."

"Good work, NAIL. What happened with Sandy Lead?"

"He rushed in and ordered everyone out of the area while we had pickups in progress. If we'd followed his instructions, they would've known where two of our guys were located. Not only that, I don't think he was prepared to handle all of the different planes in the area."

"We'd like a written report sent to SAR Operations at 7th."

"No sweat, Crown. We'll send a report."

"You saved eight of nine on that crew, NAIL. That's quite an accomplishment. There won't be any difficulty with the Sandy. Crown out."

"NAIL Four Five, Cricket."

"Roger, Cricket. This is NAIL Four Five."

"Are you OK, NAIL?"

"Fine, just fine, Cricket. I'm headed for NKP."

"The TACC passes their congratulations. The "Man" was listening to you work the rescue. He sends his personal thanks."

"Did you guys relay it back to Saigon?"

"That is affirmative. He asked to be patched in and heard it all, including the Sandy screw-up."

"Thanks, Cricket. I really appreciated the help. If you hadn't called for those Hobos, we would've lost the last man."

"Take care, NAIL. Cricket out..."

Sean watched the gaggle of Jollies, Sandys and Hobos as they outran him westward towards the Mekong and NKP.

He started to shake and his breathing became ragged. The adrenalin was wearing off...fear was grabbing him with both hands. There had been no time for fear, only for control, reaction, and planning during the SAR.... but now he was exhausted and it tried to overwhelm him. He quickly regained control...it was not a conscious effort...it just happened The tremors passed and a massive smile erupted on his face as he pounded the glare shield and screamed,

"SHIT HOT!"

Historical Note: Sam Weaver was the O-2 FAC that actually ran this SAR. This was the largest single rescue in Southeast Asia up to that time and was fully reported in "National Geographic." The OP-2E commander, Commander Paul Milius, was listed as missing in action and

was never recovered. Commander Milius flew the AC as his crew bailed out and then actually bailed himself. Eyewitnesses interviewed in 1994 said his chute did not have time to open. In 1996, an Arleigh Burke-class guided-missile destroyer was named USS Milius. Also on board the OP-2E for the mission was PO2 John Hatzhiem, who was mortally wounded when the radar compartment was hit by ground fire. He was on board when the plane crashed. PO2 Hatzhiem's remains were recovered in 1994, 1995 and 1996.

CHAPTER SIXTY FIVE
Nakhon Phanom Royal Thai Air Base (NKP)
16 February 1968, early afternoon in the Nail Ops

"Go right in, Sirs, the colonel is expecting you," said Eddie as he rose from his desk, a gesture of respect for the two captains as they entered the office area. Bill was accompanied by Phil Masters, a former O-1 pilot and one of the few NAILs who had spent thirty days at Khe Sanh during the summer of 1967.

Bill and Phil knocked and heard from inside, *"Come in."* They entered and saluted the commander, who was sitting at his desk. Ed Hardy was there and both seemed to be exhibiting very serious expressions. Colonel Benjamin returned the salutes and motioned for the two captains to sit down.

"You two are aware of the fight going on in South Vietnam, right?"

Both nodded and the colonel continued, *"It is really bad over there. The Gooks have attacked nearly every provincial capital in the country, have occupied Hue, and over ran the US Embassy in Saigon. Nineteen sappers got onto the embassy grounds. Fortunately we killed them all. We are* beating them back pretty well everywhere, but at Khe Sanh."

Both nodded and the colonel continued, *"This Khe Sanh thing has developed into a siege and we are supplying everything they need via C-130s, C-123s and a few helicopters. But since the twelfth of February, 7th Air Force has suspended all C-130 landings at Khe Sanh. The road from Dong Ha is blocked. The general ... General Westmoreland ... is concerned that this not be turned into another Dien Bien Phu. Actually, the President is concerned—Hell, everybody is concerned...the damn place is surrounded by NVA regulars."*

"Hell, Colonel, it was surrounded by NVA the whole time I was there last summer. What's new?" injected Phil.

"What's new is that the NVA appear to want to take it, overrun it...now. Haven't you noticed the increase in Trail traffic? The increase in big stuff going south? The bad guys have been getting ready for months and now they are playing hardball. That's why everyone is so interested in this."

Both captains started to realize the severity of the situation and they now began wearing more serious expressions as Bill asked, *"Okay, Sir, what do you want us to do?"*

"There's more. They just shot down a C-130. Nick Johnson was on board. Recognize the name? He was with AP news. He has a world-wide reputation. Well, he's dead now...shot down trying to land at Khe Sanh."

"Shit!" said Phil.

7th wants the 23rd to get in there and develop tactics that will safely get the cargo planes in and out of Khe Sanh and they want it tomorrow. Phil, since you spent thirty days living there last summer and flying into the North, you know the area and the base. Bill, since you seem to be our resident tactician, I want you to go with Phil and set up the tactics."

"Tomorrow?"

"Tomorrow, Bill. The grunts can barely make it through each day without the daily supplies. There are no extra supplies at Khe Sanh. Hell, the ammo dump was hit with a rocket as they started the attack on January 12th and the grunts barely have enough ammo. They need every bullet, every shell and every meal delivered every day. This is serious…very serious. There's talk of Arc Lights; the B-52s are coming."

"Okay; got it, Sir."

"I want you guys to go to INTEL and get all the poop that they have on the current Khe Sanh situation and then develop the tactics now, today. We must be able to safely supply these guys or General Giap will win another one. You can test your tactics tomorrow at Khe Sanh. By the way, this had better work as a lot of Marines are depending on your tactics."

"What resources will we have?" asked Phil.

"Whatever you need, so get out of here and start developing tactics."

Both captains rose quickly saluted and passed through the door. Ed said to the commander, "Do you really think they can do it?"

"Hell if I know, but they're our best shot. Have them brief you on their plans and resource needs. If it sounds even slightly good, order up the resources and notify 7th that the cavalry is *coming in tomorrow. I'm leaving for Saigon in a few hours for a group hand holding at 7th or I would do it myself.*

Historical Note: The shoot down of a C-130 with an international newsman on board did precipitate the NAIL involvement with the Khe Sanh airlift.

CHAPTER SIXTY SIX
Steel Tiger, Eastern Central Laos
17 February 1968, late morning climbing to 9,000 feet and heading towards Khe Sanh

Phil is in the left seat; Bill in the right, with his seat all the way back and a map on his lap.

After crossing the Mekong and leveling off at 9,000 feet Bill asked, *"Did you hear about the Colt story?"*

"The what?"

"Chuck Hill and his bi-wing air-to-air combat."

"What the hell is that?"

"Really, you haven't heard?"

"No, I don't know what you are talking about."

"All right. Zack told me this story last night at the club. It seems as though Chuck ran into a funny plane a few days ago."

"Funny plane? I know all about funny bombs, but planes?"

"Wrong word. Let me start from the beginning; you will love this. A few nights ago, Chuck takes off out of NKP in his Duck with a half moon and almost unlimited visibility. It was one of those gorgeous nights, just so clear. Anyhow he had put in a couple Nimrods (A-26) and a Zorro (T-28). It was so nice they didn't need flares; it was great. They got the front and then the rear trucks in a pretty-good-size convoy somewhere north of Golf. Then they started cleaning them up." Bill looks over to Phil.

"So far so good. I'm with ya'."

"Chuck was "Christmas Tree" with the ice cream cone shielding the rotating beacon so the strikers could see him from above. As usual, his strike aircraft were working NOSTAR (Blackout). After the Zorro RTB'd and the Nimrod was "Winchester" and rolling off from a bomb run, Chuck saw what he thought was 51 cal. (12.7mm) tracers zip diagonally across his nose and then saw them explode on the ground. He thought, "Where did <u>that</u> come from?"

"Getting interesting," said Phil over the intercom.

"Since Nimrod was out of ammo," he thought to himself, "who was that??" At that moment, a movement on his port side caught his eye and he saw what he thought was a P-40 tail (a WWII fighter aircraft) flash by. It had a radial engine and square-tipped wings. But Hell, he had NO idea what it was."

"This was really WIERD SHIT," he thought, "If those headquarters pukes were going to try this shit out here over the Trail, they should at least brief us on it."

"Alleycat told him there was no special stuff going on and only the Nimrod and Zorro were in the sector. He suddenly realized that he was the only one flying around with lights on and that the tracers were being shot at him! He turned off his lights."

"He was fired at again and from ABOVE. He saw the plane again and actually got into a Luffberry (a turn in which both aircraft were on opposite sides of the circle trying to get to each other's six o'clock position). The "P-40" had more airspeed and could out turn the Duck, so Chuck dives for the ground and the story is over. Don't know what happened to the intruder."

"You've got my attention; what about the Colt?"

"Turns out that when Chuck and the Nimrod, who thought he saw the intruder, were asked independently to find the airplane in Jane's, they both identified the Antonov AN-2 Colt."

"I still don't know what the shit that is."

"Sorry, Dumb Ass. It's a small Russian transport built in 1947. They are all over, hundreds of them."

"I got it now."

"No you don't. It's a bi-wing. How about that?"

"You gotta be shitting me, a bi-wing in 1968?"

"The story gets better! Apparently, just yesterday four of these Colts were seen bombing, or trying to bomb, Lima Site 85. You know, where the 81 is that we use to radar bomb Hanoi. Four of these things. Four. Ain't that something?"

"What did they do? The guys on the site?"

"Shit, they couldn't do anything. Now hang on for the finale."

"The finale?"

"An Air America helicopter went after them and with an AK-47 shot one down. Ain't that something?"

"Great story. Is it true?"

"According to Zack, it is."

Historical Note: The AN-2 Colt story is true and the NAIL was Jerry Stephan, Nail 57. On January 12, 1968, two Antonov AN-2 Colts attempted to destroy Lima Site 85 by dropping 120 mm mortar shells from a hole in the bottom of the aircraft. The attack was ineffective. The TACAN installation was down for a few days due to a damaged antenna, but the radar equipment was not harmed. One AN-2 crashed into the side of a mountain as a result of small-arms fire from the ground. The other was brought down by an Air America sharpshooter. The Air America warriors were Ted Moore, pilot of the Huey and Glenn Woods, the mechanic who did the firing with the AK-47. This was the only shoot down of a fixed-wing aircraft by a rotary-wing aircraft in the Vietnam War.

Glenn was KIA on 12 August 1969.

CHAPTER SIXTY SEVEN
Steel Tiger, Eastern Central Laos
17 February 1968, later that morning while continuing towards Khe Sanh

After a few minutes of limited conversation and radio chatter, Bill breaks the silence, *"I heard you were a Raven. Is that true?"*

"No, shit no. I have been a NAIL since I got here in May. Where did you hear that?"

"Last week some one in the NAIL Hole told us all that you flew with the Ravens soon after you got back from your first trip to the States. You know...a good deal followed by a bad deal."

"Yeh, I guess I did, but I was never a real Raven. You had to be there a certain length of time, fly a certain number of missions and get shot. You know all that Raven shit. I was only there for two months."

"You must have really fucked up to be thrown out in two months."

"No, no. The assignment was a short term deal. The Nails were ordered to send a guy to Pakse to cover until the real Ravens showed up. For some reason this was a quickie deal and the 23rd had to send some one quickly. Turns out that Colonel B and Colonel Hardy were both in Saigon and Major Farenmiller was in charge. What an asshole. He thought he owed me one so he sends me."

"I got to hear that one."

"NAIL FOUR EIGHT, this is Cricket. Do you read?"

"Cricket, this is 48, go ahead." Bill continued handling the radios.

"NAIL, your resources as fragged are off and running and plan to be on time in the target area. We have been advised, actually ordered, to ask if you need anything else. Do you?"

"Cricket, NAIL FOUR EIGHT could use a case of Jack."

"Forty Eight, good luck, Cricket out." replied Cricket, not laughing.

"Bill, you handled that nicely. You are so smooth on UHF."

"Yep, now what did you do with the Ravens?"

"First thing I had to do was select a call sign. They don't have any order or it seems any rules when it comes to call sign numbers. 'Just pick one,' they said. They also said it had to be a double-digit number. So I said, "I'm Raven 69." I always liked that number. Say hello to Raven 69."

"69?"

"Yep, all the Americans understood, but none of the Lao had a clue."

"What did Raven 69 do for two months to maintain the safety of the free world?"

"Shit, I didn't do anything. Just flew around and looked out the window. Most of the time I was with a real Raven....me in the back seat. We practiced landings at Lima sites and once in a field. Ravens are nuts, but I went along. We were south of Route 9 all the time so I got to see some of Laos that most NAILs never see   It looks the same as Steel Tiger. Eventually more guys volunteered to be Ravens and when they arrived at Pakse I was a goner."

Historical Note: *Several experienced* NAIL *pilots were asked and did volunteer to transfer into the Raven unit in Laos. They were "sheep dipped" and went off to fly in civilian clothes. Phil Maywald was one of them.*

CHAPTER SIXTY EIGHT

Steel Tiger, Eastern Central Laos
17 February 1968, later that morning heading towards Khe Sanh

They remained silent for most of the rest of the trip to Khe Sanh, but as they approached Route 9 just north of Tchepone, Bill asked, *"How was it living at Khe Sanh with the Marines last summer?"*

"It was something else and nothing like living at NKP. We lived in bunkers underground. We FACs had a bunker and so did some Air Force radio or comm outfit. The grunts had dug foxholes and they slept in them. Showers were outside. There were a few facilities, like the mess hall, some 8 person tents; some structures for other stuff and of course the 12-holer."

"The what?"

"A 12-holer outhouse. You will love this! The building was about 12 by 12, maybe a little larger. When you opened the door and walked in, you could see six seats on the right and six seats on the left...no doors, no privacy at all but plenty of odor. I met the battalion commander there. I'm sitting there, minding my own business, if you will, when this older guy sitting on the other side says 'Are you one of those FACs?' He wasn't a genius. I was wearing a white T-shirt, no hat, Bermuda shorts and combat boots. The Marines all had to wear uniforms. We Air Force types wore civvies. Anyhow, I said "yes" and he introduced himself as the commander and offered to give us a situational briefing, which I took him up on."

"So you met the commander of Khe Sanh on the shitter?"

"No shit, I did. Maybe I did shit. Maybe he did, too. Anyhow, we went to his tent at about 1800 hours that night. Me and a couple other FACs. He goes up to a map of the area and starts showing us where the NVA and Cong are located around Khe Sanh and it's all of a sudden real clear that we were surrounded. I said 'Colonel, we will get our planes out of here immediately.' I wasn't too concerned about the planes but, truth be told, I was damned concerned about my own ass! The Colonel said 'Ease up, Captain; we Marines are always surrounded.'"

Phil took a breath, "Can you believe that shit, always surrounded?"

"What did you do then?"

"We didn't do anything. Just went back to our bunker and continued flying night sorties into North Vietnam.

"What the hell were you trying to do?

"We were doing night search-and-kill missions just north of the DMZ."

"How was it?"

"I wasn't worth shit. We almost never got any ordnance. We were supposed to get the leftovers from strikes in the north, except there never was any. It was so bad that we went to Dong Ha one day and bribed a Gunny Sergeant into giving us some grenades. We dropped them on trucks when we found some but, really, we hardly ever saw anything. It was the pits."

"How do you bribe a Gunny?"

"Booze, man, booze. The grunts had a limit on their booze rations and never could get enough. I think they were allowed two cokes and two beers per day. That is what they told us at Khe Sanh."

"All right, where did you get the booze?"

"Easy, man. When I first got to Khe Sanh and talked with our senior NCO, Sergeant Estep, I asked him what we needed to enjoy our time at Khe Sanh. We needed all kinds of stuff and especially food and we needed it at all times of the day and night. Since the Marines owned the place and controlled everything, I needed to know how to crack the Marine code. Sergeant Estep said the grunts would do anything for booze so that was what we needed. I got donations from all the Air Force guys and flew to NKP, loaded up the O-1 with Jack Daniels and took it to Khe Sanh. Sergeant Estep took care of bribing the local Marines. We were kings of the hill. Booze bought us happiness at Khe Sanh."

After a few minutes Phil continued, *"We were so frustrated that the very few times we did see trucks, we attacked them with the O-1 by firing our .38s or M-16s at them or dropping the grenades. Nobody ever hit anything but one night a trucker got one of our guys. He got tired of being shot at so he stopped his truck, got out and started shooting at the attacking O-1. The FAC was so low and the moon was so bright that the trucker could see him easily. He laced the O-1 cockpit with his AK-47 and hit the FAC in the left leg. The FAC returns to Khe Sanh and tries to land with an unusable left leg and a left crosswind. He rolled it but wasn't killed. I put him on a chopper the next morning and then saw him at the Wright-Pat hospital during one of my two leaves to the good ol' USA. The ward he was on was filled with many with orthopedic injuries so I told him I was surprised that so many Air Force guys had been* shot. He said 'Hell, I'm the only combat injury in this entire room! These guys are all motorcycle and auto accident victims.' Funny, isn't it?"

"What is this 'my two leaves to the good ol' USA shit?" asked Bill.

"Did you know Major Farenmiller? replied Phil.

"No, but you just told me that he's an asshole."

"Right, he is. Anyhow the day I returned to NKP after 30 days at Khe Sanh, he calls me into his office. He must have been the squadron personnel guy or something. Anyhow, he was in charge of the leave schedule for all the NAILs. He says, 'Captain, you are making me look bad and I don't like it.' I hardly know this dumb fuck so you can imagine how confused I am. He continued 'You have been here for over ninety days and you have not taken leave. Don't you know that we have to follow the 7th Air Force R&R policies and have elected to also use the 13th Air Force leave policy? You have to take some leave and take it now.' So I say 'Ok, Major, I'll go tomorrow. How long do I go for?' He says 'Take two weeks. Where will you be going?' "Make that destination Springfield, Ohio," I tell him.

"Now I've got him really worked up. He says 'You can't go to Ohio!' So I calmly, or as calmly as I can, say to him, 'Where does it say I can't go to Ohio?' He is now <u>really</u> agitated and his comeback is, 'You know, I can't find that in the regs, but no one goes to Ohio from NKP.' So I said 'Major, book me for Ohio; I'm leaving tomorrow." The Major is about to explode and he says 'All right, smart ass, you are not going to do that to me again! You must have another leave so I want to know when it is. I want the date now, right now.' I say, 'Okay, Major, I will take December 21st to January 4th. That's about two weeks, Sir.'"

"Now he's even madder and he says "Nobody gets Christmas and New Years, so pick another set of dates.' I remained as cool and collected as possible and asked him what were the rules on leave scheduling. He said, 'First come, first served. Who ever signs up first for the dates gets them.' 'Well, Major,' I tell him, 'Let's look at your book and see who signed up for my dates.' As he opens the book to December, he says, "Son-of-a-bitch, you did it to me again! No one has signed up for your dates.'"

"*He must have been really pissed,*" stated Bill.

"He sure was. He remained long enough to get me into the Ravens, but fortunately he PCS'd out of here about a month later and could do me no more harm. But the story doesn't end there.

"Now what?

"That very night, the eve of my departure for la la land, I was drinking in the club when Sam Jackson runs in and yells to me 'Phil, your plane is getting ready to leave.' 'My plane,' if you will, was a C-141 that we had been advised would be departing NKP the next morning. I would be on board and on my way to Ohio. Sam and I left the club, stole a jeep, drove to the NAIL hootch area, I packed a B-4 bag in about a minute and raced off to the flight line as fast as that little thing would go. As we get to the ramp, we see the 141 starting to turn onto the active runway. Sam says 'Hang on, ol' buddy.' He mashes the accelerator and heads towards the takeoff end of the runway. As the C-141 turns on his landing lights (a sign he is ready to take off) and starts increasing the engines thrust, Sam drives the jeep onto the active runway, directly in front of the giant aircraft...25 feet in front. They pull the engines back to idle and a ladder comes down from the front left side of the 141. I jumped out of the jeep and climbed the ladder. As I got to the cockpit, the aircraft commander said, 'What the fuck is going on?' I told him, 'I am a FAC and I am going to Ohio.' He said 'Well...I'll get you to the States, but you'll have to get that goddamn jeep out of my way first!' Sam passed up the B-4 and off I went."

"Did you get there?"

"Yep; I had two wonderful weeks and then I hitchhiked back. Actually, I've been home twice so far and I may go again in a few weeks. We have a requirement to take our R&R and leaves and, as the major said, there are no regs that say I can't go to Ohio. War ain't all bad."

Historical Note: Several NAIL pilots, navigators and maintenance personnel were assigned to Khe Sanh in the spring and summer of 1967. They did fly every night into North Vietnam looking for targets. All of the above incidents were observed by Pat Sweeney. The 23rd TASS did execute the 7th Air Force and the 13th Air Forces policies on R&R and leave (vacation). NAILs normally got two R and Rs and one leave. Pat Sweeney actually returned to Springfield, Ohio three times during his one-year tour. We are unaware of anyone else in this conflict who returned to the States that often in one year. Sam Weaver was the jeep driver who stopped the C-141 on the runway at NKP.

CHAPTER SIXTY NINE
Steel Tiger, Eastern Central Laos
17 February 1968, even later that morning heading

towards Khe Sanh

After a few minutes, Phil opened the conversation again as they approached the Laos-Vietnam border, **"See just ahead? It's kind of a Special Forces camp and village."**

"U.S. Special Forces?"

"Yep, but not very big; just a few Green Berets."

"We are still in Laos, right?"

"Yep, I flew in there last summer in an O-1. Landed in a field. There it is. Not too long, but it's flat. We were taking beer to the locals. Dick Naybig, a Covey, led a flight of three in there one afternoon. We only stayed about an hour. But your pilot had his boots on the ground in Laos. Damn there ain't much left of the place. There must be NVA all over. You have been in Laos?"

"No, and I don't plan on going there today. Now where is Khe Sanh, pilot?"

"Not so fast. We gotta give you the tour. Next on the agenda is Lang Vei, former home of more Special Forces and home to a group of Montagnards. It was overrun by the NVA with tanks about ten days ago. Do you see it on your map?"

"Yes, just south of Route 9 inside Vietnam." Shortly thereafter, Bill added, *"There it is. I got it. Not much there now. And now, Khe Sahn?"*

Phil was silent but after only a couple of minutes, he couldn't resist stating the obvious, **"Why Mr. Navigator, <u>there</u> it is, just to the right of the mountain at 11 o'clock. See the little village just a little bit further south about 1 o'clock?"**

In a few seconds, *"Got it."*

They continued flying eastward generally over Highway 9 and as they approached the Marine base at Khe Sanh, Phil said, *"We are really lucky today. The fog is gone."*

"Fog?"

"Yep, during the spring monsoon this place is covered with chronic fog and rain. As we get closer to the airstrip, you will see an 800-foot drop-off on the east end. Since the prevailing winds come from the west, often the runway is fog-shrouded and well below minimum instrument landing conditions."

"That drop off reminds me of the drop off at Guam."

"This runway is not 15,000 feet though. It is only 3,900 feet long and 60 feet wide and covered with pierced steel planking. I almost forgot....the runway slopes at 3% from west to east. Normally we landed going west which was into the prevailing wind, but this meant that we were landing on a runway that was sloped into us. When we brought new guys over here, I always bet them I could make the first turn off landing east bound, but they couldn't. I never lost on this. Landing with a tail wind on a runway that slopes away from you and that you don't know is a bitch."

They circled the base a couple times at 9,000 feet as Phil described the local terrain so Bill could locate all the important sites and mark his map. The elevation of the runway was 1,500 feet above sea level. The mountains to the north went to 5,581 feet and generally the high hills in the area went to 3,000 feet. Hills 881 (hills were named by their height in meters) north and south were just off to the north west of Khe Sanh and Hill 861 was in the same direction, just closer. After a few circles, Phil flew the plane eastward over Route 9 and soon turned north.

"See that mountain just north of where the river and the road turn east?"

"Yes."

"That is the Rockpile and that is what it is...a pile of rocks. It's been an artillery position but I don't have a clue as to who owns it now."

Continuing eastbound over Route 9, Phil pointed out Camp Carroll just a few more miles down the road and explained that this also was an artillery-battery position. The U.S. Army had some 175mm long guns here that would shoot a big shell over 32,000 meters (20 miles). They continued on to Cam Lo and then Dong Ha and finally over the delta that flowed into the South China Sea.

"That's the tour of Quang Tri Province. Now when the transports say they are over Cam Lo or the Rockpile or whatever, you will know where they are. I suggest that we make this local tour a part of the FAC indoctrination for those who will support Khe Sanh's airlift."

"Nice tour and I agree. Now let's get back to Khe Sanh...."

Historical Note: Dick Nadig, a Covey FAC, did lead a flight of three O-1s, including Pat Sweeney and another Nail, from Khe Sanh into eastern Laos just south of Route 9 on a beer run to the locals. Pat Sweeney never lost a bet on the eastbound landings at Khe Sanh.

CHAPTER SEVENTY
Steel Tiger, Eastern Central Laos
17 February 1968, moments later heading west to Khe Sanh

As they turned to fly back towards Khe Sanh, *"NAIL FOUR EIGHT, this is Checkers 7; do you read me?"* came the voice interrupting Bill's deep thought. This was the expected C-130 transport.

"Roger, Checkers, this is 48. We will want you to hold offshore opposite Dong Ha until after the fighters does their air show. What is your ETA for Dong Ha?" Bill was now doing all the radio calls.

"Should be there in 15 minutes, NAIL."

"Checkers, we understand that you are a C-130 scheduled for a Low Altitude Parachute Extraction System drop at Khe Sanh. Is that correct?"

"Roger, NAIL, we will do a LAPES."

"Stand by, Checkers, and remain on this frequency for further instructions. This is NAIL FOUR EIGHT. Crow flight, are you on 287.4."

"Roger, NAIL, Crow a flight of four Fox Fours with wall to wall 82s just off the tanker. We'll have about 15 minutes when we get there. We have been listening and are about 10 minutes out from Khe Sanh. What do you want us to do?"

"Stand by, Crow. Khe Sanh tower do you read NAIL FOUR EIGHT?"

"Roger, NAIL. We have been on frequency and have copied all the traffic from you, Checkers and Crow."

"Roger, Tower. Monitor our progress and if anything should happen to prevent a successful LAPES or any other flight-safety item, call ABORT, ABORT."

"Roger, NAIL. Copied and will do."

"Crow, our mission is to get the C-130 safely in and out. When we ask, we will want your flight to fly over Khe Sanh at about 4,000 feet going east

to west. Then climb to 10,000 and circle Khe Sanh so our troops and the NVA can see you. This is an air show run. We want them all to know that you're there and ready to drop on any NVA who shows us where he is. Any questions?"

"Negative."

"After the air show, we will clear Checkers, the C-130, to depart the South China Sea and head for Khe Sanh at 8,000 feet. NAIL FOUR EIGHT will be at 8,500 and will be looking for Checkers. Checkers, you will be generally south of a road and a river running east to west. When you get to your tactical descent point, begin your descent. The NAIL will join up on your right wing and fly formation with you to about 2,500 indicated. After the drop, you will clear left to the south and begin a rapid climb. The NAIL will try to stay with you as best we can. Any questions so far?"

"Checkers negative."

"Crow negative."

"OK, now if any gook is dumb enough to shoot at us...either NAIL or Checkers can call "break" and will state the clock direction of the fire. Checkers will break left and climb rapidly, going south. The NAIL will roll in, mark the target and clear the Crow flight in hot. The NAIL will go south after the C-130 and the F-4s will come in east to west and drop half a load on the first pass, then the other half on the second pass coming in from west to east this time. Crow flight you have everything north of Khe Sanh. Remember the mountains north of the base go up to almost 6,000 feet. Any questions?"

"NAIL, we have you in sight just east of the base."

Roger, Crow flight. We are at 8,500 feet and now have you in sight. You are cleared for your air show pass. Make it good."

"Crow flight go trail, 10 second spacing, left rejoin off target"

"Two!...Three!...Four!"

Bill and Phil watched as the F-4s rolled in East to West and seemed to merge with their shadows as they rocketed towards Khe Sanh. *"Crow flight, watch your altitude."*

"Not to worry, NAIL. We want to scare the shit out of them."

They flashed over the PSP runway at 200 feet... going the speed of heat...lit their burners briefly... aileron rolled... then pulled off to the south and, seemingly instantly, were at 10,000 feet orbiting the base!

"Holy shit! Did you see that!!."

Bill was clearly impressed as he said, *"Those sons-a-bitches were well below 500 feet. Great show. Didn't you love the victory roll, before the fight?"*

With the air show over and the fighters now circling Khe Sanh at 10,000, Bill radioed, *"Checkers, you are cleared in."*

"Roger, NAIL, we are feet dry," came the call as the big transport flew from the South China Sea over the South Vietnamese shoreline, heading towards Khe Sanh.

Within seconds Bill called, *"Checkers, we have you. Continue your approach."*

Phil began to put the O-2 into a favorable location so that he could join up with the C-130 just prior to the descent, which would be rapid and steep. These transport guys really knew how to descend steeply so as to avoid as much ground fire as possible. This was going to be fun...an O-2 flying formation with a C-130.

The O-2 joined the C-130 and followed it to 2,500 feet, then leveled off.

"Bill, see anything yet?"
"Nope, they got their heads down."

The C-130 pilot continued his rapid descent until he was about 100 feet above the PSP runway where he shallowed his approach. He then abruptly leveled off about 10 feet above the runway and released a large drogue chute which inflated immediately and yanked the pallets full of supplies out of the 130 and onto the runway. The 130 immediately began a climb in a left turn. The cargo hit the landing area hard and skidded for what seemed to be a couple hundred yards before stopping. The O-2 following the C-130 was well off the right wing and initially higher, but the 130 soon out climbed the Duck.

As the transport passed about 7,000 feet, Phil called **"Checkers, nice job. The package stopped almost directly in the middle of the target. You should be clear of any anti-aircraft fire now. Thanks for a great job."**

"NAIL, that fighter-FAC formation seemed to work. Keep your head up. We are off for Danang. Thanks for the help."

"Crow, are you ready to unload some ordnance?"

"You bet, NAIL. Give me a mark."

"Crow, it will only take us a couple minutes to be in position to mark a suspected regimental headquarters that was located and identified by acoustic sensors. It will be north and west of the base about a mile. You will not be able to see any people or equipment, but the Willy Pete will be on target."

"Shit, when did you learn to shoot?" asked Bill.

"Watch me, old fighter pilot."

In a few minutes **"Crow, NAIL is rolling in to mark.... "**

Phil rolled the Duck inverted...pulled it down to a 45-degree dive angle...rolled right side up......pointed the Duck where he wanted the smoke....centered the controls and pickled off a WP.

"*Crow, the smoke is about 30 meters too far west. Start your drop about 50 yards east of the smoke going east to west. Do you see the FAC?*"

"*NAIL, we have you. Crow, push 'em up. Lets drop it all on one pass... One's in.*"

"*Two is in.*"

"*One is off; no gunfire.*"

"*Two, put yours a little further south....50 meters,*" said Bill.

"*Three is in.*"

"*Two is off.*"

"*Three, put yours between the other two.*"

"*Four is in.*"

"*Four, see if you can put yours between the first two.*"

"*Three is off.*"

"*So far, so good, you guys,*" said Bill.

"*Four is off.*"

"*Crow rejoin left, call in sight*", the wingmen responded "*Two Tally, Three Tally, Four Tally*"

"*Nail, that was fun! You got any BDA for Crow*"

"*Out fucking standing gents! We won't have any BDA for you, ... target is obscured by smoliage ... 100 percent of ordnance on target*"

"*Say again Nail?*"

"*No BDA...the target area is obscured by 'Smoliage' ...smoke and foliage!*"

Chuckling, Crow lead replied," *See ya later, NAIL. Our best to Bill Thompson, if you see him.*"

"*This is him. Who are you?*"

"Billy boy, it is your old IP from F-86 school, Burl McClin. I guess the F-4s jets are still too fast for you."

"Yeh, right. The FAC outfit needed a fighter pilot and lucky Pierre is the boy. You okay?"

"No problem. Two months to go and back to la-la land. Take care. Crow flight, go to 264.8."

Phil and Bill stayed in the Khe Sanh area for about two more hours and assisted in two more drops and one C-123 landing, all with out a shot fired.

<u>Historical Note</u>: The Khe Sanh tactics did seem to work and the NAILs continued to provide this assistance on a daily basis until the Khe Sanh base was resupplied by Highway 9 and the Battle of Khe Sanh was over. Few transports took hits and when they did, it was mostly small-arms fire. The transport crews were totally dedicated and often made drops when the weather was marginal and/or a FAC was not on scene. Unfortunately, on March 6th, a C-123 was hit by anti-aircraft fire when attempting a landing and crashed about a mile south east of Khe Sanh trying to return to Danang. It is not known if a NAIL FAC was assisting at that time. Don Brown and Pat Sweeney actually developed the tactics and flew this mission as described above. The acoustic sensors around Khe Sanh were instrumental in providing targets for every type of aircraft, including the B-52s.

CHAPTER SEVENTY ONE
Nakhon Phanom Royal Thai Air Base (NKP)
22 February 1968, after lunch at NAIL Ops

The Navy took its nine remaining aircraft and departed NKP. They'd initially flown into Nakhon Phanom with nine OP-2Es, and then soon added three more for a complete dozen. However, in less than four months, they had lost three airplanes and twenty crew members. The Navy unit had been decimated but, surprisingly, these losses were about half of what the war planners in the Pentagon had estimated for such a dangerous mission. Their war in Laos was finished and they had dropped their last sensor along the Trail. ADSID emplacement would now be reserved for fast movers...F-4s... which could survive in the increasingly-hostile anti-aircraft environment. Both the Army and the Navy were now out of the sensor business in Laos....their war was over.

General Holland was called to Washington to explain the severity of the OP-2E losses. Needless to say, he and his staff were in the process of attempting to shift the "blame" on to the FACs who led the drop "missions." Just in case that didn't work, they were compiling data to prove that the sensors found and destroyed three times as many trucks with radar bombing as the FACs normally destroyed using flares and marking rockets. The general also reported that as the battle of Khe Sanh continued, there were reports that the sensors dropped by the Navy were responsible for locating many NVA and Viet Cong units that were destroyed near the base. The sensors found them and the fighter bombers and the B-52s killed them.

Sharon had accompanied the general on this trip to Washington. For some odd reason, Sean was happy that Sharon had gone. No, happy wasn't it; what he actually felt was relief. Things had been going very badly between the two, on all fronts. It didn't seem to matter what Sean told her concerning the downed OP-2E. Sharon was getting her info from TFA...the all-seeing, all-knowing Almighty TFA...and they had officially blamed him, personally and solely, for leading the Neptune into a cloud-covered mountain. The casualties had become Sean's fault. Sharon was not the least bit receptive to any of his explanations. Things became even more awkward after she turned down his most recent proposal of marriage.

Then to make things even worse...if that were possible...good old friend Bill gave Sharon one of his famous lectures on "Warriors and Woosies" when he drove her back to her TFA trailer.

For Sean, some of the magic was gone but he was still captivated by her. He wondered if they'd ever get their acts together but decided if they did; it would most likely be after the war.

That afternoon in NAIL Admin Sean was approached by Eddie, the three- stripe Admin clerk.

"Sir, Major Palmer just dropped off Lt. Stiewe's OER (Officer Effectiveness Report) material and I think you should look it over before I type it." He handed the file to Sean.

Sean read the hand-written draft of the OER that Eddie would have to type so that the major could sign it. Sean quickly scanned the OER and realized it was far below what the lieutenant deserved and that is was surely a "career ender."

"Eddie, thanks for sharing this with me. This is the worst ER I've ever seen! This lieutenant has done a great job. He is an Academy grad. He is third in gun kills. He would be in Stan Eval if he were a Captain. I knew Palmer was an asshole, but this is too much. This 6.1 (out of a possible 9.4) as a combat effectiveness report would end his career. He couldn't make captain with that. In fact, he would probably be relieved of duty altogether if he was that ineffective and incompetent."

"That's what I thought, Captain. What should we do?"

"Let me think a minute. What is Major Palmer's schedule?"

"Sir, he expects to come back here and sign the OER and then go directly to Base Ops and get on the afternoon Klong to Bangkok so he can make his scheduled flight for home."

"When does the Klong take off from here?"

"I think 1630 hours, Sir."

"Okay, he will drop in here just before take off and hope to do the signing. I got it! Eddie, type this up and make three obvious misspellings or typos. He will see the typos and not be able to sign this OER as they must be error free. He will be pissed. Then I'll jump in see the problem.... and I'll chew your ass very vehemently. Then I'll ask him to sign a blank and promise that I will make sure what goes out is error free. He will have no time, will sign the blank OER, go get on the plane and the problem is solved."

"But, Sir, if you promised him that, what has changed?

"Eddie, I promised him it would be error free; I never said it would be the same as his draft."

About two hours later, Major Palmer came in to the NAIL admin offices, noted the typos, yelled at Eddie, as did Sean. Then he signed the blank forms after Sean promised to have the ER re-done, "error free." The major departed NKP.

The "error free" OER went to headquarters the next day. The "error free" version noted that Lt. Stiewe was "exceptional" in all areas and was recommended for promotion "well in advance of his peers." The "error free" OER was a 9.4, a "perfect OER".

Historical Note: This is a true story. The lieutenant continued to excel in his career and retired as a major general. No one knows what happened to the major. Clearly, the authors cannot name names on this one.

CHAPTER SEVENTY TWO
Nakhon Phanom Royal Thai Air Base (NKP)
26 February 1968, about 0730 on the NAIL aircraft
 parking ramp

Everywhere but at TFA, Sean was treated as one of the good guys. He had taken care of the Army's sniffer program, flew almost daily NAIL support to Khe Sanh, led many Navy sensor drops and developed a complete tactical plan for the 23rd TASS. He was exhausted. Colonel Benjamin and Lieutenant Colonel Hardy, good commander and good Ops officer that they were, decided it was time to send him and Ralph to Bangkok for a few days to relax and blow off some steam. Bill and Joe Brown were due for an R&R break and the colonel sent them with Sean and Ralph. Per procedures of the 23rd TASS, these pilots would fly an O-2 to Bangkok and turn it over to four other 23rd guys for the return flight. The plane was gone for only seven or eight hours and the crew members enjoyed four days in this fantastic Asian capitol city.

The NAIL FACS, flying four to five hours a day, seven days a week, quickly found themselves running up against the medical limits for flight hours. They were allowed to fly a hundred and twenty hours in a single month, but only three hundred hours in a thirteen-week period. There was also a 300-hour quarterly limit.

The mathematics of these limits normally afforded the NAIL pilots and navigators with approximately one week off every five to six weeks. The limits were based on a sliding calendar and were monitored daily by the staff at the 23rd and at 7th Air Force HQ.

Most of the flight commanders and the operations staff watched the crew's flying time carefully and were able to avoid the monthly limits but everyone was caught by the three-hundred-hour quarterly limit. Colonel Benjamin usually took his golf clubs to the resort at Chang Mai in northern Thailand but most the others went to Bangkok and stayed in the Chao Phraya Hotel.

This was Bill and Sean's first visit in several months and they were happy to have Joe and Ralph along to show them Bangkok's delights. The crews usually stayed together and watched out for each other. So far, no one had failed to return on time and no one wanted to be the first one to miss their plane back to NKP.

They were scheduled to land at Don Muang airport in Bangkok and meet the returning crews at USAF Base Ops, which was on the opposite side of the runways from the commercial terminal. The flight plan was filed at NKP as a round trip with a thirty-minute stop at Don Muang.

"Are we ready?" Sean asked.

"Ready and rarin' to go," Joe replied. He put Sean and Bill's hang-up bags behind the rear seats of the O-2. The four quickly climbed into the plane and Ralph started the engines. Bill and Sean rode in the rear seats.

"How do you like it back there?" Joe asked.

"This isn't my idea of a four-passenger plane," Sean commented as he tried to find room for his feet in the cramped rear.

"It is. Says so right in the Dash-1 description. I know. I read it." Joe was laughing at them, waving his pointing finger in their faces.

"How long's the flight?" Bill wanted to knows

"A little over three hours, depending on the winds. We're due at Don Muang at noon," Ralph answered.

"Ask the stewardess to bring me some coffee or a beer, if she has one," Bill said, as soon as they leveled off.

Ralph had climbed the O-2 to five thousand feet for the trip south. Joe reached for the container at his feet and handed a coke to Ralph. He had cold beers for the rest of them. **"Why did you think I selected the lieutenant as our pilot,"** he asked"

It was a bright day with a clear blue sky and no clouds. The flights to Bangkok were always scheduled to depart early in the morning, to insure that the return flight arrived before the typical late-afternoon thunderstorms. Clouds usually built up around three and it would rain by four. At six, the sky would be clear again.

Sean enjoyed the flight to Bangkok but Bill went to sleep as soon as he finished his beer. Sean studied the countryside for the first time. It was lush, green and mainly open, except for occasional rice paddies and dirt roads. Only rarely did he see any villages or people. Their route took them well to the west of Korat Air Base so they could avoid any fighters on the way to or from the war.

Bill woke up immediately as Ralph turned onto final approach and reduced the power for landing.

"How do we get into town?"

He asked the question because he thought these "experienced Bangkokers" might have something special lined up.

"We'll use the cab that brings the returning NAILs back from town. It's about a forty-minute ride. If there isn't a cab waiting, we can get one from the commercial side of the airport. That's where the airliners park. Don Muang is Bangkok's international airport," Joe replied.

"No shit," said Bill.

"Don't you guys remember any of this from your other trips here?" Ralph asked.

"This is our first real trip being led by expert Bangkokers. We came through Bangkok on our

way to NKP but we only stayed one night at the Chao Phraya with the C-130 crew," *Sean replied.* "We just went where they went ... "

"The Chao Phraya is a lousy place to stay," Ralph answered.

"It seemed nice enough when we were there," Bill commented, "and it was only a buck a night. We have stayed there the couple times we were here. "

"Oh, it's a nice hotel and it's cheap. It's under Army contract as the transient and visitor quarters for the area. That isn't the problem. Bangkok's still an accompanied tour. You'll meet everyone you know there, with their wives. I just don't want to spend the evening watching other guys with their wives," Joe replied.

"Now that you mention it, I don't either," Sean said.

"You should talk," Bill gave Sean a wry look.

"Yeah, Captain. You're the only one of us with an American honey at NKP," Ralph said, turning to look at Sean.

"Where do we stay?" Bill wanted to know.

"At the Northeast. It has a twenty-four hour bar and restaurant with some American food. The rooms are clean and reasonable. Not only that, they don't bother you about the girls or anything," Ralph replied.

"Lead on, MacDuff, we're in your capable hands," Bill said.

As they landed and taxied to the USAF parking ramp near the Base Operations building, a light blue Toyota taxi pulled onto the ramp. It continued slowly toward them, coming to a stop in front of the O-2. The doors opened and four NAILs piled out, dressed in their flight suits. They went to the trunk where each grabbed a hang-up or B-4 bag.

"Right on time, Joe. Any problems with the plane?"

Ralph shook his head negative and Joe handed the returning NAILs their copy of the flight plan. They swapped baggage locations while Ralph headed for Operations to close out the first leg of the flight plan.

CHAPTER SEVENTY THREE
Don Muang Airport, Bangkok, Thailand
26 February 1968, about 1100 hours on the military aircraft parking ramp

They found a six-pack of Budweiser in the cab, compliments of the departing NAILs. On the way into Bangkok, Joe kept up a steady stream of information. He told them a little more about the hotel, the food, the temples, the klong, the massage parlors, the girls and the American aircrews' usual haunts. Both Bill and Sean were anxious to visit and sample everything. Having experienced Bangkokers sure seemed like a great idea now. By the time they pulled into the Northeast Hotel's entranceway, they were ready for some serious partying. This had the makings of the best time they ever had in Bangkok.

The cab dropped them off at the door and Joe paid for the trip with an American five-dollar bill. When they entered the foyer, this hotel looked much like any first-class hotel anywhere in the world. The lobby was spacious and clean and it was attended by a uniformed bellman. Behind the registration desk was a businesslike clerk attired in a dark blue suit and dark tie. Also behind the desk and, just as professionally dressed, were two beautiful young Thai women.

While they were registering, Joe sent the bellman to the bar for more beer. By the time they finished signing the room cards, the Thai beer was served. They agreed to meet in the bar as soon as they had showered and changed into civilian clothes. The temperature was a pleasant seventy-five degrees so the uniform of the day was slacks and short-sleeve sport shirts.

"Well, what's first?" Sean asked as the four of them departed their hotel in a cab.

"We usually go for a massage and then to dinner," Joe answered. *"How does that sound?"*

"I'm game," Bill replied.

Sean nodded as well and Joe gave directions to the driver.

They drove for about ten minutes and turned down a street crowded with people, the small Bangkok taxis and three-wheeled tuk-tuks. The street was narrow and dominated by a large hotel at the far end. There were taxis lined up at the hotel and at two other modern-looking buildings on the street.

"Here we are," Ralph said. *"Pick one."*

"Pick one what?" Sean asked.

"Both of these massage parlors are clean. We've been to them many times."

"Do you have a preference?" Sean asked.

"I like the one on the right." replied Ralph.

"I'll go with Ralph's choice," Bill said. *"He doesn't seem to have caught anything."*

Joe laughed and Sean frowned at Bill's remark. *"What's he supposed to catch?"* Sean wanted to know.

"Who brought him?" Joe asked, kidding Sean.

"What I'd like to know is how someone as naive as Sean ends up with the only good looking round eye in Thailand. Are you sure she won't mind your dallying around in Bangkok?" Bill chuckled at his friend's embarrassment.

"Haven't you ever been to one of these massage parlors, Sean?" Joe asked. Sean shook his head, no.

"Well, it's hard to catch anything here. That's for later. Here they only relieve your tensions and pressures," Joe replied, grinning.

The four exited and Joe again paid the driver. *"We need to settle with you for the cab fares,"* Sean said.

"Later. I'm ready for some relaxation," Joe replied and followed Ralph into the building. The door was being held open by a liveried doorman. Bill smiled, nodded in appreciation and said, *"Sawadee,"* which is the Thai greeting that Joe taught them in the taxi. The doorman responded by smiling, placing his hands together as if in prayer and bowing as he said, *"Sawadee, Kup."*

They entered a dark lounge and when their eyes adjusted to the dimly lit room, they could see girls seated along one wall and at tables with mostly Caucasian men throughout the club. The four sat at a table and Joe ordered beers for everyone from a cute Thai waitress. Ralph wasn't paying much attention to anyone in particular but he was looking around the room intently.

"Haven't you seen girls before?" Bill asked.

Joe replied for him. *"Ralph has a special honey who works here. He's looking for her."*

Bill smiled and nodded. *"They're certainly good looking. The only fat one's the Mamasan over there. You know, some of these girls don't look over fifteen or sixteen years old. What're the numbers for? The ones they're wearing?"* Each girl wore a number, either on a large round lapel button or on a card pinned to her waist.

"You pick out a number that you like. Then the Mamasan arranges payment and you get your massage." Ralph answered while he was looking around.

"I have my number," Sean said, excited. *"This is easy."*

"It will be if you didn't pick the one I want," Bill replied.

The Mamasan was watching them and she came over to their table as soon as it appeared that they were ready. *"Sawadee. Message?"* She bowed slightly as she greeted them.

"Yes, Ma'am. Number Thirty-four," Joe said.

"Is Twenty-eight here today?" Ralph asked.

"She with customer. Be done soon. You wait?" the fat lady replied.

"I wait," Ralph nodded in agreement. Bill and Sean picked their numbers and as they paid their forty Baht (two dollars, American); the Mamasan motioned for the appropriate girl to come forward. One at a time the girls came over, bowed and motioned for the pilot to follow. Ralph remained at the table, waiting for his number twenty eight to appear.

Neither Bill nor Sean was completely prepared for the Bangkok massage. The girls took each of them to a separate small room that was dimly lit with a single shaded light and furnished with a bathtub and a table that resembled an examining room table in a medical facility. The girls undressed them, hung their clothes on a hook and then bathed them. Obviously, being bathed by an attractive female, clad in only a bra and panties, had an effect upon the young men. The girls would giggle at the emerging rigid members and using a soft cream, relieved the "situation" with their hands. Bill got slapped a couple times for attempting to have his masseuse relieve his "problem" in a more traditional fashion.

When they were bathed and toweled, they lay on the tables while the young girls gave them a massage. For certain it relieved a lot of tension, in every sense of the word.

Joe was sitting in the lounge when Sean appeared, followed shortly by Bill. Both wore slightly embarrassed grins. Joe laughed. *"What did you think of it?"*

"We need one of these next to the O'Club at NKP," Bill said. *"I could really use a massage after a flight ... "*

"Wouldn't that be nice? I wonder what the Air Force would do if we opened one?" Sean offered.

"They couldn't handle it. The staffies would monopolize it in any case," Joe answered.

They'd almost finished their second beer when Ralph returned. He had a gorgeous young girl with him. She was beautiful, tiny, with exquisite oriental features. She as slightly dark skinned as the Thais were, with blue-black hair down to her shoulders and full breasts, not flat chested like the Vietnamese women. Ralph's friend was in an evening dress. She was dressed to go out, not as the masseuses, who wore shorts and halters. *"This is Tomi,"* He said, getting her a chair. The others stood when they walked up to the table. They were introduced and Tomi joined them. It was a little after five in the afternoon.

"What now, Ralph?" Bill asked.

"Let's go to dinner. Tomi knows the best places and with her as interpreter, we save a bunch of money, particularly with the damn taxis."

"I'm happy that you're going with us," Bill said to Tomi as he stood and bowed slightly. *"I would much rather be in the company of a pretty woman, than with just these three ugly people. Do you have any friends?"*

"Many, many friends. We see later," Tomi answered, smiling broadly. She had perfect teeth as well. Bill was impressed. He assumed that she was a friend of Ralph's, not a working masseuse.

"What're you doing here?" Bill asked.

"Work here," she replied. Bill looked a little puzzled. Tomi is number twenty eight he thought, but did not say any more.

"Let's go find something to eat," Joe interjected and started toward the door. The rest followed. Ralph was last, with Tomi holding his arm.

They dined at a well known restaurant, Nick's Number One, and ordered the Kobe beef, for which Nick's is famous. When dinner was finished, Tomi asked Ralph to go dancing. Bill and Sean weren't very interested in watching other people enjoy themselves and it showed in their depressed expressions. The two said they would go off on their own and meet the others back at their hotel. Tomi thought she'd offended them and Joe was laughing aloud.

"That's where the girls are, you dumbasses. We're going to find us some dancing partners. Actually, we're going to find us some dancing and other activities partners for the next few days," Joe said gleefully.

Joe, Ralph and Tomi rose and started for the door. Bill and Sean were confused, but got up and followed without speaking. The group departed Nick's and hailed a taxi which took them to the Copa Cabana Night Club, which was near the Northeast Hotel. It was dark now and the club was brightly lit on the outside. A liveried doorman ushered them inside and, like the massage parlor, they found themselves in a dimly lit corridor. There is a window all the way down the length of the corridor and behind the window on a three-tiered bench were at least twenty five seated girls. Each of the girls was wearing panties, a bra, and a number and each was watching the window.

"Does this work the same way? I love numbers," Bill said.

"Make your choice and when we go through that door, you negotiate with the Mamasan for the

desired services, the same as before. You can hire one for the evening, the night or the week, if you want," Ralph said.

"What about money. I don't know if I have enough," Bill said. *"Will they take American Express?"*

"In the first place, it doesn't cost very much, maybe five dollars a day. A week is about twenty-five dollars," Joe replied, *"and they do accept American Express."*

"I should've guessed," Sean said.

"Tomi, do you have any suggestions? Are these your friends?" Bill asked.

"Friend number forty-two and sixty-one," she answered, *"Good friends, no sick."*

Bill caught Tomi's comment and whispered to Sean, *"Tomi means they don't have anything you can take back to your friend."*

Sean was glad the corridor was dark. He was bright red. *"I'll take sixty-one,"* he managed to stammer. Bill looked for forty-two and discovered that, like sixty-one, she was another young and attractive Thai girl.

"Forty-two's fine for me. Are we going for the whole trip?"

"I am," Joe said. *"Who wants to go out looking every day? Ralph has Tomi, so we've got an interpreter if the girls don't speak very good English. I'm taking number twelve."*

When they got to the end of the corridor, they went through the door. Tomi nodded to the Mamasan and they were shown to a table. To everyone's surprise, the girls they'd selected walked out of another door and joined them at the table. The girls seemed to know who selected which number.

Tomi spoke to the Mamasan and then turned to them and said, *"Five hundred Baht for girl. Stay with you in hotel, come back here in taxi when you go to airport, you pay taxi. Stay with you all time. Nice girls, polite, clean, speak good English."*

"That's fine with me," Bill said.

"Me, too," Joe added. Sean nodded in agreement.

The Mamasan collected their money and the girls held onto the arms of their partners. Bill looked at Ralph and shook his head. *"How many times have you been down here?"*

"Seven and, God, it's better each time. I've been with Tomi for the last five trips."

It was then that Bill realized that Ralph was contracting for Tomi's services the same way that they were. The war did have some compensation after all.

They remained at the club for a couple of hours, dancing and drinking with their new partners. Joe finally stood and announced, *"It's time to head back. We can have a snack at the hotel, if anyone is still hungry."*

The group exited and they summoned two taxis. On the way to the hotel, Bill wondered what sort of tip they'd have to give the doorman to get the girls in without a fuss. He was pleasantly surprised. Everyone seemed to know everyone else and the doorman treated the young ladies with deference. Bill didn't find out until weeks later that the girls paid percentages to the doormen.

Joe and Ralph led the way to a small restaurant and lounge adjacent to the hotel lobby. The girls ate but the four pilots ordered only drinks. As the evening wore on, each couple broke off and left the table. Bill and his new friend were the last ones at the table. He was left with the bill and resolved to be more careful in the future. Number forty-two, Sansi, as she was called, held tightly to his arm. He was definitely looking forward to the rest of the night and the rest of the week.

Bill wasn't disappointed. The girls couldn't do enough to please their hosts. Bill slept soundly and awoke to find the lovely young girl snuggled tightly up against him. Without any conscious effort, he found himself aroused. Some quiet giggling told him that his condition had not gone unnoticed. Sansi proved as adept in the morning as she had been at night. He thought, *"A week of this and I'll have to go back to the war for some rest."*

They got up and jointly showered, another pleasant experience, then dressed and headed for the restaurant. Sean and his friend were already eating. When they finished breakfast, Sean opened a tour-guide brochure that he'd found at the desk. *"What do you say we hire a car and go see the sights?"*

"It sounds OK to me. Just be sure we get a chance to do some shopping. I've got to buy some things to send home," Bill replied.

"What kind of shopping, PX or local?" Sean asked.

"Local. We can get PX stuff at NKP. I want to see some of this jewelry that Bangkok is so famous for."

Sean's girl spoke halting English but got the idea across that the girls would make the arrangements for a taxi and for the shopping. They would learn back at NKP that the girls received a percentage of the taxi fare and everything they bought at the shops, another Bangkok custom. Everyone involved seemed to get a percentage of every financial transaction in Bangkok ... and all of Thailand for that matter.

Neither objected. They left a note at the desk for Joe and Ralph telling them that they'd meet at the hotel at about 5:00pm for dinner and drinks.

Bangkok was well worth the sightseeing effort. They spent the next three days touring and shopping, with the girls arranging for drivers and even securing an English-speaking guide for the tour of the Grand Palace, the Reclining Buddha and the Temple of the Emerald Buddha. The most interesting day was the second, when they took a three-and- a-half-hour boat trip, a leisurely, powered excursion on Bangkok's klongs, or canals. Here they saw the "Floating Market," and people everywhere, washing, cooking and relieving themselves in the same water. One day the four played golf at the Bangkok Country Club.

Bill and Sean learned how to "Wai" properly. The "Wai," clasping both hands together and bowing politely, is the Thai manner of greeting and has an implicit recognition of status. The hands are held higher for more important persons and the fingers nearly touch the nose. It is considered poor taste to "Wai" social inferiors first. The "Wai" is usually accompanied with the words, "Sawadee," the Thai equivalent of "Good Morning, Good Evening," etc... this is the Thai version of "Aloha". Sean seemed to understand how to use the "Wai" but Bill tended to "Wai" everyone first, much to the delight of the girls.

In the afternoons they shopped, visiting jewelry stores catering to the Americans where they purchased rings, pins and assorted gems as gifts for their families and friends at home. In the evenings they enjoyed dinners, drinking, socializing and intimate time with the girls.

Historical Note: The NAILS did fly the O-2s to Bangkok for R and R just as described above. They typically flew 26 to 28 missions in 26 to 28 days and spent 3 to 4 days away from NKP. Bangkok was <u>much more exciting</u> than described above.

CHAPTER SEVENTY FOUR
Bangkok, Thailand
28 February 1968, middle of the night in Bill's hotel Room

Bill was roused from sleep by a loud banging on the door. Next to him, Sansi cringed and huddled under the blankets. **"Who is it?"** he yelled. He looked at his watch; it was nearly one in the morning.

"Mike Miller, Bill. Colonel Hardy and Major Hersey are down. You need to head back to NKP. A plane's waiting for you at Don Muang."

"Gimme a minute, Mike."

"Get moving! I'm holding a cab. What room is Sean in?"

Bill told him the room number and hurried into the shower. He was dressed in his flight suit and packed in less than ten minutes. Sansi was with him when he walked into the lobby in his flight suit. Mike was at the door.

"I told Colonel Benjamin that I'd send you back if I could find you. Sean's coming. There's a Skatback T-39 at Don Muang. It'll depart in about an hour and ..." Mike looked at his watch, **"ten minutes. They're holding two seats for you. I'll call and let them know you're on the way."**

"Thanks, Mike," Bill said. He turned to Sansi, but was interrupted by Mike.

"Ralph must be here with Tomi. Hi, Sansi," Mike said. The Thai girl was smiling and bowed gracefully. Mike was obviously another of her clients. **"Bill, I'll see that she is OK."**

"Thanks, Mike. Take care of Sean's girl, too, will you?"

"What're friends for?" Mike said with obvious relish. Sansi giggled just as Sean and his girl walked into the lobby.

"Come on Sean. We've got a plane to catch. Mike'll take care of things here," Bill said.

"I'll bet," Sean said. Both girls were holding onto Mike and grinning.

"Have you guys checked out?" Mike asked.

"You mean we have to pay, too?" Sean said an innocent look on his face. They quickly cleared their bills and went out the front door to the waiting taxi.

"What happened?" Sean asked.

"I don't know. Mike just said that Ed and Jerry are down. We can call from Base Operations," Bill was worried. *"What were those two lunatics doing flying together at night, Jesus!"*

"They were up at night?" Sean asked disbelief in his voice.

"Mike said that the plane was hit about 1930. He was leaving for Bangkok on the T-39 courier when Colonel Benjamin caught him at Base Operations."

"That's all we know? Are they okay?" Sean looked at Bill.

"We'll have to call on TUOC line at Base Ops. Mike couldn't tell us any more than that. He wasn't flying at the time."

"Tell the driver to hurry," Sean said.

"Tell him yourself. I don't speak Thai," Bill replied.

Bill thought for a second....then his expression brightened as he remembered Sansi's words to the cab driver the day before...

"Lao, Lao, Kup!!!"

The cab accelerated as if shot from a cannon....scattering late night samlars and pedestrians in all directions.

The normal 45-minute trip to Don Muang took 35...they slid sideways into the Base Ops parking lot...paid the driver and tipped him a red note. He was a happy camper.

The T-39 was parked in front of Base Operations. Sean headed for the small jet with their bags while Bill hurried into Operations.

As soon as he entered, Bill said loudly, **"Is the T-39 pilot here?"**

A major looked up from the map table and said, **"That's me."**

Bill walked up to him and stuck out his hand. **"I'm Captain Thompson. Are you headed for NKP?"**

The major smiled and took Bill's hand, **"We sure are. Are you the two we're taking to NKP?"**

"Yes, Sir. How soon do you lift off?"

"Five minutes. Are you ready?"

"Yes, Sir. I just need to check in with TUOC first," Bill replied. He walked toward the counter and asked for a phone line to NKP.

"NKP, this is Captain Thompson, NAIL Five Five. Put me through to Colonel Benjamin," Bill said into the phone.

In less than five seconds he said, **"Yes, Sir. We're leaving now. It's less than an hour and a half. Have a Duck ready. Sean and I will take off as soon as we get there. Ask Ari to put our survival stuff in the bird, preflight it and tow it to Base Operations. Thanks, Colonel, we'll be there as soon as we can. Is there any word yet?"** Bill frowned as he hung up.

He turned away from the phone and looked at several faces staring at him. They had been listening to one side of the conversation. It was clear that this captain was important to someone with enough clout to divert a T-39 from its regular schedule. They were waiting for Bill to speak. He said, **"Let's go, Major. We have men down and we need to be there. Get this bird to NKP as fast as you can."**

"Come on, Captain. We can do better than you think."

The T-39 crew was much more motivated than the NAILs expected, and in no time at all the plane broke ground, the right wing dipped and the T-39 turned on a heading for NKP. The pilots had a priority clearance and were using it to the hilt. The crew chief came back and asked the passengers if they would like some coffee. Both Bill and Sean shook their heads negative. Bill asked to be roused twenty minutes out of NKP and closed his eyes. Sean nodded in agreement and tried to sleep himself, but couldn't. *"That damned Bill could sleep on a roller coaster,"* he thought.

The next thing Bill knew, he was awakened by the crew chief that held a cup of hot coffee for him. Bill took the coffee and thanked the sergeant. He looked up and saw the co-pilot motioning for him to come forward. Bill checked his watch, 0312, unstrapped and moved forward to the cockpit.

"How's it going?" he asked when he reached the pilots.

"We're making great time, Captain. Alleycat wants to talk to you. Use Jim's headset," the major said, motioning toward his right seater. The captain in the right seat gave his headset to Bill. Then the major yelled to Bill, *"You have Alleycat on UHF."*

"Alleycat, this is NAIL Five Five," Bill called.

"Where are you, Five Five?" came back immediately.

"In a T-39 on the way to NKP. How're they doing?"

"There are lights reported in their vicinity. No one knows what they are. Can you get out there and take a look?"

"Not in this plane. It'd be too obvious. We have an O-2 waiting at NKP. I'll be on site as soon

as possible, probably within the hour. Have you established contact with them?"

"Colonel Hardy called once. The Zorros haven't been able to raise him again. They talked to Major Hersey several times but haven't heard anything for the past three hours. Something's wrong."

"Roger, Alleycat. We'll be there in less than an hour. I'll call back as soon as we get airborne from NKP."

When Bill looked at the major, he said, *"We're fifteen minutes out, Captain. Good luck. Who are you guys anyway? You aren't Rescue."*

"We're the NAILs, FACs. The 23rd TASS; we <u>own</u> most of Laos and the Trail," Bill said as he handed the headset to the right seater. The T-39 pilots looked at him with amazement. They weren't used to being right in the middle of actual combat operations. Rescues were something they read about, not participated in.

When the major tuned in NKP Tower, he was even more impressed. The tower responded immediately. *"Land on Runway 33 and stop at midfield. Captain Thompson's plane is warmed up and waiting for him at the center taxiway. Stop adjacent to the O-2. Do not delay."*

The two T-39 pilots responded quickly and brought the plane in on Runway 33. They could see the activities at midfield and were waved into position by someone wielding night wands. It turned out to be Lt. Colonel Benjamin.

Bill bounded from the T-39 and headed for the O-2. Colonel Benjamin was still holding the lighted wands he used to park the T-39. He handed Bill a packet of maps. *"This'll tell you what you need to know. Zach marked them for you. Get out there and tell us what's going on.*

Are you taking Sean or do you want someone else? We've got some other people here."

"I'll take Sean. Is Charley up there?"

"No. He's resting. John Patterson is holding down the fort and Ken Sommers is flying top cover for you. He just took off."

"Great," Bill said. *"Will you be in TUOC?"*

Benjamin nodded. *"Good,"* Bill said and ran for the plane.

Sean was holding the door. As Bill climbed in, Sean followed and gave the signal for the chocks to be pulled. The de-arming pins had already been removed. The rear engine started to turn and Bill began moving the plane to the runway. He started the front engine about 100 yards before they were turned onto the runway.

Colonel Benjamin watched them take-off and then turned and walked to the T-39. *"Give me their things. I'll see that they get to their hootches. Many thanks for getting them here so fast. You can take your T-39 to Base Ops now."*

As they turned out of the pattern on a heading of 090, off their left wing they watched a Zorro T-28 rejoin on them. Bill transmitted, *"Alleycat, this is NAIL Five Five, airborne at NKP."*

"We have you, Five Five. Cleared to the downed plane. There's one T-28 on night watch, Zorro Two Six. We show you with Zorro Four Three."

"Roger, Alleycat we have Zorro Four Three covering us," Bill replied.

"Find out what those lights are, Five Five. We need to know what to do in the morning," Alleycat requested.

"We'll be there in fifteen minutes," Bill radioed.

"Why don't we see what they know at the squadron?" Sean suggested.

"Good idea," Bill replied and switched to FM as the Mekong slipped underneath them in the moonlight, *"Dullness, this is Five Five, crossing the fence."*

"Hi, Bill. We've got you off at 0341 hours. How're you doing?" It was Milt Feldman and Bill recognized his voice.

"Hi, Milt, we're fine. What were they doing up together at night?" Bill asked.

"They were checking out the test scope. The new one that was brought in from Hanscom Field."

"I told them that it was useless. What were they doing out there with that pile of junk?"

"Major Martin, the guy from ESD, insisted that if we used it we could fly a couple of thousand feet higher. Jerry and the colonel went up to check it out," Milt radioed.

"I'm surprised that they could both fit in the bird with that scope. It takes up the whole right side of the plane. Thanks, Milt, Five Five out."

A few moments later Sean said, *"Right here, see this is where it's plotted. The area isn't very hilly. There usually isn't much activity around this place."*

Bill looked over at the map Sean was holding and lit it with his flashlight. The downed NAILs weren't far into Laos. Ed and Jerry had jumped out of their wounded Duck when it had run of steam. It was about twenty miles from any roads. *"Ed and Jerry should be fine. What could be causing all of the lights that have been reported?"*

Bill turned off his flashlight. He was still flying the O-2, but sat back in his seat. He was trying to imagine what sort of weapon could be causing the flashes.

"NAIL Five Five, this is Zorro Two Six."

"Hi, John. What've you got?" Bill answered.

"They told me you were in Bangkok. What're you doing out here?"

"I was rudely dragged from my rest and recuperation at the Bangkok YMCA, John."

"Is that what you call it? I'd have used another term but, if that's your story, it's good enough for me. Mike was sure he could find you by finding Ralph. Was he right?"

"Why do I think you also know the young ladies in question?" Bill asked.

"I'll never tell. I never knew Sansi's name," John answered.

Bill turned bright red, *"Did everyone on the base sleep with that damn girl?"* he thought.

"Have you heard from our friends?" Bill asked.

"Not for several hours. Every twenty minutes or so there's a flash of light down there. I wish I knew what it was. There! It's another one." John yelled.

"Down where, John? Jesus! How the hell am I supposed to know where there is?"

"Sorry, it's north. Look north. There it is again! Did you see it?"

Bill watched…then there was a minute flicker of yellow light.

"I'll be damned. Jesus, John, you dragged me out of bed for that? I can't believe you did that," Bill said. "You cheated me out of two more nights with Sansi so I could watch Jerry Hersey light another fucking cigarette. John, you dumb bastard. It's nothing but Hersey lighting cigarettes. I'll bet Ed Hardy won't talk because he doesn't want to be near him. That dumb chain-smoking bastard is lighting a cigarette every twenty minutes."

There was a long pause. John finally answered. *"I'm sorry, Bill. I didn't know. Now who's going to tell Alleycat? We've got Intelligence Analysts alerted all over the globe trying to identify those flashes."* John sounded very contrite.

"It doesn't matter whether you tell them or not, Boss. I will," came over the radio from Ken Somers in Zorro 43. *"This's too good to pass up."*

"Ken, are you relieving John?"

"Yeah, Five Five ... What do you need?"

"Nothing. I'll make the report to Alleycat. We don't need anything to interfere with the morning pickup or they could be in trouble. We can settle with everyone at the club tomorrow."

"Gotcha, Five Five. I'll wait until tomorrow. Who do you have with you?"

"There isn't anyone with me, unless you're talking about Walter Winchell O'Malley, here. He's rolled into a little ball trying to keep from laughing over the radio."

"I thought so. There isn't any chance of keeping this quiet, then?" It was John.

"Not one goddamn solitary chance, John," answered Sean, laughing at them.

"The only way I can keep him quiet is to toss him out," Bill radioed.

"Then toss him out."

"Alleycat, this is Zorro Two Six,"

"Go ahead, Two six."

"We've deduced that the flashes are probably one of the downed crewmen lighting cigarettes," John radioed. The pause was extensive. The answer, when it came, failed to conceal the speaker's amusement, *"Roger, Zorro Two Six. We understand cigarette lighter flashes."*

"That's affirmative, Alleycat," John answered.

"Who gets to tell 7th Air Force, Zorro? You or us?" The pause was again an extended one.

"I will," came from the chagrinned Zorro.

"Thank you, Zorro. Give NAIL Five Five our regards. I'll bet he doesn't like being dragged from bed for that one."

"I'm sure he understands," John answered, hopefully.

Bill didn't enter the conversation but Sean was still laughing aloud. *"We left Mike with two freebies for the next two days. Damn!"*

"I never got a chance to ask, but how does your little friend compare with the girls in Bangkok?" Bill inquired, grinning broadly.

Sean didn't answer right away. When he spoke it was with a low voice, *"The Thai girls are sure uninhibited. They'll do anything, and I mean anything, to please you. Sharon isn't that way,"* he paused again. *"I'm going to marry her, you know. I really am. She just doesn't know it yet."*

Bill chucked at his friends discomfort. *"The Orientals sure are different. I'd like to try that again but, you're right, it isn't worth screwing up a marriage for. It's nice, but not that nice."*

"It does make it a little easier to understand why some of the older troops are so taken with the local girls." Sean commented, *"They probably do think they've died and gone to heaven."*

"Well, partner, what now?" Bill asked.

"We might as well get some sleep. Who's first?"

"I'll go first. Wake me when you get tired," Bill said. He leaned back and closed his eyes as Sean turned the

plane to start a very large orbit a couple of miles south of the two downed NAILs.

CHAPTER SEVENTY FIVE
Steel Tiger, Western Central Laos
1 March 1968, on the ground at nearly sunrise

That morning, a few moments before sunrise, from his position on the side of a hill Ed saw an approaching plane coming from the west, minutes before the engine sound could be heard. He transmitted on his survival radio, *"This is NAIL Zero Two and you're right on time."*

"Ed, are you OK?" It was Colonel Benjamin.

"I'm OK, Boss. Jerry's down here in the same field; he's a little south of me. I'm near the north edge of the field at your eleven o'clock position."

"I've got the field. The Jolly's are right behind me and there are some Sandys up high. Bill and Sean are a couple of miles to the east..."

"Roger, Boss. Do you have contact with One Seven?"

"Not yet. Stand by while I give him a call. NAIL One Seven, do you read Zero One?"

After a short few seconds a very soft response was heard by all, except Ed for some unknown reason, *"One Seven here. I am surrounded by about two dozen well-armed uniforms. I am hiding. Can't talk. Will call later."*

Ed was standing looking toward the spot where he'd seen the lights from Jerry's cigarettes. He couldn't see anything and he didn't hear the transmission from Jerry. *"I don't see him,"* he said to Benjamin.

"We heard him but he's in trouble," Benjamin replied.

"He must be low on battery power," replied Ed, *"Is he okay?"*

Ed saw and heard the two Jolly Green helicopters at that time. He was standing near the tree he'd used for cover when he was startled by two A-1s as they skimmed over the field.

"This is Sandy Lead. One crewman is in sight. Jolly One Three, you're cleared for pickup. Two Three hold to the south. No signs of enemy forces. Make it quick."

"Jolly One Three's in for the pickup. We've got our man at the northeast edge."

"Roger, One Three. Northeast edge."

"NAIL Zero One, this is Sandy Lead. Stay out of the way!"

"Roger, NAIL Zero One will remain at three thousand, over the west side of the field."

When the Jolly came to a stop above him, Ed was surprised at the noise and force of the downdraft created by the big rotor blades. They were churning up so much debris that he had a difficult time keeping his eyes open. Every time he did open them, they filled with dirt. The air was full of swirling particles. He covered his eyes with an arm and squinted, looking for the tree penetrator being lowered at the end of a steel cable.

He was happy to see the metal penetrator. He let it touch the ground to discharge its static charge, then he opened one of the seats and then the other one, unsnapped the retaining strap, and sat in the seat, hugging the penetrator. He passed the strap under one arm, around his back and under the other arm before re-hooking it to the penetrator. He was ready to be winched up. Giving the thumbs-up signal, he felt the seat start to rise rapidly. As soon as he was off the ground, the air cleared and he could open his eyes. Although the engine noise from the Jolly was louder than any of the other engines, Ed could see and hear a number of planes in orbit around the field. He was amazed at the effort it took to carry out a rescue but he was glad that it was done and that he was headed back to NKP.

He was surprised after he was hauled into the helicopter and unstrapped from the penetrator. The PJ said that they still hadn't found the other crewman. Ed quickly scrambled to the cockpit. *"Let me have a radio,"* he said to the pilot.

"Five Five, this is Zero Two," Ed called.

"Go ahead, Zero Two. Five Five is here," Bill replied.

"Where's Jerry?"

"We can't see anything. I've got the spot marked where we saw the flashes a couple of hours ago but there's no sign of him. All we have so far is that one call."

"Did you see him?"

"No. We never talked and I never saw anything but the flashes. Do you suppose he's OK?"

"Sandy, this is Five Five. One Seven should be at the west edge of the field. How about making a low pass?"

"Sandy Lead's in," came over the radio. The A-1 skimmed the trees and then pulled up rapidly. *"I'm taking fire. Ground fire! There are some big guns here."*

"Sandy Two's in."

"No, no! Sandy, pull off, pull off! That's our man down there. Pull off," Bill was shouting into the mike.

"I've got him in sight. Look at the edge of the field," shouted Bill over the UHF radio.

They could clearly see the NAIL in the middle of a large circle of uniformed troops.

"It's him. Who are the other guys?" came from Dave Benjamin, his voice excited and high pitched.

"Shit! They're getting him. God dammit! They're getting Jerry. Look, he's got his hand in the air," Ed Hardy was shouting.

"I'll make a pass. Cover me, Sandy," Bill called.

Dave Benjamin's call was too late, *"No! Don't. That's an order."*

Then over Guard Channel….. obviously from Jerry, *"Stop it, guys. They are all over down here and I heard some loud guns. We can't do this. I'm fine. I'll be destroying this radio in three seconds. Thanks for trying. See you after the war."*

The others watched as the O-2 dropped to treetop level and flew around the men on the ground. The little plane abruptly pulled up and turned to the west, back over the trees. *"It's definitely him. He looks unharmed, but there are a dozen men around him and more in the tree line. Can we get some ground troops, fast?"* Bill asked.

"This is NAIL Zero One, break it off. We can't risk more planes. Return to NKP. Acknowledge."

The voices of the other pilots reflected their disappointment and frustration. There was nothing they could do to help Major Hersey. He was now a POW.

'Well, at least he's alive,' Bill thought to himself as he followed Dave Benjamin back to NKP. Sean was still looking out the side with his binoculars.

"Can't we do anything?" he asked Bill.

*"Nah. They'll kill him for sure if we try something cute. We don't have any ground units in

this part of Laos," Bill answered, solemnly. Then he added, *"I wonder if he gave himself away with the lighter or if the lighter was an enemy trick to lure someone there like Ed."*

"We'll have to wait till the war is over and ask him. Sure wouldn't want to be a POW," Sean said, with a shudder.

"Me neither. I'd rather be dead than a prisoner," Bill stated, flatly.

"Oh, sure. That's easy to say now. What if you were down there with Jerry's choices?" Sean chided his friend. *"Let's hope neither of us ever has to face that option."*

Bill nodded in agreement and turned the O-2 to follow Colonel B's bird into the pattern. The other planes were making their approach to NKP and the helicopter was hovering, waiting for the rest of the planes to recover. It would be the last to land.

It seemed like most of men in the 23rd TASS were on the ramp, waiting to see that their Buds were okay. Most were at the NAIL hootches when they got the word of the rescue and did not know of Jerry's fate. Until Ed stepped off the helicopter alone, they didn't realize that Jerry was still missing. Ed's expression conveyed that message more quickly than the spoken word.

"You had us worried," Dave Benjamin said as he held Ed's hand. *"I'm glad you made it. I'm terribly sorry about Jerry."*

"I can't believe it," Ed said, despair on his face. *"He was fine. I didn't go near him last night because he kept using that God damned lighter."*

"It wasn't your fault, Colonel," Bill said as he and Sean walked up to them, *"They must've seen the plane crash and come looking for you. Jerry led them*

right to himself with his cigarettes. If they didn't see the flashes, they smelled the damn smoke."

"*I'm glad you're OK,*" Sean added, reaching out to shake Ed's hand.

"*Was it the scope?*" Dave asked.

"*Yeah, Boss,*" Ed replied. "*That scope isn't worth a shit! If we had a hand-held scope, we wouldn't have taken so long to mark. I think I got too close. We didn't get under the flares but we held the run in too long for our mark, and we got stitched by a ZPU...might have been a twin ZPU.*"

Benjamin nodded in understanding. "*We'll send the test team back. They don't have another scope anyway.*"

"*I sure wouldn't want anyone else to fly it,*" Ed Hardy added. "*The pilot can't tell what's going on, or where he is. You can't really tell where the big scope is pointed.*"

"*Is there any chance that a ground team can get Jerry out?*" Sean asked Colonel Benjamin.

"*They'll try. The Laotians have some special teams and there's always Air America. We have to hope that someone finds out where they take him,*" Dave Benjamin didn't sound too hopeful.

"*What do we need to do to get the Lao teams on the way, Colonel?*" Bill wouldn't let go.

"*I'll call Cricket right now. I am sure that they have already got some of General Vang Pao's people going in there as soon as possible. Now, all of you...Ed, you too...get some rest. I'll see all of you tomorrow unless I hear something from the teams,*" Dave Benjamin turned and headed toward his office.

Historical Note: The statement "***See you after the war***" *was the exact quote made by an F-4 pilot just as he called off his* *own rescue, destroyed his survival radio and was seen being captured by a dozen NVA troops near interdiction point Golf in 1968.*

CHAPTER SEVENTY SIX
Nakhon Phanom Royal Thai Air Base (NKP)
2 March 1968, early morning in the NAIL Ops

Ed Hardy and Bill were in Colonel Benjamin's office at 0700. They were anxiously awaiting the second report from General Vang Pao's Free Laotian troops who had gone looking for signs of Major Hersey.

Yesterday, the day Jerry was captured; the teams reached the pickup site and reported finding a broken survival radio, pieces of parachute snagged in a tree and twenty or thirty cigarette butts scattered around the area. They were going to contact local farmers to see if anyone had seen enemy troops with a Caucasian prisoner in the area.

"Ed, who do you want to replace Jerry in Operations?" Dave Benjamin asked.

"I'm not going to name anyone just yet. I'll borrow Milt for the short term scheduling work," Ed replied, quietly.

"What'll happen to Jerry?" Bill asked, looking from Colonel Benjamin to Ed Hardy.

"Prisoners will be kept somewhere, moved often, and then released after the war is over. Generally, the return of prisoners is a condition of the eventual peace agreement. It can be part of a truce or surrender as well," Dave Benjamin spoke in a low voice. He was sick about the loss.

"Even here?" Bill asked. Both Dave Benjamin and Ed Hardy looked at him.

"What about here?" Ed said.

"We aren't at war in Laos. We better try to have the Ravens find where they're keeping him," Bill suggested.

"We don't have the means of attempting a rescue, if that's where you're headed, Captain; don't you try anything stupid, either," Dave Benjamin spoke sharply.

"I won't. I'm having a hard time accepting that he's gone. I saw him standing there with his hands in the air...," Bill didn't finish his sentence.

They all turned toward the door when they heard a knock. It was the Laotian interpreter, who had flown the morning flight with Colonel Benjamin.

"Good Morning, Colonel, Sir. We find prisoner. Pathet Lao take north. Farmer see eight soldiers with tall round eye in chain," the interpreter said bowing to them.

"Can we get him back?" Bill asked anxiously.

"Report day old, Captain, Sir. No find now. Major pilot prisoner," the interpreter finished and bowed again as he left the office. *"I go to airplane,"* he said to the Colonel.

"Damn, damn, damn! We can't do shit!" Bill wasn't happy with the news. He looked at Colonel Benjamin and Ed Hardy for an answer but they didn't have one. Jerry was gone. He was a prisoner and no one could do anything for him until the end of the war ... whenever that would be.

CHAPTER SEVENTY SEVEN
Nakhon Phanom Royal Thai Air Base (NKP)
3 March 1968, early morning in the NAIL Ops

The next morning Colonel Benjamin and Ed Hardy could be heard arguing in the colonel's office. The door opened suddenly and Ed came out. He went into Operations and motioned for Bill to come with him. Bill followed him back into the colonel's office and sat when Colonel Benjamin pointed to a chair.

"We have a problem, Bill," the Colonel started.

"Yeah. We sure do. Your general friend is now running the night war," Ed Hardy said.

"Read this," Dave Benjamin said, handing Bill a teletype message.

Bill glanced at the address block. It was from 7th Air Force and its subject was night interdiction. He read the message: control of the major sections of the Ho Chi Minh Trail, Routes 91 and 911, was transferred to TFA based on their success with the new sensor technology and their accuracy with radar-controlled bombing. All other units would be fragged to attack alternate or bypass routes.

"What's it mean?" Bill asked.

"We stay away from Golf and Foxtrot and we only work with Nimrods and Zorros. That's until midnight. After that we can fly where we like. Candle will fly one sortie a night for the foreseeable future. They only have two planes," Ed said, disgusted.

"They got the results, Ed. It's what we're out here for. We came here to stop the traffic on the Trail and they are stopping it." Dave Benjamin said.

"How'll TUOC handle it?" Bill asked.

"They're getting their instructions from the TACC at 7th Air Force. If I believed the TFA reports, I'd be in complete agreement," Ed Hardy argued.

"Let's not get parochial, Ed," Dave Benjamin cautioned him, *"It's tough enough when everyone's on the same side."*

"Boss, what about Bill and Sean's tricks with the engine noises? What if those computers are only picking up reciprocating engines, things like trucks, jeeps, NAILs, Zorros and Nimrods? If Bill's right, the whole thing's a farce. The goddamn war is picking up and we're playing with ourselves on the main resupply route."

"Ed, and you, too, Captain," Benjamin stood and scowled at them. They both got to their feet *"I don't want you to say a goddamn thing about it. We've got our orders and they're legal and proper. Just shut up and go do your jobs. I don't want to hear about this, not ever! Understood?"*

"Yes, Sir," came from both Ed and Bill, quietly. Bill left the room.

There were sounds of continued arguing from the office but no one could make out what was being said. When Ed came out he didn't make reference to the conversation. He did scowl at Bill and Sean when he found them at Sean's desk.

Bill left the squadron at 1100 to get something to eat and then go to bed. He'd need a few hours of sleep before he flew that night. He'd scheduled himself for Route 12 from 1800 to 2100. Briefing was at 1600 in TUOC.

CHAPTER SEVENTY EIGHT
Nakhon Phanom Royal Thai Air Base (NKP)
3 March 1968, early evening on the ramp at Base Ops

At 1930 that night Sean drove a jeep to Base Operations. Sharon was due back with the general at 1945 on a T-39 from Danang. They'd flown from California to Danang on a commercial contract carrier and then changed to a T-39, the U.S. Air Force's neat little passenger jet, the Saber Liner. He got their ETA from the TFA Duty Officer.

They landed right on time. After the general departed in his staff car, Sean drove the jeep to the plane. Sharon stepped from the stairs just as he stopped. *"Your transportation,"* Sean said, with a smile.

Sharon put her baggage in the back and got into the front seat. She kissed him gently and he drove off.

"Where to, O beautiful one?"

"The club. I'm starved and I cleaned out the trailer before I left."

"How was the trip?"

"It ended well. The general caught hell for losing the P-2s, but they really liked the results of the sensor tests. The Secretary himself directed that we implement the TFA program in Laos." Sharon's enthusiasm was apparent. She, like everyone in the chain of command, believed General Holland's reports. Sean elected to keep his opinions to himself.

"We dropped some sensors around Khe Sanh and they really worked well finding gun emplacements, large groups and tanks. The Marines were highly complimentary about the sensors," Sharon continued.

"You know we used some sensor-generated Intel to bomb a regimental headquarters north west of Khe Sanh?"

"You did?"

"Yep, the Marines are really catching hell over there. I'm glad we are helping them with the resupply," he said. *"You, know we haven't lost a*

transport since we developed the approach tactics over there?"

"*You did that well. Now we can put a crimp in the NVA plans by stopping the truck traffic, that's for sure,*" Sharon said.

"*There isn't anyone else. Foxtrot is the last place to catch them if they're running supplies down Route 9 to Khe Sanh,*" Sean remarked.

"*Don't get defensive. I told you it would save lives and it will. We don't need to lose anyone else attacking the convoys. How many trucks can you put on a dirt road anyway?*" Sharon laughed.

Sean looked at her and realized that she was repeating what she'd heard in Washington. The Secretary and others at that level didn't understand what the Ho Chi Minh Trail was. They had no idea of the amount of war materials that were being moved through Laos every day. Well, he decided, he couldn't change things all by himself and he wasn't going to argue with Sharon about it. He didn't want to argue with her; he wanted to take her to bed.

"*Not many, I guess,*" Sean answered. "*Did you have time to go home?*"

"*For a day. I flew into Dayton and then met our plane on the west coast for the trip back,*" she smiled at him.

"*I missed you,*" Sean whispered.

"*Me, too.*" she answered, "*Let's go to my trailer. We can eat later.*"

CHAPTER SEVENTY NINE
Nakhon Phanom Royal Thai Air Base (NKP)
10 March 1968, late afternoon in TUOC

The widespread fighting throughout South Vietnam caused an increase in vehicular traffic along the Trail. Prior to the Tet Offensive, during the day, NAIL FACs would occasionally find a single vehicle dashing from cover to cover or a vehicle damaged during attacks the previous night, sometimes with troops attempting to get it unloaded or moved out of sight under the trees.

In the weeks since the Tet Offensive, these daytime sightings had been increasing. The NAIL FACs were finding vehicles every day and were becoming concerned about the number of trucks moving south. Hostile anti-aircraft gunfire along the Trail was increasing significantly.

Candlestick was now the primary FAC from Golf to Foxtrot at night and all of the jet fighters were assigned to Skyspots or to attacks along that stretch of roadway. The computer experts at TFA would acquire the sounds of convoys moving south when they passed through the sensor array north of Golf. They would count the vehicles and estimate the speed of the convoy. Using radar-controlled bomb drops, they would hit the road between Golf and Foxtrot where the convoy was expected to be. They would check for sounds of the convoy continuing south with the next sensor array, count the vehicles again and credit themselves with kills for the difference in their counts.

There were no operating sensors south of Foxtrot, so Candle would orbit Foxtrot and following a Skyspot bomb drop, flare the cliff face. They would visually acquire the survivors of the TFA attack, if there were any, and light up the road for assigned fighters to bomb them. The road across the face of the cliff was so obvious that marks were not required. Candle couldn't mark; it had no capability to fire a marking rocket. The C-123 could only drop flares. At Foxtrot at night this was sufficient.

The Candlestick/TFA results were impressive. Not one night passed with less than thirty trucks being reported destroyed in the Golf to Foxtrot interdiction trap. There was little anti-aircraft gunfire since the fighters dropped from high altitude. Only rarely did Candle require an attack along Foxtrot; the radar bomb drops were so effective that few trucks escaped TFA's vigilant controllers.

After a week of glowing reports and little action on the alternate routes, the traditional NAIL, Nimrod and Zorro night fighters were feeling a letdown. In the past seven days, only three trucks had been spotted on the bypass routes. The crews were at the night briefing discussing the changes in the war.

"OK, Zach, what's going on out there?" Bill asked.

"We don't know. I can't figure why the trucks keep heading down Route 91 with all of those losses. Why haven't they moved west to 23?" the lieutenant answered.

"Well, my boss said for us to be grateful. We aren't getting shot down or captured. We're not even being shot at," Charlie Green commented.

"Knock it off; we're here to do our jobs, nothing else," John Patterson said, *"even if we don't understand. We support the Candles whether or not we believe them."*

"Does anyone believe that Candlestick who, on their best night in the past, claimed six truck kills and is now accounting for thirty or more using Skyspots?" Bill raised his eyebrows.

"It's not our problem, Bill," Charlie said.

"What if it's a mistake? Notice I used the word "mistake," not "lie." What if they're wrong, completely, totally, out-to-lunch wrong?" Bill asked his voice serious.

"So? What can we do? You've been trying to make that point ever since they started dropping

the sensors. No one believes you, Captain," Denny Cutter was standing at the back of the room.

"Follow me on this, Sir. If I'm right, we aren't seeing trucks on the alternate routes because they're all moving down 91. They aren't being bombed. They're on a wide open road to Khe Sanh. Imagine ...,"

"Knock it off, Bill. That sort of talk will get you sent home and thrown out of the service," Colonel Cutter stood and glared at Bill.

"Hold it, Colonel. I didn't say someone was intentionally letting them through. I believe that TFA is doing the best they can. I also believe that Candlestick is a plane full of good guys trying to do their jobs, but it's piloted by assholes. They probably don't exaggerate any more than they did in the past. The bulk of the kills are determined by some fucking TFA clerk who subtracts truck counts. The people in TFA think they are playing at a fucking arcade. It's just a game. The general down there is playing it to make another star. The only thing is some good guys could get real dead, if anyone cares."

From the expression on most of the pilots' faces, it was apparent that they believed Bill. John Patterson moved to the back of the room and pulled Denny Cutter aside. Everyone else watched the two have a heated, whispered conversation. They suddenly left the room and closed the door. The night crews sat for the next five minutes, refilling coffee or just talking among themselves. Lieutenant North merely shrugged and stood at the podium. He was as confused as everyone else.

The door banged open and everyone looked up. Colonel Benjamin stormed in, followed by Ed Hardy, Denny Cutter and John Patterson. Benjamin walked to the podium and waved the Intelligence Officer away.

"Close the door. This briefing is now restricted. No one will discuss anything they are about to hear with anyone not now in this room, ever. Do you understand?"

The assembled group looked confused but they all nodded in unison in agreement.

"Captain Thompson, I told you never to mention the TFA-Candlestick relationship again. Why have you disobeyed my orders?"

"No excuse, Sir. I ...," Bill started.

"Sit down and shut up," Dave Benjamin barked, then looked slowly around the room. *"Does anyone else want to bitch about TFA or Candlestick?"*

There was no movement, and then several hands were raised. Benjamin looked around the room again. He sighed and looked at Denny Cutter, *"We have to do this?"*

The group was looking back and forth between Cutter and Benjamin, waiting for Denny's answer. He only nodded.

"I will not allow a mutiny or anything sounding like it. Do you understand?" He was looking directly at Bill, who nodded in agreement.

"I will accept that this group is concerned about TFA control of a critical resupply route. I do not accept that someone is deliberately allowing trucks through!" his words were clipped and forced.

"It's not deliberate, Colonel, Sir!" Bill stood and said loudly. *"The dumb fucks think they're doing a good job."* The entire group was nodding and muttering in agreement.

Dave Benjamin sighed, *"Do you know what you're asking me to do?"*

"I'll do it," Bill stated.

"This time, you can't," Ed Hardy said.

"What exactly is it that we're supposed to do?" Dave Benjamin asked.

"We're going to go out there and watch. We're going to cover Route 91 north of them and Routes 9 and 92 south plus the backside of Foxtrot. We're also going to put someone on top of Candle. Then we're going to get a photo reconnaissance plane for pictures," Bill said.

"Is this all worked out?"

"No, Sir. We need to get started. The first planes are due off in less than an hour," Lieutenant North said.

The regular night crews departed on schedule. To the Candlestick and to TFA everything appeared normal. If they could've seen into the cockpits, they wouldn't have liked the sight. Bill and Ed Hardy were the control ship for the night. Ed was flying and Bill was beside him with his starlight scope and several large clipboards. He had maps of the entire area and a list of radio frequencies that were reserved for their use. They were going to maintain inter-plane contact using FM. Candlestick, TFA and Alleycat did not have the FM-band radio equipment.

Colonel Cutter and Colonel Benjamin were flying in Denny's A-26. They were going to look for trucks on the bypass roads, particularly looking for a way around Foxtrot to the east.

Bill called Sean and asked him to fly in the back seat with John Patterson. The Zorro would back up Ed Hardy as control ship and cover the area North of Golf, counting the trucks coming down from Mu Gia onto Route 91.

Charlie Green was assigned to look for a new way around Foxtrot to the west. The trucks had to be going somewhere. Ken Sommers was to look south along Route 9 into Khe Sanh. Ralph Langer was sent south on Route 92 to see if anything got through toward A Shau and points south.

All reports were to be relayed to Bill and Ed Hardy. They'd review the sightings and decide what to attack, if anything. No one was to give away their position unless directed by the control ship. Alleycat wasn't in on the plan, so they were to fake their usual radio calls and report "no sightings," if queried. Bill with his contacts had done it again.

There was little conversation in the control plane. Ed Hardy wasn't used to a situation which called for him to sneak around checking on his bosses. Neither was Bill for that matter, but Bill saw nothing unusual in actions taken to improve truck kills.

"Where do you want me?" he asked Bill.

"Over Foxtrot. Climb to eleven thousand or so. As soon as we find Candlestick we can set up our position," Bill answered,

"You're quiet tonight, Colonel."

"I've got a lot on my mind."

"Are you angry?"

"Not really. I wonder how we got into this situation." Ed didn't sound confident.

"I think it's the breaks. Some times things go wrong, even when everyone is trying to do them right."

"Yeah."

"It's your fault we're here, you know," Bill said to him, grinning.

"My fault?" Ed replied with disbelief.

"Remember the 'staff officers outrank you' lecture, Colonel?"

"I do."

"That started me thinking. What if the TACC acted the same way or if TFA did. The more I considered TFA and their sensors, the more I realized that they were the perfect example of your 'private agenda.' TFA has a private agenda and it has its own set of priorities. There are so many careers dependent upon the success of these

sensors that no one's left to care whether or not they work. It's a perfect example of the fox guarding the hen house. Who's gonna call them a liar even if they're wrong?"

"I can't believe anyone would make up false reports," Ed said, *"People aren't that callous, even if they do have private goals."*

"You gotta be shitting me. They can, so they do, because it helps their careers. I come out of a different Air Force, Sir. In fighters there are few real bullshitters; you can't lie. In a single-seat aircraft, you make it or you don't. You hit with the bombs or you don't. You land safely or you don't. It's like individual sports. There isn't any team to hold you up. If you fuck up then you're a fuckup. If you lose a match, there isn't anyone else to blame. If you win then, by God, you get all the credit. I win, Colonel. When I do things, I win!"

"I've heard you guys bullshitting in every club in the Air Force. Fighter pilots just seem to be full of more shit than everyone else."

"You missed it, Colonel. We don't bullshit ourselves. That's for girls and for outsiders. We know who and what we are. We've seen who can fly and who can bomb and who's afraid and who isn't."

"You're a puzzling person, Bill Thompson. You really do think. Your damn head is full of more ideas than anyone I've ever met but you're so goddamn cocky, people don't like working with you. Hell, most don't even like you." Ed was smiling. He liked the captain, but he wasn't sure why.

"*We're coming up on Foxtrot, Colonel. I see the road under us,*" Bill was looking out the right side, "*I'm looking for Candlestick now.*"

"*What frequency is Candle on?*" Ed asked.

"*Lemme see,*" Bill sat back and picked up a clipboard. He turned on a muted penlight and said, "*286.7, Sir.*"

"*286.7. I'll get it now.*"

They settled into a wide orbit to the east of Foxtrot at 11,000 feet and waited. It didn't take long for the action to start.

"*This is Zorro Two Six on FM,*" came over the radio.

"*Hi, Sean. Whatcha got?*" Bill replied.

"*A big convoy passing under us. There are seventeen trucks that we count, including three big vans and something on a flatbed under a tarp,*" Sean was excited.

"*What's next?*" from the Zorro.

"*Stay out of the way and let it move south. Let's see what TFA comes up with,*" Bill replied. "*What do you think of that, Colonel? We have seventeen trucks headed for the sensors. Let's see what happens.*"

"*This is NAIL Zero Two on FM. We have movers coming down to Golf. Everyone on their toes. Charlie, you watch the backside of Foxtrot,*" Bill called.

"*I'm here,*" Charlie replied.

They all heard Alleycat calling Candlestick, "*TFA reports a large convoy moving through Golf.*"

"*Roger, Alleycat. Candle's in position. Will we Skyspot or use flares?*"

"*TFA recommends a Skyspot. We've got a flight inbound. Stay east of the road.*"

"Roger, Candle will stay to the east. How many movers, Alleycat?"

"TFA reports fifteen to twenty vehicles of different tonnage. They hear some large vehicles in this group. The convoy speed is twelve, repeat twelve miles, per hour."

"Thank you, Alleycat. Candle is standing by."

Ten minutes passed and then they heard Alleycat. "Stand by for Skyspot. Bomb drop in thirty seconds. Stay clear of the road until after impact."

"Candle, roger."

In the dark, the explosions startled everyone within sight of Golf when they hit the ground. It was like a single hit. Each fighter dropped twelve five-hundred-pound bombs on a radar mark. There was no delay. They all impacted within one second.

"Wow!" came over the FM. It was Charlie Green.

"That's the first time I got to watch one of those. Did they hit the road?"

"It looks like it. We'll go over and check," Bill replied.

"We've got eight more!" Sean shouted over the FM.

"Eight more trucks?" Bill asked.

"No, dumbass. Eight more elephants," he paused. "Of course I mean trucks. What did you send me out here for?"

"Sorry, Sean. That makes twenty five so far tonight. You should see a lot more if the past week is any indication."

"We're on it," Sean replied. "It's noisier in this thing, but it sure flies nice."

"Glad you like it," came from someone.

Over the UHF they heard, "Candle, this is Alleycat. TFA reports only five vehicles entering Foxtrot. We have a flight inbound for you."

"Roger, Alleycat. Five vehicles at Foxtrot. Please pass the flight to us on this frequency."

Bill and Ed remained to the east at 11,000 feet. They would not want to be visible in the flare light from Candle. As soon as the flares were lit, they saw the large trucks starting across the face of the cliff. Bill wondered why only the large trucks had escaped the Skyspot.

"I've got movers! I've got trucks! The bastards are driving around Foxtrot," came from Charlie Green.

"Where are you, Charlie?" Bill asked.

"I'm behind the hill. There's a new road around the mountain. I can make out about a dozen trucks moving through the trees. What do you want me to do?"

"Keep watching. Ken and Ralph, stay on your toes. Nimrod Two One, can you go around to the south and be ready to help NAIL Four Nine go after the trucks?"

"We're on the way. We couldn't find any lights to the east," came from Colonel Benjamin.

"Are we hearing right? It sounds as though that last convoy split in two parts?"

"It sure looks like it," Bill answered. *"We're checking now. I want to see where Charlie made his sighting. We're going to have to find where that road comes out."*

"Ralph, are you there?" Bill called.

"I'm over Route 9, where 91 comes into it. Ken Sommers is with me. We're watching 91, 9 and 92 south," Ralph radioed.

"Stay there. Nimrod Two One is on the way to you. Don't start anything until I call. Let's make sure we've got them set up first."

"Roger, Bill. I'm waiting for Nimrod Two One and I've got Zorro Four Three."

They heard Alleycat call Candle with a report of the second group of trucks, *"Candle, TFA reports a ten-truck convoy passing Golf. They're going to use another Skyspot."*

"This is Candle, roger on the Skyspot. Our attack on the five trucks crossing Foxtrot is complete. We destroyed two, damaged one and two made it through."

"Roger, Candlestick, good work. TFA reports an estimated fifteen trucks destroyed out of the first convoy."

"Bill, did you hear that?" came over the FM. It was Colonel Benjamin.

"Yes, Sir. We're not done yet. Ralph, do you have the first five?"

"Here they come. There's only four of them, though. Candle must've actually got one."

"What are they, Ralph"

"These trucks are different."

"Be sure to get a good look at them," Ed Hardy broke in. *"Bill, you and the Colonel better come down here. These look special. I can't tell what they're carrying, but it isn't like anything I've ever seen,"*

Ralph came back. *"This is Two One. Bill, it looks like a missile launcher and control vans plus a fuel truck."*

Denny Cutter's voice suddenly jumped in volume and intensity. *"Jesus! They're moving missiles south. We've got to stop it!"*

"Slow down, Sir. Ralph, move east of the 92 intersection and hit them there. Don't get in the way of traffic down 91."

"OK, everyone, NAIL Four Nine is moving about ten miles east. Nimrod and Zorro, let's go.

We better let Alleycat know what we're doing and get a proper strike frequency."

"*Charlie, where are you?*" It was Bill on FM.

"*The trucks on the bypass have reached Route 9. They're turning east. What do you want me to do?*"

"*Leave them for Ralph. Go back up and see if there are any more on the bypass.*"

"*Ralph, did you hear?*"

"*He's with Alleycat, Bill. We've got it, a dozen trucks coming east on 9,*" Ken radioed.

An excited voice broke in on the FM. "*Here comes the biggest fucking convoy I've ever seen. It's just coming up on Golf. At least thirty trucks, maybe more. They're really moving,*" it was Sean again.

"*Roger, Zorro Two six. Charlie, look for them on the bypass.*"

"*I've already got another string on the bypass. It's smaller than the first one. Must be that second group,*" Charlie reported on FM.

"*Charlie, let them through. If the last convoy turns your way, go after them with Two One. OK? Hit them about halfway around so we can plot the road,*" Bill called.

"*Roger, NAIL Zero Two. We're going to hit the big one after it's committed to the bypass.*"

"*Right on, Zorros. Good hunting. Switch to UHF before you attack, but give us a call first.*"

"*Nimrod Two One, this is NAIL Zero Two. Do you read me?*"

"*We're here,*" came back over the FM.

"*Do you believe us now?*"

"*We'll talk about it back at NKP, but yes, I do,*" came from Colonel Benjamin.

"*Four Nine, do you need help?*" Bill asked.

Bill started talking to himself, *"This has the makings of the perfect strike on a convoy of great importance. First, a well-directed bomb will stop the lead truck in a location that is difficult to go around. Next, we drop one on the "tail end Charlie" and we have them boxed in....no way out. The roads are all very narrow and there are bomb craters full of water everywhere. It is dark, but with a few burning trucks it will be possible to see most of the convoy and particularly the larger trucks with the naked eye. If bomb droppers can't see well enough, they can just drop between the two fires....works every time. We get a couple burning and the rest are easy.....visible sitting ducks. This is going to be fun....a piece of cake."*

"We got it. Alleycat is sending some more fighters."

The Zorro and the Invader, under Nail 49's control plastered the totally unsuspecting convoy. Both "night fighters" made repeated bomb and gun passes!

"Zero Two...49 here.... Ken got the missile truck and the colonel's blowing the shit out of a van. We won't have anything left for the next convoy. I'll be out of flares and these two will be out of weapons," Ralph radioed.

"Get them from Alleycat. Don't let the missiles through. Ask Alley for the Gunfighters if you need to 49."

"Roger, NAIL Zero Two. We're on it."

"Charlie, how're you doing?" Ed asked calling Sean's Zorro control ship

"We're up to our ass in flak and burning trucks. We could use some help. We're out of flares and these damn T-28s don't pack a lot of ordnance," Sean's voice was excited.

"Did you call Alleycat, yet?"

"No, we didn't. How about covering us. Get up here with your flares and take over."

"We're on the way." Ed replied

"Alleycat, this is NAIL Zero Two. Request immediate fighter support for us on the Foxtrot bypass. We have a large convoy under attack with two Zorros."

"NAIL Zero Two, TFA has all ordnance committed."

"Roger, Alleycat. This NAIL Zero TWO, request immediate radio hookup with TACC, repeat, immediate hook up with 7th Air Force TACC," Bill radioed. Ed Hardy was smiling to himself, shaking his head back and forth.

"Roger, NAIL Zero Two. Your request is being passed to the senior controller."

"Alleycat, immediate means immediate. Request hook up with 7th right now. This is NAIL Zero Two. Do not delay."

"NAIL Zero Two, TFA requests you come up their frequency."

Ed Hardy looked at Bill and shrugged his shoulders. Bill said, **"Fuck them all. We'll see who's running this war."**

He switched the radio to Guard Channel and called, **"This is NAIL Zero Two on Guard Channel. Is there any aircraft in range that can patch us to the TACC at 7th? We have a serious problem."**

Everyone in Central Laos heard that transmission. Within seconds, a remarkably clear voice answered on Guard, **"Calling 7th Air Force, a patch is available on 346.2. Come up 346.2 and identify yourself."**

Bill changed channels, **"This is Nail Zero Two on 346.2. We have convoys carrying missiles and** radar-control vehicles south and east toward Khe Sanh. Request priority support from fighter aircraft. Unable to get help from TFA and the computer dinks at NKP. We need some help!"

"*Jesus, Bill. Was that necessary?*" Bill recognized Colonel Benjamin's voice on the FM radio."

"*Yes, Sir. There are a lot of people who will get hurt if the NVA get SAMs south of us. We'll get some help pretty quick now.*"

"*NAIL Zero Two. This is Alleycat. We would've helped if you had explained.*"

"*There isn't time to work this through TFA. The convoys that are getting through with the missiles are the ones that TFA and Candle already reported as destroyed.*" Bill replied.

"*NAIL Zero Two, this is Iron Hand. Do you read?*" another voice, deep and gravely.

"*Roger, Iron Hand. What can you do for us?*" Bill replied, quickly.

"*This is the 7th Duty Officer. You should have help in minutes. Gunfighters and Triple Nickel alerts have been scrambled. Redbird is launching their spare from Phan Rang and two flights from Korat are being diverted. You have priority. You'd better be right!*"

"*Thank you, Iron Hand. Please find us a recce bird with photoflash capability and we'll get you your proof. You've got a serious problem with the acoustic sensors and that program currently has priority up here. Request you send someone to NKP to review the situation. It'll take a Code Five at least,*" Bill radioed.

"*Who do you think you're talking to? Iron Hand, out.*"

"Who was that?" Ed looked at Bill. The voice acted like he knew who they were talking to, but a Code Five is a major general. Ed wondered what was going on that he did not understand.

The fighters and bombers arrived right on schedule....flares were dropped....trucks were killed...as the Nails and Zorros directed the show from on high. It was Grand!

Before the night was over, the NAILs and Zorros accounted for nearly twenty trucks destroyed. The RF-101 came by and photographed the face of Foxtrot, the new bypass, and route 9. They were littered with burning trucks and the remains of a missile carrier, a control van and a large support vehicle on Route 9, less than twenty-five miles from Khe Sanh.

Historical Note: This actually happened as described above

CHAPTER EIGHTY
Nakhon Phanom Royal Thai Air Base (NKP)
11 March 1968, early morning in the O'Club

The next morning, Bill, Sean and Ralph met at the O'Club for breakfast. They were to be at TUOC at 0800 for a review of the previous night's action. When they'd finished their attacks and landed, they were ordered to keep their mouths shut and be back at 0800. Colonel Benjamin, Colonel Cutter and Major Patterson were taking care of the mission debriefings at TUOC.

The three captains were walking toward the flight line and TUOC when they saw a T-39 making its landing approach. Bill looked at his watch and said, *"It looks like the photos are right on time. I wonder if they sent a general as well?"*

"They might, if General Holland put up a stink," Sean offered. *"I can't see him backing off, plus he's got a lot of backing at the Pentagon."*

"Well, we're about to find out. There goes his staff car," Ralph pointed to a blue sedan with the two-star general's blue flag on the right front headed toward the runway.

The large briefing room in TUOC was filled when the three walked in. Lieutenant North was at the podium and the unit commanders were seated around the big conference table at the front of the room. A major general in a flight suit was seated at the end of the table and Brigadier General Holland in his 1505s was sitting to his left. Colonel Benjamin had the seat to his right. The visitor was none other than General Jack Johnson, the 7th Air Force DCS/Operations.

"Sir, are you ready?" Lieutenant North asked.

"Just a minute, Lieutenant," the visitor looked around.

"Are the Candlesticks here? The ones who flew last night?"

Five hands were raised from one side of the room.

The General continued, *"Alleycat?"* Three hands lifted. He continued until all of the units were called and identified. When he got to the NAILs he asked, *"Which one of you shot at the helicopter?"*

Bill turned a bright shade of red and raised his hand. He wondered who'd told that story. Next to him, Sean was having difficulty holding in his laughter.

"Lieutenant, before you go through the action, let me remind everyone that this briefing is

restricted. ***Nothing said here will leave this room. Any decisions made here will be implemented by written order. There will be no verbals. Does everyone understand?*** " his voice rose and he left no doubt that his wishes would honored.

Lieutenant North traced the actions of the previous evening. He had the routes marked on a large map and he showed where the sensors were located and where the NVA had bypassed the checkpoints. He listed the number of vehicles sighted coming down from Mu Gia Pass. He traced them along the routes and then listed the claimed kills. Of the approximately sixty trucks sighted by the Zorro, TFA counted sixty at the sensor array north of Golf. Five were counted crossing Foxtrot and approximately forty likely made it through on Route 9 or were hidden in truck parks. TFA claimed thirty destroyed by Skyspot radar-controlled bombing and three by fighters under Candlestick's control at Foxtrot.

The NAILs directed strikes against approximately sixty trucks and claimed nineteen destroyed and four damaged. All of the missile system vehicles were included in the destroyed trucks.

"***Tell me about these missile carriers.***" said the two star.

"***They were in the first convoy sighted and didn't use the bypass. We surmise that the bypass route likely wouldn't handle the big rigs. A narrow gap or an un-bridged stream could easily cause that.***" replied Colonel Benjamin.

"***They were spotted by Candlestick?***"

"***Yes, Sir. Candle directed fighters against the trucks. They destroyed two and damaged a third.***"

"***They destroyed two and damaged a third. What does damaged mean?***" No one was asking questions except General Johnson.

"*Damaged means hit but not destroyed. It usually means not moving. A lot of our damaged vehicles are towed to truck parks for repairs. Almost all are towed out of sight,*" Zach answered.

General Johnson looked toward the Candlestick crew, "*What did damaged mean last night?*"

"*Not moving. It didn't pull out with the ones that were moving,*" replied a major.

"*Enough; let's see the photographs. Someone turn down the lights.*"

Zack began, "*These photographs were taken at approximately 2200 hours by an RF-10l from the wing at Tan Son Nhut, General. From the top, the first series is of Interdiction Point Golf. Note that there are no trucks in the Golf photographs. This is the site of the TFA Skyspots and it has been confirmed by Invert radar. The next is Foxtrot and we can clearly identify one large burned-out vehicle.*"

"*This next series, all seven photographs are of Route 9 between the turn off from Route 91 and the South Vietnamese border. There are eight hulks either burning or burnt on the roadway. There are six more vehicles identified as partially off the road. They are not on fire, but all of them have visible damage.*"

"*The next series of photographs are difficult to interpret. The bright spots are fires and where the trees have been blown away, you can see roadway. This is the new Foxtrot bypass. We've estimated that there are ten vehicles on fire in these photos,*" Zach finished and looked at the general.

"*Let me see. Between approximately 1830 and 2130 we sighted sixty trucks coming down from Mu Gia Pass. TFA through Skyspot radar bombing* accounted for thirty of them. Candlestick got another four and the NAILs stopped twenty-three. Out of sixty sighted, we reported stopping fifty-seven. We immediately take pictures and can only find fourteen for sure and ten highly probable because they are still burning. Of the fourteen certains, we can positively identify a missile carrier, a radar control van and a support van," the General paused and looked around the room, scowling at them, daring someone to speak.

"I'd like to send the whole bunch of you prima donnas to South Vietnam and make you earn your pay. I'm disgusted with the lot of you. General Momyer can't make decisions if his data is as useless as you're reporting it. Who allowed technical support people to report combat BDA from an air-conditioned office in Thailand?" he looked right at General Holland, "Who the fuck authorized these reports to bypass 7th Air Force?"

No one answered. The general stood and went to the podium. He looked at the assembled crews, "Either you people learn to work together or I'll shut you down."

He then added loudly, "Everyone out of here except the unit commanders and operations officers. The rest of you, go!"

Bill and Sean walked out and headed for the squadron offices. They would have to wait for Colonel Benjamin to tell them what happened.

"Did you see your lieutenant?" Bill asked Sean.

"No. I saw some of the TFA staff but the aide wasn't there."

"It sounded like he was about to get his ass chewed good. I'll bet he didn't want his aide to hear it," Bill offered.

"We plastered those missile trucks, didn't we? Did you see the wrecks and what was left of that long missile carrier? Ralph blew them away," Sean said.

"You guys did all right with the convoy on the bypass," Bill said. *"Most of the damage was done by the time I got there."*

"You took a big chance going to Guard Channel. Alleycat must be pissed," Sean said. *"Why didn't you explain it to them?"*

"When they told me that TFA wanted to talk to me, I knew the Alleycat duty controller wasn't going to make waves. We didn't have time for them to politely work through channels."

"It turned out that you were right. Have you got any idea who patched you through to the TACC?"

"I sure don't. From the quality of the radio transmission, it was someone with better equipment than Alleycat. Maybe it was one of the tankers. They probably have the best communications gear in the Air Force. They didn't identify themselves but if they were on a tanker, they didn't want SAC involved. I wonder if 7th knows who they were?"

"I'll ask around. I'd like to know who's up there at night," Sean said, *"It might even be some of my old friends."*

Soon after they reached the NAIL Ops building, *"Here comes Ed Hardy. The meeting must be over,"* Bill said. He was looking out the door toward Base Operations.

"Get everybody into Ops," Ed directed, as soon as he reached the steps. *"I have an announcement ..."*

Bill and Sean turned away and collected everyone in the offices. They filed into Ops and sat wherever they could find a chair or an open desk top.

"Thanks to our resident smartass," Ed started and looked at Bill, *"We've lost our commander."*

Everyone in the room, including Bill looked shocked. He felt sick. Strangely, Ed was smiling. They waited for him to continue.

"Effective today, Lieutenant Colonel Benjamin is now Colonel Benjamin, the Wing Commander of the 56th Air Commando Wing. He has replaced Colonel Arnholt, who has been called to Vientiane to assist Ambassador Sullivan. We're no longer under TFA's operational control. The colonel's got to integrate the TFA project with the NAILs, but the NAILs get priority. I'm acting boss of this squadron until we get a replacement in a couple of days."

"Wow!" Bill said aloud. *"General Johnson didn't waste any time."*

"Alleycat got put on the carpet and their commander actually apologized for ignoring us last night. He apologized to me for making me call the TACC directly. They think I was on the radio because we were using my call sign," Ed was looking at Bill.

"That's true, Sir," Bill replied. *"I was on the scope."*

"Keep it that way."

"What about TFA?" Sean asked.

"General Holland has to make his reports to the 56th. Everything that goes to higher headquarters will come from the wing and go through 7th Air Force. We'll be able to make them sensible and integrate the results."

"What do we do different?" Sean asked.

"Nothing. We go on as usual, except that Foxtrot and Golf are back under our control. Candlestick is just another FAC being fragged by TUOC. The changes are up to Dave Benjamin. He said to tell you that if he needs our help he'll call." Ed and Sean laughed and Bill reddened.

CHAPTER EIGHTY ONE
Nakhon Phanom Royal Thai Air Base (NKP)
15 March 1968, early evening in the O'Club

The net result of the changes was a smoother operation all around. Dave Benjamin was a positive, direct sort of officer. He quickly organized the Wing units to share information and, using the NAIL knowledge of the road structure, started daily traffic tabulation in TUOC. Within days, sensors were being requested to fill in gaps in the road structure and to test areas for hidden roads.

When Sharon did meet with Sean again, it was four days later. TFA had just finished a no-notice inspection by a team from Systems Command headquarters. General Johnson's report to 7th had sent a rocket up the chain to PACAF and then up to USAF itself and then back to the Systems Command which basically said *"What the hell is going on in TFA?"* To General Holland's credit, the inspection found little out of place.

"You aren't exactly one of the general's favorite people," Sharon said, smiling at Sean.

"Me, in particular, or NAILs in general?" Sean asked.

"*Both, I think, although most of his anger was directed at your friend for calling in 7th Air Force. I don't think I've ever seen him so angry.*"

"*What did the generals talk about?*"

"*I don't know. The general from 7th sent everyone else out of the room except Colonel Benjamin and General Holland. He must have used strong words, because my general can't do enough for Colonel Benjamin.*"

"*The activities on the Trail have really increased. We're getting more guns, more trucks and we're even finding an occasional radar-controlled gun out there. It's getting more dangerous every day,*" Sean's eyes switched out of focus as he remembered something and he drifted off.

It scared Sharon. "*Don't start taking chances. You aren't flying at night again, are you?*" her voice was strained.

"*I'm still in Stan/Eval, but I do have to fly at night once in a while. Bill never flies anything but nights. He only goes out in the daytime about once a month. It isn't fair.*"

"*What he does is his business. I'm worried about you. Please don't try to be like him, even if that major general likes him. That man actually told my boss to leave the captain alone. Imagine that, at 7th Air Force they think he's doing a great job.*"

Sean chuckled at her. "*It's different in combat, Sharon. Bill's a natural leader. He doesn't ask anyone to do anything he wouldn't do and, if they do it his way, they get better results. That's what it's all about.*"

Sharon wasn't buying it. "*I won't argue about him. He's a despicable person and I don't want *anything to do with him,"* she was whispering to be sure they couldn't hear her in the bar.

"Come on," Sean stood and took her hand. *"Let's go to your Trailer."*

"We can't. The general's taking names when people enter and leave the compound. If I take you back there, everyone's going to know we slept together."

"They don't now?" Sean looked surprised, *"Come on. It's time you saw how we lived in the lower echelons."*

"Can we?" she asked.

"There isn't anyone there taking names. Ralph's flying tonight and he won't be back until after midnight."

"If you're sure."

"I'm sure," Sean replied, putting his arm around Sharon. He loved the feel and smell of her. He wasn't about to take a chance of losing her. He'd raise the marriage question again, after the war if necessary, but not tonight.

CHAPTER EIGHTY TWO
Steel Tiger, Eastern Central Laos
20 March 1968, mid-afternoon at 8,000 feet

Bill flew the O-2 at eight thousand feet, heading for Route 9 where it came out of South Vietnam. He was flying a day mission to make sure he remained familiar with the road network. All of the night FACs were required to fly during the daytime at least once a month to maintain current knowledge of the road structure and key interdiction points. Everything looked different at night so it was important to have a mental picture of the road network to keep from losing sight of trucks in the darkness. The night scope had a very narrow field of vision and it was easy to become disoriented if you weren't absolutely sure of the road network. Ed Hardy had insisted that Bill follow his own rules so here he was, flying his required monthly day sortie. The rules were Bill's but, for him with his near-photographic mind, this was all a waste of his time.

He planned to work the southernmost NAIL sector around Route 9 for the mission and return to NKP on a roundabout flight that would carry him north to Mu Gia and then west to NKP. That way he could get a good look at Foxtrot and Golf on the way home.

He was feeling rested and alert. He hadn't flown yesterday and had slept nearly nine hours last night. Take off had been at 1400 hours and he expected to be back at NKP by at least 1900 hours. Sean was meeting him for dinner at 2030. They had a couple of problems to discuss regarding the new crews and the night check rides.

On the way out to the Trail, he had to avoid a couple of rain showers but the weather was generally clear. There were scattered buildups, but they weren't large and were moving northeast. He'd be able to see the roads easily. He flew southeast until he reached Route 122, turned south and followed that until it joined Route 23. When he reached Route 9, he turned east towards Khe Sanh. The roads appeared to be in fairly good repair and mostly open.

When he reached the South Vietnam border, Bill checked in with Cricket and then called NAIL One One on the FM radio. He was relieving Major Martin, who was covering the sector from 1200 to 1500 hours.

"NAIL One One, this is NAIL Five Five on FM. I'm at eight thousand feet."

"Roger Five Five, I'm RTB at 1452, ten thousand feet. You've got a strike scheduled at

1600 hours. Cricket didn't have any fighters available for me."

"Do you have a target, One One?" Bill asked.

"Affirmative. There is some sort of open storage along the road immediately north of highway 9 at WD 8433," Martin replied. *"I didn't bother to go down for a closer look, since I didn't have any fighters. It looks like oil drums and there are people around them and a couple are in uniforms."*

"Thanks, Sir. I'll check it out," Bill replied. *"I've got you in sight at my eleven o'clock high."* He was looking at the other O-2 about a mile in front of him. As he watched, the O-2 rocked its wings in acknowledgement. Bill did the same.

He opened his map and found the location of WD 8433. From there his eyes moved west to the road and he picked his spot. Looking out, he made a quick assessment of his position and turned the plane toward the major's sighting. The terrain below him was mountainous, reaching as high as six thousand feet in some spots, so he decided to stay at eight thousand feet. The roads ran through the valleys and were at an average height of three thousand feet in this vicinity. Bill took out his binoculars and focused them. He was approaching the target location from the east and slightly north of Route 9.

He turned the O-2 to the left to cross the road and looked east/southeast with his binoculars. As he crossed Route 9, he could see several miles of roadway and found the oil drums. They were about two miles east of his position and he could see five or six people around them. When he flew in an arc south to a position abeam the drums, he could see the reason they were there. A truck had gone off the road. He didn't know whether it was from a strike or an accident, but there was a truck on its side thirty or forty yards down the hill from the road. It appeared that the oil drums had been moved from the damaged truck up to the road for pickup.

He thought, *'This is going to be easy. We can hit the truck and the troops and it's broad daylight. It'll be a turkey shoot.'*

"Cricket, NAIL Five Five," Bill called.

"Go ahead Five Five, this is Cricket," came the reply.

"Confirming NAIL One One's target. There are five or six troops unloading a damaged truck on Route 9. They've got oil drums or barrels piled on the side of the road."

"Thank you, NAIL Five Five. We'll have a flight of two F-4s for you at about 1600. That's the earliest we can get them."

"Thank you, Cricket. I'll hang around and keep my eye on them until the fighters arrive," Bill replied.

Bill decided to make wide circles of the area. He set up an easy left turn and was watching the movement on the road, when he heard popcorn popping. It didn't register for a split second. Then he jerked the plane to the left. *"Shit, they're shooting at me. Those sons-a-bitches."*

Bill looked for the guns while turning the plane back and forth. Then he heard the popcorn again. *'They're getting serious. I better let Cricket know.'* He was moving his thumb for the radio switch when he heard and felt the jolt of an explosion. Bill's heart jumped into his throat. The instruments seemed OK and the engines were still running, but the airplane didn't want to stay level. The left wing wanted to climb. He looked out to the left and could see nothing. When he looked to the right, he found the problem. Part of his right wing was gone. Not only was part gone, there were flames coming from the jagged edges of the wing.

He was barely able to control the plane but when he saw the fire, he panicked. If the damn thing blew up he was going to die. He pushed down on the wheel and tried to blow the fire out by diving. It didn't work. The flames were still there. Bill's heart was pounding so hard he could hear it. He realized that the ground was coming closer, so he pulled back on the wheel. The airplane was still flying but it wanted to roll to the right, toward the fire. He realized that he had to get out of the plane, but the door was on the side with the fire.

Finally, his panic gave way to training and he made a call. Switching to the Guard channel, he said, in an excited and choking voice, **"MAYDAY, MAYDAY, NAIL Five Five hit by ground fire. My wing's on fire and I'm bailing out."**

To the north, NAIL Four Eight was working the adjoining sector. He came back immediately. **"Where are you, Five Five?"**

Bill heard the voice and answered, **"A little north of Route 9 at WD 8433. I'm going out now."**

His concern was mounting very rapidly. The flames had increased in intensity and he had to jettison the door. He paused, wondering if he could make it through the pilot's window. That was an alternate exit. Looking at the window and remembering all of the items he was wearing, he decided that he couldn't fit through. The O-2 made a rapid turn to the right when Bill relaxed his hold on the control wheel. He yanked hard on the wheel and returned the plane to an approximation of level flight. **'I've got to get out and the plane's going to turn into me when I jump,'** he thought. **'Now what?'**

He tried to slip the plane, putting his good wing down and stalling out the trailing wing. It worked, insofar as the fire was concerned. The flames were going away from the cabin, but the plane was now descending at a steep rate. Bill pushed the right seat all the way to the back, reached across and pulled the door-jettison lever. It immediately separated from the plane and fell away. Holding the right-side wheel, he picked up his binoculars with his free hand. When he released the wheel and reached for the map case with the other hand, the plane snapped to the right. He had one foot in the door by then, but recoiled when the flames started to come into the cabin. He didn't have a third hand for the M-16, but didn't think it would make it through the jump anyway.

The Oscar Deuce was out of control. Bill had the map case in one hand and the binoculars in the other when he dove through the flames and out the door. He hoped the plane wouldn't hit him in its death throes. As soon as he opened his eyes, which he had closed when he jumped, he realized that he was in the clear. He was tumbling though and quickly spread eagled his arms and legs. The tumbling stopped and Bill was looking at the ground coming toward him fast. He was less than half mile up and it looked as though he was going to hit any second. That's when he remembered the parachute. It wasn't going to open by itself.

He had his map case in his left hand and the binoculars in the right. So far, so good. When he started to reach for the parachute release, the D-ring, the binoculars started to whip back and forth. He didn't want them to hit him, so he released the strap. They fell away. Then he started to move his left hand toward his chest. The case of maps immediately started flapping. In disgust, Bill let it go as well. He grabbed the D-ring with both hands and pulled. The parachute opened immediately.

Bill didn't feel anything at first and then he was hit hard under his chin. The pain caused his eyes to water and when he opened them, he was hanging in his parachute. It didn't feel right because he'd forgotten to tighten his leg straps. The hit on his chin had been the buckle on his chest strap. He reached down and pulled the leg straps tighter. As he was doing that, he remembered that the book said not to loosen the straps when you were flying. In the worse case, you could even slip from the parachute harness when it opened. He was lucky this time. Like most pilots, he had loosened the leg straps for comfort when he was flying. The straps chafed, particularly when you were soaked with sweat.

Now he began to think more clearly about his situation. He estimated his altitude at about fifteen hundred to two thousand feet above the ground. His pistol was still attached and he felt the survival vest pockets. He had all of his survival gear. Then he started to look around. Below him was a large, completely barren field on the south side of a hill. It looked like a fire had burned through the area sometime in the past. There was no grass or vegetation of any sort. All he could see was the burned-out remains of trees and none of them looked to be over six feet high.

He heard sounds and looked around. The O-2 was in the process of destroying itself. It was turning and flipping end over end with both engines straining and the trim set for climb. Bill had not shut it down, because of the fire and his hurry to get away. It finally turned upside down and stayed that way until it hit the ground and exploded on contact. The plane impacted on the far north side of the hill below him. He was drifting toward trees at the west end of the barren spot. He still heard sounds and suddenly realized that someone was shooting at him. He was hearing the bullets! Bill pulled down on one set of risers and started to oscillate. He figured that they'd have a difficult time hitting him while the parachute was descending and he was swinging back and forth.

The sound of the bullets brought him back to the war. He had to do something when he was on the ground. To the south, he could see a river several miles away and decide he'd head in that direction.

As he neared the ground, the sound of bullets zipping by him stopped and he could see the trees that he was going to hit. He could also see the ground. This wasn't multiple-canopied jungle; it was more like a stand of young trees. Bill wasn't hanging straight down from the parachute when he hit. He was swinging off to the side. He crashed into the trees moving sideways and he crossed his arms in front of his face. When he stopped moving, he felt funny. Opening his eyes, he immediately figured out why the sensation was strange. He was upside down.

He looked up, which was toward the ground, and it was less than two feet away. Reaching out, he touched the dirt. Looking down toward the sky, he saw that one of his feet was caught between two small trees. The parachute was tangled in the branches of several twelve-foot-high trees. He opened the leg strap on his trapped leg and pushed the foot free of the branches. When he opened the other leg strap and finally the chest strap, he slid out and onto the ground. He was down safely, unhurt…and alive.

Bill sat down with his back against a tree and pulled out one of his two survival radios. He turned on the emergency beeper, waited for a moment and then made a voice call.

There was no answer. He put that radio away and tried the other one. This time someone answered. They identified themselves as "Motor Pool." Bill told Motor Pool that he was OK and that he'd call again when he heard or saw an airplane. He had no idea who or what Motor Pool was.

He remained in place and listened for the sound of an aircraft. The trees he'd hit were saplings. This wasn't old jungle; it was more like a forest at home. The ground was covered with brown leaves and he could see patches of sky.

Sitting there, he wondered how long it'd take for the rescue helicopters to get to him. He wasn't worried and was feeling good about not having any injuries. He'd forgotten about the war in his relief at being unhurt and in contact with Motor Pool. He knew they'd come for him.

Bill was rudely jerked from his euphoric state by the sound of voices and movement. He jumped up and nearly fainted. As he started moving to find a place to hide, the noise was deafening. The leaves all around him were dried leaves. Every step he took sounded like an elephant tramping through the jungle. It was impossible to move without making a lot of noise. He tried to pull the parachute from the trees and couldn't. It was going to signal anyone who came this way that he'd been here.

The sounds he'd heard weren't close so he decided to risk making some noise and get out of the trees. The mostly clear burned out area was to his left, so he moved carefully in that direction, which angled away from the people noises. He was at the edge of the clearing in five minutes, moving as quietly as he could. He found a place to stop but realized that he was too close to the parachute to stay for long.

He jerked his head around when he heard an airplane. It was an O-2. NAIL Four Eight had found him. Bill called him on the radio.

"Four Eight, is that you?"

"I hear you, Five Five. Are you OK?"

"I am so far. There are some people down here who are looking for me. They were shooting at me on the way down." Bill said.

"Stay put, Five Five. We've got an Air America chopper on the way; they picked up your first call," Captain Phil Masters replied.

"I'm going to get out in the open field, Phil. It'll be easier to get me and I've got to get away from here. I'll find a hole to hide in."

"Be careful, Bill. I can't see anyone but they could be hiding anywhere," Phil's voice was concerned.

Bill crept from the trees and started across the open field. He'd crouch by a dead tree, look around and then dash to the next one. The field was on the side of a hill and his path was slightly downhill. The hill was steep enough that he'd have to climb up it, but flat enough that he could run down. Bill was about twenty yards into the field when he saw the impact of several bullets in the dirt in front of him and then heard the distinctive bark of an automatic weapon. Someone was shooting at him from the top of the hill.

He dove into a depression and hit his left arm on a large tree root. The arm went numb and he thought he'd been shot. The flight suit was torn and there was blood on the sleeve. He decided he couldn't worry about it now and called Phil on the rescue radio. ***"Phil, I've got someone shooting at me from the corner of the clearing toward the northwest,"*** he was out of breath and panting.

"Keep down," Phil said.

Bill watched as the O-2 turned and dove at the field. Phil fired one of his Willie Petes at the corner of the clearing and it exploded in a large white cloud. The noise made Bill's ears ring.

"Nice shot, Phil. You were right on. I'm moving again. I think he hit me in the left arm."

"Are you OK?" came back.

Bill didn't hear Phil's call. He'd put the radio away and was running toward the center of the field, angling down for both speed and ease. He was out of breath and had to stop before he reached the center. The weight of the flack vest and the survival kit was enough to get his heart pounding every time he tried to run.

He lay down on the ground, flat on his back, gasping for breath and took out a radio. ***"Do you see any more of them, Phil?"*** he croaked.

"Five Five are you OK? I don't see anyone in the field but you. What the hell are you doing, sunbathing? I can see you laying flat on your back," Phil sounded more than a little curious.

"We need to start a PT program, Phil. I'm bushed," Bill said, still panting.

"We've got company, Five Five. Stand by for pickup," Phil was excited. *"There's an Air America chopper coming up now."*

Bill saw the blue-and-white Huey helicopter as it came screaming up the valley. He was standing now and waving at the chopper. It pulled to a hover and then started down toward him. There was a man in the open doorway wearing blue jeans and a T-shirt and holding an AK-47. He waved and turned his attention to the top of the hill. Bill waited for them to throw him a line. The helicopter was stopped about twelve feet above him, hovering when the man in the door started shooting.

Bill dove for the ground as the helicopter turned and moved off. He couldn't believe it was leaving. They were so close. He took out the radio. *"Phil, what's going on?"*

"They don't have a hoist. That's an administrative bird. They're going to try again. See if you can grab one of the skids," Phil said, his voice shaking.

Bill watched as the helicopter came back. This time the man in the door was shooting short bursts at the top of the hill. The helicopter came right at Bill, the nose lifted and it descended toward him. He stood and reached. The runners were four or five feet above him and he couldn't jump that high. He stood and looked at the man in the door, unbelieving. The man shrugged and mouthed *"Good Luck,"* then the chopper turned and left in a roar.

Bill's first reaction was one of despair. He was being left to die. He didn't know how long he stood there staring at the retreating helicopter but soon a loud explosion startled him and he looked around. Phil had just fired another rocket at the northwest corner of the field. Bill looked up and saw two fighters circling. He needed cover. To his left, another twenty yards into the field was a ravine. He headed that way on a run. When he dove into the ravine, the first of two F-105s came screaming over. Bill lay on his back looking up at the bombs falling from the plane.

The next thing he knew, he was lifted about six inches and slammed back into the ground. The Thuds must have dropped seven-hundred-and-fifty pound bombs on the top of the hill. Bill's ears were ringing and he couldn't hear anything. There was small debris falling from the sky like rain. It was pieces of trees and dirt. He covered his head and waited for number two to drop. The second drop was no less of a surprise. He was again lifted completely off the ground and showered with debris. He thought his eardrums were blown out. They hurt like hell due to the concussions.

The bombing stopped and Bill took out his radio. *"Phil, do you read?"*

"I got him. Five Five are you OK?" Phil's voice was cracking.

"I'm OK for now. What happens next?"

"We've got two Jollys on the way. You have to lay quiet until they get here. We're going to soften up the area around you."

"Do you have me?"

"No. Show me a panel."

Bill took out his orange panel and spread it on the ground.

"I see you. You moved?" Phil said.

"I'm in a ravine of sorts, looks like it was made by water running down the hill. They can't see me from the sides," Bill replied. He was beginning to sound depressed.

"Leave your radio on. I'll call you when the Jollys arrive."

"Thanks, Phil," Bill was starting to doubt that he'd get out alive. There was too much gunfire to be from a small squad of enemy. He must be near a larger force. He huddled against the bank of the ravine, behind the remains of a small

tree. It was about six inches in diameter and six or seven feet tall. The part of the ravine where he'd hidden was about five feet deep, giving him cover from the sides of the field, but he was unable to look out without standing and losing his protection.

It seemed an eternity before NAIL FOUR EIGHT called. It was more like ten or fifteen minutes but Bill was getting desperate by the time he heard the call. *"Jollys are inbound, Bill. Get ready."*

"What do they need from me?" Bill asked.

"They'll need a smoke when I tell you. They can't hear your radio when they get in close so I'll relay their instructions and your answers," Phil said.

"I'm ready. Let's go."

Bill took out a smoke flare. He didn't want to pop it before the Jolly was close since it would also let the ground troops know where he was. As soon as the helicopter approached the field, Bill popped the smoke flare and hurled it down the hill. The orange smoke billowed up and the helicopter came to a hover.

There was a sudden increase in ground fire; the helicopter jerked and then turned away. The Jolly had been sprayed by heavy automatic weapons fire.... damaging the hoist and the intercom. The pilot couldn't talk to the PJ and he couldn't lower the penetrator. The first Jolly was done for the day.

"Jolly Zero One has been hit I am unable to complete the pickup. We're exiting to the south."

"Roger Zero One, go back to the orbit point....understand you're OK"

"That's a rog"

"Sandy Lead see if you can suppress that fire from the hill to the east"

The Sandys blasted the offending hill top with 20mm cannon fire and a couple of pods of rockets. The fire seemed to quiet.

"Bill, they're going to try again with the second Jolly. Get ready," Phil said.

"I'm ready, I'm ready," he replied, tension in his voice.

The second helicopter hovered over him, at least eighty feet in the air, and began lowering the jungle penetrator. It was halfway down when Bill saw the crewman at the door jerk back and he heard the slap of rounds hitting the Jolly Green. It turned, lowered its nose towards the valley and accelerated away.

"Jolly Zero Two has been hit. We are taking fire from the top of the hill. My PJ is down."

"Bill, they can't get you until we suppress the ground fire. The two Jollys that have been hit are going home. We've got two more on the way from Danang," Phil said, in a dejected voice.

Bill knew then that he was going to be killed. There wasn't much chance that he'd be rescued. He decided that he wasn't going to be a prisoner. It was time to get out, one way or the other. He needed to stay alert now. The smoke flares let everyone know where he was and company should be arriving soon. He took out his .38 and checked it. He wanted to greet them properly.

Historical Note: Jerry Dwyer was shot down twice and was rescued both times. The first bail out ended with a routine search and rescue with no action reported by anyone. The second was different...much different. Read on.

CHAPTER EIGHTY THREE
Steel Tiger— Eastern Central Laos

20 March 1968, mid-afternoon on the ground

Bill risked a cigarette since the smoke grenade had given away his position anyway. He sat for a few moments watching the planes above him. Two more A-1s arrived and began to make firing passes at the edge of the clearing. He could see the bombs and CBU clusters falling away from the wings. They were sure beating the shit out of that edge of the jungle.

He decided to take stock of the items in his pockets and in the vest. Sitting at the bottom of the ravine and up against one of the sides, partially hidden behind a small tree stump, he began to layout the contents of his pockets. On his left leg where he normally carried a small Minox camera, what was left of the pocket dangled from one seam. The camera was gone. The pocket must have snagged on something when he landed. The right leg pocket held his survival map, his personal journal and two nylon marking panels. He re-folded the panels carefully and put the items back in the pocket. His arm hurt really badly and he decided to take an antibiotic pill while he had the chance. The medical kit was in one of the survival vest pockets and Bill took it out. The kit was sealed tightly with tear-resistant tape. Bill couldn't break the seal. He took the knife from its scabbard on the vest and started to pry the tape loose. At that instant, he saw a puff of dirt and heard a weird sound a few inches from his right shoulder and then a strange bang. He frowned and wondered what it was when he saw movement down the hill to his left. There were people in the ravine coming up from the bottom of the hill and they weren't friendly!

It suddenly dawned on Bill that what he'd seen and heard was a bullet hitting the dirt right next to his shoulder. He grabbed at his pistol, eyes wide and unbelieving. They were in the ravine and coming up toward him, shooting as they came. Bill got his pistol out and fired without thinking. He shot four times down the hill, the pistol making loud explosive sounds. The enemy scurried for cover as soon as he started shooting.

"Phil, there are people in the ravine with me," Bill called over the radio. His voice had raised a couple of octaves.

"What're they doing?" Phil came back.

"About what you would fucking well expect. They're shooting at me," Bill yelled into the radio.

The next few moments were like scenes from a western movie. Bill remained seated and tried to hide behind the tree stump. As he looked down the ravine, five enemy soldiers were coming up toward him. They were climbing slowly, cautiously moving from one dead tree or log to another. Four were carrying rifles and one had a pistol. They were wearing brown uniforms.

The tree that Bill was using for protection was only about six inches wide. That meant there was an appreciable amount of him that stuck out both sides of the stump. He looked down the hill and at the five who were moving toward him or crouching behind tree stumps. Bill decided to re-load his pistol. He took six cartridges from his belt and held them in his hand. He didn't want to completely empty the six-shot revolver, the proper method of re-loading, so he tried to gently pry the shells loose with the extractor. A movement down the hill startled him and he flinched. That caused one of the empty shells to catch under the extractor. This is the only possible way for a revolver to jam and Bill had managed to accomplish it with enemy troops shooting at him. He was cursing himself as he dropped the fresh rounds and pushed the extractor to its full open limit and shook the empty shell loose. He then scrambled to pick each of the good shells up from the ground, blow the dirt off the bullet and re-load.

When he snapped the cylinder shut and looked up, there were two of the enemy soldiers less than twenty yards from his position. He emptied the revolver at them.

Fortunately, they turned and ran when he started shooting. He didn't hit either one, but they didn't know how many shots he had so they kept running long after he'd stopped shooting. Bill re-loaded again, correctly this time, and found himself panting. He had been holding his breath since he dropped the shells on the ground.

As he tried to calm down, he looked down the hill and realized that the soldiers with rifles were eventually going to shoot him. At that moment, as if by choice, he felt a hot pain in his left arm, the left arm again. Looking down, he could see where a bullet had passed through the sleeve of his flight suit. It had creased his arm, but did little more than scratch him. He thought again about taking an antibiotic pill but couldn't get the first aid kit open with one hand, and, he sure as hell wasn't letting the pistol out of the other.

About that time, he realized that he desperately needed to relieve himself. He had to go so badly that it was beginning to hurt. He fired one shot down the hill and watched as the four ducked behind their cover.

He took a moment to realize that one was missing. He knew he should be worried but the most pressing concern was his need to piss. It bothered him to expose himself in the middle of a gun fight but it was either that or go in his flight suit. Looking around carefully, he didn't see anything about to happen. He unzipped his flight suit from the bottom, raising the zipper about five or six inches. He then held his penis out and pointed to the left, between his left boot and the tree stump. He sighed with relief as he started to empty his bladder.

Needless to say, the other occupants of the ravine were not concerned with Bill's personal problems. They picked that moment to begin inching forward. He found himself concentrating on his aim, shooting down the ravine along the right side of the tree stump. It was then that Bill noticed a warm feeling in his left foot. Looking down, he saw that he had pissed all over his left leg and foot. His boot was soaked.

"Shit," Bill muttered to himself. ***"They're going to love this when I get back."***

It was at that moment he realized that he was seriously intending to get out alive. He began to consider how to get rid of the four soldiers remaining in the ravine.

"Five Five, are you on the air," came over the emergency radio.

"I'm here," Bill answered. ***"What's up?"***

"You've got someone crawling toward you on the southeast side of the ravine," Phil radioed.

"How close?" Bill wanted to know.

"Twenty or thirty yards, no more. You have to do something about him!"

"Thanks, Phil. I'll invite him over for tea."

"Listen up, smart ass. He's not crawling that way to pass the time of day."

"Roger, Phil. I'll be careful," Bill replied, *"Thanks."*

He was wondering what to do about the enemy who was coming toward him when he heard a metallic sound, like something snapping open. When he looked up toward the noise, he saw a small dark object in the air. It only took a fraction of a second for him to realize that the object was a hand grenade. Now he knew why the man had circled around.

Bill watched with unbelieving eyes as the grenade hit the opposite bank and rolled down toward him. Then, he did what everyone should do in such a case. He closed his eyes tightly. Nothing happened and Bill slowly reopened his eyes. The grenade was less than six inches from his foot. It had rolled to the bottom of the ravine and stopped.

He picked up his radio and said. ***"It's a grenade! They're throwing grenades. It didn't go off!"***

Bill's voice had raised several octaves. He was screaming into the radio, holding down the transmit switch. As soon as he let it go, he heard voices.

"Who threw it? Where's the guy who threw the grenade? Throw it back at him."

Although he was now fully panicked, Bill heard the voices and came back to reality. He realized that he had to do something about the man who threw the grenade.

Bill moved his legs under him and eased up into a crouched position. Keeping as much of his body as possible behind the tree stump, he slowly raised himself up until he was looking out over the edge of the ravine. By that time, he was nearly standing upright.

"Damn," he muttered to himself. He was looking into the eyes of one of the enemy, ten or fifteen feet from him, inching his way toward the ravine. Bill was holding his pistol in front of him with both hands, pointing toward the soldier. He started squeezing the trigger and watched the .38 caliber bullets tear holes in the slightly-built enemy. At the range he was shooting, Bill put all six of his shots into and through the torso of the grenade thrower. The enemy soldier dropped to his knees, fell backwards, then sideways and rolled about ten feet down the hill.

Bill had lost control again but came back to reality when he heard a constant clicking sound and attempted to identify it. The sound turned out to be him, squeezing the trigger on an empty pistol. He reacted suddenly, lowering himself back down and behind the tree stump. When he saw the unexploded grenade, he panicked again and turned to scurry away up the ravine.

To his surprise, it was too steep. He couldn't run up the slope. Crawling didn't make a lot of sense, not in plain sight of several enemy soldiers shooting at him.

He reluctantly returned to the tree stump he'd been crouched behind and stared at the grenade. This just wasn't going to do. He braced himself and gingerly reached for the ugly little weapon. He gently touched it with one finger. It didn't explode. He slowly encircled the grenade and closed his hand. Lifting it gently, he brought his arm back to throw it down the hill toward the enemy. Then he thought for a moment and then stopped. He turned slightly and threw it as far as he could toward the side of the field. He didn't want someone to throw it back at him. There was no explosion; it was still a dud.

He turned his attention back to the uninvited guests in his ravine and discovered that there were only three remaining. Of the five that had entered the ravine, one was lying near his position with six great holes in his body. He could see three men with rifles, but the man with the pistol was not in sight. Bill began to worry, and then relaxed a bit when he saw a foot protruding from behind one of the logs. He didn't see the foot move, so he assumed that this man was dead or wounded.

"NAIL Five Five, are you OK?" Phil was calling him again.

"I am now," Bill replied.

"There is another pair of Jolly's inbound from Danang. You need to clear out the ravine, if they're going to be able to get to you."

"Brilliant, just fucking brilliant. Clear out the ravine! Go out there and clear out the ravine, he says," Bill replied as sarcastically as he was able.

"If you don't get those guys out of the ravine, they'll shoot up into the choppers just like they did last time. You've got to get rid of them, Five Five."

"Phil, do you have any Sandy or Hobo aircraft remaining?"

"I have two Hobos that just got here. The Sandys don't have any more ordnance, just guns," Phil answered. **"What do you want me to do with the Hobos?"**

"Do they have CBU?"

"Roger, full loads."

"Drop it on the field," Bill said.

There was a long period of quiet. The next call came from the Hobos. ***"We're not dropping it on him, for Christ's sake."***

"Bill, what's the sense of killing you before we rescue you. Can't it wait until later? That way we can at least get credit for the rescue," Phil came back. He was quick.

"I'm in a ravine. Drop the CBU along the bottom of the hill along the edge of the jungle. I'm behind a small tree, but I'm in a depression that will pretty well protect me. Have the Hobos attack in trail. As soon as they drop, I'm going down the hill to clear out the ravine."

"We can't control it that well," the Hobo leader called.

"Do it anyway," Phil directed.

Bill checked his pistol, got into a crouched position and pressed himself into the depression in the side of the ravine. His flak jacket protected most of his exposed area. When he was ready, he called. ***"I'm hunkered down, drop the CBU."***

"Hobo Lead's in. Careful Two, drop at the edge of the clearing."

"Two's right behind you, Lead."

CHAPTER EIGHTY FOUR
Steel Tiger, Eastern Central Laos
20 March 1968, past mid-afternoon on the ground

Bill heard the A-1s pass overhead and squeezed his eyes closed. His world suddenly turned into hundreds of small explosions. He felt some of the pellets hitting his flak jacket and something hit his right thigh. He looked down and was hit in the face. A pellet had bounced off the ravine in front of him and hit him in the forehead.

It was over as suddenly as it started. There were no more sounds and Bill shook his head to clear it and then looked at his leg. It was bleeding slightly but the CBU pellet must have been a ricochet. It only scratched him. Looking down the ravine, he didn't see anything moving. He stood and looked out both sides of the ravine. There was no visible movement anywhere in the clearing.

He wasn't particularly anxious to leave the relative safety of his hiding place but he knew he had to make sure that the enemy troops in the ravine wouldn't be able to shoot at the helicopter from below. The helicopters couldn't defend themselves from an attacker directly below the craft.

Bill started down the ravine with his pistol held in front of him. He'd make sure they were dead before the rescue helicopters arrived. He didn't want to touch anyone so he didn't move them. All were covered with blood. Some of the CBU had fallen right on top of them. Bill turned to climb back up the ravine when he was hit in the back. Something slammed into him and knocked him down. He heard the sound of a shot as he was falling. A rifle had been fired. The bullet hit him before the sound reached him. He rolled and looked back down the ravine. One of the "dead" men had shot him.

Bill began shooting and saw one of his bullets hit the wounded soldier in the face. He hurt and he wondered if he was hit badly or if the vest had stopped the bullet. Crawling to a stump, he sat up and leaned against the tree. Reaching under his vest, he felt for blood and found it. The vest hadn't stopped the high-speed rifle bullet. He was hit but it didn't hurt too much. **"Must be just a graze,"** he thought.

His attention was distracted by the A-1s as they made a pass over the field. He took out his radio, finding movement difficult. He was getting tired...very tired...and he wanted to close his eyes and rest. He pressed the transmit button and spoke, *"Phil, I'm hit."*

"I told you, we couldn't do it without hitting him. Now What, NAIL?"

"Hobo Lead, stay off the radio. Bill, how bad are you hit?"

"One of the guys in the ravine shot me. I thought he was dead and turned my back. Only a couple of ricochets from the CBU reached me. I'm hurt, but I don't know how badly," Bill's voice was fading. He was obviously having a difficult time talking.

"The choppers are inbound, Bill. Hang on," Phil called.

Bill heard thrashing in the brush down the hill in the tree line which was followed by shouting.

"I hear voices, Phil. There are more of them corning. You can't get me out of here. Do me a favor," Bill asked.

"Sure. What is it?"

"If the Jolly's can't get me out, level this field. Don't want them to get me," Bill was pleading, his voice hardly a whisper.

"We can't do that, Bill. Hang on. They're ten minutes out."

"Bomb the field, Phil. I don't want to be captured. I can hear them clearer now. They're coming....," Bill's voice faded out then returned, *"Please, Phil."*

"Can you see him, NAIL," came from the Hobo leader. "

"No. All I can see are bodies at the edge of the clearing. He must be one of them," Phil was desperate.

"One of them must still be alive. Someone had to shoot him. Are we going to drop the bombs?"

"I don't know," Phil answered.

"It's your decision, NAIL. He's one of yours. We don't like it, but we will drop."

Phil was holding his O-2 in a pylon turn looking almost straight down out of the left window....he saw brown uniforms burst out of the trees!

"I see more troops in the field. He hasn't got a chance. Go in, go in!" Phil was yelling over the radio.

"Lead's in; Two, take spacing. Clear out the ordnance."

"Two, Roger."

The two A-1s rolled in and dropped their remaining ordnance. Both were carrying rockets and bombs. They made one pass each with the bombs and then fired their rockets on a second pass.

Bill crawled to the edge of the jungle, away from the voices and was trying to reach a tree when the bombs hit. The last thing he remembered was thanking Phil as he was hit by the blast. He was grateful that he felt no pain and then he felt nothing and slipped into the blackness.

The two Jolly Green helicopters arrived in the area ten minutes later. They were told to wait as Phil tried in vain to raise Bill on the radio. The south end of the clearing was a smoldering mess. There were twelve bodies that he could count and they were still receiving ground fire from positions around the clearing. The enemy was still down there in force and there was no contact with the downed pilot.

"NAIL Four Eight, this is Cricket."

"Go ahead, Cricket, this is Four Eight."

"We're sorry, NAIL. You're to return to NKP. The operation is being called off," Cricket radioed.

"I have to know. I'll wait," Phil replied. *"He may still be alive."*

"NAIL Four Eight, there are two Zorros enroute to your position. They'll look around and maintain a listening watch."

"I'll wait for them," Phil replied. He couldn't believe that Bill was gone. He was the indestructible one. He couldn't be dead.

"NAIL Four Eight, this is Zorro Three Seven."

"Three Seven, this is Four Eight."

"I'm about five minutes out. Zorro Two Six will pick you up over Saravane."

"Thanks, Zorro. Will you stay here?"

"I will, NAIL. I won't leave as long as there's a chance," Charlie Green replied. He had Phil in sight and pulled into orbit around the clearing.

Phil turned toward NKP and slumped down into his seat. His friend was gone and he had ordered a strike on his position. He wasn't paying attention to his flying and was startled when a T-28 eased up to his left wing. The Zorro pilot waved and Phil waved back. They didn't talk and the T-28 moved back and away from the O-2. The pilot would keep Phil in sight and out of trouble.

The hour-long flight back to NKP was the worst Phil had ever flown. He agonized over the events in the clearing and replayed the scenes over and over again in his mind. Phil couldn't come up with a scenario that left Bill alive. He must've been badly wounded to call the ordnance in on himself.

Phil was daydreaming when he heard another voice. He looked out and saw an O-2 on his left wing. *"Are you OK,"* came over the radio.

"Yes, Sir," Phil answered. He recognized Colonel Hardy's voice.

"Any chance?"

"No, Sir. He was shot and called the last strike in on himself to keep from being captured. He sounded like he was hurt bad."

"Take it on in, Phil. I'll follow you down. There are a lot of people waiting for you at TUOC. Cricket reported that you did a superb job running the rescue attempts. Are you up to the attention?"

"I guess so. Will you be there?"

"Yeah, Phil, I will. I'll make it as short as possible."

"Thanks, Colonel. I'm going over to the tower now. The field is right in front of us."

Ed Hardy nodded to himself and allowed his O-2 to fall in behind Phil. He would follow him down and accompany the captain to TUOC. This was going to be a long night.

CHAPTER EIGHTY FIVE
Nakhon Phanom Thai Air Base
20 March 1968, late afternoon in TUOC

The toughest part of Phil's debriefing was the look on Sean's face. Phil was halfway through his report when Sean came running into TUOC. Ed Hardy got up and spoke to him for a moment and then the two of them joined the group around the table. Sean was visibly upset and couldn't keep his hands from shaking. He nodded at Phil and indicated that he should continue. Zack brought out a cup of coffee and handed it to Sean, who had difficulty not spilling it.

Sean didn't interrupt until Phil was describing the final bombing pass on the field. **"How do you know he's dead? How do you know?"** Sean demanded, loudly.

"He said he'd been shot in the back and he was hurting. He called for the bombs himself, to keep from being captured. It was his call, not mine! Shit, Man, I didn't want to do it. I had to. He told me to." Phil shouted back at Sean.

"That's it, Phil, get something to eat and go to bed," Ed Hardy interrupted. He took Sean by the arm and left the room. Ed Hardy took Sean to the O'Club and ordered for both of them. Sean wasn't talking. He didn't touch his food, but did calm down somewhat while Ed was eating.

"Where's Sharon?" Ed asked when he finished.

Sean didn't reply. He shook his head from side to side indicating that he didn't know.

"I'll call her and tell her to come over here, or do you want me to take you to TFA?"

Sean shook his head negative. He looked at Ed and said, *"I'll stay here a while, then go to my hootch. Thanks for your help, Colonel. I really don't want to see anyone else, not right now."*

Ed Hardy nodded in understanding and left Sean sitting in the dining room. He'd call Sharon and have her come to the club.

When Ed contacted the lieutenant, she told him that TFA knew about the shoot down. They had Cricket relay the radio calls and the TFA staff had listened to the rescue attempt. She was waiting for Sean to call or come over. Ed told her that the captain was in the O'Club and that he wasn't on the next day's flight schedule.

Sharon wasn't looking forward to seeing Sean. She'd never liked his friend and Bill avoided contact with her. At TFA, they listened to the rescue attempt and couldn't understand why Bill didn't surrender. At least he'd be alive and would be released when the war was over. General Holland had called Bill's actions foolish and said that he was going to cause problems for any other pilots unlucky enough to be shot down in central Laos. Now, because he'd fought back, the enemy was more likely to shoot downed crews.

Sharon walked into the O'Club and looked for Sean. He was sitting by himself in the dining room with an untouched beer in front of him. Sharon pulled out a chair and sat close to him. He didn't move until she touched his arm. When he turned to look at her, there were tears in his eyes.

"Shit, shit, shit, shit," was all that he said.

They sat for a long time without speaking. Finally, she said, *"Let's go. You need to get some rest."*

Her words broke through his thoughts. He looked at his watch and said, *"It's late. I need to sleep or I'll be the next one to have a problem. Come on let's go."*

They left the club and she drove Sean to her quarters at TFA.

CHAPTER EIGHTY SIX
Nakhon Phanom Thailand Royal Air Base (NKP)
21 March 1968, morning at Wing Headquarters

In the morning, Colonel Benjamin called Ed Hardy to come to Wing Headquarters. When Ed walked into the building, Dave Benjamin was standing at the door.

"Congratulations, Colonel Hardy. You've just been approved as commander of the 23rd. General Momyer recommended the promotion yesterday and Air Force Headquarters approved it last night, effective immediately," Dave Benjamin was smiling and holding out his hand to be the first to congratulate the new commander.

"Thanks, Dave. Why do I think this was something you arranged?" Ed asked, grinning from ear to ear.

"How's Sean?" Dave asked quietly.

"Not taking it well. I have a hard time believing it myself. He's with the lieutenant at TFA. I gave him the day off."

"That's good. Be careful we don't lose him, too."

"I will. What about this Operations Officer from Danang. Did you talk to him yet? We were going to put him in Jerry's slot, but he can have mine now," Ed suggested.

"I'll call him. If he's available, I'll ask for them to send him over in the next couple of days. What about the night program?" Dave asked.

"I'm going to put Martin in charge. We need to back off a little. I think it's getting to be a lot more risky than it's been in the past. Maybe with TFA's help we can find the convoys without going quite so low."

"Good. Martin is the timid type. It sure won't hurt to be careful for a while."

"What about Phil? He did a hell of a job out there and had to make some very tough calls," Ed asked.

"We got a message about him from 7th. Cricket recommended him for the Air Force Cross. 7th is considering pulling him off line, maybe even sending him down to FACU...keep him safe."

"When? Can I use him in Operations?" Ed wanted to know.

"The message says not later than 1 April. Base is working on transport right now. Unless I miss my guess, he'll be on next week's plane to Saigon." Benjamin said.

"That's probably smart. He was pretty broken up and he'll have a hell of a time living with his decision for a while."

"Bill called the strike in on himself, as I heard it..."

"Yeah, he did. However, Phil let the Hobos drop. He could've called it off," Ed said.

"They grow up in a hurry, don't they?" Benjamin smiled wryly. He held out his hand again. *"I've got to get back to work. Good luck with your new job, Colonel."*

"Thanks, Boss," Ed grinned and shook hands. He walked back out the door; his first flying command and it was a combat command. He felt ten feet tall.

Historical Note: Lt. Col. Pallister who is portrayed by Col Benjamin in our tale was promoted to colonel (at the ripe old age of 51) and was replaced by Lt. Col. Ben Starr, who eventually retired as a major general. Colonel Pallister retired to his home in Hawaii.

CHAPTER EIGHTY SEVEN
Nakhon Phanom Royal Thai Air Base (NKP)
21 March 1968, early evening at the O'Club

"Well, Joe, what now? Who's going to take over the night program?" Sean asked. They were in the dining room of the O'Club. Joe was eating an early dinner before going to the night briefing. Sean was waiting for Sharon to finish work.

"I don't have any idea. I wonder what Colonel Benjamin's going to do about the squadron?" Joe was obviously not pleased.

"We've lost all three of our Operations Officers. Jerry, then Bill and now Hardy's been moved up."

"Colonel Hardy will do fine as commander, but I'm going to miss him in Operations," Sean said. *"He kept a lot of the normal bullshit away from the combat crews."*

"I've heard he's to be replaced by a lieutenant colonel from Danang," Joe offered.

"Do you know his name," Sean asked, and then added, *"Hell, why should I care. I don't know any lieutenant colonels at Danang."*

Joe laughed, *"He knows you or at least he's asked for you to meet him when he arrives. He's due to land about 1000 tomorrow morning. There's a note on the board for you at the squadron."*

Sean was surprised, but not particularly interested. He didn't care about some old fart from Danang. He cared about losing his buddy. In any event, he was scheduled to fly in the morning. Someone else was going to have to meet the new lieutenant colonel.

"Here's your girl," Joe smiled, looking past Sean. They both stood.

"Hi," she said and sat down, *"Are you flying tonight?"* she looked at Joe. He nodded and continued to eat.

Sharon looked at Sean, *"You look more rested."*

"I slept some this afternoon," he replied. *"I might even be hungry in a while."*

"I am," she smiled at him, paused, and then said, *"The sensor program for Route 23 was approved this morning. We should have them in place in a couple more days."*

"It makes a lot more sense dropping sensors with F-4s, but the Navy planes would be fine for

the secondary routes. There isn't much in the way of gunfire on them," Joe commented.

"Yeah," Sean agreed.

"According to the figures, truck kills are way up. We're hearing them move all day long," Sharon said.

"I still think you're chasing a lot of engine sounds," Sean said.

"Me too," Joe offered. *"We get reports every day and there isn't anything on the roads. We have to verify every one of the sensor reports."*

"Our controllers think the trucks are moving on hidden roads," Sharon said, in a bit of a huff. She felt it necessary to defend the TFA staff.

"We'll see. It'll all come out in the wash. At least everyone is working to the same tune now," Sean smiled as he spoke. He wanted to change the subject.

Joe paid for his meal and bid them goodbye. He was off to the night briefing.

"Come on," Sharon said to Sean, *"I'll fix us something."*

CHAPTER EIGHTY EIGHT
Nakhon Phanom Thai Air Base (NKP)
22 March 1968, mid-morning in the Nail Ops

In the morning Sean found that his flight was cancelled. He was to go with Colonel Hardy to meet their new Operations Officer. The two walked from the 23rd squadron building to Base Operations. Sean was quiet and Colonel Hardy didn't make any attempt at conversation. At Operations, they were told that Covey 12 was on initial approach and would be landing in a couple of minutes.

The Coveys were the FACs from the 20th TASS based at Danang. Obviously their new Operations Officer was a Covey from Danang. Colonel Benjamin arrived at Base Operations just as the Covey O-2 landed.

When the plane taxied up to its parking spot in front of Base Operations Colonel Benjamin, Lt. Colonel Hardy, and Sean started walking toward it. To Sean's complete surprise, Fred Stebbins stepped out of the door and waved at them, a wide grin on his face and shiny new lieutenant colonel's leaves on his shoulders. Sean let out a whoop and ran forward. The two greeted each other with enthusiasm. Dave Benjamin was equally pleased, but not surprised. He and Fred had been friends for fifteen years and Dave had requested Fred's assignment to the 23rd.

"Welcome to the 23rd, Colonel," Dave Benjamin said.

"Thanks to you," Fred replied. *"I'd still be one of a dozen extra lieutenant colonels in the 20th TASS if you hadn't asked for me to come here."*

"Danang has enough brass," Dave answered. *"We need an experienced Operations Officer. We just promoted our last one. Fred, this is your new boss, Ed Hardy."*

"Nice meeting you, Sir. Thanks for the opportunity,"

Fred said, saluting and then shaking hands with Ed. He looked back at Sean, *"What happened to the tiger?"*

"Odds," Sean replied, shaking his head sadly, *"Odds. His luck ran out all at once."*

"I'm sorry," Fred said quietly. *"I know how close you two were and I know what he was doing over here. He did make a difference."*

Sean nodded, *"I'm glad to see you."*

"I'm glad to be here. This squadron has a hell of a reputation. Dave, Ed, thanks for requesting me."

"You'll earn it. Come on and meet the others. Sean, take Fred's gear to his quarters and meet us at the club for lunch. Take the Operations jeep," Ed Hardy said.

"Yes, Sir. I'll see you later, Colonel Stebbins," Sean saluted with a wide grin on his face. Fred returned the salute.

For lunch in the O'Club, Colonel Benjamin had invited all of the squadron's majors who weren't flying at the time. They were gingerly probing their new Commander and Operations Officer and wondering why Sean was included in the group. More than a few weren't happy to have had a captain running the night program and they suspected that Sean was going to replace Bill as Night Operations Officer.

It didn't turn out that way. Colonel Hardy announced the new squadron responsibilities and they pretty much followed date of rank among the field-grade officers. Major Martin was appointed Night Operations Officer and Major Tomasso remained Chief of Stan Eval, Sean's boss. Fred was going to select the Day Operations Officer in a few days.

The group was breaking up when John Patterson stopped by their table. He was introduced to Fred and then said, "There are some light flashes being reported near the place where Bill bought it. Intelligence thinks they're trying to trick us into going back for a look."

Sean brightened immediately and looked at Colonel Benjamin. Dave shook his head negatively, "There isn't any chance. I was informed of the flashes late yesterday. Someone has a mirror and is trying to lure us into landing a helicopter or putting in a ground team. It's pretty much of a standard NVA trick when we lose a pilot. They pull the survival items from the body and use them to lure other planes down. I'm sorry, Sean."

"I just wanted to pass it on," John Patterson said. "Nice to meet you, Colonel Stebbins. See you on the Trail."

John turned and left. Fred noticed the hurt in Sean's eyes and resolved to talk to Ed Hardy about sending him home. His tour wasn't over but Fred didn't want to lose Sean as well as Bill.

"Sean, Colonel Hardy tells me that you're responsible for new pilot checkouts. We start today. For the next week or so, I want you to show me the area and the squadron procedures."

"Yes, Sir. When do you want to fly?" Sean asked.

"Let's make it early afternoon. Like now. For the rest of this week anyway. Then you can show me the night action."

"I'll get a plane ready. Meet you on the line in about thirty minutes. Do you need any equipment?"

"I'll need it all. The 20th gave me orders to leave my gear in the plane."

"Yes, Sir. I'll meet you at PE in half an hour," Sean turned and hurried from the club.

"That's a good move, Fred," Ed Hardy said. "He needs to get Bill out of his mind."

"I want to see where it happened. Satisfy myself about these mysterious flashes as well," Fred replied.

"Good idea. Sean knows the area as well as anyone here and I know he wants to look for those flashes himself. He's been doing a great job with the checkouts and standardization in general. We're having fewer and fewer incidents since we started the Stan Eval program at the end of the year."

The orientation flight went smoothly. Sean showed Fred Stebbins the entire NAIL area of operations, ending up over the southern area where Bill was shot down. Sean pointed out the field where the fight had taken place three days ago.

There were no longer any bodies to be seen but the field showed all of the signs of a fierce bombardment. Trees were uprooted and lying flat along the fringes of the clearing. The southern edge was blackened by the fires which followed the final bomb attack.

"Are we going to put a ground team in?" Fred asked.

"No, Sir. There must be more NVA down there and anyway, he called the last strike in on himself. He was wounded and didn't want to be taken prisoner. Phil had a hard time giving the word to the A-1s but he did, and they leveled the place. Phil reported that there were from twelve to twenty bodies lying along the southern edge where the clearing touches the jungle. One of them had to be Bill."

"Now show me where the flashes are coming from."

"They started about a mile south of here and are moving around a little," Sean said, pointing to the south. He turned the plane and they flew in that direction. Fred looked intently in all directions; there was nothing to see but jungle. Welcome to Laos.

Fred shook his head back and forth. *"It has to be one of the NVA ground troops heading south and playing with the survival mirror."*

Sean didn't agree. *"I can't shake the feeling that it's Bill. They could've left him for dead after taking everything of value. He said he was shot.*

The mirror would be easy to miss. It's in a flat pocket in the inside of the vest. Why couldn't it be him and the only thing he has to signal with is his mirror."

"Sean, if it was Bill, he'd signal and wait for help to come. Where's he going? There's no earthly reason for someone down and injured to head in this direction. There is nothing here. It can't be Bill."

"Maybe not, Sir. But who else could it be. The enemy isn't going to keep playing with a mirror for a couple days along a route of march. There's a good reason for the flashes. I'm sure of it...

"Whatever it is, Captain. It isn't your friend. You've got to stop hoping and get back to reality," Fred answered, as gently as he could while still trying to be firm. *"You have several more months to go and you'll get yourself killed, if you're distracted by some wild hope that Bill's still alive."*

"Yes, Sir." Sean's reply was curt. *"Where to next, Colonel, Sir?"*

"Let's go home, Sean. Don't get angry with me. I'm not responsible for Bill and his problems any more. I am responsible for you and yours."

Sean was quiet on the way back to NKP. Except for pointing out major landmarks like the rooster tail and special road intersections, he didn't talk to Fred.

CHAPTER EIGHTY NINE
Nakhon Phanom Thai Air Base (NKP)
23 March 1968

Major Martin wasted no time reorganizing the night program along more traditional lines. He spent his mornings scheduling the crews and his afternoons with paperwork. It was difficult for him to fly at night and do the scheduling so he didn't schedule himself to fly at night. He flew every other afternoon. He assigned two of the majors with the responsibility for updating the tactics manual and setting up navigator training and procedures. Charles Martin was happy managing the night program, not participating in it.

On Fred's second daylight flight Sean scheduled them for the sector with the Foxtrot interdiction point. With hills all around, it was both an ideal attack location and an easily defended position.

They didn't have any strikes scheduled at that time so they flew back and forth between Foxtrot and Golf. Fred was amazed at the apparent good condition of the road and the number of bomb craters to the sides, particularly to the sides of Foxtrot where it cut along the cliff. The fighters were obviously hitting as much as a mile away from the roads during the night bombing runs.

"Why can't we do better than that?" he said to Sean.

"The fighters are restricted to minimum drop altitudes because of the anti-aircraft guns and they're distracted by the tracers and exploding shells. Hell, they drop from 15,000 feet, 3 miles up. They're lucky to hit the ground," Sean replied.

"I can understand the altitude limits. Never trade a $7,000,000 aircraft for a $20,000 truck. Why don't we move the attack points?"

"Bill did. He believed that the North Vietnamese were limited on guns and that we made their job easier by hitting the same places every night ... "

"That makes sense. Why did we hit the same places all of the time?" Fred was curious.

"The sensors. Mister McNamara's wall. They put some of their sensors between Foxtrot and Golf and the TFA general insisted that the strikes be conducted where the sensors could detect truck movement."

"That's not obviously wrong, is it?" Fred replied.

"Watch, Colonel," Sean answered sarcastically. He reached over and altered his RPM settings until the O-2 was emitting a repetitive wroom, wroom, wroom sound. The sound was common to multi-engine aircraft whose engines were not synchronized. They flew a back and forth path over the ground between Golf and Foxtrot. Fred could see all of the way from the cliff face at Foxtrot to the road intersection that marked checkpoint Golf. The roads were clear.

"NAIL Zero Two, this is Cricket," came over the radio.

Sean was wearing a large grin as he answered. *"Go ahead, Cricket. This is NAIL Zero Two."*

"We have a Spotlight report. There are movers on route 911 between Foxtrot and Golf. Please investigate."

"Roger, Cricket. We'll check it out. ZeroTwo out."

"See," he said to Fred.

"See what?" Fred answered. *"Let's check the roads. We've got a convoy somewhere down there."*

"Sure we do," Sean replied, sarcastically. He adjusted the RPM until the noise stopped. Before he could call Cricket, they got another call.

"Nail Zero Two, Spotlight reports the convoy has pulled off the road."

"Roger, Cricket. Convoy is out of sight under the trees."

"Do you want to try it yourself? Colonel," Sean asked. His amusement was evident.

"OK, smart ass. What's going on?" Fred was angry.

"This is why we have problems out here. The equipment operators at TFA can't tell the difference between an O-2 with out-of-synch engines and a convoy of trucks. If we keep it up, they'll send in some fighters and drop bombs on the convoy we just created. If that isn't enough, they used to give themselves credit for truck kills if they didn't hear the sounds after the bombs were dropped," Sean said, smugly.

Fred was livid. His face red and his voice rough, he snapped, *"Bullshit, Captain. No one's that stupid!"*

"It's your plane, Sir. Un-synch your engines and stay over the road," Sean was the instructor again.

Fred did as he was told. They flew back and forth for about ten minutes and Fred was looking at Sean with a disgusted look when the radio came to life.

"NAIL Zero Two, this is Cricket."

Fred looked back at Sean, who shrugged and indicated that Fred was to reply.

"Go ahead, Cricket."

"The convoy is moving again. We have fighters inbound, ETA seven minutes. Can you see the trucks?"

"No, Cricket we can't. I am over the road and the trucks aren't visible," Fred replied hesitantly.

"That's OK, NAIL. TFA requests that you move away from the road. They will drop on radar. The NVA must have cut a new road under the trees."

Fred turned to the west, total disbelief on his face. He motioned for Sean to take the wheel. Sean flew west and then turned to the north, so that Fred could watch the road. Soon explosions erupted over the road and nearby jungle, about midway between the two checkpoints.

"Cricket, this is Zero Two. Do you want us to check for BDA?" Sean asked.

"Go ahead Zero Two, but it's probably under the trees where you won't be able to see the damage."

"Roger, Cricket. Zero Two will take a look."

They flew over the area where the bombs fell, but couldn't find any evidence of a road or any burning trucks.

"Cricket, you're right. We can't see under the trees."

"Thanks, Zero Two. We'll let them know they'll have to use an estimate."

Fred was quiet for about ten minutes. Then he said, *"Is that normal?"*

"Bill discovered that they were chasing our engines. He used it to get them to vary the attack points once in a while, but the sensors often aren't where we need them. Not only that, the general doesn't like us to bomb the places he's dropped the sensors. It's a Catch 22."

"Until we forced their hand and called in the 7th TACC, they'd move us out of the way, drop their bombs and then give themselves credit for truck kills. We set them up about two weeks ago and General Johnson put a stop to it. He put Benjamin in as Wing Commander and made TFA report through the wing. Now TUOC puts all the unit kills together and issues one report of confirmed kills. TFA still reports its estimates to

Washington, but they aren't used for anything else."

Fred didn't answer.

"*NAIL Zero Two, this is Cricket. Is Four Five with you?*"

"*I'm here,*" Sean answered quickly.

"*We just got another report of a flash. The last set of fighters RTBing to Ubon reported seeing a mirror flash at coordinates WD 9119.*"

"*Thanks, Cricket. We'll take a look,*" Sean replied.

When he looked at Fred, the colonel was shaking his head, no. The expression on Sean's face was so despondent that Fred relented and said, "*Oh, OK. But we can't spend all day.*"

"*Yes, Sir. I'll push it up,*" Sean replied. He increased his power until the little plane was operating just below the red line. They were in level flight at one hundred and thirty three knots, a speed unobtainable with a full fuel load. Since it was nearing the end of their sortie, they'd used up about half their fuel and were considerably lighter.

Fred plotted the map coordinates and showed Sean the map. There was nothing at the coordinates but jungle; no clearing, no road and no village.

Sean didn't turn back. They flew over the location and made several wide orbits, waiting for some sign. After twenty minutes, Fred motioned for Sean to give the plane to him. He handed the binoculars to Sean and turned toward NKP. They were going home.

"*It's him, Colonel. I know it's him,*" Sean said.

"*Not a chance, Sean. It's been several days. Even if he lived through the bombing, they would've taken him when they took the other bodies.*"

CHAPTER NINETY
Nakhon Phanom Thai Air Base (NKP)
24 March 1968, early evening in the O'Club

Sean was in the O'Club when John Patterson and Charlie Green came up and sat at his table. *"You two don't seem to mind my miserable attitude,"* he said, *"Even Sharon's tired of being around me."*

"We don't really give a shit about your love life," John Patterson said, *"Charlie has something for you."*

Sean sat up and looked at Charlie and said, *"More flashes? Every time I try to get someone to listen, they tell me it's my imagination. Our new Operations Officer told me to drop it."*

Charlie was getting excited, *"This is the third day in a row. We're still seeing flashes in that area. Cricket said that they think the flashes are moving. You need to go to TUOC and talk to Colonel Bennett on Cricket. He has a theory. Give him a call."*

"I guess I might as well. It certainly won't hurt. Maybe he knows something."

Sean left the club and walked to TUOC with a little more oomph in his step.

Lieutenant Zach North was on duty. *"Hi, Captain."*

"Hello, Zach. Can I use your radio to talk to Cricket?"

"Yes, Sir. Colonel Bennett's aboard and waiting for you to call."

"Who's Colonel Bennett?" Sean asked.

"He used to be one of the Nimrods. This's his second tour and he's the Cricket controller. He's waiting to talk to you."

"Cricket, this is NAIL Four Five," Sean called.

"Stand by, NAIL Four Five. Cricket's busy. We'll call you back in a couple of minutes."

Sean waited. They couldn't hear the radio chatter between Cricket and the fighters, so they waited until Cricket called back. It would take but a few minutes.

"NAIL Four Five, this is Cricket Control."

"Go ahead, Alley. This is Four Five."

"Have you been watching the reports on the flashes?"

"It's an enemy trick," Sean replied.

"Take a few moments and plot the reports. Call me back," Cricket answered.

Sean and Zach looked at one another and then hurried to the map room. While Sean was laying out an area map, Zach retrieved the last few days of Intreps. They started marking the reported locations of the flashes being sighted along with current day/time information.

"Holy shit, Zach. They're in a line. Look at this 8833, 8929, 9119, 9215" Sean said, excited. "They're headed somewhere!"

"Where, Captain? There isn't anything out there. We don't have any people in that area.

What if they are headed somewhere..., you know, whoever is doing the flashing is going somewhere. He has a plan. What if it isn't just anybody?" Sean asked.

"Sir, it isn't him. He can't be alive. The rescue crews saw him get overrun and Captain Masters had the Hobos bomb his last known position. Sir, I'm sorry, but Captain Thompson is dead."

Sean gave Zach a disgusted look and folded up the map. He stuck it in his pocket and left TUOC. When he called Sharon from the O'Club, she was angry.

"You've got to stop talking about him!"

"I can't help it. He's still alive. I can feel it," Sean said, *"and if he's there, then he needs my help. I've got to do something."*

"What you've got to do is get your head straightened out. I've heard all I want to hear about it. Don't bother me until you come to terms with it!" She slammed down her phone.

CHAPTER NINETY ONE
Nakhon Phanom Thai Air Base (NKP)
25 March 1968, morning going to the O'Club

Sean walked to the O'Club for coffee the next morning and ran into Mike Miller coming in from a night mission. Sean wasn't sleeping well. The bags under his eyes were large enough to hold an overnight kit and the Nimrod pilot's first comment was, *"You look like shit!"*

"Thanks, Mike; I feel like shit." Sean answered, frowning at him.

"Did you talk to Colonel Bennett?" Mike continued.

"Last night," Sean nodded.

"He's waiting for you to call him back," Mike said. *"We talked to him on our way home, about an hour ago."*

"He still wants to talk?" Sean asked.

"Yeah," Mike replied. *"He's spent a lot of time flying over here and has some ideas."*

"I'll call him later," Sean replied.

"You can still get him at Cricket Control. He's waiting for you to call."

"What's so important?" Sean wondered aloud.

"Call him, Sean. He has a theory that you should hear. Get off your ass and call him now."

"Okay Mike. I'll go down and call him right now," Sean answered.

When he walked into TUOC, the crews there didn't talk to him. His preoccupation with the flashes and Bill were bothering the others, at least some of the others. It didn't seem to bother Marty Wilson who had just completed the after-action report on his night sortie. *"Sean, Cricket wants you to call."*

"So I've been told. Do you know why?"

"No. A Colonel Bennett wants to talk to you."

Sean walked into the radio room and called the control ship. *"Cricket, this is NAIL Four Five."*

"Stand by, Four Five. We're getting the controller."

"Nail Four Five, this is Cricket Control. You didn't call back."

"No, Sir. I've been told to drop it."

"We got another report. Do you have your map?"

"Yes, Sir," Sean replied as he took out his map and opened it.

"This one's at coordinates WD 9210. Plot that. What do you see?"

Sean made a mark on the map and looked. The line of sightings was moving due south. Each report was further south than the previous one. There were usually two sightings a day, one in the morning and one in the afternoon. For some reason they had only half of them but it was still a straight line going due south to somewhere or some thing.

"Captain, does that line look like anything special?"

"No, Sir," Sean was frowning, puzzled.

"Does it look special to you?" the controller waited for an answer. *"I think you should talk to the Ravens, NAIL Four Five,"* Cricket continued. *"Didn't your buddy work with them?"*

"Once in a while. He used to go down to Pakse once in a while to brief them on our operations," Sean was getting curious.

"Good luck, Four Five. Cricket out."

Sean was disturbed by the abruptness of the signoff. Colonel Bennett was trying to tell him something, but Sean couldn't figure out what. The key was obviously in Pakse. Now all Sean had to figure out was how to get there. He headed for the squadron. Fred would know.

After he explained the situation as he or should he say Colonel Bennet saw it. *"Jesus, Sean, I've told you to drop it. I'm not going to send you to Pakse on some wild goose chase. My answer is no, Hell no."* Fred Stebbins was more than a little upset at Sean's request.

Sean walked from the squadron totally dejected. He had to get to Pakse, but how. He saw Ari Comers coming toward him and waved. *"Hi, Ari."*

"What's the matter, Sean? Still looking for Bill?"

Sean nodded, yes.

"He's dead, Sean. You have to drop it or you will be too. This is no time to be working at less than full speed. You aren't paying attention."

"What attention?" Sean asked.

"You ran that engine too hot yesterday. Two cylinders burned out with the new Ops Officer aboard. I covered for you this time, but you have

to get with it," Ari said. He too was being firm and trying to be gentle. He liked Sean and didn't want to see him get hurt.

"OK, Ari. I'm sorry about the engine. We were looking over the shoot down site and I wasn't paying attention. It won't happen again."

Ari clapped Sean on the shoulder and proceeded on his way. Sean walked to Base Ops where he looked up Pakse and picked up a map of that area of southern Laos. He took the time to plot the mirror flashes on the map. *'Yep, it is a straight line,'* he thought. Some of the Ravens were based at Pakse, south of the NAIL area of Operations. *'They'd have O-1s there, and God knows what else,'* he thought.

He walked over the counter where a tech sergeant was cleaning grease pencil markings off of the clear plastic that was covering the local area weather map. *"I need to call the Ravens at Pakse, can you hook me up?"*

"No, Sir. I can't, but the major in the office may be able to."

"Thanks, Sarg." Sean walked around the counter and approached a small office with an open door. He knocked.

"What's up, Captain?"

"I need to call the Ravens at Pakse. Can I do that from here?"

"Sure, I just talked to a guy there yesterday. I needed some info on their weather....can't remember his name or rank. Hell, none of them have any rank."

The major handed Sean the phone as he dialed a number.

"Hello, NKP. What do you need this time?"

"This is NAIL FOUR FIVE, who am I talking to?"

"This is the king of southern Laos. You may call me Your Majesty. Like I said, what do you need?"

"I'll make this easy. Is there anything near Bah Khe or south of it?"

"Man, how did you find that? The French built an airstrip there in the late 50s. There ain't nothin' there now. Shit, the PL probably tore it up. They usually do when they leave. Why? Man, I keep asking why and you ask me questions."

"One more question. Do the Ravens have this strip marked on their maps?"

"Shit no, Man. Who has time to do that? Hey, we do have it marked on our map here in the "office." Now what do you need, NAIL?"

"Bill Thompson got shot down five days ago about thirteen miles north of Bah Khe, just south of Route 9."

"Okay, so…?"

"We keep getting reports of flashes from a mirror that seemed to be going towards Bah Khe or some place south. One more question. When Bill was down there talking to you guys, was that map on the wall then?"

"Man, that map has been on that wall since Christ was a corporal. So what?"

"Your Majesty, that is all I need. Fly safe." Sean handed the phone back to the major, who hung it up.

"Did you get what you need, Captain?"

"You bet your sweet ass, Major. This is a good day. Many thanks. I got to go fly." Sean departed Base Ops and headed to TUOC for his preflight briefing.

CHAPTER NINETY TWO
Nakhon Phanom Thai Air Base (NKP)
25 March 1968, later that morning at TUOC

Sean completed the standard preflight brief by Zack. He would be out for about three hours and was scheduled to cover the area north of Route 9 up to Golf. No action was expected and no resources had been fragged to support this mission. Sean knew he would have little time for the area north of Route 9 as he would be going south. He stopped by the personal equipment section to draw his survival equipment, M-16, revolver and parachute. He continued to the squadron parking area and walked onto the flight line. *"Which plane do I have?"* he asked the line chief.

"You have 473 there, Sir. It's ready to go, but I don't have any spares at this time so if you abort, you're done for the day."

"Thanks, Chief," Sean said. *"I'll take care of her."*

Sean climbed into the plane, started the engines and signaled for the crew chief to pull the chocks. He then started taxiing toward the runway. After arming, he was cleared as number one for takeoff and asked tower for clearance to take off. Clearance was given quickly and off he went with a very big smile. He was positive about what Colonel Bennett was trying to tell him and he now knew where to look.

An A-1 pulled alongside his wing about thirty minutes later. He waved and turned on his radio. *"The world is looking for a lost NAIL and has been for five days,"* came over the headset. It was Dave Montgomery.

Sean nodded, but did not answer. All of the NKP warriors were aware of the mirror flashes and many were spending mission time trying to see more flashes or figure out who was doing it or why. The A-1 pilot waved. Sean watched as the Skyraider banked away and climbed to the north.

Sean flew for an hour and a half before he reached Route 9 just west of Tchepone. He had been thinking. No he had been talking to himself. **"Could Bill be headed for that strip? It's about thirteen miles from the crash site. Not much bad terrain...mostly flat. He's such a hard head. He would never quit. He finished every thing he starts. He started south because.... because he knew about the old French strip. He knows that the mirror trail will get some results. He knows that someone will be able to figure it out."**

He banked right and headed south. This would not take long. He reduced his power and began a slow descent but continued to jink around. **"No sense taking any stupid chances."**

As he approached Bah Khe he was at about 2600 feet indicated or about 2000 feet above the ground. After a few minutes he saw what seemed to be a rectangular grass area west of the hootches and turned towards it **"That might be the old French air field,"** he thought.

He continued his descent to about 1000 feet above the ground and started to circle the possible airfield without stopping the jinking. There was no ground fire and he couldn't see any personnel or even a sign of anyone so he dropped down to tree top level to get a closer look. During his low pass from north to south a mirror flash on the left hit him just as he was looking in its direction! He yelled, **"Son-of-a-bitch! It's Bill!"**

Sean began shaking but regained control, started a left turn and climbed to about 200 feet above the trees. He started a tight circle. He saw what might be Bill, but not much movement. Now he was not so sure. Maybe it was a trap.

"Shit, I got to know," he said to himself and pushed the yoke full forward and aimed directly at "Bill," diving towards the ground. He rolled out below the trees and banked left to get a better look. He saw a guy giving him the "Touchdown Jesus," two arms up. It WAS Bill! Sean rocked the wings and started a rapid climb to about 500 feet above the ground.

Sean started talking to himself again, *"Now what? What the Hell? Let's go get him. It's an airfield. Was an airfield. The grass is pretty high. Let's go. Now to set this up. Where is the wind? Shit, it's from the east and this is a north/south field. Okay, let's go south and land going north. That should work. No, the wind again. Go the other way....north to south. Call Cricket."*

"Cricket, this is NAIL FOUR FIVE, over."

"Go 45, what's up?"

"I've found NAIL Five Five! He's alive at Bah Khe! That's about thirteen miles south of Route 9 and southeast of Tchepone about 25 miles. I'm going in to get him!"

"Four Five, hold on. We can get the Jollys. Hold on. Who owns that area?"

"Cricket, I don't know and I don't give a shit! I am getting him! Now! Gear down."

"NAIL, stop. Four Five, this is Control. Where are you?"

"Cricket, I'm going down after him," Sean replied.

"Be careful, Four Five. Call when you start your approach. I have to advise the TACC. You may be in serious trouble when you land. We don't know who owns the field," the voice said.

"Thanks for the assist."

"They're something else," Sean replied. ***"I'm setting up my approach. This is the last transmission. I'm going to try to get it down in one piece and go for him at the south end of the field. I'll call you if I can."*** Sean tightened his seat belt and shoulder harness.

As Sean lined up on the field, he could see nothing but grass. The grass looked to be about two feet high and he could see piles of dirt scattered around. The Pathet Lao hadn't tried to conceal their hole digging efforts.

Sean slowed the O-2 until it was barely maintaining flight. The airspeed showed sixty-eight knots. It wouldn't take much distance to stop but, if he hit a hole, the plane would probably flip. Sean eased it down…slowly, slowly…until the wheels were brushing the grass. He pulled up over a pile of dirt and then slammed the plane to the ground. He hit on all three wheels, a perfect three pointer. Sean was congratulating himself when the right tire dropped into a two-foot-deep hole and the plane cart wheeled. He flipped end over end twice before the plane came to a stop in a crumpled pile. It would never fly again.

Sean was badly bruised, shaken and knocked about from the pounding of the little plane as it turned end over end, but he was alive. As the stars cleared from his vision he realized that the world was upside down…or rather he was!! He was hanging from his harness contemplating the inverted view of the field of elephant grass. He wiggled his finger and toes….all worked. He said to himself ***"Great aviator you are…you go to save a Bud and end up… inverted in the middle of Laos…atta boy 45!"***

He was trying to extricate himself from the seat when something touched him on the shoulder. Sean jerked and screamed, ***"Shit."*** He stared at the apparition in front of him.

Bloody, burned and grinning, the apparition said, ***"Shitty landing, Sean."***

"Bill! God dammit, Bill. Are you OK?" Sean scrambled from the plane.

"No, I'm not. Where're the Marines? We need help. There are bad guys all over this God damn place." Bill's voice was barely a croak.

"I've got some medicine and some rations. Here, take the water. Let's get away from the plane; it could explode."

Bill and Sean were both under the plane. When Sean started to crawl away and looked back for his friend. Bill was drinking from the plastic flask, tears rolling down his cheeks. He put the top back on the plastic container, smiled at Sean, closed his eyes and appeared to pass out.

Sean hurried back to his side. Bill opened his eyes, but did not get up. Sean felt for a pulse and found one, weak and irregular, but he found one. Bill was in serious medical trouble. He looked around and couldn't see anyone. Tearing open the medical kit, he found antibiotics and some morphine. He gave both to Bill. He needed him awake for a while.

CHAPTER NINETY THREE
Steel Tiger, Eastern Laos
25 March 1968, afternoon on the ground near Chavane

Taking out his survival radio, Sean made a call. *"NAIL Four Five and NAIL Five Five are down at WD 9208. Help! MAYDAY, MAYDAY, WD 9208"*

He listened. There was no reply. He turned on the automatic beeper and put the radio beside him on the ground. Next, he turned to his friend and shook him gently. *"Bill, are you awake? Where are you hit? We have to get some bandages on you. Wake up!"*

"Tired, so tired. Lemme 'lone" the voice wasn't much more than a hoarse whisper.

"Not now. Where're you hit?" Sean was shouting. He wanted to get Bill patched up and then the two of them needed to hide.

"Shot in back. Took some bomb damage in right side, arm and leg. Burned on left side. Feet hurt," Bill whispered.

Sean shook his head. He sure as hell wasn't a doctor and he didn't know what to do other than give Bill sips from his canteen. Bill's color was ashen and it was clear that he was severely dehydrated. So he said, *"Take another pill and be quiet."*

"You sound worse than the squadron quack," Bill whispered.

A few moments later. *"Who're you talking to?"* Bill asked.

"No one. I'm not talking."

"I hear someone muttering. I thought it was someone with you," Bill was trying to look around.

Sean eased up along the fuselage until he was standing. Less than two hundred yards away; he could see several Pathet Lao troops walking toward the wreckage of their plane. He and Bill had been discovered …this was no surprise…it really is hard to miss a cart wheeling O-2 flailing through a grass field, ending up as a smoking pile of trash! The PL knew exactly where they were!

"Can you move?" he asked Bill.

Bill shook his head slowly. He couldn't move fast enough to run and he'd be lucky to even stand up. He motioned for a gun. Sean handed him the .38 and spare ammunition. Picking up his M-16, Sean tried to decide what to do. He had no idea if help was on the way. Cricket hadn't answered and he hadn't seen any aircraft. He was well below the normal NKP operating area and was afraid that they were on their own.

Bill was making motions for Sean to shoot. ***"Keep them back,"*** he croaked. ***"Don't let them get too close. Escape when it gets dark."***

Sean sighted down the barrel of the M-16 and fired three shots that went over the heads of the approaching troops. There was a lot of yelling and, much to his surprise, they turned and ran back toward the edge of the field. No one liked being out in the open, it seemed.

Bill touched Sean and whispered... ***"One or two may have hidden in the grass. Stay quiet and listen for them."***

Sean nodded. He looked toward the area where the Pathet Lao had been and watched for some telltale movement or noise. The grass suddenly started to move in a pattern different than the wind. At least one had remained hidden. Sean fired a couple of shots at the area and two more Pathet Lao soldiers jumped up and ran like hell for the jungle. This group of enemy soldiers was definitely not in the mood for a firefight.

CHAPTER NINETY FOUR
South of Steel Tiger, Southern Laos
25 March 1968, late afternoon on the ground near Chavane

Sean sat next to his sleeping friend and wondered at their ability to survive. Bill had been down, wounded and alone for the past six days. He'd hobbled and crawled for over thirteen miles to the abandoned French airstrip. Now, unless they got some immediate help, they were both going to die.

'Son of a bitch, we need some help and now," he thought.

Sean did not know that Phil Masters had heard the original "mayday" just as he arrived at Foxtrot after flying directly from NKP and had departed immediately for Sean's location south of Route 9. Phil had called Cricket for resources but there were none. He called Crown and found out that NKP and Danang had the HH-3 Jollys and the A-1 Sandys, but the rescue location was at the range limits for the choppers. Crown told him that Ubon had the HH-53s, the Super Jollys (bigger faster versions of the HH-3), but no A-1s. Crown had ordered launches from all three locations and all of them were about one hour from the downed flyers.

Phil then changed to the Air America general frequency and called for assistance, **"Air A, this is NAIL FOUR EIGHT and I need help, over."**

"This is Rancho. What do you need NAIL?"

"We have 2 NAILs down at Bah Khe and need a pick up. Can you help?"

"We are on the way. Give us about 15 minutes."

"Roger, Rancho. Thanks. Please go to 284.6 and check in."

"Okay, going to 284.6."

"NAIL, this is Rancho on 284.6. Do you read?"

"Roger, Rancho, just stay on this frequency."

"NAIL, this is Jackson flying a Porter; I heard the other stuff and will be at the site in about 20 minutes."

"Roger, Jackson. Thanks."

Back on the ground at Bah Khe, Sean assessed their situation. The O-2 was now a class 26! Both wings were broken, one tire was flat, the propellers were both twisted disasters and a landing strut was snapped in half. The airplane had essentially rolled itself into a ball on landing. The field full of holes and earth mounds was not useable for fixed-wing aircraft. He was lucky beyond belief to have landed without killing himself.

They were near the south end of the former French airstrip, now overgrown with elephant grass, effectively hiding the anti-air trenches and holes dug at intervals in the old airfield area.

Sean knew he couldn't carry Bill. They were stuck. It would be dark in another couple of hours and the Pathet Lao troops would be able to get close enough to rush them. Bill was barely alive, let alone able to help. Sean marveled at his friend's ability to drag himself to this field through enemy territory, seriously wounded and barely able to walk.

He checked to see that Bill's wounds weren't bleeding any more. They were not, since by now they were all nearly six days old. Next, he picked up his M-16 and checked it. He had two spare magazines and the one loaded in the weapon, a total of 60 rounds. For the .38, he had the rounds in the weapon plus thirty more in a survival pouch.

He didn't think it mattered. That wasn't enough ammunition to keep anyone away for very long. At least he'd give a good account of himself when they came back. He doubted that the Pathet Lao officers would be as easy to frighten as the small patrol had been. Sean picked up his radio and made another call, **"Cricket this is NAIL Four Five, over."**

There was no answer. The mountains must be blocking the transmissions to Cricket. Sean tried again, **"Anyone, this is NAIL Four Five with NAIL Five Five. We're down at coordinates WD 9208. Does anyone hear us?"**

There was no answer, but Sean thought he heard two faint clicks, just like he'd do to acknowledge a transmission if he was too busy to talk. It meant message received and understood. Sean wanted to transmit again, but didn't. Someone out there didn't want him to be on the radio or they didn't want to use their radio. At least the clicks indicated that and he hoped he was right. He put one of his survival radios on top of his damaged plane with its beacon on. The other radio went into his pocket.

He looked around again and this time was surprised to see six or seven Pathet Lao troops visible at the edge of the clearing. They looked like they were getting ready to do something but they were too far away for effective shooting, so he could only watch. Of course, they were also watching. It occurred to Sean that they might be looking for something and he started to sweat. That was it. They were definitely waiting for something to happen, but what?

Sean scanned the field. He could see nothing. However, at the northwest side of the field, a road entered from the jungle. Sean could not see more than twenty or thirty yards down the road because at that point it turned to the left into the jungle. The Laotian troops seemed to be watching in that direction.

He was becoming more nervous and sweating profusely. He couldn't understand why they were waiting to charge the two of them. **"They must be waiting for dark,"** he thought. He scanned the grass and couldn't see anything that might be troops crawling toward his position. Suddenly the Pathet Lao troops started yelling and pointing. Sean turned to see a vehicle driving from the jungle toward the field. It was some sort of an armored car. Sean thought he could see something on top, probably a machine gun. They were in trouble now. He took out his radio.

"Mayday, Mayday, Mayday. This is NAIL Four Five, we're about to be attacked by an armored vehicle. Does anyone read? Mayday, Mayday, Mayday."

There was no answer, not even the clicks he thought he'd heard earlier. Sean watched as the vehicle pulled onto the field and stopped. The armored car was too far away to effectively use the machine gun on the top, so he couldn't understand why they were waiting at the end of the field. Then he saw a puff of white come from the machine gun and realized at that instant that it was cannon, not a machine gun. The shell whistled as it passed over the wreckage of the plane and impacted about forty yards beyond them with a bang, throwing large clods of dirt and many stalks of elephant grass into the air.

They were really in trouble now. It wouldn't take the gunner many shots to zero in on the wreckage. Sean grabbed Bill by the arms and started to drag him away from their plane. The next thing he knew a round exploded twenty yards short of the plane. The next shot was certain to hit the plane and the fuel tanks would go up. He tugged at Bill, inching him further away from the plane. They were only about ten yards away, not far enough to be safe. He took out his radio.

"If anyone's there, please hurry. They're going to hit the plane with the next shot and we're too close to it..." Sean released the transmit switch and listened. There was no answer.

Then, almost as an answer to a prayer, a Willie Pete rocket exploded at the far end of the field very near the enemy soldiers and the vehicle. It exploded with a large bang and threw white phosphorous and smoke in all directions, resulting in a huge white cloud. *"Hell, those things are more impressive from down here than from up there,"* he thought!

Then suddenly a voice said, *"Keep your heads down, NAILs. NAIL FOUR EIGHT is in!"* It was Phil Master's voice!

Sean jerked his head around and looked up as the sounds reached him. There was an O-2 making a rocket pass at the approaching vehicle. Phil fired one more 2.75 rocket that hit about 50 yards north of the field. He pulled off to the east, and then curved back around a wide turn.

Sean felt the tears coming. *"Thank God, the cavalry is here"*. He watched as the armored vehicle made an abrupt turn and headed back into the jungle.

"NAIL FOUR FIVE, this is NAIL FOUR EIGHT," broadcast Phil Masters over Guard channel, *"We're gonna get you out. Hang in there."*

Sean was shaking Bill, *"Look at this, look at this. Phil's tearing the bastards up."*

Bill smiled weakly at Sean and whispered, *"Is there a helicopter anyplace? We need a helicopter. I see something."*

Sean looked around and saw a blue-and-white Air America helicopter holding off in the distance at about 4,000 feet.

"NAIL FOUR EIGHT, this is Rancho. We're ready! Is that the field with the smoke?"

"Roger, Rancho, get your ass over here and get these guys outta here."

"NAIL, we can try. We're comin' in now. Watch for guns."

The H-34 began a descent, landed in the middle of the field and near the south end and immediately started taking fire.

At the same time, small arms rounds started to hit the O-2. Sean looked around and saw four or five PL on the top of the little hill to the east firing at them.

The civilian in the door of the Air America H-34 was yelling and waving at Sean and Bill to run to the chopper. But the firing from the hill had them pinned down. They couldn't leave the security that the wreckage of the Duck provided. After less than thirty seconds on the ground, the chopper was forced into a rapid climb out.

"Rancho, what's the problem?"

"Shit, Man, there is too much coming from that hill on the east side. Can you do anything about that?"

"You bet your ass. Stay tuned and watch this."

Phil continued his circling until he was a perfect position to make a low pass and start firing rockets at the hill. He quickly trimmed the aircraft for firing, lowered the nose and began a nose dive towards the active hill. When he approached tree top level, he flattened his dive and fired his Willy Pete. He was so low and so close that he actually flew through the WP smoke during his pull out.

"Mission accomplished... got 'em."

"Rancho, let's try again. I think I got those bastards on the hill."

"Roger, NAIL, we'll try again. We're comin' in." The H-34 began a descent and barely got to the ground when...

"Shit, Rancho, they're shooting from the north side." The chopper started a rapid ascent and turned to the left, away from the north side of the field.

"We gotta go, NAIL, my loadmaster just took a hit. Good luck."

"NAIL, this is Jackson. What can I do?"

"Rancho, thanks. Hope he is okay. Jackson, just hang in there for now."

Phil flipped the UHF to the Guard position, *"Cricket, I need help. What have you got? Hurry!"*

"NAIL, we have the Jollys coming but we have no fighter assets. The Gunfighters are unable to respond due to a previous mission. We'll keep trying."

"Cricket, this is Otter 23, a flight of two Thuds. Can we go in and help the NAIL?"

Unbelievable as this sounds, Otter was an old B-52 buddy of Phil's and he recognized Phil's voice.

"*Negative, Otter. We can't do that.*" called Cricket.

"*Are you sure?*"

"*Yep, Otter, we can't do it.*"

"*Roger, Cricket, Otter out.*"

Almost unbelievably, another F-105 flight calls Phil on Guard. "*NAIL this is Atlanta 56, with a flight of two Thuds. What frequency are you using?*"

"*Atlanta, go to 284.6*"

"*NAIL, this is Atlanta, where are you?*"

"*We are 080 at 55 miles from Ubon. Do you have the frequency?*"

"*Roger, we got it. Atlanta flight push 'em up and turn to about 200 degrees. NAIL, we'll be there in five minutes. We have a full load of 750's.*"

"*Roger, Atlanta. We have two Americans on the ground on the south end of a field that goes generally north to south, about 1,000 meters long. The bad guys are on the north end. When you get here, we'll want an east/west drop to cover the north end and about 100 meters north. I'm circling at 1,000 feet. When you see me, tell me, and I'll mark for you. You'll be cleared in hot.*"

"*NAIL, got it. What's the field elevation?*"

"*Six hundred feet. Best I can tell, there's nothing but small arms. Worst case may be some ZPU. Call me.*"

"*Phil, this is Sean on Guard. Your rockets killed three or four. What is happening?*"

"*Sean, we have some Thuds coming in shortly so get under something. Choppers are still awhile out. Just hang in there. How's Bill?*"

"He's doing better. He's awake and has the .38 aimed towards the bad guys."

After what seemed like a very long time, but was in fact only two minutes since talking to Phil, *"NAIL, we have you in sight. Mark it. We are short on fuel. This has to be a one pass…haul ass drop."*

"Atlanta, give me a second as I get into position to mark. As soon as you see the smoke and have me in sight, you are cleared in east to west and hot." Phil set up, lowered the nose a little (since he was so low already) and fired.

"Got the smoke and you, NAIL. We are in hot. Two, drop it all on one pass."

"Two."

Atlanta Lead tracked, rock solid, to about 2,000 feet before he started his rolling pull to the south. His 750s, orange and black eruptions, walked across the end of the Old French Airfield…

"Lead is off." Then, an additional large explosion…a secondary, followed by greasy black smoke…POL….Atlanta's bombs had eradicated the armored car.

"Two is in."

"Great drop, Lead. Two, put yours on the north edge of the Lead's smoke."

"Two."

Atlanta Two, also showing no fear, tracked straight to the target before his 750s fell away and his Thud, enveloped in vapor up to the cockpit, pulled off to the south. Another fantastic drop! Nothing on the tree line north of the crumpled Duck and its two NAILS lived.

"Two is off."

"Atlanta, great work. The best I've ever seen. Thanks."

"See ya', NAIL, and good luck getting those guys out of there. You got any Sandys inbound?"

"*Yeah, and they should be here soon. I hope really soon.*"
"*Phil, they're shooting at us!*"
"*Who is shooting?*"
"*The guys on the hill. They've got a ZPU gun. Shit, this sucks!*"

Phil cranked the Duck around, quickly trimmed for a shot, flew to within 100 meters of the gunners at tree top level and pickled his fourth, fifth and sixth rockets. As he started his pull to clear the top of the hill… he watched his Willie Petes walk straight through the gun pit!! That ZPU would remain silent for the remainder of the SAR.

As he pulled off, Phil's Duck shuddered and the impacting rounds sounded like metal rain. A sharp pain in his left thigh!

'*Shit, they got me.*' Phil muttered to himself as he reversed his pull off.

His O-2 had been laced by an AK-47 or some other small arms fire. He quickly checked the gauges. OK. Then tried the throttles. OK. Then turned the yoke. OK. Then he pulled back on the yoke. Still OK. He continued his climb to about 3,000 feet while continuing to circle the field.

CHAPTER NINETY FIVE
South of Steel Tiger, Southern Laos
25 March 1968, later that afternoon on the ground near Chavane

"NAIL FOUR EIGHT, this is Super Jolly Zero One. We have you in sight but we are bingo fuel. We'll have to go to Crown for gas."

"Bullshit! Get your ass down here and get these guys. We ain't got time for you to go to the gas station. Get in here now!"

"Okay, NAIL, we don't have much time. Have them pop a smoke and we'll try."

Phil switched to Guard, *"Sean, pop a smoke. We have a Jolly to pick you up. Get ready."* Phil switched back to 284.6.

"I got the smoke, NAIL. I'm going in. Where are the Sandys?"

"There are no Sandys. We just put a flight of Thuds in here. Expect only minimum ground fire."

The chopper went to the wrong end of the field. *"Jolly, what the fuck are you doing? They're on the other end of the field! Go south. South... now!"*

"We're moving, NAIL."

Just as the Jolly was about to set down at about forty meters from the wrecked O-2, *"Shit, you're getting some fire from the west side of the field,"* Phil transmitted

"They're hitting us. Jolly Zero One is pulling out."

Phil's Duck was again stitched by small arms fire. One round entered the cockpit, ricocheted off of the co-pilot's seat and imbedded itself in his right leg!

"God damn! Son-of-a-bitch, that hurts!"

"NAIL, are you okay?"

"Got another one... in the other leg this time, but I'm okay. Go to Crown and get some gas. Can you come back?"

"We'll try, NAIL, but don't know what the hits did to us yet. We're off for Crown."

"NAIL FOUR EIGHT, this is Sandy One. We see the smoke. What do you want us to do? I understand there are no Jollys here now."

"Sandy, you got it. We've to keep the bad guys away from our guys on the ground. They're on the south side of the field. That is south of the smoke. Let me know when you see the field."

"I got it, NAIL. We were told that every Sandy in SEA was launched for this rescue. Now what?"

"I think we should set up a daisy chain of A-1s and drop ordnance all around the edges of the field...not too close to the south edge. We can kill everything around that field with all the A-1s that are inbound. Then when the Jollys get here, we can get them in and out safely. Whaddya' think?"

"I like it. Let's do it! Do you want me to brief the incoming Sandys on what's going on?"

"Great idea. You got all the Sandys. Use the Sandy common for the briefings. We'll run the rescue on 284.6."

"NAIL FOUR EIGHT, this is Jolly One from Danang. Do you have Sandys?"

"Roger, Jolly One, we have several flights of Sandys but understand the NAIL will be running this rescue. Any questions?"

"Seems strange. Be advised we're approaching Bingo Fuel!"

"Everybody who comes here is low on fuel! <u>How</u> low?"

"Just a minute, let us figure that one out."

After only a minute Danang Jolly Zero One continued, *"Sorry, but we don't have enough to do the pick up and get to Ubon or Vietnam."*

The ABCCC who had been monitoring the transmission broke in, *"NAIL FOUR EIGHT and Jolly One, Abort, Abort. This is Cricket on Guard... Abort the mission. We can't have a Jolly run out of fuel in that location. Acknowledge."*

Phil switched to Guard, *"Jolly One, disregard the message from Cricket. I got an idea...."*

Phil switched back to UHF just as, *"NAIL, this is Sandy. We're ready to start the race track shoot 'em up."*

"Sandy, you are all cleared in hot. I'll be at 500 to 1,000 feet directly over the field in a tight turn. Go get 'em!"

"Jolly, trust me on this. I can take you to a Lima Site that is only 20 miles away. You can refuel there. Trust me, Man. We <u>got</u> to get these guys out."

"Are you sure?

"Damn right, Jolly. It is Lima Site 294. I've been there. I'll get Air America to make sure it's ready for refueling you guys. Hold on."

Phil switched to Guard again, *"Porter, go to LS 294 and get them ready to refuel a HH-3 chopper."*

"No problem, NAIL, I'm on my way. Have fun."

Phil switched back to UHF, *"Jolly, you heard; it's all set up. Now let's get 'em out."*

The Sandys were running the racetrack pattern and dropping bombs, shooting guns and firing rockets. What a show! By now, more than six of the eventual thirteen A-1s were in the pattern or had already dropped their loads. The massive smoke pattern caused by all the bombing and shooting was starting to look like a rising smoke doughnut with the field being the doughnut hole! The instructions about not being too close to the south edge of the field were being well executed as the center of the doughnut was just a few meters north of the downed O-2. By now, Phil had fired all his rockets and had been airborne for nearly three hours since leaving NKP. He was getting very tired.

"**Okay, NAIL, now where the hell are they.**" the Danang Jolly Green asked.

Phil responded…"**Right in the middle of that Luffberry of Sandys!!**

"*Jolly has the Sandys…how about a mark?*"

"*I can't. I am out of Willy Petes. I'll lead you in and then rock my wings when I fly over them. How's that?*"

"*That'll work. Go for it.*"

Phil left his tight pattern over the airfield, ducked (so to speak!) under the swarm of Sandys that were still shooting up the Laotian country side… and led the Jolly back into the fray.

"**Sandy One, Nail Four Eight were commencing our run from the East…Cover us**"

"**Roger Nail, All Sandys… Daisy chain…NOW**"

The gaggle of A-1s miraculously transformed into an orderly procession of pairs of A-1s 'S'ing in front of, over, and behind the Jolly Green. Occasionally one would call enemy fire and break the pattern and silence it. The demonstration of air power was simply overwhelming! PL AAA fire dwindled and then ceased.

Phil flew directly over the downed aviators; with the Jolly in tow….and waggled his wings. "**Right under me, Jolly.**" Phil pulled up and started a left turn and took another hit to his airplane. "**Son-of-a-bitch, this is shitty!**" he said to himself. He leveled off at 1,500 feet.

When he looked back, the chopper was moving out. ***"Holy shit, they're leaving them!"*** he said out loud to himself.

"Jolly, what the fuck are you doing??"

"Whaddya' ya' mean? We got 'em. Both are on board."

"I didn't see you pick 'em up.

"That's because I'm Speedy Gonzalez."

"No shit, Man. Thanks, now follow me to the Lima Site. How are they doin'?"

Phil had not seen the HH-3 dive straight for Bill and Sean. The pilot screeched to a halt right in front of the wrecked O-2 and two men jumped out. The PJ and the crew chief ran to the survivors with a stretcher for Bill.

Phil had continued to make treetop passes to draw fire as the chopper did its job. The ground fire continued and the O-2 took a few more small-arms hits. Apparently, the gunners were more concerned with Phil than stopping the helicopter...it took no hits. Besides it was much safer to shoot at the FAC than to shoot at the Jolly and its swarm of A-1s!

After they lifted Bill onto the stretcher, the PJ ran over to the Duck and threw a thermite grenade into it, and then he sprinted back to the stretcher. The three of them ran with the stretcher...dumped it unceremoniously into the Jolly and piled in after it! Sean was still in the tangle of bodies and stretcher, on top of Bill, when the Jolly driver took off. They'd been on the ground less than 30 seconds. The PJ was cutting the flight suit from Bill as they flew away. Sean looked up as the crew chief, a master sergeant, thrust a cold beer into his hand.

"These chopper guys really did know how to fight a war."

Phil and the Jolly turned and headed west/southwest for LS 294.

"Sandy One, nice work. Now just put the rest in and level that place. We want them to know that

it is dangerous trying to capture our downed aviators. Many thanks. NAIL FOUR EIGHT, out."

"Rog 48...see ya at the bar! Sandy three and four escort the Jolly and the Nail"

Just as Phil level off at 5,000 feet, *"NAIL FOUR EIGHT, this is Porter."*

"Go ahead, Porter."

"We have no runway lights here and I think it's gotten too dark. What now?"

"Shit! Just a minute... Does Lima Site 298 have lights?"

"Yep, I was in there last week at night. Great lights... for Laos."

"We are going to 298; please call them and tell them we will be there in less than 30 minutes."

"Will do, NAIL. Need anything else?"

"Nope; thanks. …. BREAK BREAK. Jolly One, we'll have to go about fifteen more miles, to WC 2796. Can you make it?"

"I hope so. What other choice do we have, NAIL?"

"How are they, the pick ups?"

"NAIL FOUR EIGHT, they seem to be okay. One guy is really messed up but our PJ is taking good care of him. The other guy is having a beer. How are you? We heard you took some hits."

"I'm okay, just tired and my legs hurt." Phil replied.

Sean moved to where the medic was working on Bill. He couldn't tell if Bill was unconscious or sleeping, but either way he did have a smile on his face or at least it looked like a smile or smirk. **"How is he?"**

The PJ, a VERY young man who looked like he was at most seventeen years old, smiled back at him. **"Nothing really serious, Sir. All of the wounds are clean** hits. *The bullet in his back probably hurts like hell but it didn't do any real damage. It's under the shoulder blade, not near the spine. His lungs are OK. I've got everything else cleaned up. He'll bounce back pretty fast. It's mostly dehydration and hunger right now. That's why I have him on an IV. I'm feeding him, not giving him any medication. How are you, Captain?"*

"I'm fine; just have a headache and a very sore knee. Probably that rotten landing I just made." Sean replied.

The crew chief handed Sean another beer and the two of them sat leaning against the cockpit bulkhead. Both were soaked with sweat and grinning. The chief asked, **"We heard all about your belief that Captain Thompson was the "mirror man" and still alive. How does it feel to be right?"**

"Pretty damn good. I didn't like having to press it to the limit to prove a point. It seems like I nearly had to die to prove that he was still alive," Sean said.

"A lot of people didn't want to believe you were right, your commander for one."

CHAPTER NINETY SIX
South of Steel Tiger, Southern Laos
25 March 1968, early evening at a Lima Site 298

The airborne convoy neared the Lima Site. Darkness had not quite fallen and the HH-3 helicopter set down next to the O-2 that had just landed and taxied to an apron "parking" area. Sean jumped from the helicopter and ran to the O-2.

Sean yanked open the door, *"Phil, we'll put Bill in the back.* Then, seeing blood all over the cockpit floor, he said, *"Shit, what is that? You're hit! Are you okay??"*

"Yeah, but I hurt. How's Bill?"

"He'll make it. I'm flyin'. Get out of the seat and get in the back," Sean yelled at Phil. Phil started to get up but was having difficulty moving his right leg. Sean reached in and grabbed the right seat adjustment lever, yanked it up and pushed the seat forward. Then he reached around the seat, grabbed Phil and wrestled him into the left rear seat. Phil was clearly in pain but had tried to help with the transfer.

Bill was quickly transferred by the young medic and one of the flight crew members to the O-2. He was barely conscious as they loaded him into the back seat with Phil but he was able to croak, *"Crowded on this airliner, ain't it?"*

Before Sean could thank them, they had departed for the chopper to assist in the refueling. He quickly got into the left seat, started the engines and took off for Ubon, only thirty five minutes away. Soon his wounded passengers would have USAF doctors and nurses to take care of them.

Sean tried talking to the guys in the back, but that was not working. It was noisy in the back of the well-ventilated O-2, which now resembled a flying colander ....and neither had on headsets.

Actually, they were both slumped against opposite sides of the airplane. They were not responding to anything that Sean tried. He reached back and tried to shake each one....nothing...no movement...no response. About fifteen minutes out, Sean called for an ambulance to meet him at the mid-field taxiway. He would land, turn off at mid-field and they could get them both out then. He made another call to Ubon just prior to starting the approach,

"*Ubon, I have two unconscious pilots in the back seat. I'll turn off at mid-field. Have the ambulances ready. These guys are in bad shape.*"

Bill and Phil were both still unconscious when Sean landed the O-2 at Ubon. They were met by an ambulance at mid-field of the runway and, to Sean's great surprise, Fred Stebbins met him in a jeep.

Fred had been on an orientation ride with John Patterson, the Zorro, when all of this happened and hearing that the NAILs were enroute to Ubon, they had landed there to await their arrival. Sean shut down and piled out so the medics could remove the two wounded NAILs from the O-2. Each NAIL was loaded into the back of his own Dodge Power Wagon ambulance and immediately taken to the base hospital. The others followed in a staff car and Fred's jeep. As soon as they arrived at the hospital, Sean headed for the ER. He and Lt. Colonel Stebbins were met by a doctor just as they got to the ER door.

"*Doc, how is he?*"
"*Which one?*"
"*Bill Thompson; how is Bill?*"
"*He'll be fine, but ….*"
"*But what?*"
"*It's Captain Masters.*"
"*What do you mean?*"
"*He didn't make out so well.*"

Sean's eyes opened as wide as possible. His mouth gaped open. He couldn't speak for several seconds. "*What do you mean, he didn't make out so well? He was with us when we landed. The medics took him.*"

"Captain, he's in serious condition. We've ordered a C-9 in to pick him up and take him to Clark. The wound in his left leg was much more serious than he thought and he damned near bled out. We have him stabilized, have stopped the *bleeding, given him a blood transfusion and have him on antibiotics and morphine."*

"Can I see them?"

"No, I would prefer that they rest. The both need sleep. You can see Bill tomorrow but Phil should be out of here in less than 2 hours. You look like you need something yourself. Are you okay?"

"Thanks, Doc, I'm fine...tired, headache, and sore shoulder, but I'll be fine. I'll come by tomorrow."

The doctor said, **"Here, take these. They'll help with the pain."** as he handed Bill two white capsules.

"Thanks again, Doc."

"What now, Colonel?" Sean asked as they left the base hospital.

"Well the first thing we're going to do is go to the O'Club and thank those Jollys for saving your asses. Some one told me that some of the Sandys might also be there.. it seems that for some reason damn near everybody declared emergency fuel and landed here." Fred said with a smile

They jumped into Fred's jeep and he headed for the club. **"Maybe being a light Colonel included some bennies,"** thought Sean. As they approached the club Fred, drove to the front door and told Sean to go on in and he would park the jeep.

Sean got out of the jeep slowly and walked to the entrance door. He was stopped as he was about to open the door by a lieutenant, who was wearing an Air Police arm band. **"I'm sorry, Captain, but you are out of uniform. You have no hat and I don't know what all that stuff is on your flight suit. You will have to get a hat and clean up before I can let you into the club."**

"You gotta be shitting me, kid! I was just rescued out of Laos. My hat is in the crashed plane. Get the fuck out of my way!"

The lieutenant placed his right hand on his weapon and said sternly, *"Captain, go get cleaned up."*

Just as Sean was about to take a swing at the lieutenant, Fred walked up and very sternly said. *"Lieutenant, stand at ease. The captain and I are going in. Step out of the way."*

He did and they did. They did find the Jollys and Sandys. Sean thanked everyone profusely as everyone tried to drink Budweiser dry…they failed. After less than an hour, Sean was taken to the visiting officers' quarters where he passed out soon after he removed the bloody flight suit.

Historical Note: The two SARs recounted above really were one SAR that we split for the sake of the story. In real life Author Jerry Dwyer, on his second shoot down, was the survivor who, with great verve, out gunned the PL on the ground with his, not so powerful, Smith and Wesson Combat Masterpiece. All events on the ground in "Bill's" shoot down up to the point where we "bombed" him are fact. He was actually rescued by Phil Maywald, Nail Four Eight, who in fact, controlled the daisy chain of 13 Sandys and conducted himself as all other aviators would wish they could have. He DID lead the Jolly to a Lima site where both he and the Jolly refueled, and he did fly Jerry to Ubon. He was recommended for the Medal of Honor for his actions, but it was downgraded to an Air Force Cross. It is the author and contributor's humble opinions that this nation's highest decoration for Valor was denied to Phil because he was so good that… and so lucky that… he was not wounded and his Duck did not receive a single scratch! Or perhaps it might have had something to do with the fact he had the audacity to allow two USAF aircraft to land in a country that we were never in!

Captains Jerry Dwyer and Phil Maywald after the rescue.

CHAPTER NINETY SEVEN
Ubon Royal Thai Air Base
26 March 1968, early morning in the Visiting Officers' Quarters

The next morning Sean awoke about 0600 hours and immediately called the base hospital. He was advised that Phil had been flown out about 9pm the night before, that Bill was resting well after a good night's sleep and that he could visit him in a couple hours. He then tried to call NKP and Task Force Alpha, but eventually figured out he couldn't from the VOQ because the VOQ did not have AUTOVON authority.

He looked around the room and found about everything he needed; underwear, some civilian clothes, a full cabinet of toiletries and a pair of size nine tennis shoes, with socks. He showered, and shaved…dressed… and headed back to the O'Club for some breakfast.

As soon as he left the VOQ, he changed his mind and headed for Base Ops as he thought he could call TFA from there. It was only about a quarter of a mile out of the way to the Club anyhow. At Base Ops, he was directed to a phone on a counter near the map/weather room. When he did get through to TFA, a staff sergeant advised him that Lieutenant Stewart was not available but he could leave a message, which he did.

When he entered the main dining room at the club, he saw Fred and John and joined them. *"How you doin', Sean? Sleep well?"* asked John.

"I'm fine. Phil was flown out and I can see Bill in a couple hours. They said he was fine."

"John stayed at the hospital last night with Phil until they took him to the C-9. He seemed in good spirits, especially with the morphine."

"He was terrific out there. What do you say to the guy that saved your life…thanks?"

Fred picked up his coffee and in a toasting movement said *"You or Bill would have done the same. Hell, every Nail would have done that."*

Sean burst in, *"Colonel, begging your pardon, but you are full of shit! What he did was fantastic! He took a million hits. Got shot twice. Hung in there for over two hours. Directed a ton of A-1s and four or five helicopters. Shit, he even got a couple Thuds in there. Then he nearly bled to death. What do you mean 'every Nail would have done that?' No way, Colonel. No fucking way! It was way above the call!"*

Fred was still holding the coffee cup and now moved it up and down in kind of a 'salute.' *"I know. I really do know, and so does 7th. The Man has asked us to* put him in for the Medal of Honor. Apparently he was fully briefed on about everything you just said."

"Son-of-a-bitch. That is something," barked Sean.

"Colonel Benjamin has suggested that you write it up since you were there. That would be one way to thank the guy who saved your life. What do you say?"

"Shit Hot!! How can I say anything but "yes?" Of course I'll do it. It'll be an honor."

Fred started to smile. "Oh, I forgot. There's more."

"With you, Colonel, there's always more!"

"The colonel also wants you to write Bill up for an Air Force Cross. No one alive asked Phil more about what Bill was doing before he called in the air strike on himself than you.

You must know every move that Bill made on the ground. How many he killed. How he survived the grenade. How he shot the gomers. Everything! Then you were with him at Bah Khe during the entire rescue. You are "The Man". What do you say?"

"Well, shit, of course I'll do it. He's my best friend and he deserves the Cross. God, he walked or crawled for thirteen miles in enemy territory after we put an air strike on top of him. He ought to get it just for grit."

A lively small and young Thai waitress moved to the table, *"Sawadee, Kup. Breakfast? Coffee?"*

The three of them ordered and the conversation moved slowly through the previous day's activities in and about Bah Khe as the breakfast was delivered and consumed. Fred had told Sean that his action of trying to land in enemy territory to rescue a fellow aviator was also Air Force Cross material and that he, Fred, would be completing the paperwork. It seemed as though the big Air Force general in Saigon was well aware of Sean's landing and *"had suggested"* the Cross.

As the meal was ending Fred said, *"Oh, by the way, Colonel B told me that General Holland is in Honolulu briefing COMPAC on the success of the sensors at Khe Sanh."*

"Is Sharon with him?"

"Yes, and for some reason they will not be back to NKP until mid April."

"I guess that's why I can't get a hold of her. Thanks, Colonel."

Later that morning Sean, Fred and John visited with Bill in the hospital. His spirits were high and he felt pretty good considering what he had just endured. Fred told him about the medals and that as soon as they could move him, he would be returned to NKP. The doctors thought that might be in about five days so Fred asked Sean to stay with him, and fly Phil's Duck back to NKP when Bill was able.

CHAPTER NINETY EIGHT
Nakhon Phanom Royal Thai Air Base (NKP)
1 APRIL 1968

Sean and Bill returned to NKP on April Fool's Day (which somehow seemed appropriate!). Phil's duck, while well ventilated by enemy fire had required little serious repair...but a lot of silver tape and other patches. That the Duck had suffered no flight threatening injuries was nothing short of miraculous. The Covey O-2 maintenance troops from their FOL at Ubon, had counted over 50 AAA holes in the Duck, as well as some serious foliage damage. It had appeared that Phil, upon occasion, had really been ***"down amongst them"***.

Piloted by Sean, rarely 50 feet above the Thai country side for the two hour flight, the two Buds buzzed every water buffalo they saw and only pulled up to a "reasonable altitude" about 10 miles south of NKP.

On roll out, Sean looked right to the Ramp and was astounded to see every Nail, Zorro, Candle, and Nimrod who was not airborne awaiting them on the Nail Ramp.

"Holy Shit!! What did we do to deserve this", Sean asked

"We came back", Bill responded

CHAPTER NINETY NINE
Nakhon Phanom Royal Thai Air Base (NKP)
APRIL 1968

Sean resumed flying combat missions immediately but Bill's injuries kept him out of the air until May 2nd. By then, the rainy season had begun in Laos which meant that the HCMT would be mostly a mud-filled impassable "road network." The rains typically came torrentially, but lasted less than an hour at a time. On the few days it did not rain in central Laos, "work" on the Trail could be resumed. As a result of the rain and the efforts of the Nails, traffic on the Trail had come to a near halt. The big guns had been taken back north to protect Hanoi and Haiphong. The NAILs continued to fly night and day but rarely saw any targets of value, nor controlled any air strikes on anything but suspected truck parks.

For Sean this was a great time. The flying was fun and didn't seem too dangerous. But, most of all…best of all…he and Sharon were now clearly a couple in love. She had been briefed by the general that Sean was not in any way at fault with the crash of the P-2. She had apologized to Sean and that made Bill a happy camper. Strange as it may seem, after all of the trials and tribulations Sharon and Bill were now on good terms, maybe even friends.

With their DEROS approaching in October, Bill and Sean settled into a routine of flying nearly four hours a day or six hours with pre- and post-flight activities, sleeping about eight hours, working in the squadron offices for about three hours and then trying to relax for the remainder. Sean was able to complete the paperwork for the MOH for Phil and the AFC for Bill by April 20th. Both had been sent along with Sean's AFC paperwork to 7th Air Force in Saigon. They were able to get to Bangkok each month, but none of the trips was as exciting as the trip in February. Their lives had taken on a dullness that easily could have resulted in a loss of concentration and subsequent accidents. Fortunately, the NAIL leaders were able to keep the crews' attention focused on flying safely. It worked, and there were no NAIL losses during the 1968 wet season in Laos.

Life at NKP and over the HCMT was rather calm now in 1968. However, in Vietnam and in the USA, many significant actions had or were taking place during early 1968 and well into the Laotian wet season.

Public opinion polls taken after the Tet Offensive and published in late March revealed that President Johnson's overall rating had slipped to 36 percent and the approval of his Vietnam War policy had slipped to 26 percent.

On March 12, President Johnson edged out antiwar candidate Eugene McCarthy in the New Hampshire Democratic primary.

Six days later, the United States came off the gold standard as Congress repealed the requirement for gold reserves to back U. S. currency.

Also, late in March, it was revealed that Army Captain William Calley was responsible for three hundred civilian deaths at My Lai. Later that March, some of the nation's most brilliant, or "Wisemen," joined President Johnson at the White House and advocated a withdrawal from Vietnam. This did not become public knowledge until years later.

On April 1, The U.S. 1st Cavalry Division began the operation to re-open Route 9, the relief route to the besieged Marine base at Khe Sanh.

Three days later, on April 4, the famous civil rights leader, Reverend Dr. Martin Luther King, Jr., was assassinated in Memphis. Racial unrest erupted across America in over a hundred cities.

On April 6, the Oakland police had a shoot out with the Black Panthers, which resulted in many arrests and a few deaths.

On April 8, the siege of Khe Sanh ended with the withdrawal of NVA troops from the area. The enemy had lost an estimated 15,000 while the US recorded only 199 Marines and 92 from the 1st Air Cavalry as KIA.

Three days later, on April 11, President Johnson signed the Civil Rights Act of 1968.

Within days after opening Route 9, the U.S. command secretly abandoned and closed the Khe Sanh air base and withdrew the Marines.

Back in the U.S. on April 23, a large group of anti-war activists seized five buildings at Columbia University and shut the university down.

By May 10, the Paris peace talks had started but soon stalled. No progress was reported.

On May 22, the U. S. nuclear-powered submarine "Scorpion" sunk with 99 on board.

In Los Angeles on Jun 5, Senator Robert F. Kennedy was shot and killed, only hours after winning the California Democratic presidential primary election.

In Saigon on July 1, General Westmoreland was replaced by General Creighton W. Abrams as U.S. Commander in Vietnam.

At the Republican National Convention on August 8, Richard M. Nixon was chosen as the Republican presidential candidate.

James Anderson, Jr. was awarded the Medal of Honor on August 12. He was the first Black U. S. Marine to be awarded the MOH.

On August 28, during the Democratic National Convention in Chicago, 10,000 anti-war protesters were confronted by 26,000 police and national guardsmen. Eight hundred demonstrators were injured in this brutal confrontation that was covered in great detail on live national TV.

By September 30, the nine hundredth U.S. aircraft was shot down over North Vietnam.

Apollo 7, the first manned Apollo mission, lifted off on August 11, 1968.

These events came and went with absolutely no notice taken by the Nails. It really didn't matter who was President, or who shot whom at home. They were not at home. They were "here," and all that mattered was "here!!!"

Time was moving at what seemed a glacial pace, Oct 12th, the date of Bill and Sean's "fini flight" (final combat flight) into Laos finally arrived. They were to fly a routine and *very high and safe* two-hour mission into Laos together. This flight would be followed with a champagne toast by Colonel Hardy and many NAILS in the NAIL parking area. That evening, the 23rd would have a "Sawadee" to welcome new Nails and send the two warriors off to the U.S.

The two "old heads" stepped to their Duck with their chutes, M-16s, and map bags. They were met by the Kudy Jay's crew chief, Sergeant Ricardo, on the O-2 ramp. They were relaxed—laughing, and just fooling around. Life was good and finishing a combat tour in the Vietnam War or, more specifically, in this *secret war* was about as good as it gets.

"Good morning, Sirs," barked Sergeant Ricardo, flipping a sharp salute to both of the captains as they neared the Kudy Jay. He remained at attention.

Both Bill and Sean looked askance at their black Night O-2.

In near unison they replied, **"Good morning, Sergeant,"** as they returned the salute.

"Sergeant Ricardo, can't you tell the difference between day and night?" Bill asked with a smile.

"Certainly Sir, but we Combat Crew Chiefs thought it would be very appropriate for you two warriors to fly your final flight in an old friend who has never let you down."

Bill and Sean looked at each other, smiled and nodded.

"Sergeant Ricardo, we both have wanted to show our appreciation for all that you've done for us. You are clearly one of the best crew chiefs in the entire Air Force and we have no doubt you have the biggest set of balls this side of the Mekong. We have looked far and wide for something that you would treasure and that would help you remember your two nutty NAIL FAC's. So here is a photo of both of us." Bill handed the sergeant a small rectangular object wrapped in what looked like left over grocery bags.

He replied as he accepted the gift, *"Thank you, Sirs. Let's open this hummer!"* He tore the paper away from what was obviously a framed photo of the three of them kneeling with the Kudy Jay in the background. The picture was signed *"To Sergeant Ricardo, the AF's greatest Crew Chief, Sean O'Malley (NAIL FOUR FIVE) and Bill Thompson (NAIL FIVE FIVE)."*

The picture presented to Sgt. Ricardo.

"Sirs, this is terrific! Now my kids will know what I did during the war." He then handed the picture to a young airman and said ***"Airman, guard this with your life. I will be helping the captains pre-flight this bird."***

Bill climbed into the Duck's left seat and began working on the check list. Sean and Sergeant Ricardo circled the O-2 and performed the exterior pre-flight. Finding nothing amiss, Sean climbed into the right seat, shut the door, pulled the seat up and began completing his portion of the cockpit pre-flight check list. Soon, Bill fired up the bird and called for taxi. They departed the Nail ramp, were armed in the arming area and then were cleared for take off.

"I've been looking forward to this one. What a great day!" said Sean as they taxied onto the active runway and began the takeoff.

"Me too, Man. In a week we'll be in La La Land. I can't wait. I hope Judy can't wait either."

"Where to, O Commander?"

"You know, I'd like to go to Khe Sanh and see what's left of the base. It's been a long time since we helped the big uglies supply that place. I heard there's nothing left."

"Good idea. I was thinking we could then head up into Barrel Roll and see if we can see any jars or maybe the French trucks. Did you ever see the trucks?"

"You mean the ones the French burned out when they were leaving?" asked Bill.

"Yep, the ones they parked so neatly in rows and columns and then set on fire. You know the French...so very neat."

"Lovers, Man, not fighters."

"Nail Five Five, this is Cricket."

"Go ahead, Cricket, this is Five Five."

"Five Five, we do not expect to have any ordnance for you and have been advised that this is your final flight, you and 45. Is that correct?"

"Cricket, that is correct. We'll be on a sightseeing tour of central and northern Laos and Northwest Vietnam, but not in that order. We'll stay on this frequency in case you need us."

"Five Five, unlikely that we will need you. Have fun on the tour."

Bill continued, *"I've got to take back what I said about the French; they fought like hell against impossible odds at Dien Bien Phu. They, however, showed a total lack of imagination... not to mention judgment...by putting their heads into that noose! But fight they did!"*

"If we hadn't had the air support and air lift at Khe Sanh that would have been lost. No wonder the French lost at DBF!"

They climbed to 9,000 feet and proceeded to Khe Sanh. The one-hour trip was interspersed with little sightseeing and even less talk as both of the NAILs were thinking about what they had done here in the past year. They had controlled hundreds of attack aircraft, destroyed hundreds of trucks and guns, been on the ground in Laos delivering beer and being rescued and, last but not least, had trained those who would pick up the cause after they left. There was little to talk about, but much to think about on this last flight.

Sean broke the silence as they crossed into South Vietnam, *"Look at 1 o'clock. That's where Long Vei was. Nothing there now!"*

"You know, there wasn't very much there to begin with, but the NVA tanks took out whatever was there. Yeah, not much to look at."

Silence again overtook them as they proceeded east just a couple miles north of Route 9. Within a few minutes, Bill said *"There it is.....or was."*

"Damn, there's nothing left. Even the runway is gone! You see anything that looks like the old Khe Sanh?" Sean was as amazed as Bill.

"No, nothing. You know" Bill continued, *"this is like you read in the war novels. When you must leave an area, you leave nothing for the enemy to use against you. This is the perfect example. There's nothing here. Nothing! Let's go back to Laos."*

"Good idea. I'm glad we came here to see this, but ... "

"Yeah, I know. We lost a bunch of guys defending the place then we gave it up in less than

two months. Doesn't seem to make a lot of sense, does it?"

"*Not to me,*" replied Sean and, with that, the silence began again as they turned northwest towards Laos.

Sean broke the silence after about fifteen minutes. *"You going to just fly up 91 and 911?"*

"Yeah. I'll stay over the roads until we get to Route 12 and from there we can wing it. Do you know where the trucks are on the PDJ?"

"I know where they were and they're probably still there."

"But before we go up to the Barrel, why don't we have some fun and shoot some Willy Petes into Mu Gia Pass?"

"Sounds good to me! Lead on, McDuff."

As they got within five miles of Mu Gia, they were at 9,000 feet, flying directly towards the pass and still over Route 911 when Bill said *"Lets give it a shot from here."* Bill raised the nose of the O-2 to about thirty degrees and hosed off a Willy Pete. The range wasn't too bad but the westerly wind had moved the WP to the east by about a quarter of a mile.

"Nice shot; you hit the ground!"
"Okay, wise ass, your turn."

Sean took control of the Duck, banked to the left, took up a heading of about 340, raised the nose about 20 degrees and fired. This rocket seemed to hit somewhere in the pass.

"Any questions? Aw, shit....we got an oil pressure light on the rear engine."

"I see it. I have the aircraft....reducing power on the aft engine. Watch the pressure."

"That helped some. Pull her back some more....that's good."

"I think that has ended our last flight. I'm heading back to NKP."

"I'm with you…..now isn't that the dumbest thing you ever heard? Where else would I be going?

"The pressure's holding okay."

"No French trucks and no jars….life is full of disappointments.

"Cricket, this is Nail Five Five."

"Five Five, go."

"We got an oil pressure problem on our aft engine and are RTB to NKP. No emergency. Just being careful on this last flight."

"Five Five, we understand RTB. We're here if you need us. Call when you're over the Mekong."

"Roger, Five Five; out."

"Sorry you didn't get to see the trucks. Did you know about the story that was in the "Stars and Stripes" about the trucks?

"Story? No," replied Bill a little puzzled.

"It seems that 7th Air Force reported that a flight of Thuds had had a great day of truck killing, but the picture they used was of the dead French trucks. It was never clear to us whether 7th sent them the picture or whether they just used one from their files. It was a good picture, seeing all those burned-out trucks all lined up in rows and columns. Must have been a couple hundred of them. <u>Great picture</u>, except it was the French who burned them, not the Thuds."

The flight back to NKP was uneventful. The oil pressure remained okay with the engine in near idle and conversation was sparse. They called Cricket as they were descending over the Mekong with NKP in sight.

"Cricket, Cricket, Nail Five Five and 45 crossing the fence RTB for the last time!!

"Roger, Gents...Sawadee...say "Hi" to The Land of the Big BX for us. Cricket Out!"

The latest idea for Nail fini flight terminations would include a low smoke-dragging pass down the NKP runway at "the speed of heat" followed by a pitch up to landing. This "smoked fini" was instituted soon after the smoke generators had been installed on the day Ducks, which were normally flown on "fini flights". When operating, the generators would create dense white smoke that exited out of the rear engine cowling. However, using uncharacteristic caution, Bill decided on a straight-in approach due to the misbehaving rear engine.

As he lowered the gear, NKP tower called on Uniform....

"Hey Five Five, the SOF says to cease with the smoke if that rear engine is having a problem!"

"Tower this is Five Five... say again?"

"Don't use your smoke generator, Five Five!"

"Tower, we don't have a smoke generator...aw, shit!"

As Bill transmitted, he 'S'ed the Duck to look behind him. Sean immediately leaned out of the right-side window opening and looked aft...and there it was ....smoke...and....flames pouring out of the aft engine.

"Well, shit ...aren't we a regular ball of fire? Bill, get this son-of-a-bitch on the ground fast! We're burning."

"NKP Tower Nail Five Five on short final... for the last time. Declaring an emergency. Two souls on board with an aft engine fire. We'll stop straight ahead and egress smartly!"

"Roger Five Five...meet the fire trucks at mid field!"

Bill greased the Duck onto the PSP, piled on the brakes, and came to a quick stop opposite the two huge red Oshkosh fire trucks. Sean opened the door and threw himself out…barely managing to avoid being trampled by Bill, who was also exiting with vigor. They both ended up in a pile, laughing, beside the Duck in the middle of NKP's PSP runway. They scrambled up and beat feet for the side of the runway where they fell to the red clay earth, still laughing as the fire trucks commenced literally covering Kudy Jay with foam.

As the fire was being smothered, a long string of jeeps and line trucks pulled to a halt and out poured what appeared to be the whole 23rd TASS. Laughing and shouting **"Shit Hot!"** at the top of their lungs.

Colonel Hardy and Colonel Benjamin approached the two with a bottle of champagne and two stemmed glasses.

"Gentlemen….that was the best damn fini flight I have ever seen!"

The Colonels then put down the champagne and the glasses, came to attention, and saluted the two Nails. They, in turn, snapped to rigid attention and returned the salute.

Colonel Hardy then said, **"Gentlemen, I give you two Nails whom Uncle Ho is not going to get!"**

Then the party began…as the fire trucks completed putting out the oil fire on the Kudy Jay.

Later that week, the squadron threw its usual Sawadee party for arriving FNGs and departing old heads. This drink fest at the O'Club began at about 9pm and lasted well into the early morning hours and was punctuated with speeches, "carrier landings," "Dead Bugs" and much more juvenile hilarity.

The next morning, Bill and Sean rode the Klong to Bangkok where they boarded a contract commercial airliner to the good ol' U.S.A.

Their war was over.

CHAPTER ONE HUNDRED
The White House
24 January 1969, mid afternoon in the Roosevelt Room

A Marine Gunny Sergeant in dress blues walked into the room and stood in front of Phil, **"Major Masters, President Nixon should be finished with the Ambassador very soon. Plan on going in in about five minutes."**

"Thank you, Gunny."

It was quite a group in the Roosevelt Room directly across the hall from the Oval Office of President Richard M. Nixon, who had been in office less than a week. Phil naturally had brought his wife, Katherine and his two boys, Phil II and Jim. Phil's parents, John and Sarah, were also there. Since this ceremony was based upon what Phil had done to save the lives of Bill and Sean, they and their wives, Judy and Sharon, were also present. Bill and Sean were in Class A uniforms. All three former NAILs were wearing their recently- awarded Air Force Cross ribbons, which topped each officers resplendent array of ribbons.

Bill had recovered fully and been sent to Harvard for one of their famous MBA degrees.

Sean had been assigned to Hurlburt Field in Florida as an Instructor Pilot in the brand new FAC aircraft, the OV-10 Bronco.

Phil had been assigned to the Military Personnel Center in San Antonio, Texas so he would be near Wilford Hall Medical Center for the special medical needs he had in rehabbing his wounded right leg. The Air Force had advised him that upon re-qualification for flying duties, he would be offered an assignment of his choice. He most likely would ask to become an Operations Officer in a fighter squadron.

Sharon had returned to the USA in August and, as a result of some not-so-subtle nudging by General Holland, was assigned to the Test Wing at Eglin AFB, right next to Hurlburt Field in nearby Fort Walton, Florida. She and Sean were married in a candlelit ceremony in November. On this particular January morning she too was wearing her Class A blues. However, it would not be much longer before she would have to resign her commission. Her pregnancy had only been confirmed days before and not wanting to detract from the solemnity of this moment was a secret that she and Sean had not shared with anyone else.

"Major Masters, we can go in now."

The entourage followed the Gunnery Sergeant into the Oval Office with Phil leading the group. President Nixon met them as they entered, greeted them graciously and shook everyone's hand. An Army colonel, handsomely decked out in medals, was standing behind a small portable podium that carried the seal of the President of the United States (POTUS). He obviously would be reading the citation.

Everyone was then moved into position by the sergeant. As soon as this was done and the photographer had nodded his approval with the arrangement, the flash of the camera preserved the moment for posterity.

President Nixon began, *"Thank you all for coming. As your President, it gives me great honor and pleasure to be in the presence of one of America's greatest heroes of our day. It is very fitting that we gather in this historical room to honor one of America's bravest. In these tough times, I so enjoy taking time to honor those who have done so very much for our great country. Although as Vice President I had the privilege of meeting several Medal of Honor recipients, this is the first time I have had the honor to bestow such an award. This is a very special ceremony for me and I am sure it is for all of you. Let us proceed, Colonel..."*

The Army colonel nodded to the Commander-in-Chief and began,
"Attention to Orders. Citation to accompany the awarding of the Medal of Honor to

Captain Phillip J. Masters, U.S. Air Force

Date of Of Action: March 25, 1968

Citation:
The President of the United States of America, authorized by Title 10, Section 8741, United States Code, awards the Medal of Honor to Captain Phillip J. Masters for extraordinary heroism in military operations against an opposing armed force as an 0-2A Forward Air Controller (pilot) in Southeast Asia on 25 March 1968. On that date, Captain Masters braved an intense and deadly barrage of hostile gunfire for over two hours while he controlled the successful rescue of two fellow pilots who had been downed by antiaircraft fire deep within hostile territory. Despite the great personal risk involved to his own life, Captain Masters, with undaunted determination, indomitable courage, and professional skill, repeatedly made low passes over the rescue scene in his light unarmored observation aircraft. At times, he flew within fifty feet of the hostile forces to determine their positions, to fire all fourteen of his marking rockets at the enemy, and deliberately to draw their fire on his aircraft and away from the rescue helicopters. His aircraft took over fifty hits

by small arms fire and he was wounded in both legs and nearly lost his life due to loss of blood as he continued the rescue. Due to his courage, persistence, and professional skill the downed pilots were safely recovered. Through his extraordinary heroism, superb airmanship, and aggressiveness, Captain Masters reflected the highest possible credit upon himself, the United States Air Force, and the United States of America."

The president turned to his right and took the Medal of Honor hanging from its sky blue ribbon from a pillow held by a USAF Colonel.

As Nail FAC Phil Masters lowered his head, the President of the United States of America began to drape the ribbon around his neck and whispered, ***"God, I hope I don't screw this up."***

Phil responded in a whisper also. ***"Mr. President, I'm so nervous I hope I don't piss on your carpet!"***

Both chuckled loudly as the ribbon landed neatly around Phil's neck. The President stepped back slightly, put out his hand, shook Phil's and said ***"Congratulations, Major; you deserve this."***

Sean leaned ever so slightly toward Bill and with a solemn look on his face whispered… ***"Shit Hot!"***

"No," Bill whispered back, ***" Nails are Shit Hot!"***

To be continued ………..

EPILOGUE

General Holland went on to become Commander of the Electronic Systems Division at Hanscom Field and retired as a three-star general in 1977.

Colonel Benjamin returned the U.S.A. to retire in his home state of Hawaii and continued with his formerly-successful law practice.

Ed Hardy returned to the Strategic Air Command, first to SAC Headquarters in Omaha, Nebraska and then as Wing Commander at Dyess AFB in Texas.

Bill recovered in time to enter Harvard in the fall of 1968. There he became enamored with computers and their mathematical capabilities. He also became very interested in the entrepreneurial activities that seem to germinate in the Boston area. While a student, he obtained the financial backing to buy a small airline in Arizona. This was a special airline with a mission to fly dead Indians to the "holy burial grounds." After a dozen trips to Phoenix and at the final meeting where the papers were to be signed, the airline owner stopped the deal. When Bill asked him why, he replied, *"I don't like you, Thompson."* Bill picked up his papers and said, *"Good reason."* Bill subsequently returned all the money he had spent to his financiers and went deeply into debt. From Harvard, he was assigned to Headquarters in Europe and was the four star's daily briefing officer. He was quite talented, but when he had to report to the chief that one of the American dependants, who had just earned her pilot's license, had flown east across the iron curtain into East Germany, he was very embarrassed ... it was his wife, Judy. When Bill was selected for the War College, the chief said to Bill, *"I didn't nominate you for the War College. How did you get that assignment?"* Bill, of course, had a great answer,

"General, you aren't the only general that I know." Maybe he did know almost everyone in the Air Force. While at the War College—as the story goes—a few members of his class were showing a visiting team of senior officers from a South American country the capabilities of one of the computers at Maxwell AFB in Alabama. As the story goes...Bill told the visiting general that the computer could answer any question he could ask. Well, the visitor wasn't to be outdone and immediately asked ***"Can the computer tell me when I will die?"*** Bill responded, ***"Of course, General."*** Bill asked the general a few questions and he typed in his answers. After about nine questions and answers, out pops the answer on the printer: ***"You will die when your time comes."*** Everyone had a big laugh. Bill got into some trouble (now, there's a surprise) when he was assigned to Air Force Material Command as a middle manager on the Integrated Logistic System. He crossed a civilian and ended up in the four star's office. The general said, ***"Thompson, I don't even admit that full colonels exist so what the fuck am I doing talking to a Lieutenant Colonel?"*** No one knows what happened after that, but Bill kept his job. He just never made colonel. Imagine that. So, he put in his papers to retire. The Air Force refused because he owed them for the time at the War College. But—pure Bill—all it took was one call to the Deputy for Personnel for the Air Force (another friend) and Bill was, after twenty years and a few months, a civilian again.

With no job and a large debt as a result of the failed airline deal, he spent two months of his Air Force salary for new clothes. He selected the company he wanted to join and set up the interviews. Early in the process an interviewer, a retired two-star Army general, said, ***"Thompson, that salary is too high and way above my pay grade."*** Naturally, Bill had an answer, ***"Then, Sir, get me some one at a higher pay grade."*** He did, and Bill got the job at the salary he wanted. General Electric needed people like Bill and they got a winner. At first, he was assigned to reducing energy costs in their mid-west facilities. He did, and his contribution was recognized. Next, he moved to eastern Ohio where he and two other guys saved a factory, the major employer in that county. Then he was sent to Columbus, Ohio, where he became an expert on industrial diamonds. Next Bill found himself in Dublin, Ireland, building an industrial diamond plant from scratch. He did, and brought it in six months ahead of schedule and well below budget....another success.

But, by this time, he decided that he needed to run his own show. He left GE to build airport fueling and fire protection equipment on Long Island, New York. He owned a truck-manufacturing plant. With another success behind him, he was enticed to go into the auto parts business. He is the CEO of the parts company on Long Island.

Sean, with a Graduate degree in Civil Engineering, was to be assigned to Eglin AFB in Florida as a civil engineering officer. As the story goes, he was still at NKP when a visiting two star from the Eglin AFB field called Hurlburt ask him to prepare some notes during a "Pilots Only" meeting. Sean presented his notes for the general's perusal the following day. Peering at Sean over the top of his reading glasses, he said, **"Captain, you are coming to work for me. I want you to help me train FACs at Hurlburt."** Of course this was great news for Sean; he'd just been rescued from the "keep 'em flushing" Air Force. When Sean arrived at Eglin for his new assignment, however, a full colonel Personnel type asked him to drop by before officially signing in. This is what he heard: **"The general had me fly to MPC (Military Personnel Center in San Antonio, TX) to get your orders changed from civil engineering to flying. When I got there, I met with another colonel and he insisted that you were staying in CE. We had a**

Mexican standoff so I asked, 'What is your General's rank?" He says, 'Two star.' Now, that threw me a little so then I said, 'What is his date of rank?' You are here, O'Malley, and going to train OV-10 pilots because my general outranked his general by THREE DAYS!' Upon promotion to major, he became the training squadron Ops Officer. After a couple years at Hurlburt, he was sent to the Army Command and General Staff College at Fort Leavenworth, Kansas, where he shared a table for four months with Major Al Joulwan, the future SACEUR commander replaced by General Clark during the Bosnian conflict.

Sharon died suddenly, unexpectedly and tragically during her first pregnancy when the pain she assumed was the onset of labor turned out to be a ruptured appendix. This happened while the O'Malleys were at Fort Leavenworth. Devastated Sean volunteered for another SEA tour. He wanted to put as much distance between himself and the horror that his life had become as possible but he quickly learned that you can't leave heartache behind. When he completed ACGSC in June of 1971, he was off to SEA as an OV-10 pilot. It was hard—almost unbearable—to be back where he and Sharon had started their relationship together but he did what others have done in similar circumstances; he threw himself into his work. He flew, he read, he slept and then he flew and he read some more. He made it to SEA by early August 1971 and what happened to Sean during that tour and after is another story that will be told. .

After Phil received the Medal of Honor in 1969, the Air Force sent him on a speaking tour of the U.S. He continued in this role for about a year, returned to flying status, and joined the new A-7D fighter squadron at Luke AFB, Arizona. Like Sean's epilogue above Phil's also continues in another book.

Jerry Hersey remains in captivity somewhere in SEA, waiting for a release that may never happen.

Historical Note: The Paris Peace agreement was signed on January 27, 1973 and resulted in the withdrawal of all American troops from Vietnam. About one month later, a cease-fire agreement was signed in Vientiane and ended the war so that a coalition government could be formed for Laos. The honorable men who directed and controlled the war and U.S. policy concluded with "peace agreements" that conveniently ignored embarrassing details like missing prisoners. The Secret War in Laos remained a secret when it came to recovering our missing and dead warriors.

www.ingramcontent.com/pod-product-compliance
Lightning Source LLC
Chambersburg PA
CBHW031247230426
43670CB00005B/76